TEST BANK II

TO ACCOMPANY

PARKIN
MACROECONOMICS
FIFTH EDITION

MARK RUSH
University of Florida

and

CAROL DOLE
University of North Carolina, Charlotte

Addison-Wesley
An imprint of Addison Wesley Longman, Inc.

Reading, Massachusetts ♦ Menlo Park, California ♦ New York
Harlow, England ♦ Don Mills, Ontario ♦ Sydney
Mexico City ♦ Madrid ♦ Amsterdam

For information, address Addison Wesley Educational Publishers Inc., One Jacob Way, Reading, Massachusetts 01867-3999.

ISBN 0-201-63791-X
1 2 3 4 5 6 7 8 9 10 - VG - 03020100

Preface

■ Introduction

This book is one of six test banks, each carefully crafted to be part of the most complete package of test banks ever offered to support a beginning economics textbook. Three of the test banks are designed to accompany Michael Parkin's *Microeconomics*, Fifth Edition and three accompany Michael Parkin's *Macroeconomics*, Fifth Edition. The complete set of six books comprises *Microeconomics Test Bank*, Volumes I, II, and III and *Macroeconomics Test Bank*, Volumes I, II, and III.

Both the *Microeconomics Test Bank* Volumes I and II and the *Macroeconomics Test Bank* Volumes I and II are thoroughly revised and rewritten versions of the test banks offered with the Fourth Edition of Michael Parkin's best-selling *Microeconomics*, *Macroeconomics*, and *Economics*. If you used these test banks in the past, do not put the new volumes on your shelf in the belief that they are "tested out" for your classes. On the contrary, you will be pleased to see that these new volumes have built upon the strengths of the old editions by adding a large number of totally new questions as well as almost all the questions from the Fourth Edition in revised, rewritten form.

The *Microeconomics Test Bank* Volume III and *Macroeconomics Test Bank* Volume III, both new for the Fifth Edition of the textbook, are firmly in the Parkin tradition of offering innovations designed to increase the quality of the principles experience for student and instructor. These test banks are unique in having been written by a team of 15 dedicated and experienced instructors. The objective of this approach was to harvest the very best questions these instructors could write by requesting that each contribute only a few questions per chapter. When you look through these books, you will soon see that this effort was successful.

In the next section of the preface I describe the principles that guided writing the new questions and my revisions of the existing questions. I then discuss the revisions to this edition of the test banks and how they are designed to facilitate the test-creation process for you. I next briefly describe Volumes I and II. Then, because the Volume III test banks are unusual in being multi-authored, I discuss how you might best use these new resources. Finally, I offer some hints about how I have used these test banks to assemble my exams.

■ Test Bank Principles

Two principles guided the writing and revising of the questions:

- ◆ A question should not be a guessing game forcing the students to puzzle out what the question asks.

- ◆ An instructor must be absolutely secure in the knowledge that each question contains material covered in the textbook.

I adopted the first point as a guiding principle in revising the questions in the Volume I and II test banks. The authors of the Volume III banks also have endeavored to make each question as straightforward as possible or, as Donald Dutkowsky put it, "bullet proof."

The second principle is essential, I think, if a test bank is to be of use to an instructor. I teach large classes of approximately 1,500 students a semester and am well aware of students' propensity to argue that a question covered material that was inadequately treated in the textbook. To avoid this situation, we took pains to ensure that each and every question tests the students on information explicitly covered in the book. Each question covers only material in the book and, to the fullest extent possible, each question is on material treated only in the specific text chapter.

■ Fifth Edition Revisions

We have made substantial revisions in preparing the test banks for the Fifth Edition:

♦ All the questions from Volume I and II have been reviewed, to ensure consistency with the text and clarity for the students. Questions dealing with material eliminated from the Fifth Edition of the textbook were deleted and a large number of new questions were added to cover the new topics in the Fifth Edition of the book.

♦ The artwork has been markedly upgraded so that the figures are consistent throughout all of the books. In addition, questions now refer to "the figure above" rather than an abstruse reference to "Figure 12.67." As a result, your tests will have a more "home grown" flavor.

♦ The "Topic" listed for each question has been made more precise. Thus if you want a question dealing with, say, a perfectly price-discriminating monopoly, it will be easy to select a question covering exactly this topic.

♦ To the greatest extent possible, the questions have been reordered so that they follow the order the material is presented in the corresponding text chapter. Thus you generally will find all questions on the same topic clustered together so you can easily select the one you want. In addition, within each chapter questions are separated by each major section of the text chapter so that if you assign to the students only part of a chapter, it will be easy to select questions from that specific part.

♦ Questions covering a topic generally are ordered with non-numerical questions first, questions dealing with a numerical table second, and questions dealing with a figure third.

♦ The test banks are available in both a user-friendly computerized test bank and in Word 7.0 files. For some instructors, the ease of simply cutting and pasting from the Word files will exceed the utility of the powerful computerized test bank. With this edition, we accommodate both preferences.

■ Volumes I and II

Volumes I and II of the test bank each contain nearly 5,000 questions. Most of these are multiple choice. In addition to questions from the text, Volume I also contains multiple choice questions drawn from the *Study Guide* and *Economics in Action*. Thus if you have assigned either of these student supplements to your class, you have the means to "reward" students who are using them by asking questions drawing on what they have been studying.

In addition to multiple choice questions, Volume II also has True/False and Essay questions. Volume II thus gives you the option to mix up the style of question you use.

■ Volume III

Featuring some 4,000 questions, Volume III is, to my knowledge, unique insofar as it has been written by 15 contributors. The idea was to assemble these award-winning instructors' best questions. Each author contributed his or her best multiple choice questions for each chapter. I then put the questions in order and eliminated any that were too similar. I also lightly edited the questions to ensure that each conformed with the writing style established in the book because this style has been carefully crafted for maximum student comprehension. However, the editing was only light because we wanted each author's own unique brand of questions to come through.

The author of each question is identified by his or her initials. I expect that you will form your favorites among these authors based upon your teaching style, much as I did when ordering and editing the questions.

I have been teaching principles classes for over two decades, have written hundreds of exams, and won several teaching awards. Nonetheless, I was stunned by the quality of the questions we received. I lost count of the number of times that I marveled at a question and wished that *I* had thought of it. While creating this test bank took significantly more effort than preparing an ordinary test bank, I am sure that the quality you will find made the task worthwhile.

■ How to Assemble a Test

Because I have been teaching while working on these test banks, it has been natural to use them to create tests for my class. Having thousands of excellent questions immediately at hand made writing examinations an easy and (almost) pleasant task.

For each test, I decide *a priori* approximately how many questions I want from each chapter. Clearly my sense of the relative importance of the material plays a role here. I think this reflection is crucial because it ensures that my examinations cover the material that I deem most important for my students to know.

Because I write my tests using Word, I start the actual writing process by taking an old test and eliminating all but one question. Then, using the Word test bank files, I locate a question that I want to use, copy the question from the test bank file to my test, and immediately change the question number so that it is correct. As it happens, I prefer a slightly different paragraph style for my questions and answers than what is used in the test bank. Using the Word "Format Painter" (the paint brush symbol) I copy the format I prefer from the old question that I saved to the newly pasted question. Once I have a new question formatted with my preferred paragraph style, I delete the old question.

I change the style of the question and answers because I prefer a slightly different font and because I format the question and the first three answers using the "keep with next" command from the Format-Paragraph-Line and Page Breaks menu. The last answer for the question does not have this command. By using the "keep with next" command for the question and first three answers, I ensure that I do not have a question or answer break across a page.

As I copy and paste each question, I keep track of how many questions I have from each chapter. I do not slavishly adhere to my initial decision of how many questions I want from each chapter, but I also do not stray too far.

Finally, I print an initial copy of my examination and proofread it to be sure that I have not inadvertently given away the answer to one question with another question. I make any necessary corrections and am done. Given the quality of the test banks, I have that found I can easily write a high-quality 35-40 question examination within a little more than an hour.

■ Final Comments

Just as Sir Isaac Newton stood on the shoulders of the giants who came before him, so, too do test bank Volumes I and II reflect the superb work of the authors who initially wrote and compiled them for the Fourth Edition. Hence it is entirely fitting to thank them:

♦ Robert Whaples of Wake Forest University wrote the *Microeconomics* Volume I test bank.

♦ James Giordano and Peter A. Zaleski, both of Villanova University, wrote the *Microeconomics* Volume II test bank.

♦ Carol Dole of the University of North Carolina, Charlotte wrote both (!) *Macroeconomics* Volume I and II test banks.

The fine instructors who took part in our experiment and contributed questions to Volume III of these test banks also deserve thanks and praise. Contributing questions for all the chapters are:

♦ Melinda Nish of Salt Lake Community College

♦ Andrew Foshee of McNeese State University

♦ Nora Underwood of the University of California, Davis

♦ Virginia Shingleton of Valparaiso University

Contributing questions for the microeconomic chapters are:

♦ Jill Boylston Herndon of Hamline University

♦ Terry Olson of Truman State University

♦ Peter von Allmen of Moravian College

♦ Rochelle L. Ruffer of Youngstown State University

♦ Peter A. Zaleski of Villanova University

♦ Leo Chan of the University of Kansas

Contributing questions for the macroeconomic chapters are:

♦ Veronica Z. Kalich of Baldwin-Wallace College

♦ Kevin Carey of American University

♦ Donald H. Dutkowsky of Syracuse University

♦ Carol Dole of the University of North Carolina, Charlotte

♦ Sue Bartlett of the University of South Florida

I need once more to thank Carol Dole, who cheerfully supplied new questions for Volumes I and II of the test banks. Carol's ability to write excellent questions quickly is remarkable and made my life significantly easier. I also thank Sheryl Nelson, who drew most of the figures for Volume III. Her ability to render precisely the correct illustration is remarkable! Finally, I must acknowledge with pleasure the efforts of Deborah Kiernan, Senior Supplements Editor at Addison-Wesley, for overseeing the preparation and production of these test banks with care and unflagging good humor.

I have tried to make these *Test Banks* as helpful and useful as possible. Undoubtedly I have made some mistakes; mistakes that you may see. I have a standing offer in the *Study Guide* asking students who find any errors to notify me and promising that I will acknowledge them in all future editions of the *Study Guide*. I will make the same offer here: If you find any errors or have any comments or questions, *please* let me know and, if you want, I will note your help in all future editions of the test banks.

My address is below, or you can reach me via E-mail at RUSH@DALE.CBA.UFL.EDU.

Mark Rush
Economics Department
University of Florida
Gainesville, Florida 32611
May 1999

Table of Contents

Chapter 1

WHAT IS ECONOMICS?

■ Big Economic Questions

Topic: A Definition of Economics
Skill: Recognition
1) The fundamental questions in economics result from
 A) an excess of production over the wants of society.
 B) technological progress.
 C) distribution of income.
 D) scarcity of resources relative to the wants of society.

Answer: D

Topic: A Definition of Economics
Skill: Recognition
2) Economic scarcity arises from
 A) inefficient production.
 B) exploration.
 C) limited resources and limitless wants.
 D) limited wants and limitless resources.

Answer: C

Topic: A Definition of Economics
Skill: Conceptual
3) The problem of "scarcity" applies
 A) only in industrially developed countries because resources are scarce in these countries.
 B) only in underdeveloped countries because there are few productive resources in these countries.
 C) only in economic systems that are just beginning to develop because specialized resources are scarce.
 D) to all economic systems, regardless of their level of development.

Answer: D

Topic: A Definition of Economics
Skill: Conceptual
4) When a wealthy businessman is unable to buy tickets to the Superbowl, he experiences _____.
 A) economics
 B) scarcity
 C) opportunity costs
 D) the fallacy of composition

Answer: B

Topic: What Goods and Services Are Produced?
Skill: Conceptual
5) _____ are (is) all the things that we value and are willing to pay for.
 A) Resources.
 B) Goods and services.
 C) Points along the production possibility frontier.
 D) Capital.

Answer: B

Topic: What Goods and Services Are Produced?
Skill: Conceptual
6) When a farmer decides to raise hogs instead of cattle, the farmer is answering the _____ question.
 A) "what"
 B) "when"
 C) "where"
 D) "why"

Answer: A

Topic: What Goods and Services Are Produced?
Skill: Conceptual
7) When a farmer decides to grow sugar cane instead of radishes, the farmer is answering the _____ question.
 A) "what"
 B) "when"
 C) "where"
 D) "why"

Answer: A

Topic: What Goods and Services Are Produced?
Skill: Conceptual

8) When a country decides to produce fewer bombers and more public housing projects, it is answering the _____ question.
A) "how"
B) "what"
C) "when"
D) "who"

Answer: B

Topic: What Goods and Services Are Produced?
Skill: Conceptual

9) When a firm decides to produce more electric cars and fewer gas guzzlers, it is answering the _____ question.
A) "how"
B) "when"
C) "what"
D) "who"

Answer: C

Topic: What Goods and Services Are Produced?
Skill: Conceptual

10) When a textile firm decides to produce more cotton fabric and less synthetic fabric, it is answering the _____ question.
A) "how"
B) "when"
C) "why"
D) "what"

Answer: D

Topic: How Are Goods and Services Produced?
Skill: Conceptual

11) When a farmer decides to harvest oranges by huge machines instead of by migrant workers, the farmer is answering the _____ question.
A) "how"
B) "when"
C) "why"
D) "what"

Answer: A

Topic: How Are Goods and Services Produced?
Skill: Conceptual

12) When a lawyer decides to type a brief on a computer rather than use a typewriter, the lawyer is answering the _____ question.
A) "how"
B) "when"
C) "why"
D) "what"

Answer: A

Topic: How Are Goods and Services Produced?
Skill: Conceptual

13) When a firm decides to produce computers using robots instead of people, it is answering the _____ question.
A) "when"
B) "how"
C) "what"
D) "why"

Answer: B

Topic: How Are Goods and Services Produced?
Skill: Conceptual

14) To meet increased demand for its good, a firm decides to hire a few high-skilled workers rather than hire many low-skilled workers. The firm is answering the _____ question.
A) "how"
B) "when"
C) "what"
D) "why"

Answer: A

Topic: How Are Goods and Services Produced?
Skill: Conceptual

15) An art museum decides to offer tours by having visitors listen to cassette tapes rather than have tour guides. The museum is answering the _____ question.
A) "why"
B) "what"
C) "when"
D) "how"

Answer: D

Topic: When Are Goods and Services Produced?
Skill: Conceptual

16) If a firm decides to temporarily reduce production as a result of a recession, it is answering the _____ question.
A) "what"
B) "why"
C) "when"
D) "where"

Answer: C

Topic: When Are Goods and Services Produced?
Skill: Conceptual

17) A toy factory decides to stay open 24 hours a day during October in anticipation of the holiday season. This factory is answering the _____ question.
A) "when"
B) "who"
C) "where"
D) "why"

Answer: A

Topic: When Are Goods and Services Produced?
Skill: Conceptual

18) As the result of a severe winter, construction workers are temporarily laid off by their companies. These firms are answering the _____ question.
A) "how"
B) "when"
C) "where"
D) "what"

Answer: B

Topic: When Are Goods and Services Produced?
Skill: Conceptual

19) In preparation for back-to-school sales, a clothing store decides to have its employees work overtime. The store is answering the _____ question.
A) "how"
B) "where"
C) "when"
D) "who"

Answer: C

Topic: When Are Goods and Services Produced?
Skill: Conceptual

20) When an amusement park is open 12 hours every day of the week during the summer but open only on weekends during the rest of the year, the park is answering the _____ question.
A) "who"
B) "where"
C) "what"
D) "when"

Answer: D

Topic: When Are Goods and Services Produced?
Skill: Conceptual

21) As the result of a recession, firms temporarily lay off portions of their workforce. These firms are answering the _____ question.
A) "when"
B) "why"
C) "what"
D) "where"

Answer: A

Topic: Where Are Goods and Services Produced?
Skill: Conceptual

22) When IBM produces computers in many different locations, it is answering the _____ question.
A) "where"
B) "who"
C) "when"
D) "what"

Answer: A

Topic: Who Consumes the Goods and Services?
Skill: Conceptual

23) The fact that some people can afford to live in beautiful homes while others are homeless, is an example of an economy facing the _____ question.
A) "who"
B) "when"
C) "how"
D) "why"

Answer: A

Topic: Who Consumes the Goods and Services?
Skill: Conceptual

24) The fact that a rock star earns $5 million a year while a teacher earns $25,000 annually is an example of an economy answering the _____ question.
   A) "when"
   B) "who"
   C) "how"
   D) "why"
Answer: B

Topic: Who Consumes the Goods and Services?
Skill: Conceptual

25) Sue, who has a law degree, earns $200,000 a year while Chris, a high school dropout earns $5.00 an hour. This is an example of an economy answering the _____ question.
   A) "when"
   B) "why"
   C) "who"
   D) "how"
Answer: C

Topic: Who Consumes the Goods and Services?
Skill: Conceptual

26) A star athlete can afford a garage full of exotic cars while other people can only afford to take a city bus for transportation. This is an example of an economy answering the _____ question.
   A) "what"
   B) "when"
   C) "why"
   D) "who"
Answer: D

■ Big Ideas of Economics

Topic: Opportunity Cost
Skill: Recognition

27) Opportunity cost is best defined as
   A) how much money is paid for something.
   B) how much money is paid for something, taking inflation into account.
   C) the highest valued alternative that is foregone in making a choice.
   D) all the alternatives that are foregone in making a choice.
Answer: C

Topic: Opportunity Cost
Skill: Recognition

28) Which of the following statements are correct?
   I.   The "highest-valued alternative given up" is known as the opportunity cost of making a choice.
   II. Wealthy economies don't experience opportunity costs.
   III. Scarcity creates opportunity costs.
   A) I only.
   B) I and II.
   C) I and III.
   D) I, II, and III.
Answer: C

Topic: Opportunity Cost
Skill: Conceptual

29) You have the choice of going on vacation to Florida for one week, staying at work for the week, or spending the week doing fix-up projects around your house. If you decide to go to Florida, the opportunity cost of the week is
   A) working *and* doing fix-up projects.
   B) working *or* doing fix-up projects, depending on which you would have done otherwise.
   C) working, because you would be giving up dollars.
   D) nothing because you will enjoy the trip to Florida.
Answer: B

Topic: Opportunity Cost
Skill: Conceptual

30) Fred and Ann are both given free tickets to see a movie. Both decide to see the same movie. We know that
   A) both bear an opportunity cost of seeing the movie because they could have done other things instead of see the movie.
   B) both bear the same opportunity cost of seeing the movie because they are doing the same thing.
   C) it is not possible to calculate the opportunity cost of seeing the movie because the tickets were free.
   D) it is possible to calculate the opportunity cost of seeing the movie and it is zero because the tickets were free.
Answer: A

Topic: Opportunity Cost
Skill: Analytical

31) Bill Bonecrusher graduates from college with a choice of playing professional football at $2 million a year or coaching for $50,000 a year. He decides to play football, but eight years later, though he could continue to play football at $2 million a year, he quits football to make movies for $3 million a year. His opportunity cost of playing football at graduation was _____ and eight years later the opportunity cost of making movies was _____.

A) $50,000; $2 million
B) $2 million; $2 million
C) $2 million; $3 million
D) $50,000; $50,000

Answer: A

Topic: Marginal Benefit
Skill: Recognition

32) A benefit due to an increase in activity is called a(n)

A) marginal benefit.
B) economic benefit.
C) total benefit.
D) opportunity gain.

Answer: A

Topic: Marginal Benefit
Skill: Analytical

33) A student is studying for an exam 2 hours a day and is debating whether to study an extra hour. The student's marginal benefit

A) depends on the grade the student earns on the exam.
B) is the benefit the student receives from studying all 3 hours.
C) is the benefit the student receives from studying the extra hour.
D) is greater than the student's marginal cost.

Answer: C

Topic: Marginal Benefit
Skill: Analytical

34) A student athlete is deciding whether to work out for an extra hour. Her marginal benefit from another hour of exercise

A) is the benefit she gets from all the hours she's worked out all week.
B) is the benefit she receives from exercising the additional hour.
C) is less than the marginal cost of the additional hour.
D) depends on the cost of the workout.

Answer: B

Topic: Marginal Cost
Skill: Recognition

35) A cost due to an increase in activity is called a(n)

A) incentive loss.
B) marginal cost.
C) negative marginal benefit.
D) total cost.

Answer: B

Topic: Marginal Cost
Skill: Analytical

36) A bagel store is deciding whether to add a fifth employee to its morning shift. The marginal cost of hiring this worker

A) depends only on the wages paid to the worker.
B) depends on the total wages paid during the morning shift.
C) depends on the revenues the worker brings in.
D) depends on all the costs created by hiring the fifth worker.

Answer: D

Topic: Marginal Benefit/Marginal Cost
Skill: Analytical

37) A store remains open from 8 am to 4 pm each weekday. The store owner is deciding whether to stay open an extra hour each evening. The owner's marginal benefit

A) is the benefit the owner receives from staying open from 8 am to 5 pm.
B) depends on the revenues the owner makes during the day.
C) must be greater than or equal to the owner's marginal cost if the owner decides to stay open.
D) is equal to revenues minus operating costs.

Answer: C

Topic: Voluntary Exchange
Skill: Conceptual
38) Voluntary exchange
  A) allows sellers to gain at the expense of buyers.
  B) allows buyers to gain at the expense of sellers.
  C) allows both buyers and sellers to gain.
  D) prevents markets from working efficiently.
Answer: C

Topic: Voluntary Exchange
Skill: Recognition
39) In a market-based economy
  A) there is little room for individual decision making.
  B) buyers and sellers gain from voluntary exchange.
  C) there are reduced opportunity costs.
  D) incentives play a small role.
Answer: B

Topic: Markets
Skill: Conceptual
40) Markets are _____ because they _____.
  A) efficient; allow consumers to gain at the expense of producers
  B) efficient; allocate resources to where they are most highly valued
  C) inefficient; raise opportunity costs
  D) inefficient; require complex planning systems
Answer: B

Topic: Markets
Skill: Analytical
41) A drought destroys a large portion of the nation's wheat crop and drives up the price of wheat. The fact that some people pay the higher price for bread and continue to eat bread while others reduce their consumption of bread
  A) is an example of the fallacy of composition.
  B) shows that markets can fail.
  C) is an example of the *post hoc* fallacy.
  D) reflects that markets are efficient.
Answer: D

Topic: Markets
Skill: Recognition
42) An economic system that relies upon some people giving orders to make economic decision would be
  A) a traditional system.
  B) a market system.
  C) a command system.
  D) a incentive-failure system.
Answer: C

Topic: Market Failure
Skill: Recognition
43) _____ is (are) defined to occur when the market does not use resources efficiently.
  A) Increased opportunity costs
  B) Voluntary exchange
  C) Market failure
  D) Tradeoffs
Answer: C

Topic: Market Failure
Skill: Conceptual
44) Which of the following can lead to market failure?
  I. A single producer controlling an entire market.
  II. Producers who don't account for costs they impose on others.
  III. Goods that must be consumed by everyone equally.
  A) I only.
  B) I and II.
  C) I and III.
  D) I, II, and III.
Answer: D

Topic: Market Failure
Skill: Conceptual
45) To overcome _____ government action may help insure that resources are used efficiently.
  A) high opportunity costs
  B) market failure
  C) scarcity
  D) comparative disadvantage
Answer: B

Topic: Market Failure
Skill: Conceptual
46) Which of the following are examples of market failure?
   I.   Pollution.
   II. Low wages.
   III. High interest rates.
A) I only.
B) I and II.
C) II and III.
D) I, II, and III.
Answer: A

Topic: Market Failure
Skill: Conceptual
47) Which of the following are examples of market failure?
   I.   Scarcity.
   II. High opportunity costs.
   III. High oil prices.
A) I.
B) I and II.
C) I, II, and III.
D) None of the above are examples of market failure.
Answer: D

Topic: Market Failure
Skill: Conceptual
48) To overcome market failure, governments
A) pass antitrust laws.
B) enact environmental protection laws.
C) subsidize the production of some goods.
D) all of the above.
Answer: D

Topic: Expenditure and Income
Skill: Recognition
49) The relationship between expenditures, income and the value of production is
A) expenditure – income = value of production.
B) income – expenditure = value of production.
C) expenditure – value of production = income.
D) expenditure = value of production = income.
Answer: D

Topic: Expenditure and Income
Skill: Conceptual
50) If you spend $200 on a camera, your expenditure has generated
A) incomes less than $200 because there are production costs.
B) incomes equal to the value of production.
C) incomes equal to $200.
D) Both answers B and C are correct.
Answer: D

Topic: Expenditure and Income
Skill: Conceptual
51) If you spend $2.50 on a hamburger at Hamburger Heaven
A) your expenditure must be greater than the value of producing the hamburger.
B) your expenditure creates $2.50 in incomes to the people who have contributed to making the burger.
C) your expenditure must generate incomes greater than $2.50 so that the owner of Hamburger Heaven earns a profit.
D) None of the above answers are correct.
Answer: B

Topic: Productivity
Skill: Recognition
52) The dollar value of production can increase because
A) prices rise.
B) productivity increases.
C) population increases.
D) All of the above answers are correct.
Answer: D

Topic: Productivity
Skill: Recognition
53) Which of the following definitely causes an improvement in living standards?
   I.   Increases in output.
   II. Increases in population.
   III. Increases in productivity.
A) I only.
B) I and II.
C) II and III.
D) III only.
Answer: D

Topic: Productivity
Skill: Conceptual

54) If output in a country has increased by 10 percent and population has increased by 7 percent, we conclude that within that nation

A) productivity has increased.
B) living standards have increased.
C) output per person has declined.
D) Both answers A and B are both correct.

Answer: D

Topic: Inflation
Skill: Recognition

55) _____ occur(s) when prices rise and the quantity of money _____ production.

A) Inflation; increases faster than
B) Inflation; increases at the same rate as
C) Productivity increases; increases faster than
D) Productivity increases; increases slower than

Answer: A

Topic: Inflation
Skill: Recognition

56) A situation of "too much money chasing too few goods" is associated with

A) increasing productivity.
B) inflation.
C) rising opportunity costs.
D) market failure.

Answer: B

Topic: Inflation
Skill: Conceptual

57) If the quantity of money increases faster than production.

A) money starts to lose its value.
B) eventually production will increase.
C) eventually more jobs will be created.
D) productivity will increase.

Answer: A

Topic: Unemployment
Skill: Recognition

58) Which of the following is true regarding unemployment?

I. Unemployment is steady over the business cycle.
II. Some unemployment is productive.
III. The existence of unemployment is normal.

A) I and II.
B) I and III.
C) II and III.
D) I, II, and III.

Answer: C

Topic: Unemployment
Skill: Conceptual

59) The unemployment that results from workers searching for a suitable job and firms carefully searching for the right employee

A) shows that market failure is present.
B) improves productivity.
C) is inefficient.
D) reduces productivity.

Answer: B

■ What Economists Do

Topic: Microeconomics and Macroeconomics
Skill: Recognition

60) The analysis of the behavior of individual decision-making units is the definition of

A) microeconomics.
B) positive economics.
C) macroeconomics.
D) normative economics.

Answer: A

Topic: Microeconomics and Macroeconomics
Skill: Recognition

61) In part, microeconomics studies

A) how households spend their limited income.
B) how business firms make choices.
C) how prices are determined in markets.
D) All of the above.

Answer: D

Topic: Microeconomics and Macroeconomics
Skill: Recognition

62) Microeconomics is concerned with
  A) how prices and quantities are determined in individual product markets.
  B) changes in the economy's total output of goods and services over long periods of time.
  C) factors that explain changes in the unemployment rate over time.
  D) the causes of recessions.

Answer: A

Topic: Microeconomics and Macroeconomics
Skill: Conceptual

63) An example of a question that might be explored in microeconomics is to determine the level of
  A) employment at General Motors.
  B) savings by the household sector.
  C) investment by the private sector.
  D) the total employment within the U.S. economy.

Answer: A

Topic: Microeconomics and Macroeconomics
Skill: Conceptual

64) One topic of study for a microeconomist would be
  A) the causes of inflation.
  B) the causes of aggregate unemployment.
  C) the effects of an increase in the price of gasoline.
  D) the effects of an increase in government spending.

Answer: C

Topic: Microeconomics and Macroeconomics
Skill: Conceptual

65) Microeconomics is concerned with the study of
  A) inflation, unemployment and economic growth.
  B) the general price level.
  C) the effect government regulation has on the price of a product.
  D) total output and the money supply.

Answer: C

Topic: Microeconomics and Macroeconomics
Skill: Recognition

66) The branch of economics that deals with the analysis of the whole economy is called
  A) macroeconomics.
  B) marginal analysis.
  C) microeconomics.
  D) *ceteris paribus* analysis.

Answer: A

Topic: Microeconomics and Macroeconomics
Skill: Recognition

67) Macroeconomics is concerned with
  A) individual consumers.
  B) government decision making concerning farm price supports.
  C) economy-wide variables.
  D) the effects on a corporation of a strike by the United Auto Workers.

Answer: C

Topic: Positive and Normative
Skill: Recognition

68) A positive statement is a statement about
  A) what is.
  B) what is and what should be.
  C) what should be but is not.
  D) what is desirable.

Answer: A

Topic: Positive and Normative
Skill: Recognition

69) Positive economics
  A) prescribes what should be.
  B) is related only to microeconomics.
  C) can be tested against the facts.
  D) cannot be tested against the facts.

Answer: C

Topic: Positive and Normative
Skill: Conceptual

70) Which of the following is a positive statement?
  A) An unemployment rate of 9 percent is a national disgrace.
  B) Unemployment is not so important a problem as inflation.
  C) When the national unemployment rate is 9 percent, the unemployment rate for inner-city youth is often close to 40 percent.
  D) Unemployment and inflation are equally important problems.

Answer: C

Topic: Positive and Normative
Skill: Conceptual
71) Which of the following is a positive statement?
A) The United States should fight inflation at the expense of unemployment.
B) What to do with social security is the most important economic issue today.
C) A 5 percent increase in income leads to a 3 percent increase in the consumption of orange juice.
D) Because they have negative impact on productivity, labor unions should be eliminated.
Answer: C

Topic: Positive and Normative
Skill: Recognition
72) A normative statement concerns
A) what is provable.
B) what is correct.
C) what is incorrect.
D) a value judgment.
Answer: D

Topic: Positive and Normative
Skill: Recognition
73) Normative economics
A) describes what ought to be.
B) describes what is rather than what ought to be.
C) describes the process of economic policy-making.
D) deals with economic hypotheses that are not well-established laws.
Answer: A

Topic: Positive and Normative
Skill: Conceptual
74) The statement that peach ice cream is better than chocolate ice cream
A) can be tested using the scientific approach.
B) is a normative statement.
C) is a statement of fact.
D) provides a basis for predicting which type of ice cream will exhibit the most sales.
Answer: B

Topic: Positive and Normative
Skill: Conceptual
75) The statement "Unemployment should be kept at or below a level of 6 percent" is
A) a positive statement.
B) a normative statement.
C) a prediction.
D) an assumption.
Answer: B

Topic: Positive and Normative
Skill: Recognition
76) In order to examine the validity of positive economic statements, economists engage in
A) observation and measurement.
B) model building.
C) testing models.
D) all of the above.
Answer: D

Topic: Models
Skill: Recognition
77) Which of the following statements about economic models is true?
A) Economic models are not empirically testable.
B) The predictive power of models is not important.
C) Economic models are designed so that every detail of the real world can be analyzed.
D) Every economic model is based on a set of assumptions.
Answer: D

Topic: Models
Skill: Recognition
78) Which of the following statements apply to economic models?
I. An economic model makes assumptions.
II. An economic model is simpler than the reality it explains.
III. A good economic model is always used to make normative statements.
A) I and II.
B) I and III.
C) II and III.
D) I, II and III.
Answer: A

Topic: *Ceteris Paribus*
Skill: Recognition
79) The term "*ceteris paribus*" means
  A) the greatest good for all.
  B) the study of scarcity and choice.
  C) all other things remaining equal.
  D) value free and testable.
Answer: C

Topic: *Ceteris Paribus*
Skill: Conceptual
80) Which of the following is an example of an application of the "*ceteris paribus*" assumption?
  A) An analysis of how price changes affect people's purchases when all other factors are held constant.
  B) An analysis of how people purchase more goods when prices decline and their income increases.
  C) After reading an article on the dangers of high fat diets, an individual buys less red meat when prices increase.
  D) An analysis of how worker productivity increases when a firm invests in new machines and training programs.
Answer: A

Topic: Fallacy of Composition
Skill: Recognition
81) The fallacy of composition is the false belief that
  A) what is true for each part is also true for the whole.
  B) because event A occurred before event B, event A caused event B.
  C) because event A occurred after event B, event A caused event B.
  D) the *ceteris paribus* condition does not apply.
Answer: A

Topic: *Post Hoc* Fallacy
Skill: Recognition
82) The _____ describes the mistake of reasoning that event A causes event B just because event A occurs prior to event B.
  A) fallacy of composition
  B) *post hoc* fallacy
  C) fallacy of supposition
  D) *ceteris paribus* fallacy
Answer: B

Topic: *Post Hoc* Fallacy
Skill: Conceptual
83) "Every time wages rise, prices rise; if people would just stop asking for higher wages inflation could be brought under control." This statement is an example of a possible
  A) ceteris paribus fallacy.
  B) *post hoc* fallacy.
  C) fallacy of composition.
  D) positive normative economic statement.
Answer: B

Topic: *Post Hoc* Fallacy
Skill: Conceptual
84) "Every time I wear my school's colors on Saturday, our team wins its football game." This statement is an example of
  A) ceteris paribus fallacy.
  B) fallacy of composition.
  C) *post hoc* fallacy.
  D) a normative economic statement.
Answer: C

■ True or False Questions

Topic: Big Economic Questions
Skill: Conceptual
85) Economic scarcity applies to both the rich and the poor.
Answer: TRUE

Topic: Big Economic Questions
Skill: Conceptual
86) Economic scarcity arises because of opportunity costs.
Answer: FALSE

Topic: Big Economic Questions
Skill: Conceptual
87) A country using mainly labor to build a dam instead of using mainly machines is answering the "how" question.
Answer: TRUE

Topic: Big Economic Questions
Skill: Conceptual
88) When Nike produces shoes in Indonesia for sale around the world, it is answering the "where" question.
Answer: TRUE

Topic: Big Ideas of Economics
Skill: Conceptual
89) When a firm asks it employees to work overtime during the holiday season, it is answering the "where" question.
Answer: FALSE

Topic: Big Ideas of Economics
Skill: Conceptual
90) When I buy a $6.00 movie ticket, the opportunity cost of going to the movie is only the $6.00 I spend.
Answer: FALSE

Topic: Big Ideas of Economics
Skill: Conceptual
91) Voluntary exchange makes only sellers better off.
Answer: FALSE

Topic: Big Ideas of Economics
Skill: Conceptual
92) Air pollution is an example of market failure.
Answer: TRUE

Topic: Big Ideas of Economics
Skill: Conceptual
93) As population increases, output necessarily increases, thereby creating an increase in living standards.
Answer: FALSE

Topic: What Economists Do
Skill: Conceptual
94) Microeconomics is the study of topics like national income and expenditure.
Answer: FALSE

Topic: What Economists Do
Skill: Conceptual
95) Macroeconomics is the study of aggregate variables like inflation and unemployment.
Answer: TRUE

Topic: What Economists Do
Skill: Conceptual
96) Economic models make some assumptions in order to simplify the real world.
Answer: TRUE

Topic: What Economists Do
Skill: Conceptual
97) Keeping all but the two economic variables you are interested in constant is an example of the "*post hoc* fallacy."
Answer: FALSE

Topic: What Economists Do
Skill: Conceptual
98) "Every time I buy stock, the stock market falls. So my buying decisions must be a good forecast of the market's behavior." This statement is an example of the fallacy of composition.
Answer: FALSE

■ Essay Questions

Topic: Big Economic Questions
Skill: Conceptual
99) Explain the connection between scarcity and economics.
Answer:

Topic: Big Economic Questions
Skill: Conceptual
100) Explain why both rich and poor people experience scarcity.
Answer:

Topic: Big Ideas of Economics
Skill: Conceptual
101) What are the five big economic questions? Give an example of each.
Answer:

Topic: Big Ideas of Economics
Skill: Conceptual
102) Explain the concept of opportunity costs by using an example.
Answer:

Topic: Big Ideas of Economics
Skill: Conceptual
103) What is the difference between a total benefit and a marginal benefit?
Answer:

Topic: Big Ideas of Economics
Skill: Conceptual
104) What is the relationship between expenditure, income and the value of production?
Answer:

Topic: Big Ideas of Economics
Skill: Conceptual
105) What is the connection between output per person, productivity and living standards?

Answer:

Topic: What Economists Do
Skill: Conceptual
106) What is the difference between microeconomics and macroeconomics? Give an example of an issue each studies.

Answer:

Topic: What Economists Do
Skill: Conceptual
107) Give an example of a positive and a normative economic statement.

Answer:

Topic: What Economists Do
Skill: Conceptual
108) Why is it important that economists use the idea of "*ceteris paribus*" when testing economic models?

Answer:

Chapter 2 MAKING AND USING GRAPHS

■ Graphing Data

Topic: Graphing Data
Skill: Recognition
1) On the horizontal axis of a graph, generally
   A) values increase from left to right.
   B) values increase from right to left.
   C) values can be positive and/or negative.
   D) Both answers A and C are correct.
Answer: D

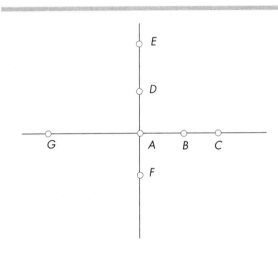

Topic: Graphing Data
Skill: Analytical
2) In the figure above, the value on the *x*-axis increases as we move from
   A) point *G* to point *A*.
   B) point *C* to point *A*.
   C) point *F* to point *A*.
   D) point *E* to point *A*.
Answer: A

Topic: Graphing Data
Skill: Analytical
3) In the figure above, the value on the *y*-axis decreases as we move from
   A) point *G* to point *A*.
   B) point *C* to point *A*.
   C) point *F* to point *A*.
   D) point *E* to point *A*.
Answer: D

Topic: Graphing Data
Skill: Analytical
4) In the figure above, point *B* is _____.
   A) on the *x*-axis
   B) on the *y*-axis
   C) at the origin
   D) a coordinate
Answer: A

Topic: Scatter Diagrams
Skill: Conceptual
5) A scatter diagram will be most useful
   A) in discerning a possible relationship between height and weight for individuals.
   B) in resolving a dispute over two normative assertions.
   C) in predicting next year's rate of unemployment.
   D) All of the above are correct.
Answer: A

Topic: Scatter Diagrams
Skill: Conceptual
6) Recording data about students' class year and GPA in a graph will yield
   A) no relationship, under any circumstances.
   B) a time-series diagram.
   C) a contour map.
   D) a scatter diagram.
Answer: D

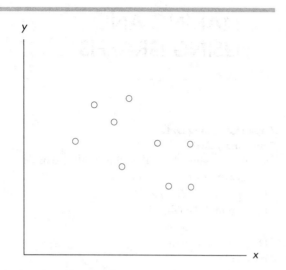

Topic: Scatter Diagrams
Skill: Recognition

7)   The figure above is an example of a

A)   time series graph.
B)   regression.
C)   scatter diagram.
D)   cross-section graph.

Answer: C

Topic: Scatter Diagrams
Skill: Recognition

8)   Compared to other types of graphs, a _____ is preferred to show the relationship between two variables like unemployment and inflation.

A)   scatter diagram.
B)   time-series graph.
C)   cross-section graph.
D)   coordinate.

Answer: A

Topic: Scatter Diagrams
Skill: Conceptual

9)   Using a graph to plot family incomes against with food expenditures results in

A)   a time series graph.
B)   a scatter diagram.
C)   a time series and a scatter diagram.
D)   neither a time series nor a scatter diagram.

Answer: B

Topic: Scatter Diagrams
Skill: Analytical

10)   The figure above shows that in 1996, unemployment was equal to about _____ and the inflation rate was equal to about _____.

A)   7.0 percent; 3.0 percent
B)   3.0 percent; 5.5 percent
C)   5.5 percent; 3.0 percent
D)   6.0 percent; 4.0 percent

Answer: C

Topic: Time-Series Graphs
Skill: Recognition

11)   To show how a variable _____, we typically use a _____.

A)   relates to another variable; time series graph
B)   relates to another variable; pie chart
C)   evolves over time; time series graph
D)   evolves over time; cross section graph

Answer: C

Topic: Time-Series Graphs
Skill: Conceptual

12)   A time series graph showing total production in Japan from 1960 to 1998 shows a positive trend. It is likely that total production

A)   fell every year between 1960 and 1998.
B)   rose every year between 1960 and 1998.
C)   was lower in 1998 than in 1960.
D)   was higher in 1998 than in 1960.

Answer: D

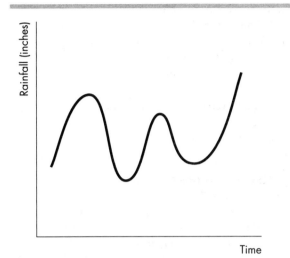

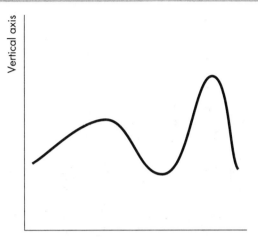

Topic: Time-Series Graphs
Skill: Recognition
13) The figure above shows a
   A) two-variable time-series graph.
   B) time-series graph.
   C) scatter diagram.
   D) regression.
Answer: B

Topic: Time-Series Graphs
Skill: Recognition
14) A time series graph reveals whether there is a ____ which represents ____.
   A) trend in a variable; a general tendency for the variable to rise or fall
   B) relationship between two variables; a cross-section graph
   C) trend in a variable; unrelated variables
   D) relationship between two variables; a trend in a variable
Answer: A

Topic: Time-Series Graphs
Skill: Recognition
15) The figure above shows a time series graph. The horizontal axis measures ____ and the vertical axis measures ____.
   A) time; x-values
   B) time; the variable of interest
   C) the variable of interest; time
   D) y-values; the variable of interest
Answer: B

Topic: Time-Series Graphs
Skill: Conceptual
16) A time series graph showing the unemployment rate between 1980 and 1998 shows a negative trend. It is likely that the unemployment rate
   A) fell every year between 1980 and 1998.
   B) rose every year between 1980 and 1998.
   C) was lower in 1998 than in 1980.
   D) was higher in 1998 than in 1980.
Answer: C

Topic: Cross-Section Graphs
Skill: Recognition
17) A ____ shows relative values for different groups at a certain point in time.
   A) time-series graphs.
   B) regression.
   C) cross-section graph.
   D) scatter plot.
Answer: C

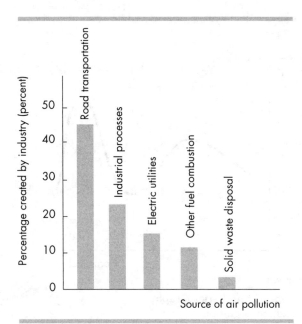

Topic: Cross-Section Graphs
Skill: Recognition
18) The above figure shows sources of air pollution. The figure is
   A) a time series graph.
   B) a cross-section graph.
   C) a multi-variable line graph.
   D) a scatter plot diagram.
Answer: B

Topic: Cross-Section Graphs
Skill: Conceptual
19) You have data for real income per person for developing countries in 1998. The type of graph to best display these data would be a
   A) cross-section graph.
   B) time-series graph.
   C) multi-variable time series graph.
   D) scatter diagram.
Answer: A

Topic: Cross-Section Graphs
Skill: Conceptual
20) You have data for sales revenues for all the pizza stores you own for the month of September. The type of graph to best display these data would be a
   A) time-series graph.
   B) cross-section graph.
   C) scatter diagram.
   D) Venn diagram.
Answer: B

Topic: Cross-Section Graphs
Skill: Conceptual
21) You have data for the amount of rainfall in 50 cities for the month of June. The type of graph to best display these data would be a
   A) time-series graph.
   B) multi-variable time series graph.
   C) cross-section graph.
   D) scatter diagram.
Answer: C

Topic: Cross-Section Graphs
Skill: Conceptual
22) You have data for average tax rates for each of the 50 states for 1998. The type of graph to best display these data would be a
   A) a cross-section graph.
   B) a time-series graph.
   C) a scatter diagram.
   D) a multi-variable time-series graph.
Answer: A

■ Graphs Used in Economic Models

Topic: Variables That Move In the Same Direction
Skill: Recognition
23) If there is a direct relationship between two variables,
   A) the graph of the relationship will be upward-sloping.
   B) the graph of the relationship will be downward-sloping.
   C) the slope of the line (or the slope of a tangent line to the curve) will be negative.
   D) Both answers A and C are correct.
Answer: A

Topic: Variables That Move In the Same Direction
Skill: Recognition
24) The variable measured on the y-axis increases whenever the variable measured on the x-axis increases. Thus the relationship between the variables will
   A) be negatively sloped.
   B) have a slope of zero.
   C) be a vertical line.
   D) be none of the above.
Answer: D

Topic: Variables That Move In the Same Direction
Skill: Recognition

25) A positive relationship exists between two variables if

A) one variable has "positively" no effect on the other variable.

B) a reduction in one variable is associated with an increase in the other variable.

C) a reduction in one variable is associated with a decrease in the other variable.

D) both variables are inflation-distorted.

Answer: C

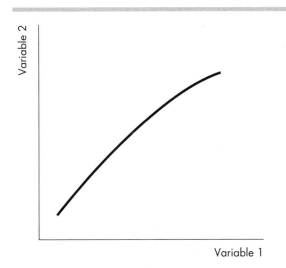

Topic: Variables That Move In the Same Direction
Skill: Recognition

26) The figure above shows _____ between the two variables.

A) a positive

B) a negative

C) no relationship

D) an inverse

Answer: A

Topic: Variables That Move In the Same Direction
Skill: Conceptual

27) "As you devote more hours to studying, your GPA increases." A graph of this relationship would show

A) a positive relationship.

B) a direct relationship.

C) an inverse relationship.

D) Both answers A and B are correct.

Answer: D

Topic: Variables That Move In the Same Direction
Skill: Conceptual

28) "As interest rates rise, people save more money." A graph displaying this relationship would show

A) an inverse relationship.

B) a positive relationship.

C) a cross-section graph.

D) a positive then a negative relationship.

Answer: B

Topic: Variables That Move In the Same Direction
Skill: Conceptual

29) "If you hire 1 worker, the worker can produce 20 pizzas a day. If you hire a 2nd worker, that worker can produce 10 more pizzas. If you hire a 3rd worker, that worker can produce 2 more pizzas a day." A graph displaying this relationship between the number of employees and *total* pizza output per day would show

A) a positive linear relationship.

B) an upward-sloping curve that becomes less steep.

C) a negative linear relationship.

D) a negatively-sloped curve that becomes less steep.

Answer: B

Topic: Variables That Move In the Same Direction
Skill: Conceptual

30) If you study 3 hours for an exam, you can raise your score by 30 points. If you study for another 3 hours your score increases by 10 points. And if you study for another 3 hours, your score will increase by 5 more points. A graph displaying this relationship between the number of hours studied and your *total* exam score would show

A) a positive linear relationship.

B) an upward-sloping curve that becomes less steep.

C) a negative linear relationship.

D) an upward-sloping curve that becomes more steep.

Answer: B

Topic: Variables That Move In the Same Direction
Skill: Conceptual

31) Suppose you produce 10 bikes a day for a total cost of $1000. Total costs increase to $1100 when you produce 15 bikes. Finally, total costs increase to $1300 if you make 20 bikes. A graph showing the relationship between total costs and the number of bikes produced would be

A) a negatively-sloped line that becomes steeper.
B) a positively-sloped line that becomes steeper.
C) a negatively-sloped line that becomes flatter.
D) a positively-sloped line that becomes flatter.

Answer: B

Topic: Variables That Move In the Opposite Direction
Skill: Recognition

32) A negative relationship exists between the variable measured along the *y*-axis and the variable measured along the *x*-axis if

A) a reduction in the variable measured along the *x*-axis is associated with a reduction in the variable measured along the *y*-axis.
B) an increase in the variable measured along the *x*-axis is associated with an increase in the variable measured along the *y*-axis.
C) the variable measured along the *x*-axis and the variable measured along the *y*-axis move in the opposite direction.
D) the variable measured along the *x*-axis and the variable measured along the *y*-axis move in the same direction.

Answer: C

Topic: Variables That Move In the Opposite Direction
Skill: Recognition

33) Along a curve, when one variable increases, the other variable decreases. The curve showing this relationship has

A) a zero slope.
B) a positive slope.
C) a negative slope.
D) an increasing then a decreasing slope.

Answer: C

Topic: Variables That Move In the Opposite Direction
Skill: Conceptual

34) "As interest rates fall, people spend more." A graph showing the relationship between interest rates and spending would have

A) an inverse relationship.
B) a negative then a positive slope.
C) a negative slope.
D) Both answers A and C are correct.

Answer: D

Topic: Variables That Move In the Opposite Direction
Skill: Conceptual

35) "As the price of gasoline increases, fewer people buy cars that are gas guzzlers." A graph showing this relationship would have

A) a negative slope.
B) a positive relationship.
C) a direct relationship.
D) a horizontal line.

Answer: A

Topic: Variables That Move In the Opposite Direction
Skill: Conceptual

36) A graph shows that as fees to use ATM machines increase, people use them less frequently. The graph of this relationship would show

A) an inverse relationship.
B) a negative relationship.
C) a direct relationship.
D) Both answers A and B are correct.

Answer: D

Topic: Variables That Move In the Opposite Direction
Skill: Conceptual

37) "The price of long distance phone calls goes down after 5 p.m. and falls further after 11 p.m. As a result, people make more long distance phone calls as it gets later each night." A graph showing this relationship between long distance phone rates and the number of calls made would show

A) a negatively-sloped curve.
B) an inverse relationship.
C) a positively-sloped curve.
D) Both answers A and B are correct.

Answer: D

Topic: Variables That Move In the Opposite Direction
Skill: Conceptual

38) As the number of days without rain increases, the amount of wheat per acre grown declines. A graph showing this relationship shows

A) a horizontal line.
B) a vertical line.
C) a positive relationship.
D) None of the above.

Answer: D

Topic: Variables That Move In the Opposite Direction
Skill: Conceptual

39) As a firm produces more and more CDs, the average cost of producing each CD falls. A curve showing the behavior of the average cost of a CD as more CDs are produced

A) would be positively and then negatively-sloped.
B) would be positively sloped.
C) would be horizontal.
D) would be negatively sloped.

Answer: D

Topic: Maximum and Minimum Points
Skill: Recognition

40) If a graph shows a negative relationship between two variables which then becomes a positive relationship, this curve would

A) always be an upward-sloping line.
B) have a minimum point.
C) have a maximum point.
D) always be a downward-sloping line.

Answer: B

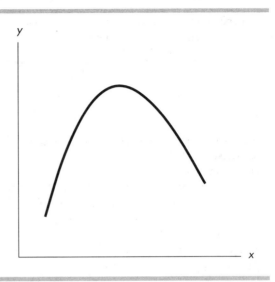

Topic: Variables That Have a Maximum or a Minimum
Skill: Analytical

41) In the figure above, the relationship between the x variable and the y variable

A) is positive.
B) is negative
C) starts by being positive and then becomes negative.
D) starts by being negative and then becomes positive.

Answer: C

Total number of workers	Total value of output (dollars)
15	10,000
16	12,000
17	9,000

Topic: Variables That Have a Maximum or a Minimum
Skill: Analytical

42) Use the table above. Place the number of workers on the horizontal axis and the total value of output on the vertical axis. The graph displaying the data provided in the table would show

A) a negative relationship among all the data points.
B) a positive relationship among all the data points.
C) a horizontal line.
D) none of the above.

Answer: D

Total number of workers	Average cost of producing a television set (dollars)
4	125
10	75
13	77
15	85

Topic: Variables That Have a Maximum or a Minimum
Skill: Analytical
43) Graphing the data in the above table with the number of workers on the horizontal axis and the average cost on the vertical axis, the graph would show

A) first a negative and then a positive relationship.
B) a horizontal line.
C) no relationship.
D) a linear relationship.

Answer: A

Year	Productivity growth rate (percent)
1990	−1.2
1991	1.9
1992	−3.3
1993	6.1
1994	7.9
1995	3.6
1996	3.4
1997	3.0
1998	4.1
1999	3.2
2000	0.7

Topic: Variables That Have a Maximum or a Minimum
Skill: Analytical
44) The table above gives productivity growth rate data for the nation of Alachua. The year when the growth rate was definitely at a minimum was

A) 1990.
B) 1992.
C) 1996.
D) 2000.

Answer: B

Topic: Variables That Have a Maximum or a Minimum
Skill: Analytical
45) The table above gives productivity growth rate data for the nation of Alachua. The year when the growth rate was definitely at a maximum was

A) 1990.
B) 1994.
C) 1997.
D) 2000.

Answer: B

Topic: Variables That Have a Maximum or a Minimum
Skill: Analytical
46) The table above gives productivity growth rate data for the nation of Alachua. Between 1994 and 1997, the trend in productivity growth was

A) negative.
B) flat.
C) positive.
D) vertical.

Answer: A

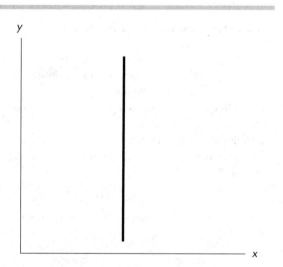

Topic: Variables That Are Unrelated
Skill: Analytical
47) In the above, as the y variable increases

A) the x variable is constant.
B) the x variable increases.
C) the x variable decreases.
D) the x variable at first increases but then decreases.

Answer: A

Topic: Variables That Are Unrelated
Skill: Analytical
48) A graph shows the price of a pound of cucumbers on the vertical axis and the quantity of new cars sold by GM on the horizontal axis. The price of a pound of cucumbers remains constant as the quantity of new cars sold increases. The graph of these data is
A) a horizontal line.
B) a vertical line.
C) a curve with a maximum.
D) a positively-sloped line.
Answer: A

■ The Slope of a Relationship

Topic: The Slope of a Relationship
Skill: Recognition
49) "The change in the value of the variable measured on the *y*-axis divided by the change in the value of the variable measured on the *x*-axis" is the definition of
A) a graph.
B) slope.
C) a curve.
D) a relation.
Answer: B

Topic: The Slope of a Relationship
Skill: Recognition
50) The slope of a curve between Y (measured on the vertical axis) and X (measured on the horizontal axis) is
A) zero.
B) the change in Y divided by the initial value of X.
C) the change in Y divided by the change in X.
D) the percentage change in Y divided by the percentage change in X.
Answer: C

Topic: The Slope of a Relationship
Skill: Conceptual
51) If a large change in the variable measured on the *x*-axis is associated with a small change of the variable measured on the *y*-axis, the line is ____ and the slope is ____.
A) downward-sloping; large
B) downward-sloping; small
C) upward-sloping; small
D) either downward or upward-sloping; small
Answer: D

Topic: The Slope of a Relationship
Skill: Conceptual
52) In which of the following cases is the slope of a line positive and less than infinity?
A) As the variable measured on the *x*-axis decreases, the variable measured on the *y*-axis decreases.
B) As the variable measured on the *x*-axis increases, the variable measured on the *y*-axis decreases.
C) As the variable measured on the *y*-axis increases, the variable measured on the *x*-axis does not change.
D) As the variable measured on the *y*-axis increases, the variable measured on the *x*-axis decreases.
Answer: A

Topic: The Slope of a Relationship
Skill: Conceptual
53) In a graph, a line has a negative slope if
A) the line is vertical.
B) the line is horizontal.
C) the line rises from right to left.
D) the line rises from left to right.
Answer: C

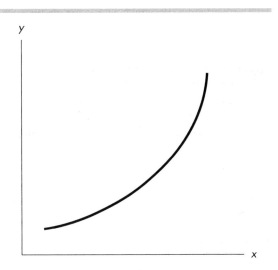

Topic: The Slope of a Relationship
Skill: Analytical
54) In the above figure, the curve has a slope that is ____.
A) positive and becoming larger in magnitude
B) positive and becoming smaller in magnitude
C) negative and becoming larger in magnitude
D) negative and becoming smaller in magnitude
Answer: A

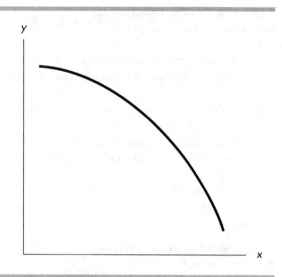

x-variable (on the horizontal axis)	y-variable (on the vertical axis)
10	28
15	31
20	34

Topic: The Slope of a Relationship
Skill: Analytical

55) In the above figure, the curve has a slope that is
     _____.

A) positive and becoming larger in magnitude
B) positive and becoming smaller in magnitude
C) negative and becoming larger in magnitude
D) negative and becoming smaller in magnitude

Answer: C

Topic: The Slope of a Relationship
Skill: Conceptual

56) Suppose that for a curve, as the variable measured on the x-axis increases, the variable measured on the y-axis decreases. The curve has a _____ slope.

A) tangent
B) positive
C) negative
D) hypothetical

Answer: C

Topic: The Slope of a Straight Line
Skill: Recognition

57) The slope of a straight line
A) is always positive.
B) is constantly changing.
C) is the change in the value of the variable measured on the y-axis divided by the change in the value of the variable measured along the x-axis.
D) equals the angle the line makes with the x-axis.

Answer: C

Topic: The Slope of a Straight Line
Skill: Analytical

58) The above table shows data on two variables. If these data were graphed, the slope of the line would be

A) 3/5.
B) 3.
C) 5/3.
D) impossible to determine from the information given.

Answer: A

x-variable (on the horizontal axis)	y-variable (on the vertical axis)
8	14
10	18
12	22

Topic: The Slope of a Straight Line
Skill: Analytical

59) The above table gives data on two variables. If these data were graphed, the slope of the line would be

A) 1.
B) −2.
C) 2.
D) −4.

Answer: C

Topic: The Slope of a Straight Line
Skill: Analytical

60) The above table gives data on two variables. If these data were graphed, their relationship would

A) be a straight line.
B) be a curved line.
C) show a negative relationship.
D) nonexistent.

Answer: A

x-variable (on the horizontal axis)	y-variable (on the vertical axis)
100	50
200	125
300	200

Topic: The Slope of a Straight Line
Skill: Analytical

61) The above table shows data on two variables. If these data were graphed, the slope of the line would be

A) 1/2.
B) 4/3.
C) 2/3.
D) 3/4.

Answer: D

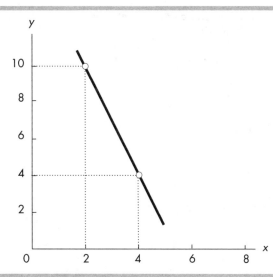

Topic: The Slope of a Straight Line
Skill: Analytical

62) The slope of the line shown in the above figure is

A) –1/3.
B) –5.
C) –1.
D) –3.

Answer: D

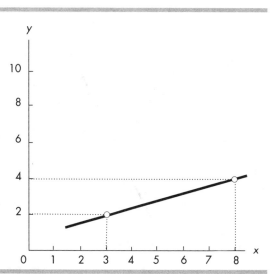

Topic: The Slope of a Straight Line
Skill: Analytical

63) The slope of the line shown in the above figure is

A) 5.
B) 2/5.
C) 2/3.
D) 5/2.

Answer: B

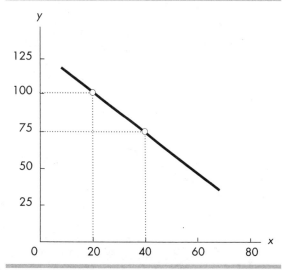

Topic: The Slope of a Straight Line
Skill: Analytical

64) The slope of the line shown in the above figure is

A) –1 1/3.
B) –1 2/3.
C) –1.25.
D) –0.80.

Answer: C

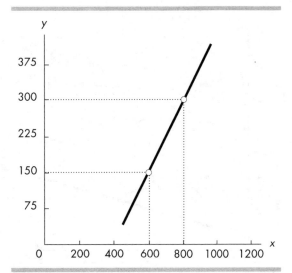

Topic: The Slope of a Straight Line
Skill: Analytical
65) The slope of the line shown in the above figure is
A) 2.
B) 0.75.
C) 0.25.
D) 1 1/3.
Answer: B

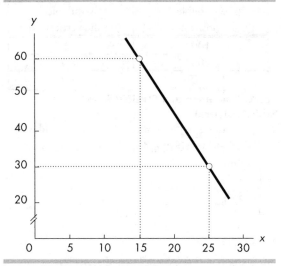

Topic: The Slope of a Straight Line
Skill: Analytical
67) The slope of the line in the above figure is
A) –1/2.
B) –3.
C) –4.
D) –1/3.
Answer: B

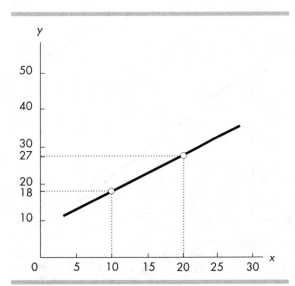

Topic: The Slope of a Straight Line
Skill: Analytical
66) The slope of the line shown in the above figure is
A) 0.90.
B) 1.5.
C) 1.11.
D) 2.
Answer: A

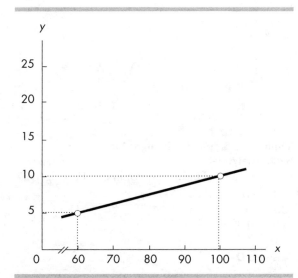

Topic: The Slope of a Straight Line
Skill: Analytical
68) The slope of the line in the above figure is
A) 8.
B) 0.05.
C) 0.125.
D) 0.10.
Answer: C

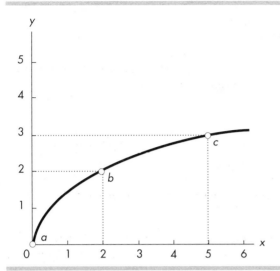

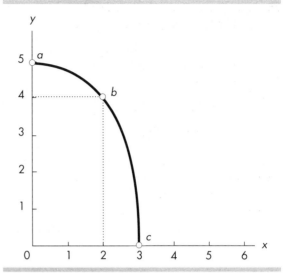

Topic: Slope Across an Arc
Skill: Analytical

69) In the above figure, using the slope across an arc, the slope of the curve between points *b* and *c* is

A) 1/3.
B) −1/3.
C) 3.
D) −3.

Answer: A

Topic: Slope Across an Arc
Skill: Analytical

70) In the above figure, using the slope across an arc, the slope of the curve between points *a* and *c* is

A) −3/5.
B) 3/5.
C) 5/3.
D) −5/3.

Answer: B

Topic: Slope Across an Arc
Skill: Analytical

71) In the above figure, using the slope across an arc, the slope of the curve between points *a* and *b* is

A) 1/2.
B) −1/2.
C) 2.
D) −2.

Answer: B

Topic: Slope Across an Arc
Skill: Analytical

72) In the above figure, using the slope across an arc, the slope of the curve between points *a* and *c* is

A) 3/5.
B) 5/3.
C) −3/5.
D) −5/3.

Answer: D

■ Graphing Relationships Among More Than Two Variables

Topic: Graphing Relationships Among More Than Two Variables, *Ceteris Paribus*
Skill: Recognition

73) To graph a relationship among several variables, we hold all but ____ variable(s) constant and use the ____ assumption.

A) one; scarcity
B) two; *ceteris paribus*
C) three; marginal benefit
D) one; *ceteris paribus*.

Answer: B

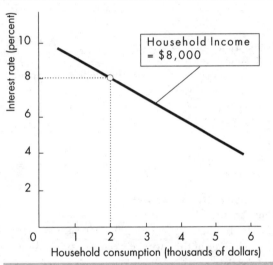

Topic: Graphing Relationships Among More Than Two Variables
Skill: Analytical

74) The slope of the line in the above figure is

A) positive.
B) negative.
C) direct.
D) independent.

Answer: B

Topic: Graphing Relationships Among More Than Two Variables
Skill: Analytical

75) In the above figure, when the interest rate is 8 percent and household income is $8,000, household consumption is

A) $0.
B) $2000.
C) $3500.
D) $6000.

Answer: B

Topic: Graphing Relationships Among More Than Two Variables
Skill: Analytical

76) The relationship in the above figure indicates that

A) a decrease in the interest rate causes a decrease in household income.
B) a decrease in household consumption causes a decrease in interest rates.
C) a decrease in household income will cause household consumption to increase.
D) none of the above.

Answer: D

Topic: Graphing Relationships Among More Than Two Variables
Skill: Analytical

77) Household consumption depends on both income and interest rates. In the above figure

A) household consumption is held constant.
B) interest rates are held constant.
C) household income is held constant.
D) no variable is held constant.

Answer: C

Topic: Graphing Relationships Among More Than Two Variables
Skill: Analytical

78) In the above figure, if household consumption is positively related to household income as well as related to the interest rate, then an increase in household income will

A) shift the line rightward.
B) shift the line leftward.
C) make the line positively sloped.
D) cause a movement along the line.

Answer: A

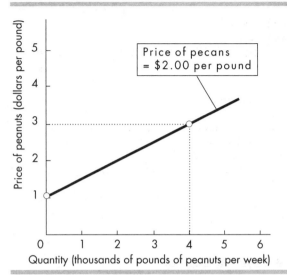

Topic: Graphing Relationships Among More Than Two Variables
Skill: Analytical
79) The above figure shows how many pounds of peanuts farmers are willing to sell at different prices per pound of peanuts. If the price of a pound of peanuts is $1 and the price of a pound of pecans is $2, peanut farmers are willing to sell

A)   no peanuts.
B)   1000 pounds of peanuts.
C)   2000 bushels of peanuts.
D)   4000 bushels of peanuts.
Answer: A

Topic: Graphing Relationships Among More Than Two Variables
Skill: Analytical
80) In the above figure, while drawing the line showing the relationship between the price of a pound of peanuts and the quantity sold, the

A)   price of a pound of pecans is held constant.
B)   price of a pound of peanuts is held constant.
C)   the quantity of peanuts that farmers supply is constant.
D)   Both answers A and B are true.
Answer: A

Topic: Graphing Relationships Among More Than Two Variables
Skill: Analytical
81) In the figure above, suppose the price of a pound of pecans is negatively related to the quantity of peanuts that farmers are willing to supply. If the price of pecans increases

A)   the curve will shift rightward.
B)   the curve will shift leftward.
C)   there is a movement along the curve.
D)   the curve will be unaffected.
Answer: B

■ True Or False Questions

Topic: Graphing Data
Skill: Recognition
82) The vertical axis of a graph shows only positive values.
Answer: FALSE

Topic: Graphing Data
Skill: Recognition
83) A scatter diagram plots the value of one economic variable against time.
Answer: FALSE

Topic: Graphing Data
Skill: Conceptual
84) A time series graph can show both the level of a variable and the speed with which the variable changes over time.
Answer: TRUE

Topic: Graphing Data
Skill: Recognition
85) A trend is a general tendency for a variable to increase or decrease over time.
Answer: TRUE

Topic: Graphing Data
Skill: Recognition
86) A cross-section graph can show how economic variables for different groups of people vary over time.
Answer: FALSE

Topic: Graphs Used in Economic Models
Skill: Conceptual
87) If the *x*-axis variable increases while the *y*-axis variable decreases, the variables *x* and *y* are negatively related.
Answer: TRUE

Topic: Graphs Used in Economic Models
Skill: Conceptual
88) A graph cannot be used to show that two variables are unrelated.
Answer: FALSE

Topic: Graphs Used in Economic Models
Skill: Recognition
89) When graphed, variables that are unrelated are shown by either a horizontal or a vertical line.
Answer: TRUE

Topic: The Slope of a Relationship
Skill: Recognition
90) The slope of a line is the change in the *y*-axis variable divided by the change in the *x*-axis variable.
Answer: TRUE

Topic: The Slope of a Relationship
Skill: Conceptual
91) The slope of a straight line increases as values get higher.
Answer: FALSE

Topic: The Slope of a Relationship
Skill: Conceptual
92) To calculate the slope of a curved line, you can calculate the slope at a point on the curve or across an arc of the curve.
Answer: TRUE

Topic: The Slope of a Relationship
Skill: Analytical
93) If the change in the *y*-axis variable is 4 and the change in the *x*-axis variable is 2, the slope of this line is 1/2.
Answer: FALSE

Topic: The Slope of a Relationship
Skill: Analytical
94) If the change in the *y*-axis variable is 6 and the change in the *x*-axis variable is 5, the slope of this line is 6/5.
Answer: TRUE

Topic: Graphing Relationships Among More Than Two Variables
Skill: Conceptual
95) To graph a relationship that involves more than two variables, we use the "*ceteris paribus*" assumption.
Answer: TRUE

Topic: Graphing Relationships Among More Than Two Variables
Skill: Conceptual
96) "*Ceteris paribus*" refers to the idea that if more than two variables are graphed, only one variable must be held constant.
Answer: FALSE

■ Essay Questions

Topic: Graphing Data
Skill: Recognition
97) Explain the purpose of using graphs.
Answer:

Topic: Graphing Data
Skill: Recognition
98) What are three main kinds of graphs?
Answer:

Topic: Graphing Data
Skill: Analytical
99) Show an example of a scatter diagram. Make sure to label the axes.
Answer:

Topic: Graphing Data
Skill: Analytical
100) Show an example of a time-series graph. Make sure to label the axes.
Answer:

Topic: Graphing Data
Skill: Analytical
101) Show an example of a cross-section graph. Make sure to label the parts of the graph.
Answer:

Topic: Graphs Used in Economic Models
Skill: Analytical
102) Show an example of a positive relationship between two variables. Explain your graph.
Answer:

Topic: Graphs Used in Economic Models
Skill: Analytical
103) Give an example of a variable with a maximum.
Explain your graph.

Answer:

Topic: Graphs Used in Economic Models
Skill: Analytical
104) Give an example of two variables that are unrelated. Explain your graph.

Answer:

Topic: The Slope of a Relationship
Skill: Analytical
105) If two points on a line are $x = 2$, $y = 5$ and $x = 7$,
$y = 10$, what is the slope of this line?

Answer:

**Topic: Graphing Relationships Among More Than
Two Variables**
Skill: Analytical
106) Give an example of a graph showing three variables. Use the price of gasoline, the price of public
transportation and gasoline consumption as your
variables. Explain your graph.

Answer:

Chapter 3 THE ECONOMIC PROBLEM

■ Resources and Wants

Topic: Resources and Wants
Skill: Recognition
1) As a student of economics, when you speak of scarcity, you are referring to
A) the ability of society to employ all of its resources.
B) the ability of society to consume all that it produces.
C) the inability of society to satisfy all human wants because of limited resources.
D) the ability of society to continually make technological breakthroughs and increase production.
Answer: C

Topic: Resources and Wants
Skill: Conceptual
2) In every economic system, choices must be made because resources
A) are unlimited, but human desires and wants are limited.
B) are limited, but human desires and wants are unlimited.
C) are unlimited, and so are human desires and wants.
D) are limited, and so are human desires and wants.
Answer: B

Topic: Limited Resources
Skill: Conceptual
3) Economists talk about scare resources. Which of the following resources would economists consider scarce?
I. Entrepreneurship.
II. Land.
III. Capital.
A) III only.
B) I and II.
C) II and III.
D) I, II and III.
Answer: D

Topic: Limited Resources
Skill: Recognition
4) Which of the following are considered resources used to produce goods and services?
I. Land
II. Labor
III. Capital
IV. Entrepreneurship
A) I and II only.
B) I and III only.
C) I, II and III only.
D) I, II, III and IV.
Answer: D

Topic: Limited Resources
Skill: Recognition
5) Which of the following is correct? Resources are
A) land, labor, the price system, and capital.
B) the inputs used to produce goods and services.
C) the fundamental source of abundance.
D) only land and labor.
Answer: B

Topic: Limited Resources
Skill: Recognition
6) Resources used for production include
A) the price system.
B) land, labor, capital and entrepreneurship.
C) labor and capital (not land, which is fixed).
D) only capital, land, and labor.
Answer: B

Topic: Limited Resources
Skill: Recognition
7) In economics, the term "land" means
A) only land that is used in agricultural production.
B) land, mineral resources, and nature's other bounties.
C) land that is devoted to economic pursuits.
D) land used for agricultural and urban purposes.
Answer: B

Topic: Limited Resources
Skill: Recognition
8)   In economics, the term "capital" refers to
A)   the money in one's pocket.
B)   plants and equipment.
C)   mineral resources.
D)   consumer goods.
Answer: B

Topic: Limited Resources
Skill: Recognition
9)   Capital goods
A)   are a special type of consumption good.
B)   are consumed because they enhance the enjoyment consumers obtain from other goods and services.
C)   are goods used to make consumer goods and services.
D)   lead to inward shifts of a production possibilities frontier.
Answer: C

Topic: Limited Resources
Skill: Recognition
10)   The term human capital refers to
A)   labor resources used to make capital equipment.
B)   buildings and machinery.
C)   people's knowledge and skill.
D)   entrepreneurship and risk-taking.
Answer: C

Topic: Limited Resources
Skill: Conceptual
11)   Which of the following is NOT an investment in human capital?
A)   A medical student's internship.
B)   The purchase of a personal computer.
C)   A mechanic attends a training workshop on a new type of engine.
D)   Johnny learns how to read.
Answer: B

Topic: Limited Resources
Skill: Conceptual
12)   A person goes to college to become an engineer. This is an example of
A)   an investment in physical capital.
B)   an investment in human capital.
C)   an increase in entrepreneurship.
D)   an increase in labor.
Answer: B

Topic: Limited Resources
Skill: Conceptual
13)   Human resources that perform the functions of organizing, managing, and assembling the other resources are called
A)   physical capital.
B)   venture capital.
C)   entrepreneurship.
D)   productive capital.
Answer: C

Topic: Limited Resources
Skill: Conceptual
14)   Keeping in mind economists' definition of resources, which of the following is NOT a resource?
A)   Money.
B)   Low-skilled labor.
C)   Coal.
D)   An engineer.
Answer: A

■ Resources, Production Possibilities, and Opportunity Cost

Topic: Production Possibility Frontier
Skill: Recognition
15)   The production possibility frontier represents
A)   the maximum amount of labor and capital available to society.
B)   combinations of goods and services among which consumers are indifferent.
C)   the maximum levels of production that can be attained.
D)   the maximum rate of growth of capital and labor in a country.
Answer: C

Topic: Production Possibility Frontier
Skill: Conceptual
16)   Which of the following is NOT true concerning a society's production possibility frontier (*PPF*)?
A)   It reveals the maximum amount of any two goods that can be produced from a given quantity of resources.
B)   Tradeoffs occur along a *PPF*.
C)   Production efficiency occurs when production is on the frontier itself.
D)   Consumers will receive equal benefits from the two goods.
Answer: D

Topic: Production Possibility Frontier
Skill: Conceptual

17) A point outside a production possibility frontier indicates

A) that resources are not being used efficiently.

B) an output combination that society cannot attain given its current level of resources and technology.

C) that resources are being used very efficiently.

D) that both goods are characterized by increasing costs.

Answer: B

Topic: Production Possibility Frontier
Skill: Conceptual

18) A production possibility frontier illustrates the maximum amount of two different goods that can be produced if

A) society is using all its resources in the most efficient manner possible.

B) the price of both goods is identical.

C) the price of both goods is held constant.

D) low-skilled workers can be prevented from getting jobs.

Answer: A

Topic: Production Possibility Frontier
Skill: Conceptual

19) Which of the following is <u>NOT</u> illustrated by a production possibility frontier?

A) scarcity.

B) opportunity cost.

C) necessity for choice.

D) who gets the goods.

Answer: D

Topic: Production Efficiency
Skill: Conceptual

20) Production efficiency can be defined as

A) producing outside the production possibility frontier.

B) minimizing opportunity cost.

C) being able to produce more of one good only if less of another is produced.

D) providing for the immediate needs of the greatest proportion of the population.

Answer: C

Topic: Production Efficiency
Skill: Conceptual

21) A society that is on its production possibility frontier is

A) under-utilizing its resources.

B) inefficient.

C) consuming too much output.

D) fully utilizing its productive resources.

Answer: D

Topic: Production Efficiency
Skill: Conceptual

22) If an economy is operating at a point inside the production possibility frontier, then

A) society's resources are being inefficiently utilized.

B) the *PPF* curve will shift inward.

C) society's resources are being used to produce too many consumer goods.

D) economic policy must retard further growth of the economy.

Answer: A

Topic: Production Efficiency
Skill: Conceptual

23) A reduction in the amount of unemployment

A) shifts the production possibility frontier outward.

B) moves the economy's production point closer to the production possibility frontier.

C) moves the economy's production point along the production possibility frontier.

D) moves the economy's production point further away from the production possibility frontier.

Answer: B

Topic: Production Efficiency
Skill: Conceptual

24) A country that *must* decrease current consumption to increase the amount of capital goods it produces

A) must be using resources inefficiently.

B) must be producing on its production possibility frontier.

C) must be producing beyond its production possibility frontier.

D) must not have private ownership of property.

Answer: B

Topic: Production Efficiency
Skill: Conceptual

25) A President of the United States promises to simultaneously produce more defense goods without any decreases in the production of other goods. Under which of the following conditions could such a promise be valid?

A) if the U.S. were producing at a point on its production possibility frontier.
B) if the U.S. were producing at a point inside its production possibility frontier.
C) if the U.S. were producing at a point beyond its production possibility frontier.
D) none of the above; the production possibility frontier must shift to the rightward.

Answer: B

Topic: Tradeoff
Skill: Conceptual

26) In the production of goods and services, tradeoffs exist because

A) not all production is efficient.
B) society has only a limited amount of productive resources.
C) buyers and sellers often must negotiate prices.
D) human wants and needs are limited at a particular point in time.

Answer: B

Topic: Opportunity Cost
Skill: Recognition

27) Opportunity cost is defined as

A) the amount of money that an individual is willing to pay to purchase a good that means a great deal to that person.
B) the amount of money lost by one individual in an exchange process so that another individual might gain.
C) the highest-valued alternative that is forgone whenever one is forced to choose among various alternatives.
D) a situation in which one individual cannot have an absolute advantage over another individual in the production of all goods.

Answer: C

Topic: Opportunity Cost
Skill: Recognition

28) A choice is made. The value of the highest-valued alternative that is foregone is the:

A) accounting cost of the choice made.
B) total cost of the choice made.
C) opportunity cost of the choice made.
D) monetary cost of the choice made.

Answer: C

Topic: Opportunity Cost
Skill: Conceptual

29) At one point along a *PPF*, 10 pizzas and 7 sandwiches can be produced. At another point along the same *PPF*, 9 pizzas and 10 sandwiches can be produced. The opportunity cost of a pizza between these points is

A) 7/10 of a sandwich.
B) 10/7 of a sandwich.
C) 1/3 of a sandwich.
D) 3 sandwiches.

Answer: D

Topic: Opportunity Cost
Skill: Conceptual

30) At one point along a *PPF* 40 tons of wheat are produced while 80 tons of rice are produced. At another point along the same *PPF*, 41 tons of wheat are produced while 70 tons of rice are produced. The opportunity cost of producing a ton of wheat between these points is

A) 1/2 ton of rice.
B) 10 tons of rice.
C) 1/10 ton of rice.
D) 4/7 ton of rice.

Answer: B

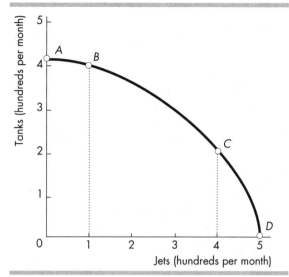

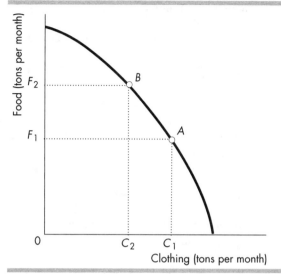

Topic: Opportunity Cost
Skill: Analytical

31) In the above figure, which of the following is
TRUE regarding the movements from point A to
B and from point C to D?

  I.   The movement from point A to B shows that
        the economy has chosen to produce 100 more
        jets.

  II.   The movement from point C to D shows that
        the economy has chosen to produce 100 more
        jets.

  III. The movement from point A to B and from
        point C to D represent the same opportunity
        cost.

  A)   I and II.
  B)   I and III.
  C)   II and III.
  D)   I, II and III.
Answer: A

Topic: Production Possibility Frontier
Skill: Analytical

32) In the figure above, the curve is known as the
  A)   production possibility frontier.
  B)   substitution options frontier.
  C)   production function.
  D)   opportunity cost curve.
Answer: A

Topic: Opportunity Cost
Skill: Analytical

33) The figure above illustrates that if this country
wishes to have $F_2 - F_1$ additional food, it will

  A)   have to find additional workers, because the
       country already is operating on its production
       possibility frontier.
  B)   be unable to do so until additional technological
       progress is made.
  C)   have to sacrifice $C_1 - C_2$ clothing in order to
       free the resources necessary to produce the addi-
       tional food.
  D)   require that all the unemployed resources in the
       country be put to work.
Answer: C

Topic: Increasing Opportunity Cost
Skill: Conceptual

34) Increasing opportunity cost while moving along a production possibility frontier is due to
A) taxes.
B) firms' needs to produce profits.
C) the fact that it is more difficult to use resources efficiently the more society produces.
D) the fact that resources are not equally productive in alternative uses.

Answer: D

Topic: Increasing Opportunity Cost
Skill: Conceptual

35) Increasing opportunity costs suggests that
A) there is no difference between inputs to a production process.
B) all labor and capital are costlessly interchangeable.
C) various types of labor are perfect substitutes for one another.
D) various types of labor are not perfect substitutes for one another.

Answer: D

Topic: Increasing Opportunity Cost
Skill: Conceptual

36) Increasing opportunity cost implies that
A) producing additional units of one good results in proportionately smaller reductions in the output of the other good.
B) producing additional units of one good results in increasing amounts of lost output of the other good.
C) the production possibility frontier will be a straight line.
D) the society will be producing inside its production possibility frontier.

Answer: B

Topic: Increasing Opportunity Cost
Skill: Conceptual

37) The production possibility frontier bows outward because
A) opportunity costs are decreasing as the production of a good increases.
B) opportunity costs are increasing as the production of a good increases.
C) opportunity costs are fixed as the production of a good increases.
D) resources are of uniform quality.

Answer: B

Topic: Increasing Opportunity Cost
Skill: Conceptual

38) The fact of increasing opportunity costs means that a production possibility frontier will
A) be a straight line.
B) reach a maximum and then gradually decrease.
C) bow outward.
D) shift outward over time.

Answer: C

Topic: Increasing Opportunity Cost
Skill: Conceptual

39) A bowed outward production possibility frontier occurs when
A) opportunity costs are constant.
B) resources are not scarce.
C) as more of a good is produced, producing additional units of it require increased reductions in the other good.
D) the society is operating on the production possibility frontier.

Answer: C

Topic: Increasing Opportunity Cost
Skill: Conceptual

40) The nation's production possibility frontier is bowed outward. Suppose that the government decides to increase the production of armaments by $20 billion, and that as a result the output of consumer goods falls by $20 billion. If a further $20 billion increase beyond the initial $20 billion increase in armaments output is sought, we can expect that the output of consumer goods and services will fall further by

A)   less than $20 billion.
B) $20 billion.
C)   more than $20 billion.
D)   There is not enough information to determine the answer.

Answer: C

Production possibilities		
Possibility	Pizza (per hour)	Soda (cases per hour)
A	0	100
B	1	95
C	2	80
D	3	60
E	4	35
F	5	0

Topic: Production Possibility Frontier
Skill: Analytical

41) In the above table, the production of 3 pizzas and 80 cases of soda is

A)   impossible unless more resources become available or technology improves.
B)   feasible but would involve unemployed or misallocated resources.
C)   possible only if the economy produces with maximum efficiency.
D)   possible only if there is inflation.

Answer: A

Topic: Production Efficiency
Skill: Analytical

42) In the above table, the production of 3 pizzas and 35 cases of soda is

A)   impossible unless more resources become available.
B)   feasible but would involve unemployed or misallocated resources.
C)   possible only if the economy produces with maximum efficiency.
D)   possible only if there is inflation.

Answer: B

Topic: Opportunity Cost
Skill: Analytical

43) In the above table, the opportunity cost of the 2nd pizza is

A)   0 cases of soda.
B)   15 cases of soda.
C)   95 cases of soda.
D)   80 cases of soda.

Answer: B

Topic: Increasing Opportunity Cost
Skill: Analytical

44) Based on the above table, as the production of pizza increases,

A)   the opportunity cost of pizza in terms of forgone cases of soda increases.
B)   the opportunity cost of pizza in terms of forgone cases of soda decreases.
C)   there is no effect on the opportunity cost of pizza in terms of forgone cases of soda.
D)   the opportunity cost of pizza in terms of forgone cases of soda initially increases then decreases.

Answer: A

Production possibilities		
Possibility	Guns (hundreds)	Butter (tons)
A	1	20
B	2	18
C	3	15
D	4	10
E	5	3

Topic: Production Efficiency
Skill: Analytical

45) The table above shows the production possibility frontier for the economy of Sauria. If this economy were to produce 3 hundred guns and 12 tons of butter,

A) it would be operating beyond its production possibility frontier.

B) it would be utilizing its resources with maximum efficiency.

C) it would be on its production possibility frontier.

D) it could utilize resources more efficiently to produce 3 more tons of butter without sacrificing any guns.

Answer: D

Topic: Opportunity Cost
Skill: Analytical

46) The table above shows the production possibility frontier for the economy of Sauria. The opportunity cost of increasing gun production from 3 hundred guns to 4 hundred guns is

A) 1 ton of butter.

B) 5 tons of butter.

C) 3 hundred guns.

D) 7 tons of butter.

Answer: B

Topic: Increasing Opportunity Cost
Skill: Analytical

47) The table above shows the production possibility frontier for the economy of Sauria. As this economy increases its production of guns along the production possibility frontier, the opportunity cost of guns

A) first rises and then falls.

B) rises continuously.

C) falls continuously.

D) remains constant.

Answer: B

Topic: Economic Growth
Skill: Analytical

48) The table above shows the production possibility frontier for the economy of Sauria. If the economy is able to produce 7 hundred guns and 10 tons of butter next year, we can conclude that next year

A) efficiency has decreased.

B) the production possibility frontier has shifted inward.

C) the supplies of resources or technology has increased.

D) the economy has moved along its production possibility frontier.

Answer: C

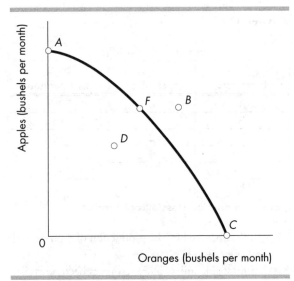

Topic: Production Possibility Frontier
Skill: Analytical

49) In the figure above, how can the economy represented by the production possibility frontier move from point C to point F?

A) Increase the available level of resources.

B) Increase the level of technology.

C) Redistribute the existing resources to produce more apples and fewer oranges.

D) Sell the excess oranges and purchase more resource.

Answer: C

Topic: Production Efficiency
Skill: Analytical

50) In the figure above, a point showing an inefficient production point is point

A) *A*.

B) *B*.

C) *C*.

D) *D*.

Answer: D

Topic: Economic Growth
Skill: Analytical

51) In the figure above, what can be said about point *B*?

A) It can be reached only after economic growth occurs.

B) It can be attained only if some resources are left unused.

C) It represents all resources being devoted to the production of apples.

D) It represents all resources being devoted to the production of oranges.

Answer: A

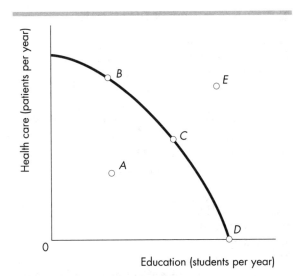

Topic: Production Efficiency
Skill: Analytical

52) In the figure above, point *D*

A) is less efficient than point *C*.

B) is efficient and point *A* is not efficient.

C) is not efficient and point *B* is efficient.

D) is efficient and point *B* is not efficient.

Answer: B

Topic: Production Efficiency
Skill: Analytical

53) In the figure above, point *A* is undesirable because

A) there is an inefficient use of resources.

B) too much health care is being produced.

C) the opportunity costs of health care is too high.

D) point *E* is a more realistic option in this economy.

Answer: A

Topic: Opportunity Cost
Skill: Analytical

54) In the figure above, the opportunity cost of moving from point *C* to point *D*

A) is the loss in production in the health care sector.

B) is the increase in production in the education sector.

C) is zero.

D) is the loss in production in the education sector.

Answer: A

Topic: Economic Growth
Skill: Analytical

55) In the figure above, point *E* could be obtained if

A) resources were shifted from education to health care.

B) resources were used more efficiently.

C) there was an increase in society's resources.

D) resources were shifted from health care to education.

Answer: C

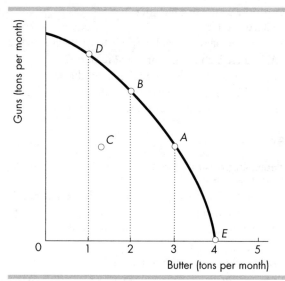

Topic: Production Efficiency
Skill: Analytical

56) In the figure above, the point labeled *C* in the production possibility frontier above

A) is unattainable; it is beyond the productive capability of this country.

B) represents a highly desirable output level in the long run, because it conserves scarce resources.

C) represents either unemployed or inefficiently utilized resources.

D) represents the maximum sustainable output level for this nation in the long run.

Answer: C

Topic: Opportunity Cost
Skill: Analytical

57) The country whose production possibility frontier is illustrated above is currently at position *A* on the production possibility frontier. If it wishes to move to position *B*, it will

A) find this change impossible to achieve given the resources it currently possesses.

B) have to employ all currently unemployed resources to accomplish this.

C) incur an opportunity cost of having to give up some butter in order to make the additional amount of guns desired.

D) be able to make the desired switch only if there is a significant improvement in the technological base available to the nation.

Answer: C

Topic: Opportunity Cost
Skill: Analytical

58) In the figure above, moving from point *B* to point *D*

A) has an opportunity cost of one ton of butter per month.

B) has an opportunity cost of one ton of guns per month.

C) requires an increase in technology.

D) Is impossible.

Answer: A

Topic: Increasing Opportunity Cost
Skill: Analytical

59) In the figure above, which of the following movements would entail the greatest opportunity cost?

A) From point *C* to point *B*.

B) From point *C* to point *A*.

C) From point *B* to point *A*.

D) From point *A* to point *E*.

Answer: D

■ Using Resources Efficiently

Topic: Marginal Cost
Skill: Recognition

60) Marginal cost

A) is defined as the opportunity cost of producing another unit of a good or service.

B) can be illustrated by moving along a *PPF* unit by unit.

C) always equals marginal benefit.

D) Both answers A and B are correct.

Answer: D

Topic: Marginal Cost
Skill: Conceptual

61) A marginal cost curve

A) is upward sloping.

B) shows that as more of a good is produced, opportunity costs of producing another unit increase.

C) is bowed inward so that its slope can become negative.

D) Both answers A and B are correct.

Answer: D

Topic: Opportunity Cost and Marginal Cost
Skill: Conceptual

62) The quantity of shoes produced is measured along the horizontal axis of a *PPF* and the quantity of shirts are measured along the vertical axis. As you move down toward the right along the *PPF*, the marginal cost of

A) shoes decreases.
B) shoes increases.
C) shirts increases.
D) shoes and shirts is equal at the midpoint between the vertical and horizontal axis.

Answer: B

Topic: Marginal Benefit
Skill: Conceptual

63) Which of the following is TRUE regarding marginal benefit?

I. The marginal benefit curve shows the benefit firms receive by producing another unit of a good.
II. Marginal benefit increases as more and more of a good is consumed.
III. Marginal benefit shows the maximum amount a person is willing to pay to obtain one more unit of a good.

A) I and II.
B) I and III.
C) II and III.
D) III only.

Answer: D

Topic: Marginal Benefit
Skill: Conceptual

64) As you consume more and more of a good

A) the marginal benefit increases.
B) the marginal benefit decreases.
C) the marginal benefit increases or decreases depending where you are or are not on the *PPF*.
D) the price of the good falls.

Answer: B

Topic: Marginal Benefit
Skill: Conceptual

65) A marginal benefit curve shows

A) the efficient use of resources.
B) the quantity of one good that must be forgone to get more of another good.
C) the quantity of one good that people are willing to forgo to get another unit of another good.
D) there are increasing opportunity costs.

Answer: C

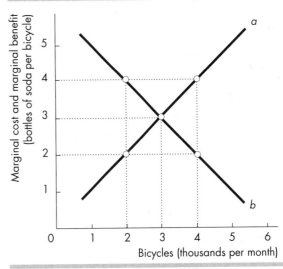

Topic: Marginal Cost and Marginal Benefit
Skill: Analytical

66) In the above figure, the curve labeled "*a*" is the _____ curve and the curve labeled "*b*" is the _____ curve.

A) marginal cost; marginal benefit
B) marginal cost; trade line
C) marginal benefit; trade line
D) production possibility frontier; trade line

Answer: A

Topic: Marginal Benefit
Skill: Analytical

67) In the above figure, curve "*b*" shows

A) the bottles of soda that people are *willing* to forgo to get another bicycle.
B) the bottles of soda that people *must* forgo to get another bicycle.
C) the benefits of producing more bicycles is greater than the benefits of producing more soda.
D) the benefits of producing more soda is greater than the benefits of producing more bicycles.

Answer: A

Topic: Efficient Use of Resources
Skill: Analytical
68) In the above figure, when 2000 bicycles are made each month, we can see that
  A) the marginal benefit from another bicycle is greater than the marginal cost of another bicycle.
  B) more bicycles should be produced to reach the efficient level of output.
  C) the economy is very efficient at the production of bicycles because the marginal benefit exceeds the marginal cost.
  D) Both answers A and B are correct.
Answer: D

Topic: Efficient Use of Resources
Skill: Analytical
69) In the above figure, if 4000 bicycles are made per month,
  A) marginal benefit is greater than marginal cost.
  B) fewer bicycles should be produced to reach the efficient level of output.
  C) the marginal cost of production is 2 bottles of soda per bicycle.
  D) Both answers A and B are correct.
Answer: B

Topic: Efficient Use of Resources
Skill: Conceptual
70) When an economist refers to choices made "at the margin" the economist is referring to
  A) an individual's margin account with a stockbroker that allows part of a stock purchase to be made with borrowed money.
  B) decisions based on the marginal benefits and marginal costs of small changes in a particular activity.
  C) an individual's all-or-nothing choice concerning a specific good or activity.
  D) All of the above.
Answer: B

■ Economic Growth

Topic: Economic Growth
Skill: Conceptual
71) Technological change
  A) generates economic growth.
  B) shifts the PPF leftward.
  C) creates inefficiency.
  D) Both answers A and C are correct.
Answer: A

Topic: Economic Growth
Skill: Conceptual
72) As an economy's capital stock increases, the economy
  A) generally experiences increased unemployment of other resources, such as labor.
  B) generally decides to engage in international trade.
  C) experiences economic growth.
  D) gains an absolute advantage in the production of capital goods.
Answer: C

Topic: Economic Growth
Skill: Conceptual
73) Economic growth is shown on the production possibility frontier as
  A) a movement from one point on the PPF to another.
  B) an outward shift in the PPF.
  C) an inward shift in the PPF.
  D) the curvature of the PPF.
Answer: B

Topic: Economic Growth
Skill: Conceptual
74) An increase in the production of capital goods
  A) must increase the current production of consumer goods.
  B) must decrease the future production of consumer goods.
  C) shifts the production possibility frontier inward.
  D) shifts the production possibility frontier outward.
Answer: D

Topic: Economic Growth
Skill: Conceptual
75) Economic growth can be pictured in a production possibility frontier diagram by
  A) making the production possibility frontier more bowed out.
  B) making the production possibility frontier less bowed out.
  C) shifting the production possibility frontier outward.
  D) shifting the production possibility frontier inward.
Answer: C

Topic: Economic Growth
Skill: Conceptual

76) Suppose a scientific breakthrough made free solar power available in unlimited quantities in the United States. The effect of this invention would be to move the

A) United States beyond its production possibility frontier.

B) United States inside its production possibility frontier.

C) United States' production possibility frontier outward.

D) United States' production possibility frontier inward.

Answer: C

Topic: Economic Growth
Skill: Conceptual

77) Suppose the United States discovers a way to produce clean nuclear fuel. The effect of this discovery would be to

A) cause the United States to produce less nuclear fuel.

B) force the United States to produce at a point inside its *PPF*.

C) shift the United States' *PPF* outward.

D) shift the United States' *PPF* inward.

Answer: C

Topic: Economic Growth
Skill: Conceptual

78) Using a production possibilities frontier, economic growth is illustrated by

A) a point inside the curve.

B) a point on the curve.

C) a movement from one point on the curve to another point on the curve.

D) a rightward shift of the curve.

Answer: D

Topic: Economic Growth
Skill: Analytical

79) In the figure above, an economy would grow fastest if it located at point

A) *A.*

B) *B.*

C) *C.*

D) *D.*

Answer: A

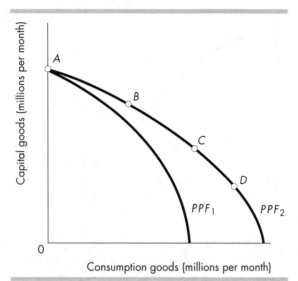

Topic: Economic Growth
Skill: Analytical
80) In the above figure, in order for this country to move from production possibility frontier PPF_1 to PPF_2, it might

A) increase the skills and productivity of its work force.
B) put all unemployed resources to work producing desired output.
C) engage in exchange with other nations.
D) increase the average level of prices for all goods produced and consumed.
Answer: A

Topic: Economic Growth
Skill: Analytical
81) In the above figure, once on PPF_2, a country would grow slowest by operating at point

A) *A.*
B) *B.*
C) *C.*
D) *D.*
Answer: D

Topic: The Cost Of Economic Growth
Skill: Conceptual
82) The opportunity cost of more capital goods today is

A) fewer capital goods in the future.
B) fewer consumer goods in the future.
C) fewer consumer goods today.
D) more unemployed resources in the future.
Answer: C

Topic: The Cost Of Economic Growth
Skill: Conceptual
83) The tradeoff between current consumption and the production of capital goods is also a trade-off between

A) the future production of capital goods and future consumption of goods.
B) economic growth and technological change.
C) satisfying today the needs of the poor and the wants of the wealthy.
D) current consumption and future consumption.
Answer: D

■ Gains from Trade

Topic: Comparative Advantage
Skill: Conceptual
84) Which of the following is a true statement?

A) Comparative advantage explains trade among nations, but not within nations.
B) Comparative advantage explains trade within nations, but not among nations.
C) Comparative advantage explains trade within nations and among nations.
D) Comparative advantage has nothing to do with trade among nations; it only is concerned with specialization within a firm.
Answer: C

Topic: Comparative Advantage
Skill: Conceptual
85) A person has a comparative advantage in an activity whenever she

A) has an absolute advantage in the activity.
B) can perform the activity at a lower opportunity cost than can another person.
C) can do the activity in less time than anyone else.
D) can do everything better than anyone else.
Answer: B

Topic: Comparative Advantage
Skill: Conceptual

86) A country possesses a comparative advantage in the production of a good if
   A) the opportunity cost in terms of forgone output of alternative goods is lower for this country than it is for its trading partners.
   B) it possesses an absolute advantage in the production of this good.
   C) it is able to produce more of this good per hour than can any other country.
   D) all of the above.

Answer: A

Topic: Comparative Advantage
Skill: Conceptual

87) Assume that Betty and Ann live on a desert island. With a day's labor, Ann can produce 8 fish or 4 coconuts; Betty can produce 6 fish or 2 coconuts. Ann's opportunity cost of producing 1 coconut is _____ and she should specialize in the production of _____.
   A) 8 fish; fish
   B) 2 fish; coconuts
   C) 6 fish; coconuts
   D) 0 fish; coconuts

Answer: B

Topic: Comparative Advantage
Skill: Conceptual

88) Assume that Betty and Ann live on a desert island. With a day's labor, Ann can produce 6 fish or 4 coconuts; Betty can produce 3 fish or 1 coconut. Betty's opportunity cost of producing 1 fish is _____, and she should specialize in the production of _____.
   A) 1/3 coconut; fish
   B) 2/3 coconut; coconuts
   C) 1 coconut; fish
   D) 4 coconuts; fish

Answer: A

Topic: Comparative Advantage
Skill: Conceptual

89) Suppose that in one week Alice can produce 5 pairs of shoes or 4 bookshelves while Roger can produce 10 pairs of shoes or 6 bookshelves. Then Alice has a(n) _____ advantage in producing _____.
   A) absolute; shoes
   B) comparative; shoes
   C) absolute; bookshelves
   D) comparative; bookshelves

Answer: D

Topic: Comparative Advantage
Skill: Conceptual

90) Suppose that in one week Alice can produce 5 pairs of shoes or 4 bookshelves while Roger can produce 10 pairs of shoes or 6 bookshelves. Then Alice should specialize in the production of
   A) shoes
   B) bookshelves
   C) either shoes or bookshelves
   D) neither shoes nor bookshelves

Answer: B

	Don's production possibilities	Bob's production possibilities
Pens	10	5
Pencils	20	15

Topic: Comparative Advantage
Skill: Analytical

91) The above table shows the number of pencils or pens that could be produced by Don and Bob in an hour. This schedule shows that
   A) Don has an absolute advantage over Bob in the production of pencils, and Bob has an absolute advantage in the production of pens.
   B) Bob has an absolute advantage over Don in the production of pencils, and Don has an absolute advantage in the production of pens.
   C) Don has a comparative advantage over Bob in the production of both pencils and pens.
   D) Bob has a comparative advantage over Don in the production of pencils.

Answer: D

	U.S. production possibilities	France's production possibilities
Steel	100	25
Concrete	200	100

Topic: Comparative Advantage
Skill: Analytical
92) The above table shows the tons of steel and concrete that can be produced by the U.S. and France in an hour. From the data in the table,
A) France has the comparative advantage in the production of concrete.
B) the United States has the comparative advantage in the production of concrete.
C) France has the absolute advantage in the production of concrete.
D) the United States has the comparative advantage in the production of both goods.
Answer: A

Topic: Achieving the Gains from Trade
Skill: Analytical
93) The data in the above table demonstrates that gains from trade can be captured if
A) the United States produced both goods.
B) the United States produced steel in exchange for concrete produced in France.
C) the United States produced concrete in exchange for steel produced in France.
D) each country became self-sufficient, produced both goods for itself, and did not engage in trade.
Answer: B

Topic: Achieving the Gains from Trade
Skill: Conceptual
94) The idea of comparative advantage implies that people or countries
A) should specialize in the production of goods.
B) can gain from trading.
C) can consume outside their production possibility frontier.
D) all of the above.
Answer: D

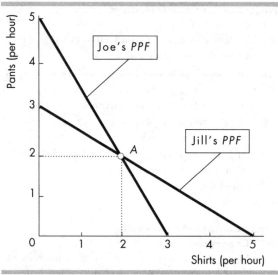

Topic: Comparative Advantage
Skill: Analytical
95) In the figure above, Joe is operating at point *A*. Joe's opportunity cost of producing a shirt is
A) 5/3 pair of pants.
B) 3/5 pair of pants.
C) 5 pair of pants.
D) 2 pair of pants.
Answer: D

Topic: Comparative Advantage
Skill: Analytical
96) In the figure above, Jill is producing at point *A*. Jill's opportunity cost producing a pair of pants is
A) 2 shirts.
B) 3 shirts.
C) 3/5 shirt.
D) 5/3 shirt.
Answer: A

Topic: Achieving the Gains from Trade
Skill: Analytical
97) In the figure above, both Joe and Jill initially produce at point *A*. If Joe and Jill realize that they each possess a comparative advantage, which outcome can we expect?
A) Joe will specialize in shirts, and Jill will specialize in pants.
B) Joe will specialize in pants, and Jill will specialize in shirts.
C) Joe and Jill each will be able to consume more than 2 shirts and 2 pairs of pants.
D) Both answers B and C are true.
Answer: D

Topic: Absolute Advantage
Skill: Conceptual

98) Dave can produce 10 pairs of shoes or 5 shirts each day. Judy can produce 9 pairs of shoes or 3 shirts each day. We can say that

A) Judy is not operating on her *PPF*.

B) Dave has an absolute advantage in the production of shoes and shirts.

C) Judy has an absolute advantage in the production of only shirts.

D) Dave has a comparative advantage in the production of shoes.

Answer: B

Topic: Dynamic Comparative Advantage
Skill: Conceptual

99) Once a country has a comparative advantage in the production of a good

A) other countries can equal but not gain a comparative advantage in the production of the good.

B) other countries might be able to gain the comparative advantage in that good through a process called learning-by-doing.

C) the country loses its absolute advantage in the production of the good.

D) None of the above answers are correct.

Answer: B

Topic: Dynamic Comparative Advantage
Skill: Conceptual

100) Dynamic comparative advantage occurs because

A) countries produce a lot of different goods.

B) people engage in learning-by-doing.

C) of absolute advantage.

D) specialization and trade.

Answer: B

■ The Market Economy

Topic: Property Rights
Skill: Recognition

101) The rights of an owner to use and exchange property are

A) capitalist rights.

B) socialist rights.

C) property rights.

D) money rights.

Answer: C

Topic: Property Rights
Skill: Conceptual

102) A system of property rights

A) encourages economic growth by creating incentives to invest in capital and to be innovative.

B) discourages economic growth by discouraging the development of new ideas and ways of doing things.

C) reduces the efficiency of government, which reduces the growth rate of the economy over time.

D) encourages investment but discourages entrepreneurial activity, so the effect on economic growth is uncertain.

Answer: A

Topic: Markets
Skill: Recognition

103) Markets are

A) arrangements where buyers and sellers get together to buy and sell.

B) specific geographic locations where people get together to buy and sell.

C) hypothetical constructs used to analyze how people form their tastes and preferences.

D) places where people can inspect goods and services carefully.

Answer: A

Topic: Markets
Skill: Conceptual

104) Which of the following is TRUE regarding markets?

I.   Economists define a market is a geographic location where trade occurs.

II. A market enables buyers and sellers to get information about each other and to buy and sell from each other.

III. Markets coordinate decisions through prices.

A) I only.

B) I and III.

C) II and III.

D) I, II and III.

Answer: C

Topic: The Circular Flows
Skill: Recognition
105) Markets in which firms sell their output of goods and services are called
  A)   resource markets.
  B)   goods markets.
  C)   command markets.
  D)   mixed markets.
Answer: B

Topic: The Circular Flows
Skill: Recognition
106) A resource market is a market in which
  A)   households buy goods and services.
  B)   households sell the services of the resources they control.
  C)   firms sell the services of resources.
  D)   firms sell goods and services.
Answer: B

Topic: The Circular Flows
Skill: Recognition
107) The market in which an individual sells the use of his or her labor is a
  A)   product market.
  B)   resource market.
  C)   foreign exchange market.
  D)   mixed market.
Answer: B

■ True Or False Questions

Topic: Resources and Wants
Skill: Recognition
108) The study of economics focuses on the fundamental problem of only demand.
Answer: FALSE

Topic: Resources and Wants
Skill: Conceptual
109) Land is not considered a limited resource because of the availability of the oceans and space.
Answer: FALSE

Topic: Resources, Production Possibilities and Opportunity Costs
Skill: Recognition
110) An economy is producing efficiently if it is producing on its *PPF*.
Answer: TRUE

Topic: Using Resources Efficiently
Skill: Conceptual
111) As long as the marginal benefit from a good is greater than its marginal cost, an economy is operating efficiently.
Answer: FALSE

Topic: Using Resources Efficiently
Skill: Conceptual
112) If marginal benefit is greater than marginal cost for the production of cars, an economy should increase the production of cars.
Answer: TRUE

Topic: Economic Growth
Skill: Conceptual
113) As long as technology increases occur, economic growth is considered "free".
Answer: FALSE

Topic: Economic Growth
Skill: Conceptual
114) To expand its *PPF*, a country may devote resources to accumulating capital.
Answer: TRUE

Topic: Gains from Trade
Skill: Recognition
115) A country has a comparative advantage in the production of a good if its opportunity cost is lower compared to another country.
Answer: TRUE

Topic: Gains from Trade
Skill: Recognition
116) Specialization and trade allow countries to consume beyond their *PPFs*.
Answer: TRUE

Topic: Gains from Trade
Skill: Recognition
117) Learning-by-doing is a process that can help a person gain a comparative advantage.
Answer: TRUE

Topic: The Market Economy
Skill: Conceptual
118) Property rights facilitate the development of trade.
Answer: TRUE

Topic: The Market Economy
Skill: Recognition
119) A circular flow diagram shows the interaction of the goods and resources markets.
Answer: TRUE

■ Essay Questions

Topic: Resources and Wants
Skill: Conceptual
120) Explain the connection between scarcity, opportunity costs and the *PPF*.
Answer:

Topic: Resources and Wants
Skill: Conceptual
121) Explain what entrepreneurship is and why it is considered a scarce resource.
Answer:

Topic: Resources, Production Possibilities and Opportunity Costs
Skill: Analytical
122) Using a *PPF*, illustrate increasing opportunity costs.
Answer:

Topic: Using Resources Efficiently
Skill: Conceptual
123) Explain the difference between marginal cost and marginal benefit.
Answer:

Topic: Using Resources Efficiently
Skill: Analytical
124) Using marginal benefit and marginal cost curves, show different levels of production when an economy is operating efficiently and when it is not. Briefly explain your answer.
Answer:

Topic: Economic Growth
Skill: Recognition
125) What factors generate economic growth?
Answer:

Topic: Economic Growth
Skill: Analytical
126) Using a *PPF* with wheat on the vertical axis and cars on the horizontal axis, show what happens when new technology improves car production. Briefly explain your answer.
Answer:

Topic: Gains from Trade
Skill: Recognition
127) What is the difference between comparative advantage and absolute advantage?
Answer:

Topic: Gains from Trade
Skill: Conceptual
128) Why does it make sense for economies to specialize and trade?
Answer:

Topic: The Market Economy
Skill: Conceptual
129) How do property rights help organize production and trade?
Answer:

Chapter 4 DEMAND AND SUPPLY

■ Price and Opportunity Cost

Topic: Price and Opportunity Cost
Skill: Conceptual
1) Joe pays $8,000.00 in tuition. The tuition Joe pays is an example of what economists call
A) a relative price.
B) a money price.
C) an indexed price.
D) an opportunity price.
Answer: B

Topic: Price and Opportunity Cost
Skill: Conceptual
2) Suppose the price of a football is $20.00 and the price of a basketball is $10.00. The _____ of a football is _____.
A) relative price; 2 basketballs
B) relative price; 1/2 basketball
C) opportunity cost; $20.00
D) opportunity cost; $10.00
Answer: A

Topic: Price and Opportunity Cost
Skill: Conceptual
3) If the money price of wheat increases and no other prices change,
A) the relative price of wheat will fall.
B) the opportunity cost of wheat rises.
C) the demand for wheat will increase too.
D) the relative price of wheat is unaffected.
Answer: B

Topic: Price and Opportunity Cost
Skill: Recognition
4) When graphing a demand curve for corn, we are showing the relationship between the quantity demanded of corn and the
A) money price of corn.
B) relative price of corn.
C) income effect.
D) substitution effect.
Answer: B

■ Demand

Topic: The Law of Demand
Skill: Conceptual
5) The "law of demand" refers to the fact that, all other things remaining constant on the demand side of the market, when the price of a good rises
A) the demand curve will shift rightward.
B) the demand curve will shift leftward.
C) there will be a movement down along the demand curve to a larger quantity demanded.
D) there will be a movement up along the demand curve to a smaller quantity demanded.
Answer: D

Topic: The Law of Demand
Skill: Recognition
6) The "law of demand" states that, other things remaining the same, the quantity demanded of any good is:
A) inversely related to its price.
B) directly related to its price.
C) positively related to its price.
D) directly related to the supply of the good.
Answer: A

Topic: The Law of Demand
Skill: Conceptual
7) The "law of demand" means that
A) consumers will buy more of a good the higher their incomes, *ceteris paribus*.
B) consumers will buy less of a good the higher its price, *ceteris paribus*.
C) consumers will buy more of a good the less is its supply, *ceteris paribus*.
D) consumers will buy less of a good the greater is its supply, *ceteris paribus*.
Answer: B

Topic: The Law of Demand
Skill: Recognition

8) Which of the following will occur in the market for soft drinks if the money price of soft drinks increases?

    I.   The relative price of soft drinks increases.

    II.   The substitution effect may cause people to switch to drinking bottled water.

A) I only.

B) II only.

C) Both I and II.

D) Neither I nor II.

Answer: C

Topic: The Law of Demand
Skill: Recognition

9) The "income effect" in the market for magazines means that

A) magazines are usually purchased by people with higher than average incomes.

B) a decrease in the price of a substitute product like books will make magazine readers feel a little poorer than they before.

C) an increase in the price of magazines will reduce the total purchasing power of magazine readers, making them able to afford fewer magazines.

D) an increase in the price of magazines will raise the relative price of magazines to books, causing magazine readers to read more books and fewer magazines.

Answer: C

Topic: Change in the Quantity Demanded
Skill: Conceptual

10) Which of the following would cause a movement along, but no shift in the demand curve for spinach?

A) Disastrous weather that destroys about half of this year's spinach crop.

B) A newly discovered increase in the nutritional value of spinach.

C) An increase in the price of broccoli, a substitute for spinach.

D) An increase in income for all spinach lovers.

Answer: A

Topic: Change in Demand, Prices of Related Goods
Skill: Recognition

11) Changes in which of the following items will shift the demand curve for hamburgers?

A) An increase in the price of the meat used to produce hamburgers.

B) An improvement in the productivity of hamburger-making machines.

C) A fall in the price of french fries, a complement for hamburgers.

D) An increase in the number of hamburger restaurants.

Answer: C

Topic: Change in Demand, Prices of Related Goods
Skill: Analytical

12) The observation that the demand curve for grape jelly shifted rightward every time the price of peanut butter fell means that grape jelly and peanut butter are

A) complements.

B) substitutes.

C) inferior goods.

D) normal goods.

Answer: A

Topic: Change in Demand, Income
Skill: Analytical

13) Which of the following can shift the demand curve for movie rentals rightward?

A) A decrease in the rental price of a movie.

B) A nationwide, 10 percent increase in household incomes if movie rentals are a normal good.

C) A decrease in the price of cable television service.

D) An increase in the quantity and quality of programming included in the basic cable television service package.

Answer: B

Topic: Change in Demand, Income
Skill: Conceptual

14) Suppose Jeep Cherokees are a normal good. Then if household income increases, the direct result will be

A) an increase in the supply of the vehicles.

B) a decrease in the demand for the vehicles.

C) an increase in the demand for the vehicles.

D) Both answers A and C are correct.

Answer: C

Topic: Change in Demand, Population
Skill: Conceptual

15) An increase in the number of consumers in a market will

A) cause only a movement along the demand curve.

B) cause a leftward shift in the supply curve.

C) cause the demand curve to shift rightward.

D) Both answers B and C are correct.

Answer: C

Topic: Change in Demand, Preferences
Skill: Analytical

16) Coke and Pepsi are substitutes. When Pepsi Cola advertises on television it is trying to cause

A) an increase in the supply of Pepsi.

B) a decrease in the supply of Coke.

C) an increase in the demand for Pepsi.

D) None of the above answers are correct.

Answer: C

Topic: Change in Demand, Preferences
Skill: Conceptual

17) A change in which of the following shifts the demand curve?

A) The number of sellers in the market.

B) The price of the resources used to produce the commodity.

C) The technology with which the commodity is produced.

D) The tastes and preferences of consumers.

Answer: D

Topic: Change In Demand
Skill: Conceptual

18) Which of the following would NOT cause the demand curve for broccoli to shift?

A) An increase in the cost of fertilizer used to grow broccoli.

B) A warning by the U.S. Surgeon General that broccoli causes schizophrenia.

C) An increase in the price of spinach, a substitute for broccoli, because rodents gobbled up much of this year's spinach crop.

D) A decrease in the price of spinach, a substitute for broccoli, because of a bumper crop of spinach this year.

Answer: A

Topic: A Change in the Quantity Demanded Versus a Change in Demand
Skill: Conceptual

19) Cable television companies nation-wide must pay increased charges by the networks for the programs the cable companies carry. As a result, they raise the price of cable television. Thus

A) the demand curve for cable television service shifts rightward.

B) the demand curve for cable television service shifts leftward.

C) there is a movement down the demand curve for cable television to a higher quantity demanded.

D) there is a movement up the demand curve for cable television to a smaller quantity demanded.

Answer: D

Topic: A Change in the Quantity Demanded Versus a Change in Demand
Skill: Conceptual

20) As the price of a pound of peanuts falls,

A) the demand for peanuts will increase.

B) the demand for peanuts will decrease.

C) the quantity of peanuts demanded will increase.

D) Both answers A and C are correct.

Answer: C

Topic: A Change in the Quantity Demanded Versus a Change in Demand
Skill: Conceptual

21) For "an increase in the quantity demanded" but not "an increase in demand" to occur, there must be

A) a rightward shift of the demand curve.

B) a rightward shift of the supply curve.

C) a movement along a supply curve.

D) Both answers B and C are correct.

Answer: B

Topic: A Change in the Quantity Demanded Versus a Change in Demand
Skill: Conceptual

22) For a "change in demand" to occur, there must be

A) a rightward shift of the supply curve.

B) a rightward shift of the demand curve.

C) a leftward shift of the demand curve.

D) Both answers B and C are correct.

Answer: D

Topic: A Change in the Quantity Demanded Versus a Change in Demand
Skill: Analytical

23) If the price per bushel of apples increased from $7.00 to $8.00 because of a poor harvest,

A) the demand for apples decreases.

B) the quantity of apples demanded decreases.

C) the quantity of apples supplied decreases.

D) Both answers A and B are correct.

Answer: B

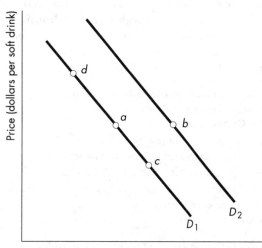

Topic: Change in the Quantity Demanded
Skill: Analytical

24) Consider the market for soft drinks shown in the figure above. Suppose the economy is at point *a*. What would cause a movement to point *c*?

A) a decrease in income.

B) an increase in the relative price of a soft drink.

C) a decrease in the relative price of a soft drink.

D) a decrease in the price of bottled water.

Answer: A

Topic: Change in the Quantity Demanded
Skill: Analytical

25) Consider the market for soft drinks shown in the figure above. Suppose the economy is at point *a*. What would cause a movement to point *d*?

A) a decrease in income.

B) an increase in the relative price of a soft drink.

C) a decrease in the relative price of a soft drink.

D) a decrease in the price of bottled water.

Answer: B

Topic: Change in Demand, Prices of Related Goods
Skill: Analytical

26) Consider the market for soft drinks shown in the figure above. Suppose the economy is at point *a*. What would cause a movement to point *b*?

A) an increase in the price of bottled water.

B) a decrease in the price of bottled water.

C) an increase in the opportunity cost of soft drinks.

D) a decrease in the relative price of a soft drink.

Answer: A

■ Supply

Topic: The Law of Supply
Skill: Conceptual

27) The "law of supply" refers to the fact that, all other things remaining constant on the supply side of the market, when the price of a good rises

A) the supply curve will shift leftward.

B) the supply curve will shift rightward.

C) there will be a movement up along the supply curve to a larger quantity demanded.

D) there will be a movement down along the supply curve to a smaller quantity demanded.

Answer: C

Topic: The Law of Supply
Skill: Conceptual

28) The "law of supply" states that, other things remaining the same,

A) firms will produce more of a good the less it costs to produce it.

B) firms will produce less of a good the more it costs to produce it.

C) firms will produce more of a good the higher its price.

D) firms will produce less of a good as the required resources become scarcer.

Answer: C

Topic: Change in the Quantity Supplied
Skill: Recognition

29) Which of the following could cause a movement along, but no shift in, the supply curve for shredded wheat breakfast cereal?

A) A report by the U.S. Surgeon General that increased wheat consumption increases nervousness and stress.

B) An increase in the cost of machinery used to shred wheat.

C) Perfect weather conditions that resulted in a large wheat crop.

D) All of the above.

Answer: A

Topic: Change in the Quantity Supplied
Skill: Conceptual

30) Which of the following would cause a movement along, but no shift in the supply curve for spinach?

A) Disastrous weather that destroys about half of this year's spinach crop.

B) A newly discovered increase in the nutritional value of spinach.

C) An increase in wages for workers in spinach fields.

D) Great weather that produces a bumper spinach crop this year.

Answer: B

Topic: Change in Supply, Prices of Resources
Skill: Recognition

31) Changes in which of the following items will shift the supply curve of hamburgers?

A) A rise in the price of soda, a complement for hamburgers.

B) A new law requiring that a health warning labels be issued when a consumer buys a hamburger.

C) An increase in the price of meat used to produce hamburgers.

D) An economy-wide decrease in family incomes due to a long recession.

Answer: C

Topic: Change in Supply, Prices of Resources
Skill: Conceptual

32) Consumers think that Honda Accords and Toyota Camrys are close substitutes. What would be the result if Honda employees all got pay increases while Toyota employees all accepted pay reductions?

A) The supply of Hondas would increase.

B) The supply of Toyotas would increase.

C) The demand for Hondas would increase.

D) The demand for Toyotas would increase.

Answer: B

Topic: Change in Supply, Number of Suppliers
Skill: Conceptual

33) An increase in the number of suppliers in a market will cause

A) a movement down along the supply curve.

B) the supply curve to shift rightward.

C) the supply curve to shift leftward.

D) Both answers A and C are correct.

Answer: B

Topic: Change in Supply, Weather
Skill: Conceptual

34) Which of the following would directly cause the supply curve of broccoli to shift?

A) An increase in the demand for broccoli.

B) A newly discovered increase in the nutritional value of broccoli.

C) A newly discovered link between broccoli consumption and tooth decay.

D) The destruction of much of this year's broccoli crop by unexpected hurricanes.

Answer: D

Topic: Change in Supply, Weather
Skill: Analytical

35) A severe drought has damaged this year's lettuce crop. The initial effect on the lettuce market would be

A) a decrease in the demand for lettuce.

B) a decrease in the supply of lettuce.

C) a decrease in both the demand and supply of lettuce.

D) a rightward movement along the demand curve for lettuce.

Answer: B

Topic: A Change in the Quantity Supplied Versus a Change in Supply
Skill: Conceptual
36) As the price of a pound of peanuts falls,
 A)   the supply of peanuts will increase.
 B)   the supply of peanuts will decrease.
 C)   the quantity of peanuts supplied will increase.
 D)   the quantity of peanuts supplied will decrease.
Answer: D

Topic: A Change in the Quantity Supplied Versus a Change in Supply
Skill: Conceptual
37) For a "change in the quantity supplied" but not "a change in supply" to occur, there must be
 A)   a rightward shift of the supply curve.
 B)   a rightward shift of the demand curve.
 C)   a leftward shift of the demand curve.
 D)   Both answers B and C are correct.
Answer: D

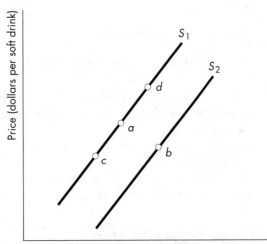

Topic: Change in the Quantity Supplied
Skill: Analytical
38) Consider the figure above showing the market for soft drinks. Suppose the economy is at point *a*. A movement to point *c* could be the result of
 A)   a decrease in technology.
 B)   a decrease in the relative price of a soft drink.
 C)   an increase in the relative price of a soft drink.
 D)   an increase in the money price of a soft drink.
Answer: B

Topic: Change in the Quantity Supplied
Skill: Recognition
39) Consider the figure above showing the market for soft drinks. Suppose the economy is at point *a*. A movement to point *d* could be the result of
 A)   an increase in technology.
 B)   a decrease in the relative price of a soft drink.
 C)   an increase in the relative price of a soft drink.
 D)   an increase in the number of soft drink suppliers.
Answer: C

Topic: Change in Supply, Technology
Skill: Analytical
40) Consider the figure above showing the market for soft drinks. Suppose the economy is at point *a*. A movement to point *b* could be the result of
 A)   an increase in technology.
 B)   a decrease in the relative price of a soft drink.
 C)   an increase in the relative price of a soft drink.
 D)   an increase in the money price of a soft drink.
Answer: A

■ Market Equilibrium

Topic: Market Equilibrium
Skill: Conceptual
41) When a market is in equilibrium,
 A)   everyone has all they want of the commodity in question.
 B)   there is no shortage and no surplus at the equilibrium price.
 C)   the number of buyers is exactly equal to the number of sellers.
 D)   the supply curve has the same slope as the demand curve.
Answer: B

Topic: Market Equilibrium
Skill: Conceptual
42) When a market is in equilibrium
 A)   there is no surplus at the existing price.
 B)   there is no shortage at the existing price.
 C)   there is no automatic tendency for either the supply curve or the demand curve to shift.
 D)   All of the above answers are correct.
Answer: D

Topic: Market Equilibrium
Skill: Conceptual
43) Which of the following is the best way to describe equilibrium in a market? At equilibrium,
 A) the price charged is the lowest possible.
 B) the price charged is usually affordable to most people.
 C) the supply and demand curves can never shift again.
 D) the quantity supplied equals the quantity demanded.
Answer: D

Topic: Price Adjustments, Shortage
Skill: Conceptual
44) Ticket scalpers at the NCAA basketball tournament last year charged prices high above the printed ticket price. This observation is evidence of
 A) a surplus at printed ticket prices.
 B) a shortage at printed ticket prices.
 C) the tournament not being televised.
 D) the tournament getting too much television exposure.
Answer: B

Topic: Price Adjustments, Surplus
Skill: Conceptual
45) Suppose the equilibrium price for soft drinks is $1.00. If the current price in the soft drink market is $1.25 each,
 A) there will be a surplus of soft drinks.
 B) there will be a shortage of soft drinks.
 C) the supply curve of soft drinks will shift leftward.
 D) the demand curve for soft drinks will shift leftward.
Answer: A

■ Predicting Changes in Price and Quantity

Topic: Predicting Changes in Price and Quantity; Demand Changes
Skill: Recognition
46) If the U.S. Surgeon General announced that increased wheat consumption could cause heightened anxiety levels among children and adults, what happens to the equilibrium price and quantity of shredded wheat?
 A) The equilibrium price rises and the equilibrium quantity increases.
 B) The equilibrium price falls and the equilibrium quantity decreases.
 C) The equilibrium price rises and the equilibrium quantity decreases.
 D) The equilibrium price falls and the equilibrium quantity increases.
Answer: B

Topic: Predicting Changes in Price and Quantity;
Skill: Conceptual
47) Suppose the equilibrium price of bottled water has increased from $1.00 per bottle to $2.00 per bottle and the equilibrium quantity has risen. These changes are a result of a _____ shift of the _____ curve for bottled water.
 A) rightward; demand
 B) rightward; supply
 C) leftward; supply
 D) leftward; demand
Answer: A

Topic: Predicting Changes in Price and Quantity; Demand Changes
Skill: Conceptual
48) During the Great Depression of the 1930s, the price of golf clubs declined quite a bit. At the same time, the number of golf clubs purchased also declined. This goes to show that
 A) the usual law of demand does not usually work in a time of economic crises.
 B) buyers and sellers all behaved in an irrational manner.
 C) the demand curve for golf clubs shifted.
 D) golf is played by people whose incomes remained high during the Great Depression.
Answer: C

Topic: Predicting Changes in Price and Quantity; Demand Changes
Skill: Analytical

49) Which of the following would increase the equilibrium price of a used car and also increase the equilibrium quantity sold?

A) A fall in income if used cars are an inferior good.

B) An increase in the wage rate paid to used car salespeople.

C) Neither of the above because the question suggests a violation of the law of demand.

D) Neither of the above because the question suggests a violation of the law of supply.

Answer: A

Topic: Predicting Changes in Price and Quantity; Demand Changes
Skill: Analytical

50) Coffee and sugar are complements. If a poor sugar harvest causes an increase in the price of sugar, there will also be

A) an increase in coffee prices as well.

B) a decrease in coffee prices.

C) a rightward shift in the demand curve for coffee.

D) a leftward shift of the supply curve of coffee.

Answer: B

Topic: Predicting Changes in Price and Quantity; Demand Changes
Skill: Conceptual

51) A decrease in the demand for beef because of concerns over cholesterol will cause

A) lower beef prices.

B) higher beef prices.

C) an increase in the supply of beef.

D) an offsetting increase in the demand for beef if the price of beef falls.

Answer: A

Topic: Predicting Changes in Price and Quantity; Demand Changes
Skill: Analytical

52) During the last decade, the price of shoes rose substantially yet people bought more pairs of new shoes each year. This experience suggests that

A) the supply curve of shoes shifted leftward.

B) the demand curve for shoes shifted leftward.

C) the supply curve of shoes shifted rightward.

D) the demand curve for shoes shifted rightward.

Answer: D

Topic: Predicting Changes in Price and Quantity; Demand Changes
Skill: Analytical

53) Throughout the 1990's, the price of four-wheel drive vehicles rose and each year more were purchased. This experience suggests that

A) there must have been tremendous technological advances in the way four-wheel drive vehicles are produced.

B) there must have been rightward shifts in the demand curve for four-wheel drive vehicles.

C) there must have movements leftward along the supply curve of four-wheel drive vehicles.

D) None of the above.

Answer: B

Topic: Predicting Changes in Price and Quantity; Demand Changes
Skill: Analytical

54) During the past twenty years, the prices of prescription drugs, relative to the prices of other goods, have risen, yet Americans buy more prescription drugs than ever. This might be because

A) with higher incomes and better health insurance coverage, we have moved rightward along our demand curve for drugs.

B) with higher incomes and better health insurance coverage, the demand curve for prescription drugs has shifted rightward.

C) more and more new firms entered the pharmaceutical industry each year, which caused a rightward shift in the supply curve of prescription drugs.

D) Both answers A and C are correct.

Answer: B

Topic: Predicting Changes in Price and Quantity; Demand Changes
Skill: Analytical

55) Every spring, motorists do more driving than during the winter months. Every spring, the price of gasoline increases and the motorists buy more gasoline. This experience suggests that

A) the law of supply does not always hold for necessities like gasoline.

B) the law of demand does not always hold for necessities like gasoline.

C) the laws of supply and demand are both contradicted for gasoline, though only during the spring driving season.

D) None of the above.

Answer: D

Topic: Predicting Changes in Price and Quantity; Demand Changes
Skill: Analytical

56) After the sugar substitute saccharin was found to cause cancer in laboratory mice, its price dropped dramatically. This change in the price was because

A) the supply of saccharin decreased.

B) the demand for saccharin decreased.

C) the government ordered the price reduction.

D) saccharin producers felt sorry for their past customers and were making an honest attempt to compensate them

Answer: B

Topic: Predicting Changes in Price and Quantity; Supply Changes
Skill: Analytical

57) Bicycles are made out of steel. If the price of steel increases, there would be a shift in the supply curve of bicycles that would lead to

A) a shift in the demand curve for bicycles.

B) a temporary surplus of bicycles.

C) a permanent surplus of bicycles.

D) an increase in the price of a bicycle.

Answer: D

Topic: Predicting Changes in Price and Quantity; Supply Changes
Skill: Analytical

58) "The recent hurricanes in Florida are bringing financial gain to California citrus growers. Due to extensive damage to the Florida citrus crop, California citrus products are commanding their highest prices ever." Which of the following statements best explains the economics of this quotation?

A) The supply of Florida oranges decreased, causing their price to increase, which then increased the demand for substitute California oranges.

B) The supply of Florida oranges decreased, causing the supply of California oranges to increase and the price of California oranges to rise.

C) The demand for Florida oranges decreased because of the hurricanes, causing a greater demand for California oranges and an increase in the price of California oranges.

D) The demand for Florida oranges decreased, causing their prices to rise, therefore increasing the demand for California oranges.

Answer: A

Topic: Predicting Changes in Price and Quantity; Supply Changes
Skill: Analytical

59) Crude oil can be refined into home heating oil or gasoline. If very cold weather caused the price of home heating oil to increase then,

A) the supply of gasoline would increase.

B) the supply of home heating oil would decrease.

C) the equilibrium price of gasoline would rise.

D) Both answers A and C are correct.

Answer: C

Topic: Predicting Changes in Price and Quantity; Supply Changes
Skill: Analytical

60) Which of the following would increase the equilibrium price of a used car and decrease the equilibrium quantity sold?

A) An announcement by the U.S. Attorney General that the windows on older cars were made with cheaper glass that can explode at high speeds.

B) New federal legislation that raises the legal driving age to twenty-four in all states.

C) A new fee that used car dealers must pay to the government on all sales of used cars.

D) All of the above because each is consistent with the law of demand.

Answer: C

Topic: Predicting Changes in Price and Quantity; Supply Changes
Skill: Analytical

61) During the last decade, the price of a computer fell every year and the quantity sold increased every year. This experience suggests that

A) the law of demand was definitely contradicted.

B) the law of supply was definitely contradicted.

C) the demand curve shifted rightward.

D) the supply curve shifted rightward.

Answer: D

Topic: Predicting Changes in Price and Quantity; Supply Changes
Skill: Analytical

62) During the 1990s, the price of compact disc players fell each year and manufacturers of compact disc players produced and sold more compact disc players each year. This result is because

A) the law of supply does not apply to companies in the "high-tech" sector of the economy.

B) the law of demand does not apply to customers in the "high-tech" sector of the economy.

C) the supply curve of compact disc players shifted rightward.

D) the demand curve for compact disc players shifted leftward.

Answer: C

Topic: Predicting Changes in Price and Quantity; Demand Increases, Supply Decreases
Skill: Analytical

63) All shredded wheat producers have decided to add a new ingredient to shredded wheat, the "crunch enhancer." Crunch enhancer keeps cereals crisper longer in milk and, as a result, consumers decide they like shredded more wheat more than before. What happens to the equilibrium price and quantity of shredded wheat now that is costs more to produce but consumers like it better?

A) The equilibrium price rises and the equilibrium quantity increases.

C) The equilibrium price rises and the equilibrium quantity decreases.

C) The effect on the equilibrium price is uncertain, but the equilibrium quantity will increase.

D) The equilibrium price will rise, but the effect on the equilibrium quantity is uncertain.

Answer: D

Topic: Predicting Changes in Price and Quantity; Demand Increases, Supply Decreases
Skill: Conceptual

64) If the demand curve for bottled water shifts rightward and the supply curve for bottled water shifts leftward,

A) the equilibrium price of bottled water definitely increases.

B) the equilibrium price of bottled water definitely decreases.

C) the equilibrium quantity of bottled water definitely increases.

D) the equilibrium quantity of bottled water definitely decreases.

Answer: A

**Topic: Predicting Changes in Price and Quantity;
Demand Increases, Supply Decreases**
Skill: Analytical
65) All shredded wheat producers have decided to add
a new ingredient to shredded wheat, the "crunch
enhancer." Crunch enhancer keeps cereals crisper
longer in milk and, as a result, consumers decide
they like shredded more wheat more than before.
What happens to the supply and demand curves
for shredded wheat now that is costs more to produce and consumers like it better?

A) The supply and demand curves both shift rightward.
B) The supply curve shifts rightward and the demand curve doesn't shift.
C) The supply curve shifts leftward and the demand
curve shifts rightward.
D) The supply curve shifts leftward and the demand
curve doesn't shift.

Answer: C

**Topic: Predicting Changes in Price and Quantity;
Demand Decreases, Supply Increases**
Skill: Conceptual
66) If the demand curve for bikes shifts leftward and
the supply curve for bikes shifts rightward,

A) the equilibrium price of bikes definitely increases.
B) the equilibrium price of bikes definitely decreases.
C) the equilibrium quantity of bikes definitely increases.
D) the equilibrium quantity of bikes definitely decreases.

Answer: B

**Topic: Predicting Changes in Price and Quantity;
Demand and Supply Both Increase**
Skill: Conceptual
67) If the demand curve for bottled water shifts
rightward and the supply curve for bottled water
shifts rightward,

A) the equilibrium price of bottled water definitely
increases.
B) the equilibrium price of bottled water definitely
decreases.
C) the equilibrium quantity of bottled water definitely increases.
D) the equilibrium quantity of bottled water definitely decreases.

Answer: C

**Topic: Predicting Changes in Price and Quantity;
Demand and Supply Both Decrease**
Skill: Conceptual
68) If the demand curve for bottled water shifts leftward and the supply curve for bottled water shifts
leftward,

A) the equilibrium price of bottled water definitely
increases.
B) the equilibrium price of bottled water definitely
decreases.
C) the equilibrium quantity of bottled water definitely increases.
D) the equilibrium quantity of bottled water definitely decreases.

Answer: D

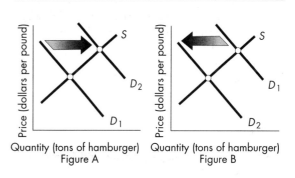

Quantity (tons of hamburger)
Figure A

Quantity (tons of hamburger)
Figure B

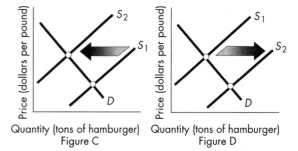

Quantity (tons of hamburger)
Figure C

Quantity (tons of hamburger)
Figure D

**Topic: Predicting Changes in Price and Quantity;
Demand Changes**
Skill: Recognition
69) The above figures show the market for hamburger
meat. Which figure(s) shows the effect of a new
report by the U.S. Surgeon General that beef consumption is healthier than previously believed?

A) Figure A.
B) Figure B.
C) Figure D.
D) Figure A and B.

Answer: A

Topic: Predicting Changes in Price and Quantity; Demand Changes
Skill: Recognition

70) The above figures show the market for hamburger meat. Which figure(s) shows the effect of an increase in the price of a hamburger bun, a complement for hamburger meat?
A) Figure B.
B) Figure C.
C) Figure D.
D) Figures A and B.

Answer: A

Topic: Predicting Changes in Price and Quantity; Demand Changes
Skill: Recognition

71) The above figures show the market for hamburger meat. Which figure(s) shows the effect of a nation-wide scare that hamburger meat is infected with "mad cow" disease?
A) Figure A.
B) Figure B.
C) Figure C.
D) Figures A and C.

Answer: B

Topic: Predicting Changes in Price and Quantity; Demand Changes
Skill: Recognition

72) The above figures show the market for hamburger meat. Which figure(s) shows the effect of a decrease in the price of a hamburger complement such as hamburger buns?
A) Figure A.
B) Figure B.
C) Figure D.
D) Figures A and B.

Answer: A

Topic: Predicting Changes in Price and Quantity; Demand Changes
Skill: Recognition

73) The above figures show the market for hamburger meat. Which figure(s) shows the effect of an increase in the price of a substitute like hot dogs?
A) Figure A.
B) Figure C.
C) Figure D.
D) Figures A and C.

Answer: A

Topic: Predicting Changes in Price and Quantity; Demand Changes
Skill: Recognition

74) The above figures show the market for hamburger meat. Which figure(s) shows the effect of a decrease in the price of a substitute like hot dogs?
A) Figure A.
B) Figure B.
C) Figure C.
D) Figures A and C.

Answer: B

Topic: Predicting Changes in Price and Quantity; Supply Changes
Skill: Recognition

75) The above figures show the market for hamburger meat. Which figure(s) shows the effect of a nation-wide strike by butchers and meat-packers?
A) Figure B.
B) Figure C.
C) Figure D.
D) Figures B and C.

Answer: B

Topic: Predicting Changes in Price and Quantity; Supply Changes
Skill: Recognition

76) The above figures show the market for hamburger meat. Which figure(s) shows the effect of a newly invented machine which grinds beef at twice the speed previously possible?
A) Figure A.
B) Figure C.
C) Figure D.
D) Figures A and C.

Answer: C

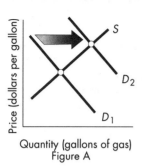

Figure A

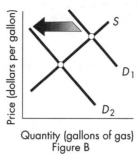

Figure B

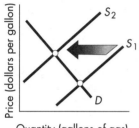

Figure C

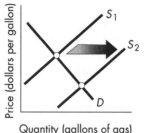

Figure D

Topic: Predicting Changes in Price and Quantity; Demand Changes
Skill: Recognition

77) The above figures show the market for gasoline. Which figure(s) shows the effect of a nation-wide strike by municipal bus drivers, which causes more people to drive their cars to work?
A) Figure A.
B) Figure B.
C) Figure D.
D) Figures A and B.
Answer: A

Topic: Predicting Changes in Price and Quantity; Demand Changes
Skill: Recognition

78) The above figures show the market for gasoline. Which figure(s) shows the effect of an increased preference for cars that are smaller and more fuel efficient?
A) Figure A.
B) Figure B.
C) Figure C.
D) Figures A and C.
Answer: B

Topic: Predicting Changes in Price and Quantity; Demand Changes
Skill: Recognition

79) The above figures show the market for gasoline. Which figure(s) shows the effect of motorists increasing their demand for taking the bus to work rather than driving their own cars?
A) Figure A.
B) Figure B.
C) Figure C.
D) Figures A and C.
Answer: B

Topic: Predicting Changes in Price and Quantity; Supply Changes
Skill: Recognition

80) The above figures show the market for gasoline. Which figure(s) shows the effect of a decision by the OPEC countries in the Middle East to export less oil to the rest of the world?
A) Figure B.
B) Figure C.
C) Figure D.
D) Figures B and C.
Answer: B

Topic: Predicting Changes in Price and Quantity; Supply Changes
Skill: Recognition

81) The above figures show the market for gasoline. Which figure(s) shows the effect of a freezing cold winter which drives up the price of home heating oil (a substitute in production for gasoline because each is made from crude oil)?
A) Figure B.
B) Figure C.
C) Figure D.
D) Figures B and C.
Answer: B

Topic: Predicting Changes in Price and Quantity; Supply Changes
Skill: Recognition

82) The above figures show the market for gasoline. Which figure(s) shows the effect of a new U.S. tax on oil that suppliers must pay?
A) Figures A and C.
B) Figures B and D.
C) Figure A only.
D) Figure C only.
Answer: D

Topic: Predicting Changes in Price and Quantity; Supply Changes
Skill: Recognition
83) The above figures show the market for gasoline. Which figure shows the effect of the end of a nine month strike by workers at all U.S. oil refineries?
A) Figure A.
B) Figure B.
C) Figure C.
D) Figure D.
Answer: D

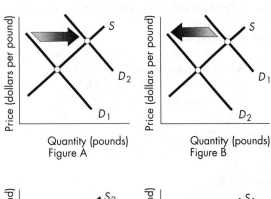

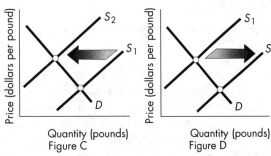

Figure A   Figure B   Figure C   Figure D

Topic: Predicting Changes in Price and Quantity; Demand Changes
Skill: Recognition
84) The above figures show the market for oranges. Which figure shows the effect of changing consumer preferences for more orange juice and less coffee in the morning?
A) Figure A.
B) Figure B.
C) Figure C.
D) Figure D.
Answer: A

Topic: Predicting Changes in Price and Quantity; Demand Changes
Skill: Recognition
85) The above figures show the market for oranges. Which figure(s) shows the effect of a new government program that provides each public school child with an orange to start the day?
A) Figure A.
B) Figure D.
C) Figures A and C.
D) Figures A and D.
Answer: A

Topic: Predicting Changes in Price and Quantity; Demand Changes
Skill: Recognition
86) The above figures show the market for oranges. Which figure(s) shows the effect of an increase in the price of bananas, a substitute for oranges?
A) Figure A.
B) Figure C.
C) Figure D.
D) Figure A and C.
Answer: A

Topic: Predicting Changes in Price and Quantity; Demand Changes
Skill: Recognition
87) The above figures show the market for oranges. Which figure(s) shows the effect of new successful advertising campaigns to eat more oranges?
A) Panel A.
B) Panel B.
C) Panel D.
D) Panels A and D.
Answer: A

Topic: Predicting Changes in Price and Quantity; Demand Changes
Skill: Recognition
88) The above figures show the market for oranges. Which figure(s) shows the effect of a nation-wide consumer boycott of eating oranges?
A) Figure B.
B) Figure C.
C) Figures B and C.
D) Figures A and D.
Answer: A

Topic: Predicting Changes in Price and Quantity; Supply Changes
Skill: Recognition

89) The above figures show the market for oranges. Which figure shows the effect of great growing conditions that produce an above-average sized crop?
   A) Figure A.
   B) Figure B.
   C) Figure C.
   D) Figure D.

Answer: D

Topic: Predicting Changes in Price and Quantity; Supply Changes
Skill: Recognition

90) The above figures show the market for oranges. Which figure shows the effect of a new technology called "the orange picker", which harvests oranges less expensively than ever before?
   A) Figure A.
   B) Figure B.
   C) Figure C.
   D) Figure D.

Answer: D

Topic: Predicting Changes in Price and Quantity; Supply Changes
Skill: Recognition

91) The above figures show the market for oranges. Which figure(s) shows the effect of existing orange growers increasing the size of their orange groves?
   A) Figures A and C.
   B) Figures B and D.
   C) Figure A.
   D) Figure D.

Answer: D

■ True or False Questions

Topic: Demand
Skill: Conceptual

92) An increase in the incomes of baseball fans in New York causes a rightward movement along the demand curve but no shift in the demand curve for Yankee's tickets.

Answer: FALSE

Topic: Demand
Skill: Conceptual

93) Young drivers often buy used cars. An increase in the legal driving age to twenty-one causes a leftward movement along the demand curve for used cars, whereas lowering the age to fifteen causes a rightward movement.

Answer: FALSE

Topic: Demand
Skill: Conceptual

94) Young drivers often buy used cars. An increase in the legal driving age to twenty-one shifts the demand curve for used cars leftward, whereas lowering the age to fifteen shifts the demand curve rightward.

Answer: TRUE

Topic: Supply
Skill: Conceptual

95) An increase in the hourly wage of hot dog vendors at Yankee Stadium shifts the supply curve of hot dogs leftward.

Answer: TRUE

Topic: Predicting Changes in Price and Quantity
Skill: Analytical

96) If house purchases and apartment rentals are substitutes, then an increase in the price of a new house causes an increase in apartment rents.

Answer: TRUE

Topic: Predicting Changes in Price and Quantity
Skill: Analytical

97) During the 1990s, the average price of a used car fell by nearly $500 and the quantity sold nationwide decreased by several thousands each year. This set of results is a contradiction of the law of demand.

Answer: FALSE

■ Essay Questions

Topic: Predicting Changes in Price and Quantity
Skill: Analytical

98) What will happen to the equilibrium price and
     quantity in the market for shredded wheat if (a)
     the producer purchases and applies a "crunch en-
     hancer" food additive to shredded wheat and (2)
     consumers begin to eat more shredded wheat be-
     cause they like the way the crunch enhancer keeps
     it crisper longer in milk.

Answer: The supply curve shifts leftward because the
     purchase and application of the crunch enhancer
     creates one more cost of production. The demand
     curve shifts rightward because tastes and prefer-
     ences for shredded wheat have improved. Both
     shifts cause the equilibrium price of shredded
     wheat to increase. Whether the equilibrium
     quantity increases or decreases depends on
     whether the demand curve shift is greater than the
     supply curve shift, or vice versa.

Topic: Predicting Changes in Price and Quantity
Skill: Analytical

99) During the real estate boom of the mid-1990's,
     the prices of new and existing homes rose year af-
     ter year yet people purchased more homes year
     after year. Can this outcome be explained as an
     exception to the law of demand?

Answer: No; it is explained by a rightward shift of the
     demand curves for new and existing homes. The
     rightward shift was caused by rising consumer in-
     comes and lower mortgage interest rates.

Topic: Market Equilibrium
Skill: Analytical

100) If the equilibrium relative price for a two-liter
     bottle of Coca-Cola is $1.50 today, just like it was
     ten years ago, can we safely say that all supply and
     demand conditions in the market for Coke have
     remained very stable all these years?

Answer: Not necessarily. The demand curve might
     have shifted rightward continuously due to popu-
     lation growth in the U.S. and growing demand
     for Coke in other countries world-wide. Although
     that alone would have driven up the price, there
     could have been other factors shifting the supply
     curve rightward and pulling the price down. Some
     possibilities would be improved technology for
     producing and transporting Coke, or declining
     sugar prices due to some great sugar harvests.

Chapter 5 A FIRST LOOK AT MACROECONOMICS*

■ Origins and Issues of Macroeconomics

Topic: Origins and Issues of Macroeconomics
Skill: Recognition
1) Which of the following is TRUE regarding macroeconomics?
   I.   Economists only started to study macroeconomic topics like long-term economic growth and international payments in the 1960s.
   II. The origins of macroeconomics started in the 1700s.
   III. "Modern" macroeconomics emerged as a result of the Great Depression.
   A) I and II.
   B) I and III.
   C) II and III.
   D) I, II and III.
Answer: C

Topic: Origins and Issues of Macroeconomics
Skill: Recognition
2) As a result of the Great Depression
   A) people questioned the ability of markets to work properly.
   B) people believed that capitalism was the only solution to the economic depression.
   C) modern macroeconomics developed.
   D) Both answers A and C are correct.
Answer: D

Topic: Origins and Issues of Macroeconomics
Skill: Recognition
3) The Great Depression made a lasting impression on all Americans who experienced it. During the Depression, at its worst the unemployment rate was approximately ____ percent of the labor force.
   A) 50
   B) 40
   C) 25
   D) 15
Answer: C

Topic: Origins and Issues of Macroeconomics
Skill: Conceptual
4) John Maynard Keynes was the author of ____, which was published in 1936.
   A) *Explanations of the Great Depression*
   B) *The Wealth of Nations*
   C) *The General Theory of Employment, Interest and Money*
   D) the first macroeconomics textbook.
Answer: C

Topic: Short-Term Versus Long-Term Goals
Skill: Recognition
5) John Maynard Keynes' work focused on
   A) short-term economic problems.
   B) solutions for long-term economic growth.
   C) the long-term consequences of inflation.
   D) collecting better statistics to better understand the Great Depression.
Answer: A

---

* This is Chapter 22 in *Economics*.

Topic: Macroeconomics
Skill: Recognition
6) Macroeconomic theory addresses the question of how to
   A) price each of the products the economy produces.
   B) generate full employment, price stability and long-term economic growth.
   C) organize resources within a given industry.
   D) ensure that consumers maximize the satisfaction possible from their incomes.
Answer: B

Topic: Macroeconomics
Skill: Recognition
7) Macroeconomics studies many issues including:
   A) long-term economic growth.
   B) international deficits.
   C) inflation.
   D) all of the above.
Answer: D

■ Economic Growth

Topic: Economic Growth
Skill: Recognition
8) The expansion of an economy's production possibilities is known as
   A) inflation.
   B) economic growth.
   C) the business cycle.
   D) economic fluctuations.
Answer: B

Topic: Economic Growth
Skill: Recognition
9) On a production possibility curve, economic growth is represented by
   A) a movement downward along the production possibility curve.
   B) a movement upward along the production possibility curve.
   C) an outward shift of the production possibility curve.
   D) an inward shift of the production possibility curve.
Answer: C

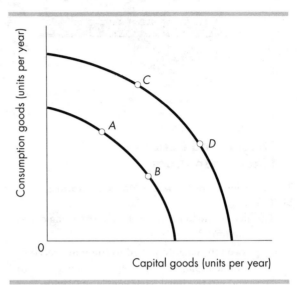

Topic: Economic Growth
Skill: Analytical
10) In the above figure, economic growth is shown as the movement from point
   A) *A* to point *B*.
   B) *C* to point *D*.
   C) *B* to point *D*.
   D) None of the above because it is not possible to show economic growth using a production possibility frontier
Answer: C

Topic: Economic Growth
Skill: Conceptual
11) Economic growth is measured by increases in
   A) resource use.
   B) real GDP.
   C) satisfaction.
   D) employment and unemployment.
Answer: B

Topic: Real GDP
Skill: Recognition
12) _____ gross domestic product is the value of _____ linked back to the prices of a single year.
   A) Real; total production
   B) Real; production possibilities
   C) Nominal; the consumer price index
   D) Nominal; total production
Answer: A

Topic: Real GDP
Skill: Conceptual
13) Which of the following is TRUE regarding the use of real GDP to measure economic growth?
   I.   Real GDP is the value of the total production of the country's farms, factories, shops, and offices.
   II.   Real GDP rises whenever inflation occurs.
   III. Real GDP does not measure all that is produced.
   A) I and II.
   B) I and III.
   C) II and III.
   D) I, II and III.
Answer: B

Topic: Potential GDP
Skill: Recognition
14) When all of the economy's resources are fully employed, the value of production is called
   A) real GDP.
   B) nominal GDP.
   C) actual GDP.
   D) potential GDP.
Answer: D

Topic: Potential GDP
Skill: Conceptual
15) Long-term economic growth
   A) is unlikely to occur when inflation is present.
   B) is measured by the growth rate of potential GDP.
   C) is measured using a consumer price index.
   D) generally requires a high rate of present consumption to build a base for future consumption.
Answer: B

Topic: Productivity Growth Slowdown
Skill: Recognition
16) In comparing economic growth today versus growth in the 1960s, which of the following is TRUE?
   I.   Economic growth in the 1960s averaged about 4.4 percent a year.
   II.   Economic growth in the 1990s has averaged about 5 percent per year.
   III. A productivity growth slowdown occurred in the 1970s.
   A) I only.
   B) I and II.
   C) I and III.
   D) I, II and III.
Answer: C

Topic: Productivity Growth Slowdown
Skill: Recognition
17) The productivity growth slowdown refers to the
   A) years following the 1930s depression.
   B) period during the 1970s and for some years afterwards.
   C) years during the 1990s.
   D) situation in foreign nations but not in the United States.
Answer: B

Topic: Productivity Growth Slowdown
Skill: Recognition
18) ____ refers to a period when the ____ decreases.
   A) Recession; growth rate of nominal GDP
   B) Recession; growth rate of output per person
   C) Productivity growth slowdown; growth rate of real GDP
   D) Productivity growth slowdown; growth rate of output per person
Answer: D

Topic: Business Cycles
Skill: Conceptual
19) In any year, the real GDP of an economy
   A) must always be less than potential GDP.
   B) may be greater or less than potential GDP.
   C) will always be greater than potential GDP because of the tendency of developed nations to incur inflation.
   D) always equals potential GDP.
Answer: B

Topic: Business Cycle
Skill: Conceptual
20) When real GDP is less than potential GDP
   A) people work longer hours than usual.
   B) some capital equipment is underused.
   C) some labor is unemployed.
   D) Both answers B and C are correct.
Answer: D

Topic: Business Cycle
Skill: Recognition
21) The series of ups and downs the economy tends to move in is called
   A) the business cycle.
   B) a recession.
   C) a depression.
   D) economic growth.
Answer: A

Topic: Business Cycle
Skill: Recognition
22) The term "business cycle" most closely refers to the
   A) fluctuating profits of firms.
   B) fiscal year.
   C) accounting period used by firms.
   D) alternating periods of expansions and recessions.
Answer: D

Topic: Business Cycle
Skill: Recognition
23) Which of the following is not a phase or turning point of the business cycle?
   A) recession.
   B) expansion.
   C) shutdown.
   D) trough.
Answer: C

Topic: Business Cycle
Skill: Recognition
24) The four parts of the business cycle occur in the following order:
   A) recession, trough, peak, expansion.
   B) expansion, trough, peak, recession.
   C) recession, trough, expansion, peak.
   D) expansion, trough, peak, recession.
Answer: C

Topic: Business Cycle
Skill: Conceptual
25) Which of the following is TRUE regarding business cycles?
   I.   Cycles are predictable.
   II.   In each cycle, a peak follows an expansion.
   III. Potential GDP fluctuates around real GDP.
   A) I and II.
   B) I and III.
   C) II and III.
   D) II only.
Answer: D

Topic: Business Cycle
Skill: Recognition
26) In the most general terms, a recession is a time with
   A) a decline in the price level.
   B) a decline in interest rates.
   C) a decrease in the level of total production.
   D) a decrease in the unemployment rate.
Answer: C

Topic: Business Cycle
Skill: Recognition
27) A recession is defined as
   A) at least 6 months during which real GDP decreases.
   B) an increase in real economic output from one period to the next.
   C) no change in real GDP over a period of time.
   D) no change in the dollar (money) value of economic output over a period of time.
Answer: A

Topic: Business Cycle
Skill: Recognition
28) A recession is defined as occurring when
   A) real GDP decreases for a period of 12 or more months.
   B) real GDP decreases for a period of 6 or more months.
   C) the unemployment rate rises above 7.5 percent for 6 or more months.
   D) the unemployment rate rises above 5.0 percent for 12 or more months.
Answer: B

Topic: Business Cycle
Skill: Conceptual

29) During a recession, real GDP ____ and unemployment ____.

A) increases; increases
B) increases; decreases
C) decreases; increases
D) decreases; decreases

Answer: C

Topic: Business Cycle
Skill: Recognition

30) In the U.S., the most recent recession occurred in

A) 1973-1975.
B) 1980-1982.
C) 1990-1991.
D) 1998.

Answer: C

Topic: Business Cycle
Skill: Recognition

31) When a recession ends, the turning point that immediately follows is called a

A) trough
B) peak
C) depression
D) None of the above answers are correct.

Answer: A

Topic: Business Cycle
Skill: Recognition

32) The low point of economic activity during a business cycle is called the

A) trough.
B) recession.
C) peak.
D) pits.

Answer: A

Topic: Business Cycle
Skill: Recognition

33) The times during which real GDP increases are referred to as

A) contractions.
B) expansions.
C) anti-cycles.
D) corrections.

Answer: B

Topic: Business Cycle
Skill: Conceptual

34) An economy recovering from a recession

A) moves up from its trough to a period of expansion.
B) moves up from its peak to a period of expansion.
C) moves down from its trough to a period of depression.
D) moves down from its peak to a period of expansion.

Answer: A

Topic: Business Cycle
Skill: Conceptual

35) During an economic expansion, real GDP ____ and unemployment ____.

A) increases; increases
B) increases; decreases
C) decreases; increases
D) decreases; decreases

Answer: B

Topic: Business Cycle
Skill: Conceptual

36) An observer of the economy notices that over the past 12 months the unemployment rate has fallen from 7.0 percent to 6.5 percent. During the same time, the rate of growth in real GDP has been positive. From this information we might conclude that

A) inflation is not occurring.
B) an expansion is occurring in the economy.
C) a recession is in progress.
D) a trough in the business cycle will soon be reached.

Answer: B

Topic: Business Cycle
Skill: Recognition

37) When an expansion ends, the turning point that immediately follows is called a

A) peak
B) trough
C) zenith
D) depression

Answer: A

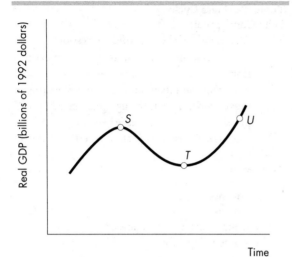

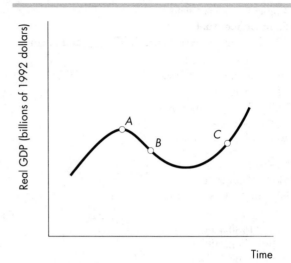

Topic: Business Cycle
Skill: Analytical

38) In the above figure, the distance between points S and T represents

A) an expansion.

B) a trough.

C) a peak.

D) a recession.

Answer: D

Topic: Business Cycle
Skill: Analytical

39) In the above figure, the distance between points T and U represents

A) an expansion.

B) a trough.

C) a peak.

D) a recession.

Answer: A

Topic: Business Cycle
Skill: Analytical

40) In the above figure, the letters A, B, and C represent which positions in the business cycle?

A) peak, expansion, and recession, respectively.

B) recession, expansion, and peak, respectively.

C) expansion, peak, and recession, respectively.

D) peak, recession, and expansion, respectively.

Answer: D

Topic: Long-Term Economic Growth in the United States
Skill: Conceptual

41) The historical record for the United States since 1900 shows

A) mostly positive economic growth, though the Great Depression caused actual GDP to dip well below potential GDP.

B) economic growth for about half the years and economic decline for the other half.

C) growth until 1970 and then a period of constant per capita real GDP.

D) continuous economic growth for each year, although at different rates, throughout the entire century.

Answer: A

Topic: Economic Growth Around the World
Skill: Recognition

42) To compare economic growth across countries, the best measure is
A) population growth rates.
B) potential GDP.
C) growth rates of real GDP per person.
D) real GDP.

Answer: C

Topic: Economic Growth Around the World
Skill: Conceptual

43) Growth rates of real GDP per person
A) are usually greater for industrial countries than for developing countries.
B) for the world, on average, are positive.
C) for developing and transition countries are all positive.
D) have been most rapid in Latin America.

Answer: B

Topic: Japanese, German, and U.S. Economic Growth
Skill: Recognition

44) Which of the following is TRUE regarding Japan, Germany and the U.S.?
I. All three experienced productivity growth slowdowns.
II. Real GDP per person is higher in the United States than in Germany or Japan.
A) I only.
B) II only.
C) Neither I nor II.
D) Both I and II.

Answer: D

Topic: Japanese, German, and U.S. Economic Growth
Skill: Conceptual

45) Between 1990 and 1998, the growth rate of real GDP per person in the U.S.
A) became negative.
B) has been higher than that in Germany.
C) has been higher than that in Japan.
D) has been lower than that in Japan and Germany.

Answer: C

Topic: Benefits and Costs of Economic Growth
Skill: Conceptual

46) Which of the following are potential benefits of economic growth?
I. Greater consumption today.
II. More resources for health care.
III. A cleaner environment.
A) I.
B) I and II.
C) I and III.
D) II and III.

Answer: D

Topic: Benefits and Costs of Economic Growth
Skill: Conceptual

47) A cost of economic growth is
A) a more equal income distribution.
B) lower current consumption.
C) higher spending for environmental protection.
D) a lower level of future living standards.

Answer: B

Topic: Benefits and Costs of Economic Growth
Skill: Conceptual

48) A cost of economic growth is
A) increased life span.
B) more political instability.
C) more frequent job changes.
D) forgone future consumption.

Answer: C

■ Jobs and Unemployment

Topic: Jobs
Skill: Recognition

49) Every year, the U.S. economy creates an average of close to _____ new jobs.
A) 0.
B) 10 million.
C) 100 thousand.
D) 2 million.

Answer: D

Topic: Jobs
Skill: Conceptual
50) Which of the following is TRUE regarding job creation?
- I.   The number of jobs created increases during an expansion.
- II. Job creation is fairly steady over the business cycle.
- III The number of jobs created decreases during a recession.

A) I and II.
B) I and III.
C) II and III.
D) II only.
Answer: B

Topic: Unemployment
Skill: Recognition
51) Over the last 100 years in the United States, the unemployment rate reached its highest rate

A) in the 1920s.
B) in the 1930s.
C) in the 1970s.
D) in the 1990s.
Answer: B

Topic: Unemployment
Skill: Conceptual
52) Which of the following is TRUE regarding the U.S. unemployment rate?
- I.   During the Great Expansion in the 1940s, the unemployment rate actually fell to 0 percent.
- II. The highest unemployment rates during the last 30 years occurred during recessions.
- III. Since the Great Depression, the unemployment rate has averaged about 6 percent.

A) I and II.
B) I and III.
C) II and III.
D) I, II and III.
Answer: C

Topic: Unemployment
Skill: Conceptual
53) Which of the following is TRUE regarding the social costs of unemployment?
- I.   The costs of unemployment are spread equally across economic classes.
- II. Prolonged unemployment causes a loss of human capital.
- III. Because of unemployment benefits, there is no loss of income to an unemployed worker.

A) I only.
B) II only.
C) I and II.
D) I and III.
Answer: B

■ Inflation

Topic: Inflation
Skill: Recognition
54) Inflation is

A) a general rise in all macroeconomic variables– prices, interest rates and unemployment.
B) a general rise in prices.
C) a rise in prices that is faster than the rise in wages.
D) a rise in wages that is faster than the rise in prices.
Answer: B

Topic: Inflation
Skill: Recognition
55) Inflation refers to the situation when

A) the prices of necessities increase.
B) the prices in general are increasing.
C) all prices rise by the same rate.
D) the rate at which prices rise is rising.
Answer: B

Topic: Inflation
Skill: Conceptual
56) In 1999, the price level was seven times higher than that of 1947. From this information, we can be sure that

A) the unemployment rate rose during this period.
B) the rate of inflation was greater in 1999 than in 1947.
C) the average annual inflation rate was positive between these years.
D) the unemployment rate fell during this period.
Answer: C

Topic: Inflation
Skill: Recognition

57) Deflation refers to the situation when
A) the inflation rate decreases.
B) the price level is falling.
C) there is a recession and inflation.
D) prices generally are not changing.

Answer: B

Topic: Inflation
Skill: Recognition

58) Deflation is defined as a situation in which
A) the rate of inflation is below 2 percent.
B) the price level is falling.
C) the government is running a budget surplus.
D) the GDP's growth rate is less for a given quarter than it was for the prior quarter.

Answer: B

Topic: Inflation
Skill: Conceptual

59) The CPI tells us
A) changes in prices of a group of goods and services bought by a typical urban household.
B) the increase in prices of those goods that are rising fastest.
C) the rate at which wages are rising.
D) the increase in the prices of those goods that are rising slowest.

Answer: A

Topic: Inflation
Skill: Analytical

60) If the CPI in 1999 is 220 and is 200 in 1998, the annual inflation rate between the two years is
A) 5 percent.
B) 10 percent.
C) 20 percent.
D) 2 percent.

Answer: B

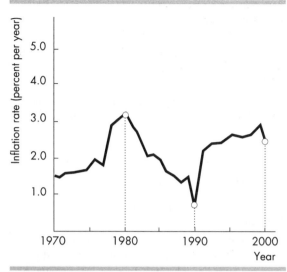

Topic: Inflation
Skill: Analytical

61) In the above figure, which period(s) show deflation?
A) Only from 1990 to 2000.
B) Only from 1980 to 1990.
C) From both 1970 to 1980 and from 1990 to 2000.
D) None of the above because there is no year with deflation in the above figure.

Answer: D

Topic: Inflation in the United States
Skill: Recognition

62) In the United States, between the 1960s and 1990s, the price level has _____. Within that period, the rate of inflation began to _____ sharply in the mid-1960s, but started to _____ in the 1980s.
A) generally risen; fall; rise
B) generally risen; rise; fall
C) generally fallen; fall; rise
D) generally fallen; rise; fall

Answer: B

Topic: Inflation Around the World
Skill: Conceptual

63) Which of the following is TRUE?

    I.   The U.S. inflation rate is less variable than the rate of other industrial countries.

    II.   The inflation rate in industrial countries is less than in developing countries.

    A)   I only.

    B)   II only.

    C)   Both I and II.

    D)   Neither I nor II.

Answer: B

Topic: Is Inflation a Problem?
Skill: Conceptual

64) The cost of inflation to society includes

    I.   The opportunity costs of resources used by people to protect themselves against inflation

    II.   The diversion of productive resources to forecasting inflation.

    A)   I only.

    B)   II only.

    C)   Both I and II.

    D)   Neither I nor II.

Answer: C

Topic: Is Inflation a Problem?
Skill: Conceptual

65) The cost of inflation to society includes

    A)   unpredictable changes in the value of money.

    B)   higher interest rates paid by borrowers.

    C)   higher interest rates paid by the government on its debt.

    D)   the lost spending when people do not have enough money.

Answer: A

Topic: Is Inflation a Problem?
Skill: Recognition

66) A period of time during which prices are rising at more than 50 percent a month is known as

    A)   hyperinflation.

    B)   superinflation.

    C)   deflation.

    D)   deficit inflation.

Answer: A

■ Surpluses and Deficits

Topic: Government Budget Surpluses and Deficits
Skill: Recognition

67) A government budget deficit occurs when

    A)   U.S. consumers buy more than U.S. producers produce.

    B)   foreign holdings of American assets exceed American holdings of foreign assets.

    C)   government spending is more than what it collects in taxes.

    D)   the value of U.S. imports exceed the value of U.S. exports.

Answer: C

Topic: Government Budget Surpluses and Deficits
Skill: Recognition

68) Since 1970, the government's budget deficit has been as much as ____ of GDP and in recent years the government has had a budget ____.

    A)   5 percent; surplus

    B)   12 percent; surplus

    C)   5 percent; deficit

    D)   12 percent; deficit

Answer: A

Topic: International Deficit
Skill: Conceptual

69) When the United States ____ the rest of the world, we ____.

    A)   imports goods and services from; run a trade surplus

    B)   imports goods and services from; make payments to foreigners

    C)   exports goods and services to; run a trade deficit

    D)   exports goods and services to; make payments to foreigners

Answer: B

■ Macroeconomic Policy Challenges and Tools

Topic: Macroeconomic Policy Challenges
Skill: Recognition

70) Macroeconomic policy challenges economy include all but which one of the following?

    A)   Reducing unemployment.

    B)   Keep inflation low.

    C)   Increasing the rate of economic growth.

    D)   Equalizing the distribution of income.

Answer: D

Topic: Macroeconomic Policy Challenges and Tools
Skill: Conceptual

71) _____ is a goal of macroeconomic policy and _____ is a tool that may help achieve the goals.
   A)   Boosting economic growth; fiscal policy
   B)   Reducing unemployment; keeping inflation low
   C)   Monetary policy; reducing unemployment
   D)   Fiscal policy; monetary policy

Answer: A

Topic: Fiscal Policy
Skill: Recognition

72) Fiscal policy involves
   A)   the use of interest rates to influence the level of GDP.
   B)   the use of tax and spending policies by the government.
   C)   decreasing the role of the Federal Reserve in the everyday life of the economy.
   D)   the use of tax and money policies by government to influence the level of interest rates.

Answer: B

Topic: Fiscal Policy
Skill: Conceptual

73) Fiscal policy might be used to increase long-term growth in real GDP by
   A)   motivating an increase in investment.
   B)   encouraging saving.
   C)   reducing unemployment.
   D)   Both answers A and B are correct.

Answer: D

Topic: Fiscal Policy
Skill: Conceptual

74) Fiscal policy might be used to smooth fluctuations in real GDP by
   A)   increasing taxes during a recession.
   B)   raising taxes during an expansion.
   C)   decreasing government spending during an expansion.
   D)   Both answers B and C are correct.

Answer: D

Topic: Monetary Policy
Skill: Recognition

75) Monetary policy is controlled by which of the following?
   A)   The U.S. Congress and the president.
   B)   The U.S. Federal Reserve.
   C)   The Interstate Commerce Commission.
   D)   The Federal Trade Commission.

Answer: B

Topic: Monetary Policy
Skill: Recognition

76) Monetary policy consists of
   A)   changing the amount of money in the economy.
   B)   tax policy.
   C)   change government spending.
   D)   following congressionally established rules concerning the interest rates.

Answer: A

Topic: Monetary Policy
Skill: Conceptual

77) The Federal Reserve is observed increasing the money supply in order to diminish the effect of a downturn in the business cycle. This action is an example of
   A)   a policy to promote economic growth.
   B)   the Fed avoiding inflation.
   C)   monetary policy.
   D)   fiscal policy.

Answer: C

Topic: Monetary Policy
Skill: Conceptual

78) As part of monetary policy, the Federal Reserve may _____ in an effort to _____.
   A)   raise taxes; decrease the international deficit
   B)   increase government spending; decrease the inflation rate
   C)   increase the amount of money; eliminate a recession
   D)   reduce taxes; lower interest rates

Answer: C

Topic: Monetary Policy
Skill: Conceptual

79) In order to smooth fluctuations in the business cycle, the Federal Reserve can

A) lower interest rates during a recession.

B) inject money into the economy during an expansion.

C) decrease taxes during a recession.

D) Both answers A and C are correct.

Answer: A

■ True Or False Questions

Topic: Origins and Issues of Macroeconomics
Skill: Recognition

80) Modern macroeconomics had its origins in the 1930s.

Answer: TRUE

Topic: Productivity Growth Slowdown
Skill: Conceptual

81) A productivity growth slowdown can be shown as year-to-year fluctuations of real GDP around potential GDP.

Answer: FALSE

Topic: Business Cycle
Skill: Recognition

82) Phases and turning points of the business cycle are expansion, peak, recession and trough.

Answer: TRUE

Topic: Business Cycle
Skill: Recognition

83) A recession occurs when real GDP decreases for at least 6 months.

Answer: TRUE

Topic: Japanese, German, and U.S. Economic Growth
Skill: Conceptual

84) The U.S., Germany, and Japan have all experienced similar rates of economic growth.

Answer: FALSE

Topic: Benefits and Costs of Economic Growth
Skill: Conceptual

85) Benefits of economic growth include expanded consumption possibilities in the future.

Answer: TRUE

Topic: Benefits and Costs of Economic Growth
Skill: Conceptual

86) Costs of economic growth include high interest rates.

Answer: FALSE

Topic: Unemployment
Skill: Recognition

87) Over the past 70 years, the unemployment rate in the U.S. has ranged from near 0 percent to near 25 percent.

Answer: TRUE

Topic: Unemployment
Skill: Conceptual

88) Lost production and lost human capital are some of the costs of unemployment.

Answer: TRUE

Topic: Inflation
Skill: Conceptual

89) To calculate the inflation rate, you must use a price index.

Answer: TRUE

Topic: Inflation Around the World
Skill: Conceptual

90) Developing countries tend to have higher inflation rates than do industrial countries.

Answer: TRUE

Topic: Macroeconomic Policy Challenges
Skill: Recognition

91) Agreed upon goals of macroeconomic policies include stabilization of the business cycle and keeping inflation low.

Answer: TRUE

■ Essay Questions

Topic: Origins and Issues of Macroeconomics
Skill: Recognition

92) Briefly explain John Maynard Keynes' role in the development of modern macroeconomics.

Answer:

Topic: Actual and Potential GDP
Skill: Recognition

93) What is the relationship between actual and potential real GDP?

Answer:

Topic: Business Cycle
Skill: Recognition
94) Using a graph, draw and label the phases and turning points of the business cycle.
Answer:

Topic: Business Cycle
Skill: Recognition
95) What is a recession?
Answer:

Topic: Benefits and Costs of Economic Growth
Skill: Recognition
96) What are some of the benefits of economic growth? Name at least two.
Answer:

Topic: Unemployment
Skill: Conceptual
97) Why is unemployment a problem?
Answer:

Topic: Inflation Around the World
Skill: Conceptual
98) What is the difference between inflation rates in developing versus industrial countries?
Answer:

Topic: Government Budget Surpluses and Deficits
Skill: Conceptual
99) What is the government budget surplus and deficit? How has the U.S. budget deficit and surplus behaved over the past 25 years?
Answer:

Topic: Fiscal Policy
Skill: Conceptual
100) Define and give an example of fiscal policy.
Answer:

Topic: Monetary Policy
Skill: Conceptual
101) Define and give an example of monetary policy.
Answer:

Chapter 6 MEASURING GDP, ECONOMIC GROWTH, AND INFLATION*

■ Gross Domestic Product

Topic: Gross Domestic Product
Skill: Recognition
1) Gross domestic product
   A) includes all the goods and none of the services produced in an economy in a given time period.
   B) measures the value of the aggregate production of goods and services in a country during a given time period.
   C) measures the value of labor payments generated in an economy in a given time period.
   D) is generally less than federal expenditure in any time period.
Answer: B

Topic: Flows and Stocks
Skill: Recognition
2) The distinction between a flow and a stock is that the former measures
   A) liquid items, while the latter measures solid items.
   B) an account on a monthly basis, while the latter measures it on an annual basis.
   C) a value in dollars, while the latter measures it in real terms.
   D) a quantity per unit of time, while the latter measures a quantity that exists at a point in time.
Answer: D

Topic: Flows and Stocks
Skill: Conceptual
3) When dealing with anything that is measured as a flow, one must
   A) use dollar values.
   B) make sure the thing can be measured accurately.
   C) specify a time period.
   D) specify the point in time one is using.
Answer: C

Topic: Flows and Stocks
Skill: Conceptual
4) GDP is a
   A) stock because it measures income for the entire country.
   B) stock because it measures wealth at a distinct point in time.
   C) flow because dollar values are used.
   D) flow because it measures production over a period of time.
Answer: D

Topic: Flows and Stocks
Skill: Conceptual
5) An economist giving a lecture mentions that positive net investment creates growth in capital equipment, which increases worker productivity. In this statement a flow variable is _____ and a stock variable is _____.
   A) net investment; capital
   B) capital; productivity
   C) productivity; net investment
   D) capital; net investment
Answer: A

---

* This is Chapter 23 in *Economics*.

Topic: Capital and Investment
Skill: Recognition

6) A capital good is
  A) one produced by the government.
  B) a good that is immediately consumed by consumers.
  C) a good that is used to make other goods and services.
  D) not part of GDP because it is an intermediate product.

Answer: C

Topic: Capital and Investment
Skill: Recognition

7) Economists define investment as the
  A) purchase of stocks and bonds.
  B) purchase of raw land for later resale.
  C) difference between people's income and their spending.
  D) purchase of equipment, plants, and inventories.

Answer: D

Topic: Capital and Investment
Skill: Recognition

8) Two flow variables that change the stock of capital are
  A) investment and productivity.
  B) productivity and depreciation.
  C) depreciation and investment.
  D) money and depreciation.

Answer: C

Topic: Capital and Investment
Skill: Recognition

9) Depreciation is
  A) added to GDP to equal net domestic product.
  B) the decrease in the stock of capital goods from physical wear and tear.
  C) not included in GDP from the income side.
  D) always larger than the capital consumption allowance.

Answer: B

Topic: Capital and Investment
Skill: Recognition

10) Depreciation
  A) equals gross investment minus net investment.
  B) is the reduction in inventories per year.
  C) is also called capital consumption.
  D) Both answers A and C are correct.

Answer: D

Topic: Capital and Investment
Skill: Conceptual

11) The capital stock _____ depreciation and _____ investment.
  A) increases because of; is unaffected by
  B) decreases because of; increases because of
  C) is unaffected by; is unaffected by
  D) increases because of; decreases because of

Answer: B

Topic: Capital and Investment
Skill: Recognition

12) Gross investment equals
  A) net investment – depreciation + change in inventories.
  B) net investment + depreciation.
  C) net investment + change in inventories.
  D) depreciation + change in inventories.

Answer: B

Topic: Capital and Investment
Skill: Recognition

13) Net investment
  A) is equivalent to replacement investment minus depreciation.
  B) is the only measure of investment used to calculate GDP.
  C) equals gross investment minus depreciation.
  D) is equivalent to the existing capital stock in the economy.

Answer: C

Topic: Capital and Investment
Skill: Recognition

14) Net investment during a year equals
  A) the change in capital stock over the year.
  B) the change in inventories over the year.
  C) the change in investment spending and the change in government expenditures on infrastructure.
  D) exports minus imports.

Answer: A

Topic: Capital and Investment
Skill: Conceptual

15) Wyatt's Widgets had 14 machines at the start of 1999. During the year, 2 machines were scrapped. In December 1999, Wyatt bought 3 new machines for $100,000 each. Wyatt's net investment for 1999 was

A)   14 machines.
B)   12 machines.
C)   1 machine.
D)   3 machines.

Answer: C

Topic: Wealth and Income
Skill: Recognition

16) Wealth is

A)   a flow variable.
B)   the amount spent on goods and services.
C)   the same as income.
D)   the value of all the things that people own.

Answer: D

Topic: Wealth and Income
Skill: Recognition

17) Saving

A)   decreases wealth.
B)   equals capital consumption.
C)   increases wealth.
D)   Both answers B and C are correct.

Answer: C

Topic: Circular Flow
Skill: Recognition

18) The circular flow model shows that consumer goods and services produced by business firms are sold in the

A)   goods market.
B)   resource market.
C)   labor market.
D)   financial market.

Answer: A

Topic: Circular Flow
Skill: Conceptual

19) In the circular flow of income

A)   households demand goods and services that are supplied by firms, and the firms demand resources that are supplied by intermediate firms.
B)   households demand goods and services that are supplied by firms, while supplying resources that are demanded by firms.
C)   households sell goods and services while firms sell resources.
D)   households buy goods and services while firms sell goods and services. Firms obtain labor from households, capital from government, and raw materials from other firms.

Answer: B

Topic: Circular Flow
Skill: Conceptual

20) The circular flow of income shows

A)   that households transact only in the goods market.
B)   that governments purchase goods and services.
C)   firms generally are the demanders in the goods markets and suppliers in the resource markets.
D)   None of the above answers are correct.

Answer: B

Topic: Circular Flow
Skill: Conceptual

21) Which of the following is true regarding the circular flow diagram?

I.   "Aggregate income" is the flow of income earned by firms.
II.   Retained earnings are considered income earned by firms rather than part of households' income.
III. The government, households, firms and foreigners all operate in the financial market.

A)   I only.
B)   I and II.
C)   I and III.
D)   III only.

Answer: D

Topic: Circular Flow
Skill: Recognition

22) The circular flow diagram shows that
   A) the flow of payments to the resources used to produce goods and services exceeds the flow of payments for final goods and services.
   B) product and resource markets are independent.
   C) the total amount of income generated by the economy equals the total purchases of final goods and services.
   D) consumption expenditure equals saving.
Answer: C

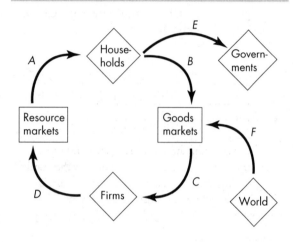

Topic: Circular Flow
Skill: Analytical

23) In the above figure, flow E represents _____.
   A) household borrowing.
   B) government borrowing.
   C) net taxes.
   D) government lending.
Answer: C

Topic: Circular Flow
Skill: Analytical

24) In the above figure, flow B represents _____.
   A) household purchases of goods and services.
   B) household borrowing.
   C) household income.
   D) firms' payments for labor services.
Answer: A

Topic: Circular Flow
Skill: Analytical

25) In the above figure, household income is shown by flow
   A) A.
   B) B.
   C) C.
   D) F.
Answer: A

Topic: Circular Flow
Skill: Analytical

26) In the above figure, consumption expenditure is shown by flow
   A) A.
   B) B.
   C) C.
   D) F.
Answer: B

Topic: Net Taxes
Skill: Recognition

27) Net taxes are equal to
   A) government purchases – consumption expenditures.
   B) government purchases – transfer payments.
   C) consumption expenditures – taxes paid.
   D) taxes paid – transfer payments – government interest payments on its debt.
Answer: D

Topic: Rest of the World Sector
Skill: Conceptual

28) Which of the following is TRUE regarding net exports?
   I.   U.S. net exports are positive if the value of U.S. exports exceeds the value of U.S. imports.
   II. If U.S. net exports are negative, we must borrow from the rest of the world or sell foreign assets.
   III. The value of net exports equals the value of imports + exports.
   A) I.
   B) I and II.
   C) I and III.
   D) II and III.
Answer: B

Topic: Borrowing from the Rest of the World
Skill: Conceptual

29) If the U.S. spends _____ on foreign goods and services than foreigners spend on U.S.-made goods and services, the U.S. _____.
   A) more; borrows from the rest of the world.
   B) more; lends to the rest of the world.
   C) less; must save more.
   D) less; borrows from the rest of the world.

Answer: A

Topic: Expenditure Equals Income
Skill: Recognition

30) According to the circular flow diagram, the dollar value of a nation's output is equal to
   A) profits.
   B) total income.
   C) net income minus taxes.
   D) wages.

Answer: B

Topic: Expenditure Equals Income
Skill: Recognition

31) Total output and total income in the circular flow model
   A) are measures of the economy's level of savings.
   B) include only intermediate goods.
   C) are equal to each other.
   D) are related because national income is less than national product.

Answer: C

Topic: Expenditure Equals Income
Skill: Conceptual

32) The circular flow shows that
   A) aggregate production equals aggregate expenditure.
   B) aggregate expenditure is less than aggregate income.
   C) GDP equals aggregate income.
   D) Both answers A and C are correct.

Answer: D

Topic: Expenditure Equals Income
Skill: Recognition

33) Gross domestic product (GDP) is
   A) the value of all final goods and services produced in a country during a year.
   B) the sum of consumption expenditure, investment, government purchases of goods and services, and net exports.
   C) the sum of compensation of employees, proprietor's income, net interest, rental income, corporate profits, depreciation, and indirect business taxes minus subsidies.
   D) All of the above.

Answer: D

Topic: Expenditure Equals Income
Skill: Recognition

34) Gross domestic product can be calculated
   A) either by valuing the nation's output of goods and services or by valuing the income generated in the production process.
   B) by adding up the personal consumption of all members of the society.
   C) by adding up the value of all intermediate goods used in the economy.
   D) by adding up the income tax returns of all members of the society.

Answer: A

■ Measuring U.S. GDP

Topic: Measuring U.S. GDP
Skill: Recognition

35) Two methods of measuring GDP are
   A) the income approach and the expenditure approach.
   B) the income approach and the receipts approach.
   C) the goods approach and the services approach.
   D) the saving approach and the investment approach.

Answer: A

Topic: Expenditure Approach
Skill: Recognition

36) In the equation, GDP = $C + I + G + NX$, G refers to

A) federal government expenditures plus all transfer payments.

B) local, state, and federal government spending for all purposes.

C) the taxes and expenditures of all government units.

D) local, state, and federal government purchases of goods and services, but does not include transfer payments.

Answer: D

Topic: Expenditure Approach
Skill: Recognition

37) The components of the expenditure approach to measuring GDP include all of the following EX-CEPT

A) net exports.

B) government purchases of goods and services.

C) investment.

D) the implicit payments for unpaid household work.

Answer: D

Topic: Expenditure Approach, Consumption Expenditures
Skill: Recognition

38) The largest component of GDP in the expenditures approach is

A) personal consumption expenditures.

B) gross private domestic investment.

C) government spending on goods and services.

D) net exports.

Answer: A

Topic: Expenditure Approach, Consumption Expenditures
Skill: Recognition

39) In 1998, the largest component of GDP was

A) personal consumption expenditures.

B) gross private domestic investment.

C) government purchases of goods and services.

D) net exports of goods and services.

Answer: A

Topic: Expenditure Approach, Consumption Expenditures
Skill: Conceptual

40) Which of the following purchases is included in personal consumption expenditures when determining gross domestic product?

A) purchase of a new house because of the arrival of a new baby.

B) purchase of a new office building.

C) vacation expenses for a spring trip to Fort Lauderdale.

D) purchases of jeans to add to a store's inventory.

Answer: C

Topic: Expenditure Approach, Consumption Expenditures
Skill: Conceptual

41) Personal consumption expenditures include all of the following EXCEPT

A) spending on consumer durable goods.

B) spending on consumer nondurable goods.

C) spending on consumer services.

D) spending on residential housing.

Answer: D

Topic: Expenditure Approach, Investment
Skill: Conceptual

42) Which of the following are examples of the gross private domestic investment component of GDP?

I. The purchase of production machinery by IBM.

II. An increase in the finished goods inventory at Intel.

A) I only.

B) II only.

C) Both I and II.

D) Neither I nor II.

Answer: C

Topic: Expenditure Approach, Investment
Skill: Conceptual

43) Which of the following is an example of the gross private domestic investment component of GDP?

A) You buy a share of GM stock.

B) GM buys a new drill press.

C) You put money into your savings account.

D) You put money into your checking account.

Answer: B

Topic: Expenditure Approach, Investment
Skill: Conceptual
44) Which of the following items is <u>NOT</u> a part of gross private domestic investment?
A) purchase of a share of IBM stock.
B) purchase of a new house.
C) net additions to inventory.
D) equipment for a new wing on a factory.
Answer: A

Topic: Expenditure Approach, Investment
Skill: Conceptual
45) In the calculation of gross domestic product by the expenditure approach, the "investment" component is
A) net investment.
B) gross investment minus depreciation.
C) gross investment plus depreciation.
D) gross investment.
Answer: D

Topic: Expenditure Approach, Investment
Skill: Conceptual
46) Of several purchases made by a family farm, which of the following would be included in GDP as part of investment expenditure?
A) 10 acres of land.
B) 100 shares of corporate stock.
C) a new tractor.
D) a U.S. government bond.
Answer: C

Topic: Expenditure Approach, Government Purchases
Skill: Conceptual
47) Which of the following is included in government expenditures when measuring GDP?
A) Social security payments.
B) Unemployment compensation payments.
C) Pension payment made to past presidents.
D) The current president's salary.
Answer: D

Topic: Expenditure Approach, Government Purchases
Skill: Conceptual
48) Which of the following items is <u>NOT</u> part of government purchases of goods and services in the GDP accounts?
A) gasoline purchases for government carpools.
B) Social Security expenditures.
C) new computer hardware for use by the IRS.
D) drapes to brighten up the president's office.
Answer: B

Topic: Expenditure Approach, Government Purchases
Skill: Conceptual
49) Transfer payments are not included in GDP because
A) their market value cannot be accurately determined.
B) they do not generate additional income.
C) they are not purchases of goods or services.
D) their value is included in government expenditure.
Answer: C

Topic: Expenditure Approach, Government Purchases
Skill: Conceptual
50) Which of the following transfer payments is included in GDP?
A) Social Security payments.
B) welfare payments.
C) veteran's benefits.
D) none of the above.
Answer: D

Topic: Expenditure Approach, Government Purchases
Skill: Conceptual
51) Transfer payments
A) are included in the government expenditure category in gross domestic product.
B) refer to all payments made to households by governments.
C) refer to payments made by the government that are not made to purchase a good or service.
D) are made by households to firms in exchange for goods and services.
Answer: C

Topic: Expenditure Approach, Net Exports
Skill: Recognition

52) The value of net exports is negative if
  A) the value of exports exceeds the value of imports.
  B) the value of imports exceeds the value of exports.
  C) the value of tariff payments is included in the value of imported and exported items.
  D) too much production occurs in the exporting country during the year.
Answer: B

Topic: Expenditure Approach, Net Exports
Skill: Recognition

53) In 1998, net exports in the U.S. were
  A) zero.
  B) positive.
  C) negative.
  D) greater than personal consumption expenditures.
Answer: C

Topic: Expenditure Approach, Net Exports
Skill: Recognition

54) To calculate GDP, in part one
  A) adds imports and exports.
  B) adds imports and subtracts exports.
  C) adds exports and subtracts imports.
  D) subtracts both exports and imports.
Answer: C

Topic: Expenditure Approach, Net Exports
Skill: Conceptual

55) An increase in exports of goods or services with no change in imports of goods or services
  A) decreases GDP.
  B) increases GDP.
  C) may increase or decrease GDP depending on whether it is the export of goods or the export of services that increased.
  D) has no effect on GDP.
Answer: B

Topic: Expenditure Approach, Net Exports
Skill: Conceptual

56) By itself, an increase in exports
  A) causes GDP to increase.
  B) causes GDP to decrease.
  C) causes a decrease in imports of the same size.
  D) can cause GDP to either increase or decrease, depending on whether the exports are durable or nondurable.
Answer: A

Topic: Expenditure Approach, Net Exports
Skill: Conceptual

57) If Ford sells 200 Explorers for a total of $400,000 to Germany, while the U.S. imports 100 BMWs for a total of $500,000 from Germany,
  A) U.S. GDP increases because it sells more Explorers.
  B) U.S. GDP decreases because net exports are negative.
  C) Germany's GDP decreases.
  D) U.S. net exports is positive.
Answer: B

Topic: Expenditure Approach, Net Exports
Skill: Conceptual

58) If an American firm produces output that is sold to a German household, then
  A) German GDP increases but not that of the United States.
  B) U.S. GDP increases.
  C) the transaction is considered an export in the German GDP accounts.
  D) net exports in the United States will not change because an export immediately generates an off-setting import.
Answer: B

Topic: Expenditures Not In GDP
Skill: Conceptual

59) If you buy stocks and bonds, the dollar value is
  A) included in GDP under investment.
  B) included in GDP under consumer expenditures.
  C) not included in calculating GDP.
  D) included in GDP if the stocks and bonds were issued by business firms but not if they were issued by government bodies.
Answer: C

Topic: Expenditures Not In GDP
Skill: Conceptual

60) Which of the following transactions would be included in GDP?
  A) The purchase of 100 shares of Microsoft.
  B) The purchase of an 1880 Monet painting.
  C) The purchase of a gallon of gasoline to run a lawn mower.
  D) The purchase of a used car.
Answer: C

Item	Billions of dollars
Government purchases of goods and services	250
Compensation of employees	1,675
Gross private domestic investment	325
Rental income	20
Personal consumption expenditures	1425
Net interest	40
Net exports of goods and services	100
Indirect business taxes and depreciation	300

Topic: Expenditure Approach
Skill: Analytical
61) The above table shows some (but not all) national income accounting data for hypothetical country. According to these data, the value of GDP is _____ billion.
   A) $2100.
   B) $1850.
   C) $2000.
   D) $2050.
Answer: A

Item	Billions of dollars
Personal consumption expenditure	100
Gross private domestic investment	10
Government purchases of goods and services	50
Exports of goods and services	30
Imports of goods and services	30
Net taxes	50

Topic: Expenditure Approach
Skill: Analytical
62) The above table shows data from the GDP accounts of Hypothetica. Hypothetica's GDP is _____ billion.
   A) $270.
   B) $210.
   C) $190.
   D) $160.
Answer: D

Topic: Expenditure Approach
Skill: Analytical
63) If imports are $100 million less than exports, government purchases are $500 million, consumer expenditures are $1 billion, and gross investment spending is $500 million, then GDP is
   A) $1 billion.
   B) $1.9 billion.
   C) $2 billion.
   D) $2.1 billion.
Answer: D

Topic: Expenditure Approach
Skill: Analytical
64) If consumption expenditures are $500 million, net investment is $100 million, depreciation equals $5 million, imports are $50 million, exports are $55 million, government purchases of goods and services is $220 million, and government transfer payments are $20 million, then GDP is
   A) $790 million.
   B) $800 million.
   C) $830 million.
   D) $850 million.
Answer: C

Topic: Intermediate Goods and Services
Skill: Recognition
65) Goods and services used as inputs by another firm are called
   A) value added goods.
   B) intermediate goods.
   C) national income goods.
   D) final goods.
Answer: B

Topic: Intermediate Goods and Services
Skill: Conceptual
66) GDP does not directly include intermediate goods because
   A) intermediate goods are not valuable.
   B) intermediate goods are not useful to consumers.
   C) that would count the intermediate goods twice.
   D) that would understate the true size of GDP.
Answer: C

Topic: Intermediate Goods and Services
Skill: Conceptual

67) The calculation of the final goods and services sold in an economy would NOT include

A) the purchase of a lawnmower by a household.

B) General Motors' purchases of tires for new automobiles.

C) Ford Motor Company's purchase of a new industrial robot to be used to produce cars.

D) the purchase of a service by a household.

Answer: B

Topic: Intermediate Goods and Services
Skill: Conceptual

68) In computing GDP, it is essential to

A) avoid double counting.

B) include government transfer payments.

C) include government tax revenues.

D) count all intermediate products directly as they are produced.

Answer: A

Topic: Intermediate Goods and Services
Skill: Conceptual

69) Double counting (counting the same thing twice) in GDP accounting is avoided by not including

A) net exports.

B) intermediate goods.

C) illegal activities.

D) depreciation.

Answer: B

Topic: Income Approach
Skill: Recognition

70) Which of the following expressions equals GDP?

A) compensation of employees + consumption + depreciation + net investment.

B) compensation of employees + net interest + rental income + depreciation + corporate profits + proprietors' income + indirect taxes – subsidies.

C) compensation of employees + net exports + depreciation + corporate profits.

D) compensation of employees + gross investment + rental income + depreciation + corporate profits + indirect taxes – subsidies.

Answer: B

Topic: Income Approach
Skill: Recognition

71) Which of the following is NOT a part of the income approach to determining GDP?

A) rental income.

B) gross private domestic investment.

C) net interest.

D) indirect business taxes.

Answer: B

Topic: Income Approach, Compensation of Employees
Skill: Recognition

72) The largest component of income is

A) proprietors' income.

B) corporate profits.

C) net interest.

D) compensation of employees.

Answer: D

Topic: Income Approach, Compensation of Employees
Skill: Recognition

73) Compensation paid to employees represented ____ of GDP for the United States in 1998.

A) about 5 percent.

B) approximately 15 percent.

C) 35 percent.

D) more than 50 percent.

Answer: D

Topic: Indirect Tax
Skill: Conceptual

74) An indirect tax is exemplified by a(n)

A) income tax.

B) sales tax.

C) subsidy.

D) None of the above answers are correct.

Answer: B

Topic: Income Approach
Skill: Conceptual

75) Gross domestic product is the sum of factor incomes ____ indirect business taxes minus subsidies ____ depreciation.

A) plus; plus

B) plus; minus

C) minus; plus

D) minus; minus

Answer: A

Topic: Income Approach, Depreciation
Skill: Recognition
76) Depreciation is
   A) the part of investment that is equal to all the existing capital stock.
   B) the decrease in the value of capital from wear and tear.
   C) included in net interest in the income approach to calculating GDP.
   D) equivalent to the value of resources purchased by producers.
Answer: B

Topic: Net Domestic Product
Skill: Recognition
77) Net domestic product is equal to gross domestic product minus
   A) indirect business taxes.
   B) depreciation.
   C) net investment.
   D) government subsidies to corporations.
Answer: B

Item	Billions of dollars
Personal income	1,200
Net domestic income at factor cost	2,100
Government purchases of goods and services	400
Depreciation	200
Gross private domestic investment	100
Indirect taxes	600
Subsidies	100

Topic: Income Approach
Skill: Analytical
78) The above table shows some national income accounting data for a nation. In this nation, gross domestic product is equal to _____ billion.
   A) $2,000.
   B) $2,300.
   C) $2,500.
   D) $2,800.
Answer: D

Item	Dollars
Personal consumption expenditure	1500
Gross private domestic investment	355
Government purchases of goods and services	590
Exports of goods and services	70
Imports of goods and services	50
Depreciation	200
Indirect business taxes	75

Topic: Expenditure Approach
Skill: Analytical
79) Based on the data in the above table, gross domestic product equals
   A) $2,190.
   B) $2,840.
   C) $2,465.
   D) $2,750.
Answer: C

Topic: Gross Domestic Product and Net Domestic Product
Skill: Analytical
80) Based on the data in the above table, gross domestic product equals _____ and net domestic product equals _____.
   A) $2,550; $2,550
   B) $2,465; $2,265
   C) $2,750; $2,550
   D) $2,650; $2,850
Answer: B

Item	Dollars
Net interest	239
Government purchases of goods and services	136
Compensation of employees	1,735
Rental income	37
Proprietors' income	128
Indirect taxes minus subsidies	259
Corporate profits	194
Exports of goods and services	249
Imports of goods and services	289
Depreciation	333

Topic: Income Approach
Skill: Analytical
81) Using the data in the above table, gross domestic product as calculated by the income approach equals _____.
A) $2,333
B) $2,592
C) $2,925
D) $2,205
Answer: C

Topic: Net Domestic Product
Skill: Analytical
82) Using the data in the above table, net domestic product equals _____
A) $2,259 billion.
B) $2,592 billion.
C) $1,872 billion.
D) $2,486 billion.
Answer: B

Topic: Value Added
Skill: Recognition
83) A firm's value added is
A) the value of its production.
B) the value of its production minus profits.
C) the value of its production minus purchases of goods and services other firms.
D) total sales revenue at market prices.
Answer: C

Topic: Value Added
Skill: Recognition
84) A firm's value added is found by subtracting the value of _____ from total sales.
A) corporate profits tax
B) intermediate goods the firm buys from other firms
C) wages and dividends
D) retained earnings
Answer: B

Topic: Value Added
Skill: Recognition
85) Industry A buys $100 worth of products from other firms. If the sales of industry A are $300, industry A's value added is
A) $400.
B) $300.
C) $200.
D) $0.
Answer: C

Topic: Value Added and Gross Domestic Production
Skill: Conceptual
86) In Bakersville, a farmer takes $200 worth of inputs and produces wheat, which is sold to the miller for $400. The miller then sells flour to the baker for $700, and the baker later sells $1200 worth of bread. These are the only products produced in Bakersville. The gross domestic product for this economy equals
A) $1200.
B) $1000.
C) $2500.
D) $2300.
Answer: A

Topic: Final Goods and Intermediate Goods
Skill: Recognition
87) GDP counts only final goods and services because
A) this method avoids including any goods that are produced this year and sold next year.
B) this method avoids double counting of goods going through several stages of production.
C) this amount can be more easily determined in the marketplace.
D) this method avoids understating the value of GDP produced during a given year.
Answer: B

■ The Price Level and Real GDP

Topic: Consumer Price Index
Skill: Recognition

88) When computing the consumer price index (CPI), the base year is

A)   the earliest year for which the CPI was ever calculated.

B)   the year that is chosen as the point of reference for comparison of prices with other years.

C)   the most recent year for which data are available.

D)   the most recent year in which the inflation rate was close to zero.

Answer: B

	Market basket quantity	1998 price	1999 price
CDs	10 discs	$16 per disc	$12 per disc
Gasoline	200 gallons	$1.00 per gallon	$1.25 per gallon

Topic: Consumer Price Index
Skill: Conceptual

89) If 1998 is the base year, what is the price index for a market basket of goods for 1999 in the above table?

A)   97.3.

B)   102.8.

C)   128.0.

D)   Zero because the price of CDs fell and the price of gasoline increased.

Answer: B

Topic: GDP Deflator
Skill: Recognition

90) The GDP deflator is

A)   an index that measures real production.

B)   a measure of the average level of prices of all goods and services included in GDP.

C)   an index used to calculate inflation at the wholesale level.

D)   the least used price index because it is so costly to calculate.

Answer: B

Topic: Chain-Weighted Growth Rate
Skill: Conceptual

91) Which of the following is TRUE regarding a chain-weighted output index?

I.   It is the method used to measure the growth rate of nominal GDP.

II.   It uses data from the current year and from the previous year.

III. It is a method of measuring the growth rate of real GDP.

A)   I and II.

B)   II and III.

C)   I and III.

D)   I, II and III.

Answer: B

Year	Price level	Nominal GDP
1979	100	$1,600
1989	150	$3,000
1999	300	$6,000

Topic: Real and Nominal GDP
Skill: Analytical

92) In the above table, using 1979 as the base year, what was real GDP in 1989?

A) $1,600.

B) $2,000.

C) $2,400.

D) $3,000.

Answer: B

Topic: Real and Nominal GDP
Skill: Analytical

93) In the above table, using 1979 as the base year, what was real GDP in 1999?

A) $1,600.

B) $2,000.

C) $3,000.

D) $6,000.

Answer: B

Topic: Real and Nominal GDP
Skill: Analytical

94) In the above table, which of the following is true concerning changes between 1989 and 1999:

A) Nominal and real GDP both increased.
B) Nominal GDP increased, but real GDP was unchanged.
C) Nominal GDP increased, but real GDP decreased.
D) None of the above statements are true.

Answer: B

■ Measuring Economic Growth

Topic: GDP and Economic Welfare Comparisons
Skill: Conceptual

95) Real GDP does not show the state of economic welfare in a country in part because GDP omits

I.   household production.
II. leisure time available.
III. the quality of the environment.

A) I only.
B) I and III.
C) II and III.
D) I, II and III.

Answer: D

Topic: GDP and Economic Welfare Comparisons
Skill: Conceptual

96) A country that has a large real GDP per person may not necessarily have a high level of economic welfare because it may have

A) very little political freedom.
B) environmental problems.
C) a high crime rate.
D) All of the above answers are correct .

Answer: D

Topic: Household Production
Skill: Recognition

97) Which, if any, of the following causes reported GDP to be less than total economic production?

A) The exclusion of household production.
B) The exclusion of government transfers.
C) The inclusion of government purchases.
D) All of the above cause reported GDP to be less than total production.

Answer: A

Topic: Household Production, Underground Economic Activity
Skill: Conceptual

98) Which of the following changes causes reported GDP to increase when, in fact, total production is unchanged?

A) A shift from household production to market production.
B) The legalization of previously illegal activities.
C) Neither of the above will cause reported GDP to increase when total production does not change
D) Both of the answers in A and B are correct.

Answer: D

Topic: Underground Economic Activity
Skill: Conceptual

99) In part, the underground economy exists because of the

A) irrationality of people who choose to evade taxes.
B) high tax rates.
C) ease of entry into the occupations that compose it.
D) greater efficiency of barter transactions compared to monetary ones.

Answer: B

Topic: Purchasing Power Parity Prices
Skill: Conceptual

100) The use of purchasing power parity prices

A) decreases the real GDP per person statistics published by the International Monetary Fund.
B) weakens the validity of cross country comparisons of economic welfare.
C) increases the amount by which U.S. GDP is larger than that of any other nation.
D) accounts for differences in the prices of the same goods in different countries when measuring real GDP.

Answer: D

Topic: GDP and Business Cycle Assessment
Skill: Recognition

101) Estimates of GDP are used for

A) business cycle forecasting.
B) adjusting for household production.
C) estimating the CPI.
D) Both answers A and B are correct.

Answer: A

■ Measuring Inflation

Topic: Measuring Inflation
Skill: Recognition
102) The rate of inflation can be measured by
  A) the level of the GDP deflator.
  B) the level of the CPI.
  C) the percentage change in the CPI from one year to the next.
  D) the GDP deflator minus the CPI index.
Answer: C

Topic: Biased CPI
Skill: Conceptual
103) The bias in the CPI and the GDP deflator is one that
  A) overstates inflation.
  B) understates inflation.
  C) about half the time overstates and about half the time understates the inflation rate.
  D) cannot be measured or estimated.
Answer: A

Topic: Biased CPI
Skill: Conceptual
104) The currently used method for calculating the CPI
  A) fails to account for people increasing consumption of a good that falls in relative price.
  B) probably overstates inflation by about 1 percentage point.
  C) can cause government expenditures to be higher than otherwise.
  D) All of the above answers are correct.
Answer: D

Topic: The Biased CPI, New Goods Bias
Skill: Conceptual
105) As currently calculated, the CPI tends to overstate the true inflation rate because
  A) we cannot know what the true inflation rate is.
  B) it fails to consider the effects of new products in the marketplace.
  C) the market basket actually selected is inappropriate.
  D) the market basket fails to weigh housing costs sufficiently.
Answer: B

■ True Or False Questions

Topic: Flows and Stocks
Skill: Recognition
106) A flow is a quantity per unit of time while a stock is a quantity that exists at a point in time.
Answer: TRUE

Topic: Capital and Investment
Skill: Conceptual
107) The capital stock decreases because of depreciation.
Answer: TRUE

Topic: Circular Flow, Aggregate Expenditures
Skill: Conceptual
108) The circular flow diagram shows only the aggregate expenditures measure of GDP.
Answer: FALSE

Topic: Expenditure Approach
Skill: Recognition
109) The expenditure approach to measuring GDP includes firms' spending on wages.
Answer: FALSE

Topic: Expenditure Approach
Skill: Recognition
110) Intermediate goods and services are one of the largest components of the expenditure approach to measuring GDP.
Answer: FALSE

Topic: Income Approach
Skill: Conceptual
111) To calculate GDP when using the income approach, you must add indirect business taxes and depreciation.
Answer: TRUE

Topic: Value Added
Skill: Recognition
112) Value added is the value of a firm's production minus purchases of intermediate goods.
Answer: TRUE

Topic: The Price Level
Skill: Conceptual
113) The CPI and GDP deflator usually move in opposite directions.
Answer: FALSE

Topic: GDP Deflator
Skill: Recognition
114) To calculate the GDP deflator, real GDP is divided by nominal GDP.
Answer: FALSE

Topic: GDP Deflator
Skill: Conceptual
115) The GDP deflator is not biased while the CPI is biased.
Answer: FALSE

Topic: GDP and Household Production
Skill: Conceptual
116) The omission of household production causes actual economic production to be underestimated.
Answer: TRUE

Topic: GDP and Leisure Time
Skill: Conceptual
117) If a measure of real GDP could include the value of leisure time, measured real GDP would increase.
Answer: TRUE

Topic: GDP and Purchasing Power Parity Prices
Skill: Conceptual
118) The fact that prices for similar goods differ across nations complicates comparisons of real GDP across countries.
Answer: TRUE

■ Essay Questions

Topic: Flows and Stocks
Skill: Conceptual
119) Give an example of a flow and a stock variable.
Answer:

Topic: Expenditure Approach
Skill: Recognition
120) List the components of the expenditure approach to measuring GDP.
Answer:

Topic: Income Approach
Skill: Recognition
121) List the components of the income approach to measuring GDP.
Answer:

Topic: Intermediate Goods
Skill: Conceptual
122) Briefly explain why intermediate goods are not included in GDP.
Answer:

Topic: Consumer Price Index
Skill: Conceptual
123) Briefly explain the construction of the CPI.
Answer:

Topic: GDP and Underground Economic Activity
Skill: Conceptual
124) Explain how underground economic activity affects measurement of GDP.
Answer:

Topic: Biased CPI
Skill: Conceptual
125) List sources of bias in the CPI and briefly explain them.
Answer:

Topic: Biased CPI, Quality Change Bias
Skill: Conceptual
126) Give an example of the quality change bias in the CPI.
Answer:

Topic: Biased CPI
Skill: Conceptual
127) What is at least one consequence of CPI bias? Explain your answer.
Answer:

Chapter 7 MEASURING EMPLOYMENT AND UNEMPLOYMENT*

■ Employment and Wages

Topic: Population Survey
Skill: Recognition
1) All people in the working-age population can be divided into
A) labor force participants.
B) either employed, unemployed, or not in the labor force.
C) either over-employed or under-employed.
D) potential employees.
Answer: B

Topic: Population Survey
Skill: Recognition
2) The _____ is the total number of people aged 16 years and older (and not in jail, hospital or institutional care) while the _____ is the number of people employed and the unemployed.
A) labor force; working-age population
B) labor force participation rate; labor force
C) working-age population; labor force
D) working-age population; labor force participation rate
Answer: C

Topic: Population Survey
Skill: Recognition
3) The labor force is defined as
A) the number of people over 16 years of age.
B) the number of people who are working.
C) the sum of employed and unemployed people.
D) the number of people in blue-collar jobs.
Answer: C

Topic: Population Survey
Skill: Recognition
4) The labor force is defined as
A) the number of employed people plus the number of unemployed people.
B) the number of people who are working.
C) the number of people who are working in labor-type jobs.
D) the number of union members who are working.
Answer: A

Topic: Population Survey
Skill: Recognition
5) The labor force includes
A) only the number of people employed.
B) discouraged workers.
C) only the number of people unemployed.
D) both employed and unemployed workers.
Answer: D

Topic: Population Survey
Skill: Recognition
6) Which of the following individuals is counted as an unemployed worker in the United States?
A) an individual who works ten hours part-time but would like to work full-time.
B) a worker who has quit looking for work because he or she is convinced that no jobs are available.
C) an individual who in the past month actively looked for work without finding it.
D) a person working in the home without pay.
Answer: C

---

* This is Chapter 24 in *Economics*.

Topic: Population Survey
Skill: Recognition

7) The official unemployment estimates
A) include persons without a job who say they are actively searching for a job.
B) include persons without a job, whether they are actively searching for work or not.
C) count discouraged workers as unemployed.
D) count as unemployed people with part-time jobs who want full-time jobs.

Answer: A

Topic: Population Survey
Skill: Recognition

8) In the official statistics, a person who is working at a half-time job but wants to work full-time is
A) counted as employed.
B) counted as unemployed.
C) counted as half employed and half unemployed.
D) counted as unemployed if the job is unsatisfactory and counted as employed if the job is satisfactory.

Answer: A

Topic: Population Survey
Skill: Recognition

9) Which of the following best fits the definition of unemployed?
A) retired and not working.
B) working less than a full work week.
C) not working but looking for a job.
D) not working and not looking for work.

Answer: C

Topic: Population Survey
Skill: Conceptual

10) Which of the following people would be considered unemployed by the Bureau of Labor Statistics?
 I. Mrs. X retires from her job at the age of 55 and does not look for another job.
 II. Mr. Y was laid off from his job as a welder, but expects to be rehired in 8 months.
A) I only.
B) II only.
C) Both I and II.
D) Neither I nor II.

Answer: B

Topic: Population Survey
Skill: Conceptual

11) Which of the following would NOT be considered unemployed?
A) a new entrant to the labor force.
B) a job leaver who is looking for a better job.
C) an individual fired by her employer.
D) a newly retired worker.

Answer: D

Topic: Population Survey
Skill: Conceptual

12) Using the definition of unemployment, which of the following individuals would be unemployed?
A) A full-time student quits school, enters the labor market for the first time, and searches for employment.
B) Because of the increased level of automobile imports, an employee of General Motors is laid off but expects to be called back to work soon.
C) Because of a reduction in the military budget, your next door neighbor loses her job in a plant where nuclear warheads are made and must look for a new job.
D) All of these individuals are unemployed.

Answer: D

Topic: Unemployment Rate
Skill: Recognition

13) The unemployment rate equals 100 times
A) the number of unemployed workers.
B) the number of unemployed workers divided by the population.
C) the number of unemployed workers divided by the number of employed workers.
D) the number of unemployed workers divided by the labor force.

Answer: D

Topic: Unemployment Rate
Skill: Recognition

14) The unemployment rate equals 100 times
A) (the number of unemployed workers)/(the number of employed + unemployed workers)
B) (the number of unemployed workers)/(the civilian population)
C) (the number of unemployed workers)/(the U.S. population older than 16 years of age)
D) (the number of unemployed + employed workers)/(U.S. population older than 16 years of age)

Answer: A

Topic: Unemployment Rate
Skill: Recognition
15) The unemployment rate equals
  A) the total number of people without jobs in a given period.
  B) the percentage of the population not currently employed.
  C) the rate of change in unemployment figures from one period to another.
  D) the percentage of the labor force currently unemployed.
Answer: D

Topic: Unemployment Rate
Skill: Recognition
16) To calculate the unemployment rate, which of the following are necessary pieces of information?
  I. The number of unemployed persons.
  II. The population.
  III. The number of people in the labor force.
  IV. The working age population.
  A) I, II III and IV.
  B) I and II.
  C) I and III.
  D) I and IV.
Answer: C

Topic: Unemployment Rate
Skill: Recognition
17) The unemployment rate is found by
  A) dividing the number of unemployed people by the number of working individuals, and multiplying by 100.
  B) dividing the number of unemployed people by the number of the working-age population, and multiplying by 100.
  C) dividing the number of unemployed people by the sum of working individuals plus unemployed workers, and multiplying by 100.
  D) dividing the number of unemployed people by the number in the labor force, and dividing by 100.
Answer: C

Topic: Unemployment Rate
Skill: Recognition
18) The _____ is calculated as the number of people _____ divided by the labor force multiplied by 100.
  A) unemployment rate; unemployed
  B) employment-to-population ratio; unemployed
  C) employment rate; employed
  D) employment-to-population ratio; in the working age population
Answer: A

Topic: Unemployment Rate
Skill: Analytical
19) In the U.S. in 1996, the population was 265.5 million and the working age population was 200.6 million. There were 133.9 million people in the labor force and 126.7 of them were considered employed. The unemployment rate equaled _____.
  A) 7.2 percent
  B) 5.4 percent
  C) 3.6 percent
  D) 33 percent
Answer: B

Topic: Unemployment Rate
Skill: Analytical
20) Suppose there are 100 million in the labor force, and 6 million unemployed people. During the next month, 200,000 people lose their jobs and 300,000 find jobs. The new total of employed persons is _____ and the new unemployment rate is _____.
  A) 100.1 million; 5.8 percent
  B) 100 million; 6.1 percent
  C) 94.1 million; 5.9 percent
  D) 93.9 million; 6.1 percent
Answer: C

Topic: Unemployment Rate
Skill: Conceptual
21) If a part-time worker becomes a full-time worker,
  A) the measured unemployment rate will fall.
  B) the measured unemployment rate will remain the same.
  C) the economy will move towards the natural rate of unemployment.
  D) there will be less excess supply of output.
Answer: B

Topic: Unemployment Rate
Skill: Conceptual
22)   Which of the following is <u>FALSE</u>?
  A)   New young workers who enter the labor force and start looking for jobs increase the official unemployment rate.
  B)   Workers who quit their jobs to look for better positions increase the official unemployment rate.
  C)   A recession that causes many firms to lay off workers will increase the official unemployment rate.
  D)   Full-time workers who are cut to thirty-two hours a week will increase the unemployment rate.
Answer: D

Topic: Unemployment Rate
Skill: Conceptual
23)   Which of the following is <u>FALSE</u>?
  A)   When workers seeking full-time jobs get part-time jobs, the official unemployment rate falls.
  B)   When older unemployed workers give up looking for jobs and take early retirement, the official unemployment rate falls.
  C)   When part-time workers become full-time workers, the official unemployment rate falls.
  D)   When young unemployed workers stop looking for jobs and go to school, the official unemployment rate falls.
Answer: C

Topic: Unemployment Rate
Skill: Conceptual
24)   An increase in the number of discouraged workers will _____ the measured unemployment rate; a shift of workers from part-time to full-time work will _____ the measured unemployment rate.
  A)   decrease; increase
  B)   increase; increase
  C)   decrease; not affect
  D)   not affect; increase
Answer: C

Topic: Labor Force Participation Rate
Skill: Conceptual
25)   The labor force participation rate shows the percentage of
  A)   people not working, but who want to work.
  B)   people who are not actively participating in meaningful economic activity.
  C)   new entrants into the labor force.
  D)   non-institutionalized working-age people who are actually working or seeking employment.
Answer: D

Topic: Labor Force Participation Rate
Skill: Recognition
26)   Which of the following is TRUE regarding the labor force participation rate?
  I.   The labor force participation rate has gradually trended higher over the last thirty years.
  II.   Discouraged workers can affect the labor force participation rate.
  III.   Adding the labor force participation rate plus the unemployment rate equals the employment-to-population ratio.
  A)   I only.
  B)   I and II.
  C)   I and III.
  D)   II and III.
Answer: B

Topic: Labor Force Participation Rate
Skill: Recognition
27)   Which of the following pieces of information do you need to calculate the labor force participation rate?
  I.   The number of employed persons.
  II.   The number of unemployed persons.
  III.   The population.
  IV.   The working age population.
  A)   I and II.
  B)   I and III.
  C)   I, II and III.
  D)   I, II and IV.
Answer: D

Topic: Labor Force Participation Rate
Skill: Conceptual
28) An increase in the labor force participation rate
   A) means that the unemployment rate definitely must fall.
   B) means that the unemployment rate definitely must rise.
   C) means there are more discouraged workers.
   D) may be associated with either a rise or a fall of the unemployment rate.
Answer: D

Topic: Labor Force Participation Rate
Skill: Conceptual
29) In the United States, over the past 30 years, the labor force participation rate has _____ for males and _____ for females.
   A) increased; increased
   B) increased; decreased
   C) decreased; increased
   D) decreased; decreased
Answer: C

Topic: Labor Force Participation Rate
Skill: Conceptual
30) Which of the following is true of the labor force participation rate of females?
   A) The rate has decreased over the last 30 years.
   B) The increase in that rate have led to a reduction in the natural rate of unemployment.
   C) Technological advances have played little role in the rate's change.
   D) The rate has increased over the last 30 years.
Answer: D

Topic: Labor Force Participation Rate
Skill: Recognition
31) In the U.S., the labor force participation rate for males has been
   A) increasing while their employment-to-population ratio has been falling.
   B) decreasing and their employment-to-population ratio has been falling.
   C) increasing and their employment-to-population ratio has been rising.
   D) decreasing while their employment-to-population has been rising.
Answer: B

Topic: Labor Force Participation Rate
Skill: Recognition
32) In the U.S., the labor force participation rate for females has been
   A) increasing while their employment-to-population ratio has been falling.
   B) decreasing and their employment-to-population ratio has been falling.
   C) increasing and their employment-to-population ratio has been rising.
   D) decreasing while their employment-to-population has been rising.
Answer: C

Topic: Discouraged Worker
Skill: Recognition
33) An individual who has stopped looking for a job because he is convinced that he cannot find a job is referred to as
   A) a contingent worker.
   B) a productive worker.
   C) a discouraged worker.
   D) an unemployed worker.
Answer: C

Topic: Discouraged Worker
Skill: Conceptual
34) Discouraged workers
   A) are considered unemployed because they are not working.
   B) are considered unemployed because they are still in the labor force.
   C) are not considered unemployed because they are not qualified to work.
   D) are not considered unemployed because they are not actively seeking work.
Answer: D

Topic: Discouraged Worker
Skill: Conceptual
35) Including discouraged workers in the calculation of the unemployment rate would
   A) increase the reported rate.
   B) lower the reported rate.
   C) not change the reported rate.
   D) change the reported rate, but in an unpredictable manner.
Answer: A

Topic: Discouraged Workers
Skill: Conceptual
36) When an individual who has not been working but has been looking for work decides to terminate the search process, the official unemployment rate
A) will fall.
B) will rise.
C) will remain unchanged.
D) may fall or rise depending on whether or not the individual resumes his education.
Answer: A

Topic: Employment-to-Population Ratio
Skill: Recognition
37) The employment-to-population ratio equals
A) (labor force)/(working-age population) X 100.
B) (number of people employed)/(labor force) X 100.
C) (number of people with full-time jobs)/(labor force) X 100.
D) (number of people employed)/(working-age population) X 100.
Answer: D

Topic: Employment-to-Population Ratio
Skill: Recognition
38) The percentage of people employed aged 16 years and older divided by the working-age population is known as the
A) employment rate.
B) employment-to-population ratio.
C) labor force participation rate.
D) working-age population ratio.
Answer: B

Topic: Employment-to-Population Ratio
Skill: Conceptual
39) The employment-to-population ratio
A) has increased over the past 30 years.
B) shows that the U.S. economy has created jobs at a faster rate than the working-age population has grown.
C) falls during a recession.
D) All of the above answers are correct.
Answer: D

Topic: Aggregate Hours
Skill: Conceptual
40) Which of the following is TRUE regarding the number of hours worked in the economy?
I.   Since 1960, aggregate hours in the U.S. have increased.
II.   Since 1960, average hours per worker have increased.
III. Fluctuations in aggregate hours vary directly with the business cycle, so that they rise during an expansion and fall during a recession.
A) I and II.
B) I and III.
C) II and III.
D) I, II and III.
Answer: B

Topic: Wage Rates
Skill: Recognition
41) Over the past 40 years, average weekly hours per person has ____ and the real wage rate ____.
A) increased; increased
B) increased; decreased
C) decreased; decreased
D) decreased; increased
Answer: D

Topic: Wage Rates
Skill: Conceptual
42) Which of the following is TRUE regarding the behavior of the average hourly real wage?
I.   Since 1960, the average hourly real wage has increased regardless of the measure used.
II.   Since 1960, the average hourly real wage may or may not have increased, depending on the measure used.
III. No matter the measure used, the average hourly real wage rate reflects the productivity growth slowdown in the 1970s.
A) I only.
B) I and III.
C) II and III.
D) III only.
Answer: B

Topic: Wage Rates
Skill: Recognition
43) "Total labor compensation" includes
A) wages.
B) salaries.
C) fringe benefits.
D) All of the above are part of "total labor compensation."

Answer: D

Topic: Wage Rates
Skill: Conceptual
44) Suppose the money wage rate increases from $10 to $12. If nothing else changes,
A) the real wage increases.
B) the real wage decreases.
C) the quantity of goods and services that an hour of work can buy increases.
D) Both answers A and C are correct.

Answer: D

■ Unemployment and Full Employment

Topic: The Anatomy of Unemployment
Skill: Recognition
45) If a person is laid-off from a job, the person is considered to be a
A) job loser.
B) reentrant.
C) job leaver.
D) new entrant.

Answer: A

Topic: The Anatomy of Unemployment
Skill: Recognition
46) Suppose Percy was laid off from his job at the pickle factory and he decides to look for another job. Percy is considered
A) a discouraged worker.
B) a job loser.
C) a job leaver.
D) not in the labor force.

Answer: B

Topic: The Anatomy of Unemployment
Skill: Recognition
47) If a person voluntarily quits his or her job, the person is considered to be a
A) job loser.
B) reentrant.
C) job leaver.
D) new entrant.

Answer: C

Topic: The Anatomy of Unemployment
Skill: Conceptual
48) Fluctuations in the unemployment rate may reflect which of the following?
A) people moving in and out of the labor market.
B) an absence of change.
C) too many jobs.
D) too few employees.

Answer: A

Topic: Sources of Unemployment
Skill: Recognition
49) The largest category of the unemployed are
A) job losers.
B) reentrants.
C) job leavers.
D) new entrants.

Answer: A

Topic: Sources of Unemployment
Skill: Conceptual
50) From highest to lowest, which of the rankings of sources of unemployment is correct?
A) job leavers, job losers, entrants and reentrants.
B) entrants, job leavers, job losers.
C) job losers, job leavers, entrants.
D) job losers, entrants, job leavers.

Answer: D

Topic: Duration of Unemployment
Skill: Conceptual
51) The average duration of unemployment is high when
A) more people leave their jobs rather than lose their jobs.
B) the number of entrants to the labor force exceeds the number of re-entrants.
C) the economy is at a business cycle peak.
D) the economy is a business cycle trough.

Answer: D

Topic: Demographics of Unemployment
Skill: Recognition

52) Of the following, which group tends to have the lowest unemployment rate in the United States?

A) white teenagers.
B) white males over twenty years of age.
C) black teenagers.
D) females who are reentering the labor force.

Answer: B

Topic: Demographics of Unemployment
Skill: Recognition

53) Of the following, which group tends to have the highest unemployment rate in the United States?

A) white teenagers.
B) white males over twenty years of age.
C) black teenagers.
D) females who are reentering the labor force.

Answer: C

Topic: Demographics of Unemployment
Skill: Conceptual

54) Which of the following is TRUE regarding teenage unemployment?

I. The job loss rate is higher for teens.
II. Teens tend to leave jobs more frequently.
III. Teenage unemployment rates are lower than those of older workers.

A) I and II.
B) I and III.
C) II and III.
D) I, II and III.

Answer: A

Topic: Frictional Unemployment
Skill: Recognition

55) Frictional unemployment is

A) unemployment associated with business cycle recessions.
B) unemployment associated with the changing of jobs in a changing economy.
C) long-term unemployment.
D) unemployment associated with declining industries.

Answer: B

Topic: Frictional Unemployment
Skill: Conceptual

56) When an individual is frictionally unemployed, the unemployment arises in part from

A) a short-term elimination of jobs because of a slowdown in business activity.
B) individuals searching for appropriate employment.
C) the permanent elimination of jobs because of a change in the structure of the economy.
D) a reduction in the overall demand for workers' skills.

Answer: B

Topic: Frictional Unemployment
Skill: Conceptual

57) Frictional unemployment increases when

A) real GDP decreases and the unemployment rate rises.
B) the number of workers who quit one job to find another increases.
C) discouraged workers drop out of the work force.
D) workers are replaced by machines and the unemployed workers do not have the skills to perform new jobs.

Answer: B

Topic: Frictional Unemployment
Skill: Conceptual

58) Which of the following events causes an increase in frictional unemployment?

A) A decrease in real GDP.
B) An increase in unemployment benefits.
C) An increase in steel imports that displaces steel workers.
D) A decrease in the minimum wage.

Answer: B

Topic: Frictional Unemployment
Skill: Conceptual

59) To prevent frictional unemployment, we would have to

A) eliminate recessions.
B) eliminate the business cycle.
C) prevent people from leaving their jobs.
D) make sure everyone went to college.

Answer: C

Topic: Frictional Unemployment
Skill: Conceptual

60) A person quits her job in order to spend time looking for a better-paying job. This is an example of

A) frictional unemployment.
B) cyclical unemployment.
C) seasonal unemployment.
D) structural unemployment.

Answer: A

Topic: Frictional Unemployment
Skill: Conceptual

61) An individual with good job prospects who is between jobs is best considered as

A) structurally unemployed.
B) cyclically unemployed.
C) not in the labor force.
D) frictionally unemployed.

Answer: D

Topic: Frictional Unemployment
Skill: Conceptual

62) Suppose that Matt quits a job with the XYZ Corporation in order to look for more rewarding employment. Matt would be best be considered as

A) still being employed.
B) included in the economy's "hidden employment."
C) frictionally unemployed.
D) cyclically unemployed.

Answer: C

Topic: Frictional Unemployment
Skill: Conceptual

63) Catherine quit her job in order to look for a new one; therefore, she is best considered as

A) frictionally unemployed.
B) structurally unemployed.
C) cyclically unemployed.
D) seasonally unemployed.

Answer: A

Topic: Frictional Unemployment
Skill: Conceptual

64) A recent accounting graduate from a major business school is searching for a place to begin his career as an accountant. This individual is best considered as

A) structurally unemployed.
B) seasonally unemployed.
C) cyclically unemployed.
D) frictionally unemployed.

Answer: D

Topic: Frictional Unemployment
Skill: Conceptual

65) The best example of a frictionally unemployed individual is

A) Charles who has lost his job as an autoworker because of increased imports and can't find a good job that utilizes his skills.
B) Mary who quit her job to find work closer to her home.
C) Sam who lost his job as a real estate salesperson when the housing market went soft because of a recession.
D) Sandy who has few skills and is no longer looking for work.

Answer: B

Topic: Structural Unemployment
Skill: Recognition

66) Structural unemployment is best described as the

A) unemployment of individuals who are in the process of finding jobs.
B) unemployment of individuals who refuse job offers in their area of expertise.
C) unemployment of individuals who are willing to work at prevailing wages but cannot find jobs.
D) unemployment caused by a mismatch between the skills of the unemployed workers and the available jobs.

Answer: D

Topic: Structural Unemployment
Skill: Conceptual

67) Structural unemployment is
  A) associated with the changing of jobs in a dynamic economy.
  B) associated with general downturns in the economy.
  C) associated with changes in technology that change required job skills.
  D) very short-term unemployment.

Answer: C

Topic: Structural Unemployment
Skill: Recognition

68) Suppose that over a period of years the country of Quasiland switched from being an agriculturally-based economy to a technologically-based economy. As a result, many people lost jobs because they lacked the correct skills. These people would be considered part of
  A) frictional unemployment.
  B) structural unemployment.
  C) cyclical unemployment.
  D) discouraged workers.

Answer: B

Topic: Structural Unemployment
Skill: Conceptual

69) An individual is structurally unemployed if
  A) there is a recession and the individual is laid off.
  B) the individual wants to work just during certain months of the year.
  C) the individual quits a job in order to search for a better one.
  D) the individual lacks marketable job skills.

Answer: D

Topic: Structural Unemployment
Skill: Conceptual

70) The nation's structural unemployment will increase when
  A) bad economic policies send the economy into a recession.
  B) there is influx into the labor market of new college graduates.
  C) there is an increase in post-Christmas layoffs of workers.
  D) an increase in textile imports displaces older textile workers who do not have the skills necessary to find new jobs.

Answer: D

Topic: Structural Unemployment
Skill: Conceptual

71) A major characteristic of structural unemployment that differentiates it from frictional unemployment is that structural unemployment
  A) exists only during a recession.
  B) exists in an expansion whereas there is no frictional unemployment in an expansion.
  C) is a short-term problem.
  D) usually lasts longer than frictional unemployment.

Answer: D

Topic: Structural Unemployment
Skill: Conceptual

72) Which of the following individuals is the best example of a structurally unemployed worker?
  A) A recent college graduate who has entered the labor force.
  B) An individual who has been laid off from his job because of a business cycle recession.
  C) An automobile worker who has lost her job because of an increase in automobile imports and does not have the skills currently needed by businesses.
  D) An individual who quits one job in the hope of finding a better job.

Answer: C

Topic: Structural Unemployment
Skill: Conceptual

73) Nicholas does not possess marketable job skills; therefore, he is
  A) frictionally unemployed.
  B) structurally unemployed.
  C) cyclically unemployed.
  D) seasonally unemployed.

Answer: B

Topic: Cyclical Unemployment
Skill: Recognition

74) Cyclical unemployment occurs when
  A) individuals enter into the labor market making the rounds of potential employers.
  B) individuals with skills no longer valued in the labor market cannot find employment.
  C) individuals give up the search for employment.
  D) a business cycle recession decreases employment.

Answer: D

Topic: Cyclical Unemployment
Skill: Conceptual

75) Unemployment that is caused by recessions is called

A) frictional unemployment.
B) cyclical unemployment.
C) downtime unemployment.
D) structural unemployment.

Answer: B

Topic: Cyclical Unemployment
Skill: Recognition

76) Suppose the country of Quasiland experienced a decrease in real GDP and people were laid off from their jobs. The people would be considered part of

A) frictional unemployment.
B) structural unemployment.
C) cyclical unemployment.
D) discouraged workers.

Answer: C

Topic: Cyclical Unemployment
Skill: Recognition

77) The primary cause of cyclical unemployment is that

A) businesses often discriminate in their hiring practices on the basis of age, sex, and race.
B) the level of overall economic activity fluctuates.
C) workers sometimes quit their jobs in order to look for higher paying employment.
D) some workers do not have marketable job skills.

Answer: B

Topic: Cyclical Unemployment
Skill: Conceptual

78) Which of the following statements about cyclical unemployment is <u>FALSE</u>?

A) Cyclical unemployment exists when actual GDP is less than potential GDP.
B) When there is unemployment in excess of frictional and structural unemployment, it is cyclical unemployment.
C) Cyclical unemployment can be negative when actual GDP exceeds potential GDP.
D) None of the above because all the statements are true.

Answer: D

Topic: Cyclical Unemployment
Skill: Conceptual

79) Cyclical unemployment exists when

A) frictional and structural unemployment is zero.
B) real national income exceeds potential income.
C) actual GDP is more than potential GDP.
D) actual GDP is less than potential GDP.

Answer: D

Topic: Cyclical Unemployment
Skill: Conceptual

80) A recession causes a decrease in the demand for housing, resulting in substantial layoffs in the construction industry. The people laid off are considered

A) cyclically unemployment.
B) frictionally unemployment.
C) seasonally unemployment.
D) structurally unemployment.

Answer: A

Topic: Cyclical Unemployment
Skill: Conceptual

81) The best example of a cyclically unemployed individual is

A) Charles who lost his job as a real estate salesperson when the housing market went soft because of a recession.
B) Alice who quit her job to enter college.
C) Mary who lost her job in the textile industry following a decrease in the tariff on textiles.
D) Bob who has just graduated from college and is entering the labor market.

Answer: A

Topic: Cyclical Unemployment
Skill: Conceptual

82) Which of the following situations best describes an individual who is cyclically unemployed?

A) Catherine is a ski instructor who is not working because it is summer.
B) Matthew was an artillery man, but he has been unable to find work since he left the army.
C) Nicholas was laid-off when orders for General Motors cars fell during a recession.
D) Susan quit her job as a preschool teacher to try to find a better paying job.

Answer: C

Topic: Full Employment
Skill: Recognition

83) The economy is at full employment when
A) there are no unemployed workers.
B) all unemployment is frictional or structural.
C) there are more unemployed workers than vacancies.
D) all unemployment is cyclical.

Answer: B

Topic: Full Employment
Skill: Conceptual

84) When economists speak of full employment, they refer to the case in which the sum of frictional and structural unemployment is
A) falling over time.
B) equal to zero.
C) equal to the actual amount of unemployment.
D) greater than the level of deficient demand unemployment.

Answer: C

Topic: Full Employment
Skill: Conceptual

85) When the economy is operating at full employment, the natural rate of unemployment is greater than zero. This full employment level of unemployment consists of
A) only cyclical unemployment.
B) only frictional and structural unemployment.
C) only frictional and cyclical unemployment.
D) only structural and cyclical unemployment.

Answer: B

Topic: Full Employment
Skill: Recognition

86) Full employment means that
A) no one is unemployed.
B) there is no cyclical unemployment.
C) there is no cyclical or frictional unemployment.
D) there is no structural or frictional unemployment.

Answer: B

Topic: Natural Rate of Unemployment
Skill: Recognition

87) The natural rate of unemployment
A) is a constant figure of about 4 percent.
B) fluctuates with the rate of inflation.
C) is the unemployment rate that occurs when the economy is at full employment.
D) is equal to cyclical unemployment.

Answer: C

Topic: Natural Rate of Unemployment
Skill: Recognition

88) If unemployment is at the natural rate, then there
A) is no cyclical unemployment.
B) is no frictional unemployment.
C) will be cyclical and frictional unemployment but not structural unemployment.
D) will be only cyclical unemployment.

Answer: A

Topic: Natural Rate of Unemployment
Skill: Recognition

89) The natural rate of unemployment means that there
A) is zero unemployment.
B) is only frictional or structural unemployment.
C) are no job openings existing at the time.
D) is less than full employment.

Answer: B

Topic: Natural Rate of Unemployment
Skill: Conceptual

90) An unemployment rate of zero cannot be expected because
A) there are some people who do not want to work.
B) there will always be discouraged workers.
C) some portion of the labor force will always be between jobs.
D) cyclical unemployment will always exist.

Answer: C

Topic: Natural Rate of Unemployment
Skill: Recognition

91) The estimate of the current natural rate of unemployment is approximately
A) 0 percent.
B) 1-2 percent.
C) 4-7 percent.
D) 10-12 percent.

Answer: C

■ True Or False Questions

Topic: Population Survey
Skill: Recognition

92) The working-age population is divided between those people in the labor force and those people unemployed.

Answer: FALSE

Topic: Population Survey
Skill: Recognition

93) One way to be considered unemployed is to be without a job and looking for work.

Answer: TRUE

Topic: Unemployment Rate
Skill: Recognition

94) The unemployment rate equals (the number of people unemployed) divided by (the population) times 100.

Answer: FALSE

Topic: Aggregate Hours
Skill: Recognition

95) Aggregate hours has an upward trend over the last 30 years.

Answer: TRUE

Topic: Sources of Unemployment
Skill: Conceptual

96) The number of job leavers varies quite a bit over business cycle.

Answer: FALSE

Topic: Types of Unemployment
Skill: Recognition

97) Frictional, structural and cyclical unemployment are three classifications of unemployment.

Answer: TRUE

Topic: Structural Unemployment
Skill: Conceptual

98) Structural unemployment usually lasts longer than frictional unemployment.

Answer: TRUE

Topic: Natural Rate of Unemployment
Skill: Conceptual

99) The absence of cyclical unemployment means the economy is at the natural rate of unemployment.

Answer: TRUE

Topic: Explaining Employment and Wage Rates
Skill: Recognition

100) The natural rate of unemployment increased during the 1980s and the 1990s.

Answer: FALSE

■ Essay Questions

Topic: Unemployment Rate
Skill: Conceptual

101) How does the Census Bureau calculate the unemployment rate?

Answer:

Topic: Labor Participation Rate
Skill: Conceptual

102) What has happened to the labor force participation rate for men and women since 1960?

Answer:

Topic: Wages
Skill: Conceptual

103) What has happened to real wages since 1960? Explain your answer.

Answer:

Topic: Frictional Unemployment
Skill: Conceptual

104) Give an example of a frictionally unemployed person.

Answer:

Topic: Structural Unemployment
Skill: Conceptual

105) Give an example of a structurally unemployed person.

Answer:

Topic: Cyclical Unemployment
Skill: Conceptual

106) Give an example of a cyclically unemployed person.

Answer:

Chapter 8

AGGREGATE SUPPLY AND AGGREGATE DEMAND*

■ Aggregate Supply

Topic: Aggregate Supply
Skill: Recognition
1) Aggregate supply is
  A) desired spending on output at different price levels.
  B) the available goods and services at different price levels during a given period of time.
  C) the relationship between labor employment and the real (inflation adjusted) wage rate.
  D) the relationship between the unemployment rate and real GDP.
Answer: B

Topic: Aggregate Supply
Skill: Recognition
2) The quantity of real GDP supplied at different price levels is reflected by the
  A) aggregate supply curve.
  B) aggregate demand curve.
  C) real balance effect.
  D) total expenditures.
Answer: A

Topic: Aggregate Supply
Skill: Recognition
3) What is measured on the vertical axis of a diagram showing the aggregate supply curve?
  A) real national income.
  B) nominal income.
  C) the price level.
  D) the interest rate.
Answer: C

Topic: Aggregate Supply
Skill: Recognition
4) When talking about aggregate supply, it is necessary to
  A) focus on the short run.
  B) focus on the long run.
  C) distinguish between long-run aggregate supply and short-run aggregate supply.
  D) distinguish between long-run full employment and short-term full-employment.
Answer: C

Topic: Macroeconomic Long Run and Short Run
Skill: Recognition
5) We distinguish between the long-run aggregate supply curve and the short-run aggregate supply curve. In the long run
  A) technology is fixed but not in the short run.
  B) the price level is constant but in the short run it fluctuates.
  C) the aggregate supply curve is horizontal while in the short run it is upward sloping.
  D) real GDP equals potential GDP.
Answer: D

Topic: Long-Run Aggregate Supply
Skill: Recognition
6) The long-run aggregate supply curve is
  A) horizontal at the full employment price level.
  B) vertical at the full employment level of real GDP.
  C) upward sloping because of the effects of price level changes on output.
  D) the same as the short-run aggregate supply curve.
Answer: B

---

* This is Chapter 25 in *Economics*.

Topic: Long-Run Aggregate Supply
Skill: Recognition
7)   Which of the following statements is TRUE?
A)   The long-run aggregate supply curve is upward sloping.
B)   The long-run aggregate demand curve is upward sloping.
C)   The short-run aggregate supply curve is vertical.
D)   The long-run aggregate supply curve is vertical.
Answer: D

Topic: Short-Run Aggregate Supply
Skill: Recognition
8)   The short-run aggregate supply curve
A)   shows what each producer is willing and able to produce at each income level holding constant potential GDP and all resource prices.
B)   relates aggregate production and the price level holding constant potential GDP and all resource prices.
C)   becomes vertical if there is excess production capacity within the economy.
D)   shows a negative relationship between the price level and real national income holding constant potential GDP and all resource prices.
Answer: B

Topic: Short-Run Aggregate Supply
Skill: Recognition
9)   The short-run aggregate supply curve is
A)   vertical.
B)   positively sloped.
C)   negatively sloped.
D)   horizontal.
Answer: B

Topic: Short-Run Aggregate Supply
Skill: Conceptual
10)   The positive relationship between short-run aggregate supply and the price level indicates that, in the short run,
A)   firms produce more output as the price level falls.
B)   firms produce more output as the price level rises.
C)   wages increase along the short-run aggregate supply curve.
D)   lower price levels are more profitable for the firms.
Answer: B

Topic: Short-Run Aggregate Supply
Skill: Conceptual
11)   In the short run, an increase in the price level causes firms to expand production because
A)   the money wage rate remains constant so the higher prices for their product makes it profitable for firms to expand production.
B)   each firm must keep its production level up to the level of its rivals, and some firms will expand production as the price level increases.
C)   the higher prices allow the firm to hire more workers by offering higher wages, thereby increasing productivity and profits.
D)   firms can increase their profits by increasing their maintenance.
Answer: A

Topic: Short-Run Aggregate Supply
Skill: Conceptual
12)   Along a short-run aggregate supply curve, a decrease in the price level causes
A)   more output to be produced as consumer demand increases.
B)   less output to be produced as firms decrease production.
C)   more output to be produced as firms increase production because wages fall more than the price level falls, making it profitable to hire more workers.
D)   no change in output because firms do not change the quantity they produce.
Answer: B

Topic: Short-Run Aggregate Supply
Skill: Conceptual
13)   A change in _____ causes a movement along the short-run aggregate supply curve but no shift in the short-run aggregate supply curve.
A)   wage rates (the cost of labor)
B)   technology
C)   the quantity of capital
D)   the price level
Answer: D

Topic: Short-Run Aggregate Supply
Skill: Conceptual

14) Which of the following does <u>NOT</u> shift the short-run aggregate supply curve?
A) a change in the wage rate.
B) technological progress.
C) a reduction in the price of a raw material.
D) a change in the price level.
Answer: D

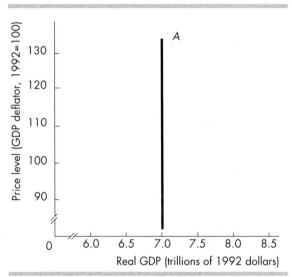

Topic: Long-Run Aggregate Supply
Skill: Analytical

15) The curve labeled *A* in the above figure is a
A) short-run aggregate demand curve.
B) short-run aggregate supply curve.
C) long-run aggregate demand curve.
D) long-run aggregate supply curve.
Answer: D

Topic: Changes in Aggregate Supply; Technology
Skill: Analytical

16) The curve labeled *A* in the above figure will shift rightward when
A) the price level falls.
B) technology increases.
C) population falls.
D) the price level rises.
Answer: B

Topic: Changes in Aggregate Supply; Capital
Skill: Conceptual

17) An increase in the capital stock causes the short-run aggregate supply curve to
A) remain as it is.
B) shift rightward.
C) shift leftward.
D) become steeper.
Answer: B

Topic: Changes in Aggregate Supply; Technology
Skill: Conceptual

18) A major technological advance causes
A) the long-run aggregate supply curve to shift rightward and the short-run aggregate supply curve to shift leftward.
B) the long-run aggregate supply curve to shift rightward and the short-run aggregate supply curve to remain where it is.
C) the short-run aggregate supply curve to shift rightward and the long-run aggregate supply curve to remain where it is.
D) both the long-run and the short-run aggregate supply curves to shift rightward.
Answer: D

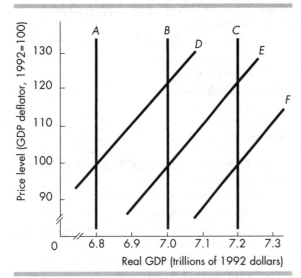

Topic: Changes in Aggregate Supply; Full-Employment Quantity of Labor
Skill: Analytical

19) In the above figure, *B* is the current long-run aggregate supply curve and *E* is the current short-run aggregate supply curve. If there is an increase in the full-employment quantity of labor, then the long-run aggregate supply curve and the short-run aggregate supply curve

A) remain *B* and *E*.
B) shift to *A* and *D*, respectively.
C) shift to *C* and *F*, respectively.
D) shift to *A* and *F*, respectively.

Answer: C

Topic: Changes in Aggregate Supply; Technology
Skill: Analytical

20) In the above figure, *B* is the current long-run aggregate supply curve and *E* is the current short-run aggregate supply curve. Technological advances cause the long-run aggregate supply curve and short-run aggregate supply curve to

A) remain *B* and *E*.
B) shift to *A* and *D*, respectively.
C) shift to *C* and *F*, respectively.
D) shift to *C* and remain *E*, respectively.

Answer: C

Topic: Changes in Aggregate Supply
Skill: Conceptual

21) All of the following shift the short-run aggregate supply curve <u>EXCEPT</u>

A) a change in the price level.
B) a change in the money wage rate.
C) a change in the price of a needed raw material.
D) technological progress.

Answer: A

Topic: Changes in Aggregate Supply
Skill: Conceptual

22) An increase in money wages shifts the short-run aggregate supply curve _____; an increase in technology shifts the long-run aggregate supply curve _____.

A) rightward; rightward
B) rightward; leftward
C) leftward; rightward
D) leftward; leftward

Answer: C

Topic: Changes in Money Wages and Other Resource Prices
Skill: Conceptual

23) Which of the following directly shifts the short-run aggregate supply curve?

A) a change in aggregate demand.
B) a change in the price level.
C) a change in resource prices.
D) all of the above.

Answer: C

Topic: Changes in Aggregate Supply
Skill: Conceptual

24) A change in which of the following shifts the short-run aggregate supply curve?

A) A change in the wage rate.
B) An advance in technology.
C) A change in the quantity of capital.
D) All of the above shift the short-run aggregate supply curve.

Answer: D

Topic: Changes in Aggregate Supply
Skill: Conceptual
25) Which of the following cause the short-run aggregate supply curve to shift?
  I.   Changes in the size of the labor force.
  II. Changes in money wages.
  A) I only.
  B) II only.
  C) Both I and II.
  D) Neither I nor II.
Answer: C

Topic: Changes in Money Wages and Other Resource Prices
Skill: Conceptual
26) The short-run aggregate supply curve shifts leftward when the
  A) price level increases.
  B) general level of technology advances.
  C) money wages paid to workers increase.
  D) availability of on-the-job training expands to all workers.
Answer: C

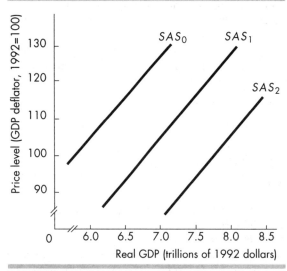

Topic: Short-Run Aggregate Supply
Skill: Analytical
27) In the above figure, the short-run aggregate supply curve is SAS_1. Suppose that the price level in the economy increases. The effect of this development is a
  A) movement upward along SAS_1.
  B) movement downward along SAS_1.
  C) shift to SAS_0.
  D) shift to SAS_2.
Answer: A

Topic: Changes in Aggregate Supply; Technology
Skill: Analytical
28) In the above figure, the short-run aggregate supply curve is SAS_1. If the level of technology in the economy increases, there is a
  A) movement upward along SAS_1.
  B) movement downward along SAS_1.
  C) shift to SAS_0.
  D) shift to SAS_2.
Answer: D

Topic: Changes in Money Wages and Other Resource Prices
Skill: Analytical

29) In the above figure, the short-run aggregate supply curve is SAS_1. If money wages in the economy increase, there is a
   A) movement upward along SAS_1.
   B) movement downward along SAS_1.
   C) shift to SAS_0.
   D) shift to SAS_2.

Answer: C

Topic: Changes in Money Wages and Other Resource Prices
Skill: Analytical

30) In the above figure, the short-run aggregate supply curve is SAS_1. If the prices of resources in the economy drop because of reductions in tariffs and quotas placed on imports, there is a
   A) movement upward along SAS_1.
   B) movement downward along SAS_1.
   C) shift to SAS_0.
   D) shift to SAS_2.

Answer: D

■ Aggregate Demand

Topic: The Aggregate Demand Curve
Skill: Recognition

31) Other things being equal, the curve that shows households and businesses buying more as the price level falls is known as
   A) aggregate demand curve.
   B) aggregate supply curve.
   C) aggregate production curve.
   D) total expenditures ($C + I + G + NX$) curve.

Answer: A

Topic: The Aggregate Demand Curve
Skill: Recognition

32) The aggregate demand curve shows
   A) total expenditures at different levels of national income.
   B) the quantity of real GDP demanded at different price levels.
   C) that real income is directly (positively) related to the price level.
   D) All of the above answers are correct.

Answer: B

Topic: The Aggregate Demand Curve
Skill: Recognition

33) Other things constant, the economy's aggregate demand curve shows that
   A) as the price level falls, GDP decreases.
   B) any change in the price level causes the aggregate demand curve to shift.
   C) the quantity of real GDP demanded decreases when the price level rises.
   D) the quantity of real GDP demanded and the price level are not related.

Answer: C

Topic: The Aggregate Demand Curve
Skill: Recognition

34) The aggregate demand curve shows the ____ relationship between the price level and ____.
   A) positive; quantity of real GDP demanded
   B) negative; aggregate labor demanded
   C) positive; aggregate labor demand
   D) negative; quantity of real GDP demanded

Answer: D

Topic: The Aggregate Demand Curve
Skill: Recognition

35) The aggregate demand curve illustrates a(n) ____ relationship between the price level and the quantity of real GDP demanded.
   A) multiplied
   B) direct and proportional
   C) direct but not necessarily proportional
   D) inverse

Answer: D

Topic: The Aggregate Demand Curve
Skill: Conceptual
36) The aggregate demand curve shows that, if other factors are held constant,
 A) a higher price level will result in a decrease in the quantity of real GDP demanded.
 B) a higher price level will result in an increase in the quantity of real GDP demanded.
 C) a higher price level will result in a lower interest rate.
 D) a lower price level will result in inflationary conditions.
Answer: A

Topic: The Aggregate Demand Curve
Skill: Conceptual
37) The quantity of real GDP demanded equals $7.2 trillion when the GDP deflator is 90. If the GDP deflator rises to 95, the quantity of real GDP demanded equals
 A) less than $7.2 trillion.
 B) $7.2 trillion.
 C) more than $7.2 trillion but less than $7.8 trillion.
 D) more than $7.2 trillion but without more information it is not possible to determine how much more.
Answer: A

Topic: The Aggregate Demand Curve
Skill: Conceptual
38) The quantity of real GDP demanded equals $7.4 trillion when the GDP deflator is 95. If the GDP deflator falls to 90, the quantity of real GDP demanded equals
 A) less than $7.4 trillion but more than $7 trillion.
 B) less than $7.4 trillion but without more information, it is not possible to determine how much less.
 C) more than $7.4 trillion.
 D) $7.4 trillion.
Answer: C

Topic: The Aggregate Demand Curve
Skill: Recognition
39) The aggregate demand curve
 A) is vertical.
 B) has a positive slope.
 C) has a negative slope.
 D) is horizontal.
Answer: C

Topic: The Aggregate Demand Curve
Skill: Conceptual
40) A movement along the aggregate demand curve but no shift in the aggregate demand curve is caused by which of the following?
 A) A change in tax rates.
 B) A change in the price level.
 C) A change in fiscal policy.
 D) None of the above because they all shift the aggregate demand curve.
Answer: B

Topic: The Aggregate Demand Curve
Skill: Conceptual
41) All of the following explain the downward slope of the aggregate demand curve EXCEPT
 A) changes in real wealth.
 B) the effect of changing interest rates on the quantity demanded of goods today versus goods in the future.
 C) the availability of foreign substitute goods.
 D) the presence of unused production capacity and unemployment.
Answer: D

Topic: The Aggregate Demand Curve
Skill: Conceptual
42) An increase in the price level causes
 A) consumption expenditures to decrease.
 B) a wealth effect.
 C) a movement along the aggregate demand curve.
 D) All of the above answers are correct.
Answer: D

Topic: Aggregate Demand, Real Wealth
Skill: Conceptual
43) An individual holds $10,000 in a non-interest-earning checking account, and the overall price level rises significantly. Hence
 A) the individual's real wealth and consumption expenditure decrease.
 B) the *individual's* real wealth decreases but real *national* wealth increases.
 C) there is no change in the individual's real wealth.
 D) the individual's wealth increases.
Answer: A

Topic: Aggregate Demand, Real Wealth
Skill: Conceptual

44) If you have 1,000 dollars in wealth and the GDP deflator increases 20 percent, then
   A) the 1,000 dollars will buy 20 percent fewer goods and services.
   B) the 1,000 dollars will buy 20 percent more goods and services.
   C) the real value of the 1,000 dollars increases.
   D) you will be able to buy fewer goods, but the real value of those goods will increase.

Answer: A

Topic: Aggregate Demand, Real Wealth
Skill: Conceptual

45) If you have 5,000 dollars in wealth and the GDP deflator decreases 20 percent, then
   A) the 5,000 dollars will buy 20 percent fewer goods and services.
   B) the 5,000 dollars will buy 20 percent more goods and services.
   C) the real value of the 5,000 decreases.
   D) the real value of the 5,000 dollars remains constant.

Answer: B

Topic: Aggregate Demand, Wealth Effect
Skill: Conceptual

46) ____ points out that a rise in the price level decreases the value of real wealth, which then decreases consumption.
   A) The wealth effect
   B) The substitution effect
   C) The open-economy effect
   D) The interest rate effect

Answer: A

Topic: Aggregate Demand, Wealth Effect
Skill: Conceptual

47) A rise in the price level will have an effect on aggregate demand because
   A) people like to spend more when prices are higher.
   B) the real value of people's wealth varies directly with the price level and so does their spending.
   C) the real value of people's wealth decreases and so they decrease their consumption.
   D) the more money people have, the more it is worth and hence the more goods and services they demand.

Answer: C

Topic: Aggregate Demand, Intertemporal Substitution Effect
Skill: Conceptual

48) Substitution effects help explain the slope of the aggregate demand curve. One substitution effect refers to
   A) the inverse relationship between the interest rate and the price level.
   B) the direct relationship between the interest rate and the real value of wealth.
   C) the effect on investment expenditures that result from a change in interest rates produced by a change in the price level.
   D) the change in wealth that results from a change in the interest rate.

Answer: C

Topic: Aggregate Demand, Intertemporal Substitution Effect
Skill: Conceptual

49) According to the intertemporal substitution effect, a fall in the price level will
   A) decrease the real value of wealth, which causes the quantity of real GDP demanded to increase.
   B) cause the interest rate to fall. As a result, investment increases and the quantity of real GDP demanded increases.
   C) lead to an increase in net exports, which causes the quantity of real GDP demanded to increase.
   D) increase the real value of wealth, which causes interest rates to increase. As a result, the quantity of real GDP demanded decreases.

Answer: B

Topic: Aggregate Demand, Intertemporal Substitution Effect
Skill: Conceptual

50) According to the intertemporal substitution effect, when the price level increases, the interest rate
   A) increases and the quantity of real GDP demanded increases.
   B) increases and the quantity of real GDP demanded decreases.
   C) decreases and the quantity of real GDP demanded decreases.
   D) is not affected.

Answer: B

Topic: Aggregate Demand, Intertemporal Substitution Effect
Skill: Conceptual

51) According to the intertemporal substitution effect, a higher price level

A) decreases the quantity of real GDP demanded.
B) lowers the costs of building new plants and equipment.
C) increases the quantity of real GDP demanded.
D) makes it less costly for people to buy houses and cars.

Answer: A

Topic: Aggregate Demand, International Price Substitution Effect
Skill: Conceptual

52) There are several reasons why the aggregate demand curve is downward sloping. Which of the following correctly describes one of these explanations?

A) A rise in the price level raises the purchasing power of consumer assets and increases desired consumption.
B) A rise in the price level raises interest rates and increases investment spending.
C) A fall in the price level, holding foreign prices and the exchange rate constant, increases net exports.
D) A rise in the price level lowers the interest rate and increases investment spending.

Answer: C

Topic: Aggregate Demand, International Price Substitution Effect
Skill: Conceptual

53) A fall in the price level

A) increases the real value of people's wealth, which causes borrowing to decrease. As a result, investment decreases and hence the quantity of real GDP demanded decreases.
B) causes exports to increase and imports to decrease, leading to an increase in the quantity of real GDP demanded.
C) leads to a decrease in the quantity of real GDP demanded because of the wealth effect.
D) causes the quantity of real GDP demanded to increase as long as the fall is less than the fall in the price level in other countries.

Answer: B

Topic: Aggregate Demand, International Price Substitution Effect
Skill: Conceptual

54) When the relative prices of American-made goods go up, the result is

A) an increase in exports.
B) a decrease in exports.
C) a decrease in imports.
D) no change in imports or exports.

Answer: B

Topic: Aggregate Demand, International Price Substitution Effect
Skill: Conceptual

55) When the price level in France increases while the exchange rate and the price level in the U.S. remain the same, the result is

A) U.S.-made goods become relatively cheaper compared to French-made goods.
B) French citizens are more likely to buy U.S.-made goods.
C) U.S. citizens are less likely to buy French-made goods.
D) All of the above answers are correct.

Answer: D

Topic: Changes in Aggregate Demand
Skill: Recognition

56) Which of the following does NOT shift the aggregate demand curve?

A) A decrease in the money supply.
B) An increase in people's expected future incomes.
C) An increase in the price level.
D) An increase in current foreign income.

Answer: C

Topic: Changes in Aggregate Demand, Investment
Skill: Conceptual

57) A change in which of the following causes a rightward shift in the aggregate demand curve?

A) An increase in saving matched by a decrease in consumption.
B) An increase in investment expenditures.
C) A decrease in net exports.
D) A decrease in government purchases of goods and services.

Answer: B

Topic: Changes in Aggregate Demand, Government Purchases
Skill: Conceptual
58) A change in which of the following causes a leftward shift in the aggregate demand curve?
   A) An increase in consumption expenditures.
   B) A decrease in taxes.
   C) A decrease in government purchases of goods and services.
   D) An increase in net exports of goods and services.
Answer: C

Topic: Changes in Aggregate Demand, Taxes
Skill: Recognition
59) The aggregate demand curve
   A) shifts rightward when the price level increases and leftward when the price level falls.
   B) shifts rightward when taxes are decreased.
   C) shifts rightward when foreign incomes decrease and shifts leftward when foreign incomes increase.
   D) does not shift, unlike market demand curves.
Answer: B

Topic: Changes in Aggregate Demand, Taxes
Skill: Conceptual
60) Which of the following causes aggregate demand to decrease?
   A) The government increases taxes on both business and personal income.
   B) Foreign incomes rise.
   C) The amount of money in the economy increases.
   D) Households believe that the economy is headed for good times, with higher future incomes.
Answer: A

Topic: Changes in Aggregate Demand, Taxes
Skill: Conceptual
61) Which of the following increases aggregate demand?
   A) A decrease in tax rates.
   B) A decrease in foreign income.
   C) A decrease in government spending.
   D) A decrease in the money supply.
Answer: A

Topic: Changes in Aggregate Demand, Money
Skill: Conceptual
62) Which of the following shifts the aggregate demand curve rightward?
   A) A decrease in the price level.
   B) A decrease in government purchases.
   C) An increase in the money supply.
   D) A decrease in transfer payments.
Answer: C

Topic: Changes in Aggregate Demand, Money
Skill: Conceptual
63) The U.S. aggregate demand curve shifts leftward if
   A) the economic conditions in Europe improve so that European incomes increase.
   B) there is a tax cut.
   C) the Federal Reserve decreases the money supply.
   D) the foreign exchange rate falls.
Answer: C

Topic: Changes in Aggregate Demand, Money
Skill: Conceptual
64) When the quantity of money in the economy increases,
   A) the long-run aggregate supply curve shifts leftward.
   B) the aggregate demand curve shifts rightward.
   C) the aggregate demand curve does not shift but the economy moves along it.
   D) the wealth effect is no longer operable.
Answer: B

Topic: Changes in Aggregate Demand, Foreign Exchange Rate
Skill: Conceptual
65) Suppose that U.S. consumers show an increased preference for imported, rather than domestic, cars because the U.S. exchange rate rises. As a result,
   A) there will be a movement along the U.S. aggregate demand curve only.
   B) there will be a rightward shift in the U.S. aggregate demand curve.
   C) there will be a leftward shift in the U.S. aggregate demand curve.
   D) there will be a rightward shift in the long-run U.S. aggregate supply curve.
Answer: C

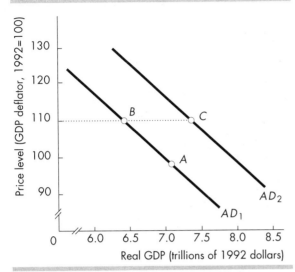

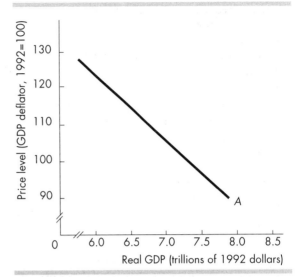

Topic: The Aggregate Demand Curve
Skill: Analytical

66) In the above figure, the movement from point B to point A may be the result of

A) an increase in government purchases because of a war.

B) an increase in government purchases because of increases in education expenditures.

C) an increase in the demand for manufacturing goods because of new technology.

D) a fall in the price level.

Answer: D

Topic: Aggregate Demand, Wealth Effect
Skill: Analytical

67) In the above figure, the movement from point A to point B may be the result of

A) an increase in the real value of wealth.

B) a decrease in the real value of wealth.

C) a decrease in interest rates.

D) an increase in exports.

Answer: B

Topic: Changes in Aggregate Demand,
Government Purchases
Skill: Analytical

68) In the above figure, the shift from point C to point B may be the result of

A) an increase in the price level.

B) a decrease in the price level.

C) a decrease in government purchases.

D) an increase in the quantity of money.

Answer: C

Topic: The Aggregate Demand Curve
Skill: Analytical

69) The curve labeled A in the above figure is

A) a short-run aggregate supply curve.

B) an aggregate demand curve.

C) a long-run aggregate supply curve.

D) a production possibilities curve.

Answer: B

Topic: Changes in Aggregate Demand, Taxes
Skill: Analytical

70) In the above figure, the curve labeled A shifts rightward if

A) expected future profits decrease.

B) the money supply decreases.

C) the substitution effect occurs.

D) taxes decrease.

Answer: D

■ Macroeconomic Equilibrium

Topic: Macroeconomic Equilibrium
Skill: Recognition

71) The equilibrium level of GDP occurs at the level of GDP at which the

A) unemployment rate is zero.

B) aggregate quantity demanded equals the aggregate quantity supplied.

C) aggregate demand curve becomes vertical.

D) All of the above answers are correct.

Answer: B

Topic: Macroeconomic Equilibrium
Skill: Recognition
72) By using only the aggregate demand curve, we can
     determine
   A)   only the price level.
   B)   only the quantity of real GDP.
   C)   both the price level and quantity of real GDP.
   D)   neither the price level nor the quantity of real
        GDP.
Answer: D

Topic: Short-Run Macroeconomic Equilibrium
Skill: Recognition
73)   In the short run, at the point of intersection be-
      tween the aggregate demand and the short-run
      aggregate supply curves,
   A)   the equilibrium price level is established.
   B)   there is neither a surplus nor a shortage of goods
        on the market.
   C)   the equilibrium level of real GDP is established.
   D)   All of the above answers are correct.
Answer: D

Topic: Short-Run Macroeconomic Equilibrium
Skill: Recognition
74) A short-run macroeconomic equilibrium occurs
   A)   at the intersection of the short-run aggregate
        supply curve and the long-run aggregate supply
        curve.
   B)   at the intersection of the short-run aggregate
        supply curve and the aggregate demand curve.
   C)   at the intersection of the short-run aggregate
        supply curve, the long-run aggregate supply
        curve, and the aggregate demand curve.
   D)   when the rate at which prices increase equals the
        rate at which resource prices increase.
Answer: B

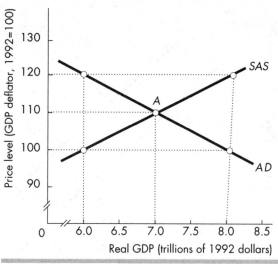

Topic: Fluctuations in Short-Run Aggregate Supply
Skill: Analytical
75)   In the above figure, the economy is at point A
      when changes occur. If the new equilibrium has a
      price level of 120 and real GDP of $6.0 trillion,
      then it must be the case that
   A)   aggregate demand has increased.
   B)   aggregate demand has decreased.
   C)   aggregate supply has decreased.
   D)   aggregate supply has increased.
Answer: C

Topic: Fluctuations in Short-Run Aggregate Supply
Skill: Analytical
76)   In the above figure, the economy is at point A
      when changes occur. If the new equilibrium has a
      price level of 100 and real GDP of $8.0 trillion,
      then it must be the case that
   A)   aggregate demand has increased.
   B)   aggregate demand has decreased.
   C)   aggregate supply has decreased.
   D)   aggregate supply has increased.
Answer: D

Topic: Fluctuations in Aggregate Demand
Skill: Analytical

77) In the above figure, the economy is at point *A* when changes occur. If the new equilibrium has a price level of 100 and real GDP of $6.0 trillion, then it must be the case that

A) aggregate demand has increased.
B) aggregate demand has decreased.
C) aggregate supply has decreased.
D) aggregate supply has increased.

Answer: B

Topic: Long-Run Macroeconomic Equilibrium
Skill: Conceptual

78) If the money wage has fully adjusted to any changes, the economy is

A) at its long-run macroeconomic equilibrium.
B) at a short-run macroeconomic equilibrium but not at a long-run macroeconomic equilibrium.
C) experiencing an inflationary gap.
D) experiencing a recessionary gap.

Answer: A

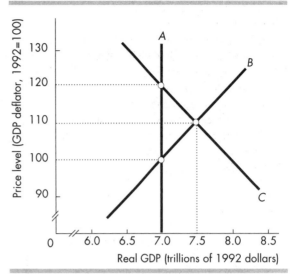

Topic: Long-Run Macroeconomic Equilibrium
Skill: Analytical

79) In the above figure, the three curves are:
A) *A* is long-run aggregate supply, *B* is short-run aggregate supply, and *C* is aggregate demand.
B) *A* is aggregate demand, *B* is short-run aggregate supply, and *C* is long-run aggregate supply.
C) *A* is short-run aggregate supply, *B* is long-run aggregate supply, and *C* is aggregate demand.
D) *A* is long-run aggregate supply, *B* is aggregate demand, and *C* is short-run aggregate supply.

Answer: A

Topic: Economic Growth
Skill: Conceptual

80) Which of the following helps determine the growth rate of potential GDP?
  I.   capital accumulation.
  II. technology advances.
  III. the money supply.

A) I.
B) I and II.
C) I and III.
D) I, II and III.

Answer: B

Topic: Inflation
Skill: Conceptual
81) Inflation occurs over time as a result of
   A) long-run aggregate supply increasing faster than aggregate demand.
   B) long-run aggregate supply increasing faster than short-run aggregate supply.
   C) decreases in aggregate demand.
   D) aggregate demand increasing faster than long-run aggregate supply.
Answer: D

Topic: Inflation
Skill: Conceptual
82) If the aggregate demand curve shifts _____ faster than the long-run aggregate supply curve, then _____ occurs.
   A) leftward; economic growth
   B) leftward; inflation
   C) rightward; economic growth
   D) rightward; inflation
Answer: D

Topic: Business Cycles
Skill: Conceptual
83) One possible result of decreases in aggregate demand coupled with a stable aggregate supply is
   A) a recession.
   B) an increase in employment levels.
   C) an economic expansion.
   D) a rise in the price level.
Answer: A

Topic: Recessionary Gap
Skill: Conceptual
84) If aggregate demand decreases and neither short-run nor long-run aggregate supply changes, then
   A) the price level will increase in the short-run and decrease in the long-run.
   B) there will be an inflationary gap.
   C) there will be a recessionary gap.
   D) in the long run, the long-run aggregate supply will decrease.
Answer: C

Topic: Inflationary Gap
Skill: Conceptual
85) If the level of real GDP exceeds potential GDP,
   A) there is a long-run and a short-run equilibrium.
   B) there is neither a long-run nor a short-run equilibrium.
   C) there can be a short-run equilibrium with an inflationary gap.
   D) there can be a short-run equilibrium with a recessionary gap.
Answer: C

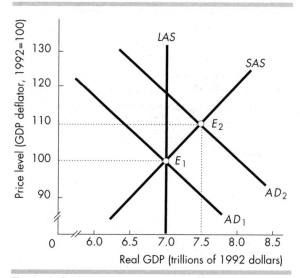

Topic: Inflationary Gap
Skill: Analytical
86) In the above figure, the inflationary gap when AD_2 is the aggregate demand curve equals
   A) the difference between 110 and 100.
   B) the difference between $7.5 trillion and $7.0 trillion.
   C) *LAS* minus *SAS* at a price level of 100.
   D) AD_1.
Answer: B

Topic: Inflationary Gap
Skill: Analytical

87) The reason that it is possible for the economy in the above figure to be at equilibrium E_2 rather than at E_1 is that

A) in the long run there is always less than full employment.

B) in the short run the economy can produce more than it can in a long-run situation.

C) AD always shifts rightward and never shifts leftward.

D) the economy must be in a recession.

Answer: B

Topic: Above Full-Employment Equilibrium
Skill: Conceptual

88) An above full-employment equilibrium occurs when

A) aggregate demand decreases while neither the short-run nor long-run aggregate supply changes.

B) short-run aggregate supply decreases while neither aggregate demand nor long-run aggregate supply changes.

C) the equilibrium level of real GDP is greater than potential GDP.

D) the equilibrium level of real GDP is less than potential GDP.

Answer: C

Topic: Fluctuations in Aggregate Demand
Skill: Conceptual

89) In the short run, an increase in aggregate demand

A) lowers the price level and decreases real GDP.

B) lowers the price level and increases real GDP.

C) increases the price level and increases real GDP.

D) increases the price level and decreases real GDP.

Answer: C

Topic: Fluctuations in Aggregate Demand
Skill: Conceptual

90) In the short-run, a decrease in government spending causes

A) a decrease in real GDP and an increase in the price level.

B) a decrease in the price level and an increase in real GDP.

C) a decrease in real GDP and in the price level.

D) an increase in real GDP and in the price level.

Answer: C

Topic: Fluctuations in Aggregate Demand
Skill: Conceptual

91) A lower price level combined with a decrease in real GDP occurs when the

A) short-run aggregate supply curve shifts rightward.

B) short-run aggregate supply curve shifts leftward.

C) aggregate demand curve shifts rightward.

D) aggregate demand curve shifts leftward.

Answer: D

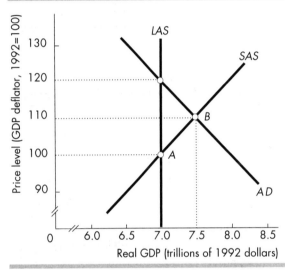

Topic: Fluctuations in Aggregate Demand
Skill: Analytical

92) In the above figure, suppose the economy had been at point A and now is at B. What could have caused the movement to B?

A) Unusually good weather causes the wheat crop to be larger than normal.

B) Government purchases increased.

C) Winter storms cause factories in the north to be shut down for several weeks.

D) Money wages rose.

Answer: B

Topic: Movement to the Long-Run Equilibrium
Skill: Analytical

93) In the above figure, suppose the economy had been at point *A* and now is at *B*. Without any economic growth, what will the new long-run equilibrium be?

A) Aggregate demand will decrease until real GDP is $7 trillion and the price level is 110.

B) Money wages will fall and the aggregate demand curve will shift leftward until the price level is 100 and real GDP is $7.0 trillion.

C) The population will increase, causing the long-run aggregate supply to increase to $7.5 trillion and the price level to fall to 100.

D) Money wages will increase and the short-run aggregate supply curve will shift leftward until the price level is 120 and real GDP is $7 trillion.

Answer: D

Topic: Movement to the Long-Run Equilibrium
Skill: Conceptual

94) Suppose the current situation is such that the price level is 120, real GDP is $4 trillion, and GDP along the long-run aggregate supply is $3.6 trillion. What will take place to restore the long-run equilibrium?

A) The price level will fall until long-run aggregate supply increases to $4 trillion.

B) The price level will fall and money wages will rise until real GDP along the long-run aggregate supply curve is $4 trillion.

C) Money wages will rise until real GDP is $3.6 trillion.

D) Aggregate demand will increase until both short-run and long-run aggregate supply equal $4 trillion.

Answer: C

Topic: Movement to the Long-Run Equilibrium
Skill: Conceptual

95) The long-run aggregate supply curve is vertical at $5 trillion but the short-run aggregate supply curve intersects the aggregate demand curve at $6 trillion. We know that

A) the economy is operating below full employment in the short run, and will adjust by hiring more workers, thus decreasing unemployment.

B) the price level is too high. The long-run equilibrium will occur with a lower price level.

C) adjustments will occur so that the long-run aggregate supply equals $6 trillion.

D) adjustments will occur so that the short-run aggregate supply eventually intersects the aggregate demand curve at $5 trillion.

Answer: D

Topic: Fluctuations in Short-Run Aggregate Supply
Skill: Conceptual

96) A decrease in short-run aggregate supply causes the equilibrium price level to _____ and the equilibrium quantity of real GDP to _____.

A) increase; increase

B) increase; decrease

C) decrease; increase

D) decrease; decrease

Answer: B

Topic: Fluctuations in Short-Run Aggregate Supply
Skill: Conceptual

97) In the short run, a rightward shift of the short-run aggregate supply curve causes

A) a decrease in real GDP and in the price level.

B) an increase in real GDP and in the price level.

C) a decrease in real GDP and an increase in the price level.

D) an increase in real GDP and a decrease in the price level.

Answer: D

Topic: Fluctuations in Short-Run Aggregate Supply
Skill: Conceptual

98) In the short run, a supply shock that shifts the short-run aggregate supply curve leftward

A) raises the price level and real GDP.

B) raises the price level and decreases real GDP.

C) lowers the price level and increases real GDP.

D) lowers the price level and real GDP.

Answer: B

■ U.S. Economic Growth, Inflation, and Cycles

Topic: Business Cycles
Skill: Conceptual
99) Which of the following is correct when describing business cycles?
   - I. The economy does not grow or shrink at a steady pace.
   - II. Short-run aggregate supply increases at a fixed pace.
   - III. There are usually a few years between recessions.
   - A) I only.
   - B) I and II.
   - C) I and III.
   - D) II and III.

Answer: C

Topic: Economic Growth
Skill: Conceptual
100) Over time in a growing economy, the long-run aggregate supply curve will
   - A) become horizontal at the long-run potential price level.
   - B) shift rightward.
   - C) shift leftward.
   - D) become increasingly steep.

Answer: B

Topic: The Evolving Economy
Skill: Conceptual
101) Since the 1960s,
   - A) growth in both real GDP and the price level have occurred.
   - B) economic growth has always been rapid.
   - C) growth in real GDP has occurred but the price level has not changed.
   - D) there have been more periods of recession than expansion.

Answer: A

■ True Or False Questions

Topic: Long-Run Aggregate Supply
Skill: Recognition
102) The long-run aggregate supply curve is vertical.
Answer: TRUE

Topic: Short-Run Aggregate Supply
Skill: Recognition
103) The level of output when there is full employment is called actual GDP.
Answer: FALSE

Topic: Short-Run Aggregate Supply
Skill: Conceptual
104) In the long-run, the quantity of real GDP supplied increases when the price level increases.
Answer: FALSE

Topic: Short-Run Aggregate Supply
Skill: Conceptual
105) The short-run aggregate supply curve shows a positive relationship between the price level and real GDP.
Answer: TRUE

Topic: Changes in Aggregate Supply, Technology
Skill: Conceptual
106) If there is an increase in technology, the long-run aggregate supply curve shifts rightward, but the short-run aggregate supply curve does not shift.
Answer: FALSE

Topic: Changes in Aggregate Supply, Capital
Skill: Conceptual
107) An increase in the quantity of capital shifts both the long-run and short-run aggregate supply curves.
Answer: TRUE

Topic: Changes in Money Wages and Other Resource Prices
Skill: Conceptual
108) If money wages increase, the short-run aggregate supply curve shifts rightward.
Answer: FALSE

Topic: Aggregate Demand Curve, Wealth and Substitution Effects
Skill: Conceptual
109) Wealth and substitution effects explain why the aggregate demand curve has a positive slope.
Answer: FALSE

Topic: Changes in Aggregate Demand, Money
Skill: Conceptual
110) An increase in the money supply causes a rightward shift in the aggregate demand curve.
Answer: TRUE

Topic: Short-Run Macroeconomic Equilibrium
Skill: Conceptual
111) The level of output at which the short-run aggregate supply curve and the aggregate demand curve intersect is the full employment level of GDP.

Answer: FALSE

Topic: Above Full-Employment Equilibrium
Skill: Conceptual
112) During an above full-employment equilibrium, actual GDP is greater than potential GDP.

Answer: TRUE

Topic: U.S. Economic Growth, Inflation and Cycles
Skill: Conceptual
113) Fluctuations in aggregate demand and aggregate supply explain why real GDP fluctuates.

Answer: TRUE

■ Essay Questions

Topic: Long-Run and Short-Run Aggregate Supply
Skill: Conceptual
114) What is the difference between the long-run aggregate supply and the short-run aggregate supply curves?

Answer:

Topic: Long-Run and Short-Run Aggregate Supply
Skill: Conceptual
115) What are the factors that can shift the short-run aggregate supply curve but not the long-run aggregate supply curve? Explain your answer.

Answer:

Topic: Aggregate Demand, Wealth Effect
Skill: Conceptual
116) Give an example of a wealth effect that changes aggregate demand.

Answer:

Topic: Aggregate Demand, Substitution Effect
Skill: Conceptual
117) Give an example of a substitution effect that changes aggregate demand.

Answer:

Topic: Changes in Aggregate Demand, Foreign Exchange Rate
Skill: Conceptual
118) What happens to the aggregate demand curve in the United States if the foreign exchange rate increases so that U.S.-made products become more expensive?

Answer:

Topic: Macroeconomic Equilibrium
Skill: Conceptual
119) Explain the relationship of the long-run aggregate supply curve, the short-run aggregate supply curve and the aggregate demand curve in determining a long-run and short-run macroeconomic equilibrium.

Answer:

Topic: Inflationary Gap and Recessionary Gap
Skill: Conceptual
120) What is the difference between an inflationary gap and a recessionary gap?

Answer:

Topic: Fluctuations in Aggregate Demand
Skill: Conceptual
121) If the world economy expands so that the demand for U.S.-made goods increases, what will happen to aggregate demand, the price level, and real GDP in the U.S.?

Answer:

Topic Inflation
Skill: Conceptual
122) In general, what has occurred to the price level over the past 35 years? What is the driving force behind this change?

Answer:

Chapter 9 — THE ECONOMY AT FULL EMPLOYMENT*

■ Real GDP and Employment

Topic: Real GDP & Employment
Skill: Recognition
1) In the *short run*, which of the following can increase real GDP?
   I. increases in the quantity of labor.
   II. increases in the quantity of capital.
   A) I only.
   B) II only.
   C) Both I and II.
   D) Neither I nor II.
Answer: A

Topic: The Production Function
Skill: Recognition
2) The production function shows how _____ varies with ____.
   A) leisure time; labor input
   B) labor input; leisure time
   C) real GDP; labor input
   D) labor input; capital input
Answer: C

Topic: The Production Function
Skill: Conceptual
3) Suppose that orange growers in Florida decide to buy new automated pickers to bring in the orange crop. As a result
   A) there will be an increase in human capital.
   B) the production function shifts upward.
   C) there will be an increase in labor input.
   D) there will be a decrease in opportunity costs.
Answer: B

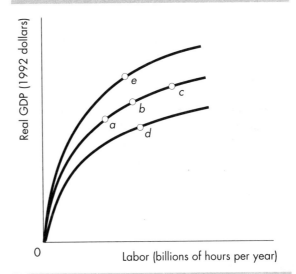

Topic: Production Function
Skill: Analytical
4) In the above figure, which of the following will cause a move from point *a* to point *b*?
   A) a decrease in leisure time.
   B) an increase in human capital.
   C) learning-by-doing.
   D) an increase in physical capital.
Answer: A

Topic: Production Function
Skill: Analytical
5) In the above figure, suppose the country of Laborious is operating at point *b*. If the country wanted to move to point *e*, it could
   A) increase the amount of physical capital used.
   B) increase the amount of human capital used.
   C) increase the level and quality of education.
   D) All of the above answers are correct.
Answer: D

---

* This is Chapter 26 in *Economics*.

Topic: Production Function
Skill: Analytical

6) In the above figure, which of the following will cause a movement from point *b* to point *c*?

   I.   an increase in human capital
   II. an increase in physical capital
   III. an increase in labor input

   A) I only.
   B) I and II.
   C) III only.
   D) I, II and III.

Answer: C

Topic: Production Function
Skill: Analytical

7) In the above figure, suppose the country of Laborious is operating at point *b*. If the country wanted to move to point *e*, it could do so by

   A) decreasing the amount of capital input.
   B) increasing labor productivity.
   C) increasing the number of hours of labor input.
   D) All of the above answers are correct.

Answer: B

Topic: Labor Productivity
Skill: Conceptual

8) Suppose a firm sells all of its typewriters and replaces them with computers and trains its workers to use them. As a result,

   A) there will be an increase in labor productivity and the production function will shift upward.
   B) the production function will shift downward.
   C) there will be a movement along the production function but there will not be a shift in the production function.
   D) there will be an increase in labor input.

Answer: A

Topic: Labor Productivity
Skill: Conceptual

9) Which of the following factors can change labor productivity? Increases in

   A) on-the-job training.
   B) physical capital.
   C) learning-by-doing.
   D) All of the above answers are correct.

Answer: D

Topic: Labor Productivity
Skill: Conceptual

10) Suppose the country of Redland wants to increase its labor productivity. Which of the following would contribute to this increase?

    A) an increase in the use of computer technology.
    B) a downward shift in Redland's production function.
    C) a movement upward along Redland's production function.
    D) an increase in the amount of labor used.

Answer: A

Topic: Labor Productivity
Skill: Conceptual

11) By using more capital in production processes,

    A) labor productivity increases.
    B) human capital increases.
    C) there is a movement downward along the production function.
    D) there is a movement upward along the production function.

Answer: A

Topic: Labor Productivity
Skill: Conceptual

12) Suppose that the country of Bluelands want to increase labor productivity. To accomplish this goal, the government can

    A) allow people to work more hours.
    B) provide training programs so that people can increase their human capital.
    C) move the nation along its production function.
    D) encourage people to take less leisure time.

Answer: B

Topic: Labor Productivity
Skill: Conceptual

13) The Council of Wise Economists advised the government of GuruLand to use more capital and provide training programs for its country's workers. As a result of the training programs, the country would experience a(n)

    A) increase in the quantity of money in the economy.
    B) increase in human capital.
    C) increase in labor productivity.
    D) Both answers B and C are correct.

Answer: D

Topic: Learning-by-doing
Skill: Conceptual

14) The first day Bab's Bicycle Factory opened, its 30 workers could produce 50 bikes per day. After 2 months of operation, the same employees could produce 300 bikes per day. This increase in output is probably due to

A) decreased leisure time.
B) increases in technology.
C) increased capital.
D) learning-by-doing.

Answer: D

Topic: Learning-by-doing
Skill: Conceptual

15) Ulysses' Umbrella Factory first opened with 20 workers making 500 umbrellas per day. After 3 months in operation, these same factory workers in the same factory were able to make 1000 umbrellas per day. This increase in output is probably due to

A) an increase in human capital.
B) an increase in physical capital.
C) an increase in real wages.
D) increases in technology.

Answer: A

■ The Labor Market and Aggregate Supply

Topic: Real Wage
Skill: Conceptual

16) Which of the following is TRUE regarding the real wage? The real wage

I. equals the 100 x (money wage)/(price level).
II. measures the quantity of goods and services an hour's work can buy.

A) Only I.
B) Only II.
C) Both I and II.
D) Neither I nor II.

Answer: C

Topic: Demand for Labor
Skill: Recognition

17) The demand for labor curve

A) shows the number of workers who demand jobs.
B) shows the quantity of labor firms plan to hire at various real wage rates.
C) slopes upward to the right.
D) has a slope equal to –1.

Answer: B

Topic: Demand for Labor
Skill: Conceptual

18) The quantity of labor demanded depends on
_____.

A) the real wage.
B) only the money wage.
C) only the price level.
D) None of the above answers are correct.

Answer: A

Topic: Demand for Labor
Skill: Conceptual

19) Which of the following is TRUE regarding the labor market?

I. The labor supply curve slopes upward because firms maximize profits as they hire more workers.
II. If the real wage falls, the quantity of labor firms demand increases.
III. The demand for labor curve slopes downward because as the real wage falls, workers demand to work fewer hours.

A) I and II.
B) I and III.
C) II only.
D) I, II and III.

Answer: C

Topic: Demand for Labor Curve
Skill: Recognition

20) If the labor demand curve shifted rightward, it may have been because

A) the marginal product of labor has increased.
B) the population has increased.
C) the natural rate of unemployment has increased.
D) labor productivity has decreased.

Answer: A

Topic: Demand for Labor Curve
Skill: Recognition
21) Which of the following will cause the labor demand curve to shift rightward?
   I.   a decrease in labor productivity
   II. an increase in technology that increases the marginal product of labor
   III. an increase in the supply of labor
   A) I and III.
   B) II only.
   C) I only.
   D) I, II and III.
Answer: B

Topic: Marginal Product of Labor
Skill: Conceptual
22) If economists in the country of Tiny Town estimate that real GDP increases by $100 when an extra hour of labor is used, the economists are calculating
   A) the *PPF*.
   B) the marginal product of labor.
   C) the real wage.
   D) the labor demand curve.
Answer: B

Topic: Marginal Product of Labor
Skill: Recognition
23) The marginal product curve is _____ which reflects _____.
   A) downward sloping; the diminishing marginal product of labor as employment increases
   B) downward sloping; increasing opportunity costs as employment decreases
   C) upward sloping; increasing opportunity costs as employment decreases
   D) upward sloping; the diminishing marginal product of labor as employment increases
Answer: A

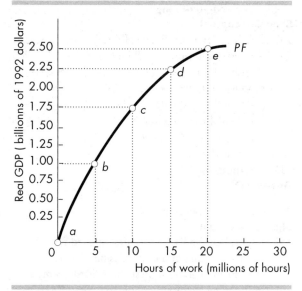

Topic: Marginal Product of Labor
Skill: Analytical
24) In the above figure, for a movement from point *a* to point *b*, the marginal product of labor equals
   A) $200.
   B) 5,000,000 hours.
   C) $1 billion.
   D) There is not enough information provided to answer the question.
Answer: A

Topic: Marginal Product of Labor
Skill: Analytical
25) In the above figure, for a movement from point *b* to point *c*, the marginal product of labor equals
   A) $75.
   B) $150.
   C) $200.
   D) 5,000,000 hours.
Answer: B

Topic: Marginal Product of Labor
Skill: Analytical
26) In the above figure, for a movement from point *c* to point *d*, the marginal product of labor equals
   A) $45.
   B) $100.
   C) $150
   D) $200.
Answer: B

Topic: Marginal Product of Labor
Skill: Analytical

27) In the above figure, for a movement from point *d* to point *e*, the marginal product of labor equals
   A) $12.50.
   B) $50.
   C) $150.
   D) $200.
Answer: B

Topic: Marginal Product of Labor
Skill: Analytical

28) In the above figure, as the economy moves from point *a* to point *e*,
   A) the demand for labor decreases.
   B) the marginal product of labor declines.
   C) there is an increase in the real wage.
   D) there is an increase in capital inputs.
Answer: B

Topic: Demand for Labor and Supply of Labor
Skill: Conceptual

29) If the money wage rate rises relative to the price level, firms _____ the quantity of labor they demand and workers _____ the quantity of labor they supply.
   A) increase; increase
   B) increase; decrease
   C) decrease; increase
   D) decrease; decrease
Answer: C

Topic: Demand for Labor and Supply of Labor
Skill: Conceptual

30) If the price level rises relative to the money wage rate, firms _____ the quantity of labor they demand and workers _____ the quantity of labor they supply.
   A) increase; increase
   B) increase; decrease
   C) decrease; increase
   D) decrease; decrease
Answer: B

Topic: Supply of Labor
Skill: Recognition

31) The supply of labor curve
   A) has a negative slope.
   B) is independent of the wage rate.
   C) shows how much labor workers are willing to supply at various real wage rates.
   D) is usually vertical.
Answer: C

Topic: Supply of Labor
Skill: Recognition

32) If the real wage increases from $15 per hour to $18 per hour, the quantity of labor supplied will increase
   A) because of the income effect.
   B) if the labor demand curve shifts rightward.
   C) because the labor supply curve shifts leftward.
   D) because the opportunity cost of not working increases.
Answer: D

Topic: Supply of Labor
Skill: Conceptual

33) People base their labor supply on the _____ because they care about _____.
   A) real wage; what their earnings will buy
   B) real wage; the equality of money wages and the price level
   C) money wage; a surplus of labor
   D) money wage; the amount of labor firms demand
Answer: A

Topic: Labor Market Equilibrium
Skill: Conceptual

34) Which of the following does the labor market determine?
   I.   the level of employment.
   II.   the real wage rate.
   III. the inflation rate.
   A) I and II.
   B) I, II and III.
   C) II only.
   D) I and III.
Answer: A

Topic: Labor Market Equilibrium
Skill: Recognition
35) If the quantity of labor supplied equals the quantity of labor demanded,
A) the income effect equals the opportunity cost effect.
B) the economy is operating on the long run aggregate supply curve.
C) the real wage equals the money wage.
D) the economy has an above the full-employment equilibrium.
Answer: B

Topic: Short-Run Aggregate Supply
Skill: Recognition
36) If the economy is at a point on its *SAS* curve such that real GDP is greater than potential GDP,
A) the real wage is less than the equilibrium real wage.
B) the economy is operating efficiently.
C) there is a shortage of labor.
D) there will be an increase in labor productivity.
Answer: A

Topic: Short-Run Aggregate Supply
Skill: Recognition
37) Suppose potential GDP equals $5 trillion and the equilibrium real wage equals $30 per hour. If the current level of real GDP equals $4 trillion,
A) the current real wage is above the full-employment equilibrium level.
B) the current real wage is below the full-employment equilibrium level.
C) there is a shortage of labor.
D) there will be an increase in labor productivity.
Answer: A

Topic: Labor Market Equilibrium
Skill: Analytical
38) In the above figure, at a wage rate of $20 per hour,
A) there is a shortage of labor.
B) there is a surplus of labor.
C) the labor supply curve will shift rightward.
D) the labor demand curve will shift rightward.
Answer: B

■ Changes in Potential GDP

Topic: An Increase in Productivity
Skill: Conceptual
39) If labor productivity increases, then
I.   the demand for labor increases
II.   the real wage rate increases
A) Only I is correct.
B) Only II correct.
C) Both I and II are correct.
D) Neither I not II is correct.
Answer: C

Topic: An Increase in Productivity
Skill: Conceptual
40) Which of the following would be a reason why both the quantity of labor employed and the real wage rate would increase?
A) Labor productivity increased.
B) The population grew in size.
C) The nation's capital stock decreased.
D) Both answers A and B are correct.
Answer: A

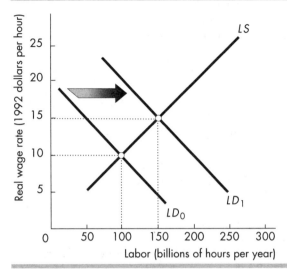

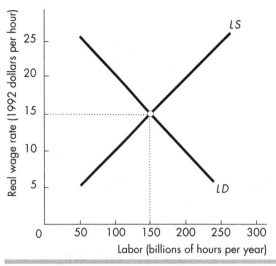

Topic: An Increase in Productivity
Skill: Analytical

41) In the above figure, which of the following might have shifted the demand curve for labor from LD_0 to LD_1?

A) Labor productivity increased.
B) The population grew.
C) The capital stock decreased.
D) Workers' human capital fell.

Answer: A

Topic: An Increase in Productivity
Skill: Analytical

42) As a result of the rightward shift in the demand curve for labor from LD_0 to LD_1, the equilibrium level of employment _____ and potential GDP _____.

A) increases; increases
B) increases; decreases
C) decreases; increases
D) decreases; decreases

Answer: A

Topic: An Increase in Productivity
Skill: Analytical

43) In the above figure, which of the following is TRUE?

A) An increase in capital would increase the wage rate.
B) As the real wage rate falls, the labor demand curve shifts rightward.
C) As the real wage rate rises, the labor supply curve shifts leftwards.
D) A minimum wage of $10 per hour will cause less labor to be hired.

Answer: A

Topic: An Increase in Population
Skill: Analytical

44) In the above figure, which of the following would be a reason why the wage rate falls to $10 per hour?

A) The nation's capital stock increased.
B) There were advances in technology.
C) The population grew.
D) The quantity of human capital increased.

Answer: C

Topic: Productivity in the United States
Skill: Conceptual

45) In the United States, over the last 15 years, labor has become ____ causing firms to ____.
A) more productive; demand more labor
B) more productive; demand less labor
C) less productive; demand more labor
D) less productive; pay higher wages to get more productive workers

Answer: A

■ Unemployment at Full Employment

Topic: Unemployment at Full Employment
Skill: Conceptual

46) Which of the following is (are) reasons why unemployment always exists?
   I.   Job search
   II.   Job rationing
A) Only I is correct.
B) Only II correct.
C) Both I and II are correct.
D) Neither I not II is correct.

Answer: C

Topic: Job Search
Skill: Recognition

47) Which of the following statements about job search is correct?
A) At the equilibrium wage rate, there is still some job search.
B) Job search is not affected by the presence of efficiency wages.
C) The extent of job search does not change because everyone needs a job.
D) Why people search for jobs is difficult to explain in the U.S.

Answer: A

Topic: Job Search
Skill: Conceptual

48) Which of the following is TRUE regarding job search?
   I.   Job search occurs only when there is equilibrium in the labor market.
   II.   Unemployment benefits affect the length of job search.
A) Only I is correct.
B) Only II correct.
C) Both I and II are correct.
D) Neither I not II is correct.

Answer: B

Topic: Job Search
Skill: Conceptual

49) Which of the following decreases job search?
A) An increase in the entry rate into the labor force.
B) An increase the number of households with two paid workers.
C) An increase in unemployment-insurance benefits.
D) None of the above decrease job search because they all increase it.

Answer: D

Topic: Job Search
Skill: Recognition

50) Suppose the amount of job search increases. This event could be a result of
A) the natural rate of unemployment being greater than the unemployment rate.
B) an increase in unemployment benefits.
C) a decrease in the real wage.
D) None of the above answers are correct.

Answer: B

Topic: Job Search
Skill: Recognition

51) Suppose the amount of job search decreases. This decrease could be a result of
A) a decrease in unemployment benefits.
B) increased structural change.
C) an increase in the natural rate of unemployment.
D) an increase in the real wage.

Answer: A

Topic: Job Search
Skill: Conceptual
52) Which of the following decreases job search?
A) An increase in unemployment benefits.
B) An decrease the number of households with two paid workers.
C) An increase in the entry rate into the labor force.
D) A wage rate that is above the equilibrium wage rate.
Answer: B

Topic: Job Rationing
Skill: Recognition
53) Which of the following can cause job rationing?
I. efficiency wages.
II. the minimum wage.
A) Only I.
B) Only II.
C) Both I and II.
D) Neither I nor II.
Answer: C

Topic: Job Rationing
Skill: Conceptual
54) Suppose the equilibrium real wage is $10 per hour. If the current real wage is $15 per hour,
A) the unemployment rate will be greater than the natural rate of unemployment.
B) the labor market is out of equilibrium.
C) job rationing is definitely not occurring.
D) Both answers A and B are correct.
Answer: D

Topic: Job Rationing
Skill: Conceptual
55) Job rationing can be created by
I. Job search
II. Efficiency wages
III. Minimum wage
A) I.
B) I and II.
C) II and III.
D) I and III.
Answer: C

Topic: Efficiency Wage
Skill: Recognition
56) An efficiency wage is a wage
A) that reduces unemployment to zero.
B) at which there are no discouraged workers.
C) that is the equilibrium wage only when the economy is producing at its potential GDP.
D) such that the quantity of labor demanded exceeds the quantity of labor supplied.
Answer: D

Topic: Efficiency Wage
Skill: Recognition
57) Efficiency wages
A) decrease productivity.
B) lead to lower real wages.
C) increase unemployment.
D) are created by job search.
Answer: C

Topic: Efficiency Wage
Skill: Recognition
58) Microsoft may pay its workers $50 per hour when the equilibrium real wage is $35 per hour. Microsoft could be paying this higher wage because
A) it believes it can attract more productive workers.
B) it believes its workers will work harder to avoid being fired.
C) it thinks the equilibrium wage is too low.
D) Both answers A and B are correct.
Answer: D

Topic: Efficiency Wage
Skill: Conceptual
59) Suppose the equilibrium real wage equals $20 per hour, but the current real wage equals $35 per hour. This difference could be a result of
A) firms' paying an efficiency wage.
B) high unemployment benefits.
C) an increase in the natural rate of unemployment.
D) an increase in labor supply.
Answer: A

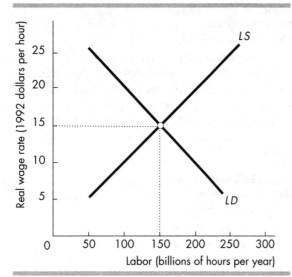

Topic: Efficiency Wage
Skill: Analytical
60) In the above figure, the wage rate paid to workers would
A) be higher than $15 per hour if firms use efficiency wages.
B) be higher than $15 per hour if the population increases.
C) fall if a minimum wage of $10 an hour is imposed.
D) depend only on how much firms are willing to pay.
Answer: A

Topic: Efficiency Wage
Skill: Conceptual
61) Which of the following is an example of an efficiency wage?
A) Paying salespeople commissions.
B) Paying some factory workers per unit of output they produce.
C) Paying a wage above the minimum wage.
D) Paying a wage higher than the equilibrium wage in order to decrease labor turnover.
Answer: D

Topic: Minimum Wage
Skill: Recognition
62) A minimum wage is set by _____ and causes an _____ of labor.
A) the government; surplus
B) unions; shortage
C) firms; surplus
D) unions; surplus
Answer: A

Topic: Minimum Wage
Skill: Conceptual
63) Suppose that the equilibrium real wage rate is $6 per hour causing 100 million hours of labor to be employed. If a $5 minimum wage is imposed,
A) less than 100 million hours will be employed.
B) more than 100 million hours will be employed.
C) firms will lower the equilibrium wage rate they pay.
D) there will be no effects on the current labor market.
Answer: D

Topic: Minimum Wage
Skill: Conceptual
64) Suppose that the equilibrium real wage rate is $6 per hour causing 100 million hours of labor to be employed. If a $7 minimum wage is imposed,
A) less than 100 million hours will be employed.
B) more than 100 million hours will be employed.
C) firms will lower the equilibrium wage rate they pay.
D) there will be no effects on the current labor market.
Answer: A

■ True Or False Questions

Topic: Production Possibilities
Skill: Recognition
65) An increase in technology will cause a movement along a *PPF*.
Answer: FALSE

Topic: Human Capital
Skill: Recognition
66) Learning-by-doing can increase human capital.
Answer: TRUE

Topic: Shift in the Production Function
Skill: Recognition

67) If the *PPF* between leisure and real GDP shifts outward because of an increase in technology, the production function shifts upward.

Answer: TRUE

Topic: Shift in the Production Function
Skill: Recognition

68) An increase in human capital will cause an upward shift of the production function.

Answer: TRUE

Topic: Real Wage
Skill: Conceptual

69) The real wage measures the quantity of goods and services an hour's work will buy.

Answer: TRUE

Topic: Demand for Labor
Skill: Recognition

70) The demand curve for labor shows how many hours workers demand to work.

Answer: FALSE

Topic: Demand for Labor
Skill: Conceptual

71) Labor demand has increased because of the increased productivity of labor.

Answer: TRUE

Topic: Marginal Product of Labor
Skill: Recognition

72) If the marginal product of labor increases, firms will demand less labor.

Answer: FALSE

Topic: Marginal Product of Labor
Skill: Recognition

73) If the marginal product of labor increases, there is a movement up along the labor demand curve.

Answer: FALSE

Topic: Labor Demand Curve
Skill: Recognition

74) The labor demand curve reflects the effect of diminishing marginal product of labor.

Answer: TRUE

Topic: Labor Productivity
Skill: Recognition

75) An increase in human capital will increase labor productivity.

Answer: TRUE

Topic: Labor Productivity
Skill: Recognition

76) Both increases in human capital and physical capital increase labor productivity.

Answer: TRUE

Topic: Labor Supply
Skill: Recognition

77) In general, a higher real wage rate decreases the quantity of labor supplied because fewer people enter the labor force.

Answer: FALSE

Topic: Full-Employment in the United States
Skill: Recognition

78) In the U.S., a combination of population growth and advances in technology have raised the real wage and the level of employment over the past 40 years.

Answer: TRUE

Topic: Job Search
Skill: Recognition

79) If job search increases, the natural rate of unemployment decreases.

Answer: FALSE

Topic: Job Search
Skill: Recognition

80) An increase in job search must increase the equilibrium real wage rate.

Answer: FALSE

Topic: Job Search
Skill: Recognition

81) Unemployment compensation and increased structural change are factors that cause job search.

Answer: TRUE

Topic: Efficiency Wage
Skill: Conceptual

82) An efficiency wage usually causes too many workers to be employed.

Answer: FALSE

Topic: Efficiency Wages
Skill: Recognition
83) Efficiency wages cause the real wage to be above the equilibrium real wage.
Answer: TRUE

■ Essay Questions

Topic: PPF and Production Function
Skill: Recognition
84) Explain the connection between the *PPF* for real GDP and leisure and the production function.

Answer:

Topic: Labor Market Equilibrium
Skill: Analytical
85) Explain the labor market using a diagram.

Answer:

Topic: Labor Market and Aggregate Supply
Skill: Conceptual
86) What is the relationship between the natural rate of unemployment, the unemployment rate, potential GDP, and actual GDP?

Answer:

Topic: Labor Market and Potential GDP
Skill: Conceptual
87) How will an increase in physical capital affect labor productivity, labor demand, and potential GDP?

Answer:

Topic: Labor Market and Potential GDP
Skill: Conceptual
88) With no change in labor productivity, what would happen to the real wage and potential GDP is population increased? What would happen if labor productivity increased?

Answer:

Topic: Job Search
Skill: Conceptual
89) What is "job search"? How does it affect unemployment?

Answer:

Topic: Job Search
Skill: Conceptual
90) Explain how unemployment insurance benefits affect job search.

Answer:

Topic: Efficiency Wage
Skill: Conceptual
91) What is an efficiency wage and how does it affect the unemployment rate?

Answer:

Topic: Efficiency Wage
Skill: Conceptual
92) Why would a firm choose to use efficiency wages? Describe 3 reasons.

Answer:

Chapter 10 CAPITAL, INVESTMENT, AND SAVING*

■ Capital and Interest

Topic: Capital Stock
Skill: Recognition
1) The total amount of plants, inventories, equipment and buildings is called

A) net investment.
B) gross investment.
C) capital stock.
D) depreciation.

Answer: C

Topic: Capital Stock
Skill: Recognition
2) Which of the following is included in an economy's capital stock?

I. inventories
II. highways
III. equipment
IV. stocks and bonds.

A) I and II.
B) III and IV.
C) I, II and III.
D) I, II, III and IV.

Answer: C

Topic: Capital Stock
Skill: Conceptual
3) Social infrastructure capital

A) includes government purchases of highways.
B) does not include schools and universities.
C) includes the government's social security expenditures.
D) affects actual GDP but not potential GDP.

Answer: A

Topic: Investment
Skill: Recognition
4) The total amount of _____ purchased is called _____.

A) new capital; net investment
B) new capital; gross investment
C) stocks and bonds; capital investment
D) stocks and bonds; gross investment

Answer: B

Topic: Investment
Skill: Conceptual
5) Which of the following would be considered gross investment?

I. Microsoft's building of a new office building.
II. IBM's issuance of new shares of stock.
III. Unsold new cars delivered to a lot at a Ford plant in Michigan.

A) I only.
B) I and II.
C) I and III.
D) I, II and III.

Answer: C

Topic: Investment
Skill: Recognition
6) _____ is gross investment minus _____.

A) The capital stock; net investment
B) The capital stock; depreciation
C) Depreciation; replacement investment
D) Net investment; depreciation

Answer: D

---

* This is Chapter 27 in *Economics*.

Topic: Investment
Skill: Conceptual

7) Which of the following is TRUE regarding net investment?

 I. Net investment equals gross investment minus depreciation.

 II. The capital stock increases by the amount of net investment.

A) I only.
B) II only.
C) Both I and II.
D) Neither I nor II.

Answer: C

Topic: Investment
Skill: Recognition

8) Investment includes

A) purchases of stocks and bonds.
B) purchases of new assembly lines.
C) additions to inventories.
D) Both answers B and C are correct.

Answer: D

Topic: Depreciation
Skill: Conceptual

9) Suppose Mail Boxes Etc. buys a new copier for its store for $1000. A year later, when the firm wants to upgrade to a new copier, it finds that the old copier is only worth $750. Over the year the copier was used, _____ has occurred.

A) replacement investment
B) gross investment
C) depreciation
D) net investment

Answer: C

Topic: Depreciation
Skill: Conceptual

10) Which of the following applies to the concept of depreciation?

 I. Depreciation includes the purchase of new capital.

 II. Equipment can depreciate but buildings cannot.

 III. Depreciation decreases the capital stock.

A) I and II.
B) II only.
C) III only.
D) I, II and III.

Answer: C

Topic: Capital Stock
Skill: Conceptual

11) Which of the following is true regarding the capital stock?

 I. The capital stock decreases during recessions.

 II. The capital stock in the U.S. has more than doubled since 1970.

 III. The capital stock grows when net investment is positive.

A) I and II.
B) II and III.
C) I and III.
D) I, II and III.

Answer: B

Topic: Investment
Skill: Conceptual

12) During recessionary periods, gross investment _____ while during expansionary periods gross investment _____.

A) increases; increases
B) increases; decreases
C) decreases; increases
D) decreases; decreases

Answer: C

Topic: Investment
Skill: Conceptual

13) Which of the following is true regarding investment's behavior over the business cycle?

 I. Net investment fluctuates over the business cycle.

 II. Gross investment fluctuates over the business cycle.

A) I only.
B) II only.
C) Both I and II.
D) Neither I nor II.

Answer: C

Topic: Investment Around the World
Skill: Conceptual

14) Compared to other countries, investment in the U.S. since 1970

A) has exceeded the percentage of GDP invested in developing countries.

B) has ranged between 15 and 20 percent of GDP, less than the percentage in many other countries.

C) is about the same as in other industrial countries.

D) None of the above answers is correct.

Answer: B

Topic: Investment Around the World
Skill: Conceptual

15) Since 1970, investment as a percentage of GDP in developing countries generally

A) has remained relatively steady.

B) has exceeded investment in industrial countries.

C) lags investment growth in the U.S.

D) has decreased sharply.

Answer: B

Topic: Nominal Interest Rate
Skill: Recognition

16) The nominal interest rate is defined as

A) the market interest rate minus the inflation rate.

B) the home mortgage loan rate.

C) the interest rate banks charge to their best customers.

D) the interest rate expressed in terms of money.

Answer: D

Topic: Real Interest Rate
Skill: Recognition

17) Which of the following approximately equals the real interest rate?

A) The nominal interest rate minus the inflation rate.

B) The nominal interest rate plus the inflation rate.

C) The nominal interest rate minus the growth rate of GDP.

D) The rate paid when the best customers of banks borrow money.

Answer: A

Topic: Real Interest Rate
Skill: Recognition

18) The nominal interest rate minus the real interest rate equals the

A) rate of increase in the amount of investment.

B) inflation rate.

C) the rate of increase in the income.

D) the rate the bank receives to cover lending costs.

Answer: B

Topic: Real Interest Rate
Skill: Recognition

19) The nominal interest rate approximately equals which of the following?

A) The real interest rate minus the inflation rate.

B) The real interest rate plus the inflation rate.

C) The real interest rate minus the growth rate of real GDP.

D) The real interest rate plus the growth rate of real GDP.

Answer: B

Topic: Real Interest Rate
Skill: Analytical

20) If the nominal interest rate is 7 percent and the inflation rate is 1 percent, the real interest rate is approximately

A) 7 percent.

B) 6 percent.

C) 8 percent.

D) –6 percent.

Answer: B

Topic: Real Interest Rate
Skill: Analytical

21) If the nominal interest rate is 8 percent and the inflation rate is 2 percent, the real interest rate is approximately

A) 4 percent.

B) 6 percent.

C) 0.25 percent.

D) 10 percent.

Answer: B

Topic: Real Interest Rate
Skill: Recognition
22) In the 1990s, the real interest rate generally has
     been between _____ percent.
   A)   7 to 9
   B)   10 to 12
   C)   4 to 6
   D)   −1 to 2
Answer: C

Topic: Real Interest Rate
Skill: Conceptual
23) Since 1970, the real interest rate
   A)   has never been greater than zero.
   B)   has risen steadily.
   C)   has risen at the same rate as inflation.
   D)   has averaged about 4 percent.
Answer: D

■ Investment Decisions

Topic: Expected Profit Rate
Skill: Conceptual
24) Which of the following are major influences on
     expected profit rates?
   I.   Technology advances.
   II.   Stock market behavior.
   III.   Accounting practices.
   A)   I only.
   B)   I and II.
   C)   I and III.
   D)   II and III.
Answer: A

Topic: Expected Profit Rate
Skill: Conceptual
25) Which of the following is true regarding expected
     profit rates?
   I.   Profit rates are highest immediately upon new
          technology becoming available.
   II.   Firms are interested mainly in pre-tax profits.
   III.   Profit rates increase during expansions.
   A)   I only.
   B)   I and III.
   C)   III only.
   D)   I, II and III.
Answer: C

Price of the computer (dollars)	Net revenue from the computer (dollars)
$5,000	$6,000

Topic: Expected Profit Rate
Skill: Analytical
26) In the above table you are given information on
     your firm's decision to buy a new computer. The
     computer will last for one year and after that will
     be thrown away. What is the expected profit rate?
   A)   17 percent.
   B)   20 percent.
   C)   83 percent.
   D)   5 percent.
Answer: B

Topic: Investment Decisions
Skill: Analytical
27) In the above table you are given information on
     your firm's decision to buy a new computer. The
     computer will last for one year and after that will
     be thrown away. For your firm to make the in-
     vestment,
   A)   the expected profit rate should be higher.
   B)   the real interest rate must be greater than 17
        percent.
   C)   the nominal interest rate must be less than 20
        percent.
   D)   the real interest rate must be less than 20 per-
        cent.
Answer: D

Price of the harvester (dollars)	Net revenue from the harvester (dollars)
$25,000	$35,000

Topic: Expected Profit Rate
Skill: Analytical
28) In the above table you are given information on
     your firm's decision to buy a harvester. The har-
     vester will last for one year and after that will be
     scrapped. What is the expected profit rate?
   A)   14 percent.
   B)   29 percent.
   C)   40 percent.
   D)   72 percent.
Answer: C

Topic: Investment Decisions
Skill: Analytical

29) In the above table you are given information on your firm's decision to buy a harvester. The harvester will last for one year and after that will be scrapped. For your firm to buy the harvester,

A) the expected profit rate should be higher.

B) the nominal interest rate must be less than 40 percent.

C) the real interest rate must be greater than 29 percent.

D) the real interest rate must be less than 40 percent.

Answer: D

Topic: The Real Interest Rate and Investment
Skill: Conceptual

30) The opportunity cost for investment

A) is the real interest rate.

B) is the nominal interest rate if the investment is funded from retained earnings.

C) is zero if the investment is funded from retained earnings.

D) is the saving rate.

Answer: A

Topic: The Real Interest Rate and Investment
Skill: Conceptual

31) The real interest rate is the opportunity cost of making an investment using borrowed funds. The real interest rate is the opportunity cost of making an investment using the owners' financial resources, such as the firm's retained earnings.

A) Both sentences are correct.

B) The first sentence is correct; the second sentence is incorrect.

C) The first sentence is incorrect; the second sentence is correct.

D) Both sentences are incorrect.

Answer: A

Topic: The Real Interest Rate and Investment
Skill: Conceptual

32) As the ____ interest rate increases, the quantity of investment demanded ____.

A) real; increases

B) real; decreases

C) nominal; increases

D) nominal; decreases

Answer: B

Topic: The Real Interest Rate and Investment
Skill: Conceptual

33) Which of the following explains why investment demand is negatively related to the real interest rate?

A) A lower real interest rate makes more investment projects profitable and hence undertaken.

B) Consumers are willing to spend less and hence save more at higher real interest rates.

C) Interest rate flexibility in financial markets assures an equilibrium in which saving equals investment.

D) All of the above are correct reasons why investment demand is negatively related to the real interest rate.

Answer: A

Topic: Investment Decisions
Skill: Conceptual

34) When Sew One On decides whether to invest in a new embroidery machine, it needs to

A) make sure the opportunity cost of the investment is greater than the expected profit rate.

B) compare the expected profit rate to the real interest rate.

C) compare the nominal interest rate to the expected profit rate.

D) only consider its expected sales for the next year.

Answer: B

Topic: Investment Decisions
Skill: Conceptual

35) Business firms will fund investment projects

A) as long as the expected profit rate from the investment is greater than the real interest rate.

B) so long as the firm has investment projects with a positive expected profit rate.

C) if the firm's management is optimistic about the state of the economy.

D) until the firm runs out of profits.

Answer: A

Topic: Investment Decisions
Skill: Conceptual

36) If the expected profit rate from an investment is 17 percent, it is profitable for a firm to invest if
A) the nominal interest rate is greater than 17 percent.
B) the real interest rate is greater than 17 percent.
C) the real interest rate is less than 17 percent.
D) the after-tax profit rate is greater than 17 percent.

Answer: C

Topic: Investment Decisions
Skill: Conceptual

37) If the real interest rate is 6.5 percent,
A) a firm will invest in projects that have expected profit rates no more than 6.5 percent.
B) the opportunity cost of investment is less than 6.5 percent.
C) investment projects with expected profit rates over 6.5 percent will be undertaken.
D) a firm will probably choose to use retained earnings to finance investment.

Answer: C

Topic: Investment Demand
Skill: Recognition

38) The _____ the expected profit rate from new capital, the greater is the _____.
A) lower; investment demand
B) greater; investment demand
C) lower; capital stock
D) None of the above answers is correct

Answer: B

Topic: Investment Demand Curve
Skill: Conceptual

39) The quantity of investment demanded increases so there is a movement downward along the investment demand curve when
A) the expected profit rate on investment decreases.
B) business expectations become more optimistic.
C) the real interest rate falls.
D) the pool of available savings falls.

Answer: C

Topic: Investment Demand Curve
Skill: Conceptual

40) The investment demand curve shifts rightward if
A) the expected profit rate increases.
B) the real interest rate falls.
C) savers increase their thriftiness.
D) the economy moves into a recession.

Answer: A

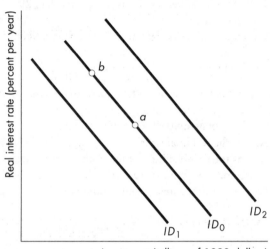

Topic: Investment Demand Curve
Skill: Analytical

41) In the above figure, the economy is at point *a* on the initial investment demand curve ID_0. What happens if the real interest rate rises?
A) There is a movement to a point such as *b* on investment demand curve ID_0.
B) The investment demand curve shifts rightward to a curve such as ID_2.
C) The investment demand curve shifts leftward to a curve such as ID_1.
D) None of the above.

Answer: A

Topic: Investment Demand Curve
Skill: Analytical
42) In the above figure, the economy is at point a on the initial investment demand curve ID_0. What happens if technology advances and increases the expected profit rate?
A) There is a movement to a point such as b on investment demand curve ID_0.
B) The investment demand curve shifts rightward to a curve such as ID_2.
C) The investment demand curve shifts leftward to a curve such as ID_1.
D) None of the above.
Answer: B

Topic: Investment Demand Curve
Skill: Analytical
43) In the above figure, the economy is at point a on the initial investment demand curve ID_0. What happens if the expected profit rate decreases?
A) There is a movement to a point such as b on investment demand curve ID_0.
B) The investment demand curve shifts rightward to a curve such as ID_2.
C) The investment demand curve shifts leftward to a curve such as ID_1.
D) None of the above.
Answer: C

Topic: Investment Demand Curve
Skill: Analytical
44) In the above figure, the economy is at point a on the initial investment demand curve ID_0. What happens during an expansion?
A) There is a movement to a point such as b on investment demand curve ID_0.
B) The investment demand curve shifts rightward to a curve such as ID_2.
C) The investment demand curve shifts leftward to a curve such as ID_1.
D) None of the above.
Answer: B

■ Saving Decisions

Topic: Saving Decisions
Skill: Recognition
45) Investment in the U.S. is financed by
A) only government saving.
B) only private saving.
C) only borrowing from the rest of the world.
D) government saving, private saving, and borrowing from the rest of the world.
Answer: D

Topic: National Saving
Skill: Conceptual
46) Which of the following is true regarding national saving?
  I.   National saving is also called government saving.
  II. The real interest rate influences national saving.
  III. National saving equals national investment.
A) I and II.
B) I and III.
C) II and III.
D) II only.
Answer: D

Topic: Household Saving
Skill: Recognition
47) Household saving is
A) what remains of personal disposable income after personal consumption expenditures.
B) the value of stocks and bonds.
C) the difference between exports and imports.
D) personal income minus taxes.
Answer: A

Topic: The Real Interest Rate and Saving
Skill: Conceptual
48) The amount of ____ by households will be less ____.
A) saving; the higher is disposable income
B) saving; the lower is the real interest rate
C) consumption; the lower is the inflation rate
D) consumption; the higher is disposable income
Answer: B

Topic: The Real Interest Rate and Saving
Skill: Conceptual
49) If the real interest rate rises, we would expect
A) you to save more.
B) you to save less.
C) you to earn a higher income.
D) you to decrease your expected future income.
Answer: A

Topic: Disposable Income and Saving
Skill: Conceptual
50) Which of the following have a positive relationship with household saving?
I. the real interest rate
II. disposable income
III. expected future income
A) I and II.
B) II only.
C) II and III.
D) I, II and III.
Answer: A

Topic: Disposable Income and Saving
Skill: Conceptual
51) Which of the following is correct?
A) As disposable income increases, the real interest rate increases.
B) As disposable income decreases, saving decreases.
C) As saving decreases, disposable income decreases.
D) As saving increases, investment by households decreases.
Answer: B

Topic: Net Assets and Saving
Skill: Recognition
52) A household's net assets are its _____ and the real value of these net assets represents _____.
A) disposable income plus assets; the purchasing power of the net assets
B) assets minus debts; the purchasing power of the net assets
C) purchasing power; assets plus debts
D) purchasing power; income minus debts
Answer: B

Topic: Net Assets and Saving
Skill: Conceptual
53) The greater a household's _____ the less is its saving.
A) return from saving
B) purchasing power of net assets
C) disposable income
D) expected future profits
Answer: B

Topic: Expected Future Income and Saving
Skill: Conceptual
54) Which of the following is true regarding expected future income's effect on saving?
I. As expected future income increases, saving increases.
II. Young people typically save very little.
III. Middle aged people, earning higher incomes, are not very big savers.
A) I and III.
B) II only.
C) III only.
D) II and III.
Answer: B

Topic: Saving Supply Curve
Skill: Conceptual
55) Which of the following is true regarding saving supply?
I. As the real interest rate increases, people increase the quantity they save.
II. The saving supply curve is downward sloping.
III. As disposable income increases, the saving supply curve becomes steeper.
A) I and III.
B) II and III.
C) I only.
D) III only.
Answer: C

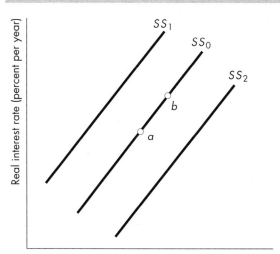

Real interest rate (percent per year)

SS_1

SS_0

SS_2

b

a

Saving (trillions of 1992 dollars)

Topic: Saving Supply Curve
Skill: Analytical
56) In the above figure, the economy is at point *a* on the initial saving supply curve SS_0. What happens if the interest rate rises?
A) There is a movement to a point such as *b* on saving supply curve SS_0.
B) The saving supply curve shifts rightward to a curve such as SS_2.
C) The saving supply curve shifts leftward to a curve such as SS_1.
D) None of the above.
Answer: A

Topic: Saving Supply Curve
Skill: Analytical
57) In the above figure, the economy is at point *a* on the initial saving supply curve SS_0. What happens if disposable incomes increase?
A) There is a movement to a point such as *b* on saving supply curve SS_0.
B) The saving supply curve shifts rightward to a curve such as SS_2.
C) The saving supply curve shifts leftward to a curve such as SS_1.
D) None of the above.
Answer: B

Topic: Saving Supply Curve
Skill: Analytical
58) In the above figure, the economy is at point *a* on the initial saving supply curve SS_0. What happens if households expect future incomes to decrease?
A) There is a movement to a point such as *b* on saving supply curve SS_0.
B) The saving supply curve shifts rightward to a curve such as SS_2.
C) The saving supply curve shifts leftward to a curve such as SS_1.
D) None of the above.
Answer: B

Topic: Saving Supply Curve
Skill: Analytical
59) In the above figure, the economy is at point *a* on the initial saving supply curve SS_0. What happens if households' real net assets increase?
A) There is a movement to a point such as *b* on saving supply curve SS_0.
B) The saving supply curve shifts rightward to a curve such as SS_2.
C) The saving supply curve shifts leftward to a curve such as SS_1.
D) None of the above.
Answer: C

Topic: Saving Supply Curve
Skill: Analytical
60) In the above figure, the economy is at point *a* on the initial saving supply curve SS_0. What happens if consumers become more interested in saving?
A) There is a movement to a point such as *b* on saving supply curve SS_0.
B) The saving supply curve shifts rightward to a curve such as SS_2.
C) The saving supply curve shifts leftward to a curve such as SS_1.
D) None of the above.
Answer: B

Topic: Saving Supply in the United States
Skill: Conceptual
61) In the U.S. there have been
  A) movements along the U.S. saving supply curve.
  B) shifts of the U.S. saving supply curve.
  C) very little response of saving to changes in disposable income.
  D) Both answers A and B are correct.
Answer: D

■ Equilibrium in the World Economy

Topic: Equilibrium in the World Economy
Skill: Recognition
62) To study how interest rates are determined in a country, we examine
  A) saving and investment in that country.
  B) world saving and investment.
  C) all industries, businesses and households' borrowing and lending decisions in that nation.
  D) the behavior of past interest rates.
Answer: B

Topic: Equilibrium in the World Economy
Skill: Conceptual
63) The fact that interest rates are different across countries is because
  A) capital markets are unique to each country.
  B) households in some countries have higher saving rates.
  C) there are higher risks in some countries.
  D) firms in some countries invest in more projects.
Answer: C

Topic: Equilibrium in the World Economy
Skill: Conceptual
64) Which of the following is true regarding capital markets around the world?
  I.   There is a capital market for developing countries and another for industrial countries.
  II.   Global saving and global investment decisions determine the world real interest rate.
  III. Riskiness causes interest rates to vary across countries.
  A) I and II.
  B) II and III.
  C) I and III.
  D) I, II and III.
Answer: B

Topic: Determining the Real Interest Rate
Skill: Conceptual
65) When the actual real interest rate exceeds the equilibrium real interest rate
  A) saving exceeds investment.
  B) borrowers find it easy to locate investment funds.
  C) lenders are unable to lend all the funds they have.
  D) All of the above answers are correct.
Answer: D

Topic: Determining the Real Interest Rate
Skill: Analytical
66) When the actual real interest rate is less than the equilibrium real interest rate
  A) the equilibrium real interest rate will rise.
  B) borrowers find it difficult to borrow.
  C) there are not enough funds for the quantity of investment demanded.
  D) Both answers B and C are correct.
Answer: D

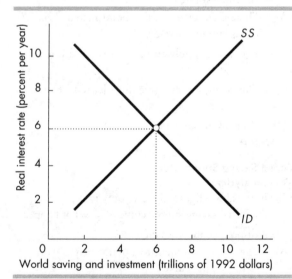

Topic: Determining the Real Interest Rate
Skill: Analytical
67) In the above figure, if the real interest rate was 8, there would be
  A) underproduction in this economy.
  B) a surplus of saving.
  C) a shortage of saving.
  D) a shortage in available funds for investment.
Answer: B

Topic: Determining the Real Interest Rate
Skill: Analytical
68) In the above figure, an 8 percent real interest rate results in
A) an increase in the equilibrium interest rate.
B) a rightward shift in the *ID* curve.
C) a leftward shift in the *SS* curve.
D) a surplus of saving.
Answer: D

Topic: Determining the Real Interest Rate
Skill: Analytical
69) In the above figure, a 4 percent interest rate results in
A) a surplus of saving.
B) equilibrium.
C) borrowers bidding up interest rates.
D) too little investment demand.
Answer: C

Topic: Changes in the Real Interest Rate
Skill: Analytical
70) In the above figure, the expected profit rate increases, the real interest rate ____ and the equilibrium quantity of investment ____.
A) rises; increases
B) rises; decreases
C) falls; increases
D) falls; decreases
Answer: A

Topic: Changes in the Real Interest Rate
Skill: Analytical
71) In the above figure, if disposable incomes increase, the real interest rate ____ and the equilibrium quantity of investment ____.
A) rises; increases
B) rises; decreases
C) falls; increases
D) falls; decreases
Answer: C

Topic: Changes in the Real Interest Rate
Skill: Analytical
72) In the above figure, if the expected profit rate decreases, the real interest rate ____ and the equilibrium quantity of investment ____.
A) rises; increases
B) rises; decreases
C) falls; increases
D) falls; decreases
Answer: D

Topic: Changes in the Real Interest Rate
Skill: Analytical
73) In the above figure, if people's expected future incomes increase, the real interest rate ____ and the equilibrium quantity of investment ____.
A) rises; increases
B) rises; decreases
C) falls; increases
D) falls; decreases
Answer: B

Topic: Changes in the Real Interest Rate
Skill: Analytical
74) In the above figure, if people's disposable incomes decrease, the real interest rate ____ and the equilibrium quantity of investment ____.
A) rises; increases
B) rises; decreases
C) falls; increases
D) falls; decreases
Answer: B

Topic: Explaining Changes in the Real Interest Rate
Skill: Conceptual
75) Since 1975, the world economy has experienced
A) a smaller increase in saving compared to increases in investment demand.
B) an increase in the real interest rate.
C) an increase in the quantity of investment.
D) All of the above answers are correct.
Answer: D

■ The Role of Government

Topic: Government Budgets
Skill: Recognition
76) In the equation, $I = S + (T - G)$, the term ____ identifies government saving (or dissaving).
A) I
B) S
C) $T - G$
D) T
Answer: C

Topic: Government Budgets
Skill: Recognition

77) When economists refer to government saving or dissaving, they are referring to

A)   government bonds.
B)   government surpluses or deficits.
C)   government transfer payments.
D)   taxes collected by the government.

Answer: B

Topic: Government Budgets
Skill: Conceptual

78) When the government's net taxes exceed its purchases,

A)   the government runs a surplus.
B)   it has positive saving.
C)   it helps increase the real interest rate.
D)   Both answers A and B are correct.

Answer: D

Topic: Government Budgets
Skill: Conceptual

79) When the government runs a budget deficit,

A)   its purchases are less than its net taxes.
B)   it is required to invest by redeeming bonds.
C)   its deficit increases private saving.
D)   its has negative saving.

Answer: D

Topic: Barro-Ricardo Effect
Skill: Conceptual

80) The Barro-Ricardo effect proposes that

A)   government budget deficits do not affect real interest rates.
B)   government budget deficits negatively affect world interest rates.
C)   government budget deficits positively affect world investment.
D)   Both answers B and C are correct.

Answer: A

Topic: Barro-Ricardo Effect
Skill: Conceptual

81) The Barro-Ricardo effect proposes that

A)   people expect government dissaving to increase their incomes.
B)   interest rates will probably increase because of government deficits.
C)   people expect lower disposable incomes in the future if the government runs a deficit.
D)   tax payers do not have the ability to neutralize the effects of government deficits.

Answer: C

■ Saving and Investment in the National Economy

Topic: Saving and Investment in the National Economy
Skill: Conceptual

82) Which of the following is true regarding saving and investment?

A)   Saving supply and investment demand in the world economy determine the world real interest rate.
B)   Saving equals investment in a national economy.
C)   In a nation, investment is financed by national saving plus borrowing from the rest of the world.
D)   Both answers A and C are correct.

Answer: D

Topic: International Saving and Borrowing
Skill: Conceptual

83) Which of the following is true regarding saving and investment?

A)   For the world as a whole, international borrowing equals international lending.
B)   If a nation's saving is less than its investment, the nation has negative net exports.
C)   A nation's funds for investment come from national saving plus borrowing from the world.
D)   All of the above answers are true.

Answer: D

Topic: International Saving and Borrowing
Skill: Conceptual

84) If a nation's saving is greater than its investment
   A) it runs a net exports deficit.
   B) there is not equilibrium between saving and investment in the world.
   C) it lends to the rest of the world.
   D) it faces a lower real interest rate than the equilibrium real interest rate in the world.

Answer: C

Topic: International Saving and Borrowing
Skill: Conceptual

85) The world real interest rate is 7 percent. Initially a country is cut off from the world financial market and its initial real interest rate is 9 percent. After the country joins the world financial market,
   A) the nation will lend to the world.
   B) the nation will run a net exports surplus.
   C) the nation's investment exceeds it saving, and it borrows from the rest of the world.
   D) the nation's investment equals its saving.

Answer: C

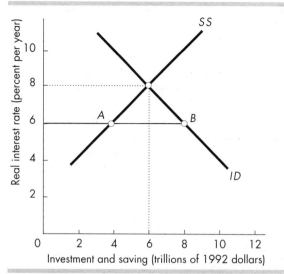

Topic: International Saving and Borrowing
Skill: Analytical

86) The above figure shows the investment demand and saving supply in a nation. The world real interest rate equals 6 percent. The distance *AB* represents the nation's
   A) international borrowing.
   B) international lending.
   C) government dissaving.
   D) difference between its real interest rate and the world real interest rate.

Answer: A

Topic: International Saving and Borrowing
Skill: Analytical

87) The above figure shows the investment demand and saving supply in a nation. The world real interest rate equals 6 percent.
   A) The country will have positive net exports.
   B) The government must have a budget deficit.
   C) The government will lend in the world market.
   D) The country will have negative net exports.

Answer: D

Topic: Government Saving and International Borrowing
Skill: Conceptual
88) Suppose that Antigua, a small country, currently borrows money in the international market. If the government deficit in Antigua increases,
A) national saving in Antigua increases.
B) Antigua's international borrowing increases.
C) the world real interest rate will increase.
D) saving and investment in Antigua will be unaffected.
Answer: B

■ True Or False Questions

Topic: Capital Stock
Skill: Conceptual
89) Social infrastructure capital includes the justice system and highways.
Answer: TRUE

Topic: Capital Stock
Skill: Conceptual
90) The capital stock is greater than gross investment in any one year.
Answer: TRUE

Topic: Capital Stock
Skill: Conceptual
91) Over the last 30 years, the growth rate of the capital stock has always been positive.
Answer: TRUE

Topic: Investment Decisions
Skill: Conceptual
92) The expected profit rate and the real interest rate affect investment decisions.
Answer: TRUE

Topic: The Real interest Rate and Investment
Skill: Conceptual
93) There is a positive relationship between investment demand and the real interest rate.
Answer: FALSE

Topic: The Real Interest Rate and Saving
Skill: Conceptual
94) The real interest rate has positive relationship to saving supply.
Answer: TRUE

Topic: Disposable Income and Saving
Skill: Conceptual
95) If Ann's disposable income increases, we would expect her saving to decrease.
Answer: FALSE

Topic: Net Assets and Saving
Skill: Conceptual
96) As the purchasing power of net assets increases, saving decreases.
Answer: TRUE

Topic: Saving Supply Curve
Skill: Conceptual
97) The saving supply curve shifts leftward if the real interest rate rises.
Answer: FALSE

Topic: Equilibrium in the World Economy
Skill: Conceptual
98) The real interest rate is determined in the world capital market.
Answer: TRUE

Topic: Crowding-Out Effect
Skill: Conceptual
99) The crowding-out effect asserts that government deficits increase the interest rate.
Answer: TRUE

Topic: Barro-Ricardo Effect
Skill: Conceptual
100) The Barro-Ricardo effect claims that government deficits increase interest rates.
Answer: FALSE

■ Essay Questions

Topic: Capital Stock and Investment
Skill: Conceptual
101) Explain the difference between the capital stock, net investment and gross investment.
Answer:

Topic: Real Interest Rate
Skill: Conceptual
102) What is the difference between the real interest rate and the nominal interest rate?
Answer:

Topic: Expected Profit Rate
Skill: Conceptual
103) What is an expected profit rate and how does it affect investment decisions?
Answer:

Topic: Expected Future Income and Saving
Skill: Conceptual
104) How does expected future income affect saving supply?
Answer:

Topic: Determining the World Real Interest Rate
Skill: Conceptual
105) What is the relationship between the real interest rate, saving supply and investment demand?
Answer:

Topic: Determining the World Real Interest Rate
Skill: Analytical
106) Explain the world capital market using a diagram.
Answer:

Topic: Government Budgets
Skill: Conceptual
107) What effect does a government budget deficit have on national saving?
Answer:

Topic: Crowding-Out Effect
Skill: Analytical
108) Explain the crowding-out effect using a diagram.
Answer:

Topic: Barro-Ricardo Effect
Skill: Analytical
109) Explain the Barro-Ricardo effect using a diagram.
Answer:

Topic: International Saving and Borrowing
Skill: Conceptual
110) Explain what would occur if the world interest rate was below the equilibrium real interest rate in the U.S.
Answer:

Chapter 11 ECONOMIC GROWTH*

■ Long-Term Growth Trends

Topic: Long-Term Growth Trends
Skill: Recognition
1) Economic growth is usually defined as
   A) the rate of increase in output divided by the increase in capital.
   B) the increase in real GDP per person.
   C) the increase in input availability.
   D) the decrease in the real cost of necessities.
Answer: B

Topic: Long-Term Growth Trends
Skill: Conceptual
2) The defining feature of economic growth is
   A) growth of potential GDP per person.
   B) business cycles.
   C) the more rapid growth of population than of output.
   D) rising prices.
Answer: A

Topic: Long-Term Growth Trends
Skill: Conceptual
3) If a nation's population grows, then,
   A) growth in real GDP per person will be less than the growth of real GDP.
   B) there can be no economic growth.
   C) growth in real GDP per person will be greater than the growth of real GDP.
   D) there must be an increase in real GDP per person.
Answer: A

Topic: Growth In the U.S. Economy
Skill: Recognition
4) The historical record for the United States for the past 100 years shows
   A) mostly positive economic growth, with two periods of substantial negative economic growth.
   B) economic growth for about half the years and economic decline for the other half.
   C) growth until 1970 and then a period of constant per person real GDP.
   D) continuous economic growth, although at different rates, throughout the entire century.
Answer: A

Topic: Growth In the U.S. Economy
Skill: Recognition
5) Which of the following statements are correct?
   I. The average economic growth rate in real GDP per person in the U.S. over the last century was 5 percent per year.
   II. The U.S. has the highest economic growth rate of any industrialized nation.
   A) I only.
   B) II only.
   C) Both I and II.
   D) Neither I nor II.
Answer: D

Topic: Growth In the U.S. Economy
Skill: Recognition
6) The average long-run growth rate in real GDP per person in the U.S. economy has been equal to approximately
   A) 2.0 percent.
   B) 3.5 percent.
   C) 5.0 percent.
   D) 7.5 percent.
Answer: A

---

* This is Chapter 28 in *Economics*.

Topic: Real GDP Growth in the World Economy
Skill: Conceptual

7) If a rich country grows at a faster rate than a poor one, then

A) the gap in their standard of living will widen over time.

B) the gap in their standard of living will close over time.

C) the difference in their living standards will not change over time.

D) whether or not the living standards gap widens or closes over time depends on the absolute size of the relative growth rates.

Answer: A

Topic: Real GDP Growth in the World Economy
Skill: Recognition

8) In 1998, _____ had the highest real GDP per person.

A) Japan.

B) Canada.

C) Germany.

D) the U.S.

Answer: D

Topic: Real GDP Growth in the World Economy
Skill: Recognition

9) Between which pair (of countries or continents) has real GDP per person converged over the past 30 years?

A) Canada and Japan.

B) U.S. and Africa.

C) U.S. and South America.

D) Canada and South America.

Answer: A

■ The Causes of Economic Growth: A First Look

Topic: Preconditions for Economic Growth
Skill: Recognition

10) A political system can foster economic growth if it provides an incentive system that includes

A) property rights.

B) markets.

C) monetary exchange.

D) All of the above answers are correct.

Answer: D

Topic: Preconditions for Economic Growth,
Markets
Skill: Conceptual

11) Which of the following explain how markets promote economic growth?

A) Markets ensure that producers make a profit.

B) Markets allow prices to send signals to buyers and sellers.

C) Markets allow people to specialize and trade.

D) Both answers B and C are correct.

Answer: D

Topic: Preconditions for Economic Growth,
Markets
Skill: Conceptual

12) Markets allow economic growth to occur by promoting

A) specialization.

B) enforcement of property rights.

C) exchange of goods and services.

D) Both answers A and C are correct.

Answer: D

Topic: Preconditions for Economic Growth
Skill: Recognition

13) Components of an incentive system include which of the following?

A) property rights.

B) guaranteed profits.

C) democratic government.

D) All of the above answers are correct.

Answer: A

Topic: Preconditions for Economic Growth,
Property Rights
Skill: Conceptual

14) The more certain private property rights are

A) the less people need to invest in education or human capital development.

B) the less entrepreneurship there will be.

C) the more investment in new capital there will be.

D) the more an economy must grow to maintain a certain living standard.

Answer: C

Topic: Preconditions for Economic Growth, Monetary Exchange
Skill: Conceptual
15) Which of the following is the best way to facilitate trade?
A) barter.
B) monetary exchange.
C) government-directed markets.
D) None of the above.
Answer: B

Topic: Preconditions for Economic Growth, Monetary Exchange
Skill: Conceptual
16) ____ help(s) to facilitate market transactions, specialization and trade.
A) Government-directed policies
B) Barter
C) Rapid economic growth
D) Monetary exchange
Answer: D

Topic: Persistent Economic Growth
Skill: Conceptual
17) Which of the following make economic growth certain?
A) incentive systems.
B) democracies.
C) markets.
D) None of the above because no factor can guarantee economic growth.
Answer: D

Topic: Persistent Economic Growth
Skill: Recognition
18) The most important sources of economic growth include all of the following EXCEPT
A) growth in government assistance to industry.
B) growth in labor productivity.
C) investment in human capital.
D) technological change.
Answer: A

Topic: Persistent Economic Growth
Skill: Recognition
19) Which of the following is NOT an important factor affecting economic growth?
A) The rate of saving.
B) The rate of fall in the price level.
C) The rate of growth of capital.
D) The rate of growth in labor productivity.
Answer: B

Topic: Persistent Economic Growth
Skill: Recognition
20) Which of the following contributes to economic growth?
A) Increases in labor productivity.
B) Capital accumulation.
C) Technological improvements.
D) All of the above contribute to economic growth.
Answer: D

Topic: Saving and Investment in New Capital
Skill: Recognition
21) An important factor in determining a country's rate of economic growth is
A) the diversity of its population.
B) its rate of saving and investment.
C) its climate.
D) its location.
Answer: B

Topic: Saving and Investment in New Capital
Skill: Recognition
22) An increase in saving that leads to more capital accumulation ____ labor productivity.
A) increases
B) does not change
C) decreases
D) probably changes but in an ambiguous direction
Answer: A

Topic: Saving and Investment in New Capital
Skill: Conceptual
23) A higher savings rate that leads to an increase in the capital stock
A) leads to higher interest rates.
B) leads to increases in labor productivity.
C) causes investment to immediately decrease.
D) is associated with a decrease in the rate of growth of the population.
Answer: B

Topic: Saving and Investment in New Capital
Skill: Conceptual
24) Labor productivity increases with
A) increases in consumption expenditure.
B) increases in depreciation.
C) increases in capital per worker.
D) All of the above answers are correct.
Answer: C

Topic: Saving and Investment in New Capital
Skill: Conceptual
25) A factory directly represents
A) learning-by-doing.
B) investment in human capital.
C) investment in physical capital.
D) technological change.
Answer: C

Topic: Investment in Human Capital
Skill: Recognition
26) Human capital is
A) the saving done by human beings.
B) people's knowledge and skills.
C) a measure of the labor productivity of workers.
D) the investment people make in industries that make capital goods.
Answer: B

Topic: Investment in Human Capital
Skill: Conceptual
27) Which of the following are examples of advances in human capital?
   I. The development of written records.
   II. The formulation of scientific knowledge.
   III. Experience gained from job specialization.
A) I and II.
B) I and III.
C) II and III.
D) I, II and III.
Answer: D

Topic: Investment in Human Capital
Skill: Conceptual
28) On-the-job-training is an example of
A) increasing labor force participation.
B) investment in human capital.
C) investment in physical capital.
D) technological change.
Answer: B

Topic: Discovery of New Technologies
Skill: Conceptual
29) In addition to saving and investment in capital, making an even larger contribution to long-term economic growth in real GDP per person is (are)
A) technological advances.
B) lower current consumption.
C) higher current consumption.
D) a larger work force.
Answer: A

Topic: Discovery of New Technologies
Skill: Conceptual
30) Most _____ is embodied in physical capital.
A) human capital
B) technological change
C) labor productivity
D) economic growth
Answer: B

Growth Accounting

Topic: Growth Accounting
Skill: Recognition
31) _____ provides a way for economists to calculate the impact of different determinants of economic growth.
A) Nominal GDP
B) Labor productivity
C) Growth accounting
D) Growth theory
Answer: A

Topic: Aggregate Production Function
Skill: Recognition
32) If Y = real GDP, and N, K and T represent the quantities of labor, capital and technology respectively, then the most appropriate representation of the aggregate production function is
A) $Y + N - K + T$.
B) $Y - N + K + T$.
C) $Y = N, K, T$.
D) $Y = F(N, K, T)$.
Answer: D

Topic: Aggregate Production Function
Skill: Recognition
33) If Y = real GDP and N, K and T represent the quantities of labor, capital and technology respectively, then the expression $Y = F(N, K, T)$ represents
A) the consumption function.
B) the demand function.
C) the aggregate production function.
D) the aggregate expenditure function.
Answer: C

Topic: Growth Accounting
Skill: Recognition
34) The growth rate of real GDP can be broken down into which of the following components?
A) The growth of capital inputs.
B) The growth of technological advances.
C) The growth of labor input(s).
D) All of the above.
Answer: D

Topic: Growth Accounting
Skill: Conceptual
35) Economic growth occurs as a result of all of the following EXCEPT
A) more labor hours.
B) growth of capital.
C) technological progress.
D) less saving.
Answer: D

Topic: Labor Productivity
Skill: Recognition
36) Labor productivity is
A) real GDP per hour of work times the hours of work.
B) real GDP per hour of work times the number of people.
C) real GDP per hour of work.
D) the rate of change in real GDP per hour of work.
Answer: C

Topic: Labor Productivity
Skill: Recognition
37) Dividing the value of real GDP by aggregate labor hours gives
A) the net domestic product.
B) labor productivity.
C) the size of the labor force.
D) the rate of capital accumulation.
Answer: B

Topic: Labor Productivity
Skill: Recognition
38) Labor productivity is defined as
A) total output attributable to labor.
B) total real GDP.
C) the growth rate of the labor force.
D) real GDP per hour of work.
Answer: D

Topic: Labor Productivity
Skill: Conceptual
39) Suppose a graph shows labor productivity in the U.S. over time. Which of the following statements would correctly describe the graph?
A) The 1960s would show a productivity growth slowdown.
B) The 1990s would show the largest productivity growth.
C) The 1970s would show a productivity growth slowdown.
D) The 1980s would show the largest productivity growth.
Answer: C

Topic: Labor Productivity
Skill: Conceptual
40) Labor growth depends mainly on _____ and labor productivity growth depends on _____.
A) population growth; increases in real GDP
B) population growth; technological advances
C) growth in real GDP per person; growth rate of capital
D) growth in real GDP per person; technological advances
Answer: B

Topic: Labor Productivity
Skill: Conceptual
41) An increase in productivity relates to
A) working harder over time.
B) working longer over time.
C) producing the same output with fewer labor hours.
D) producing the same output with more labor hours.
Answer: C

Topic: Labor Productivity
Skill: Conceptual
42) Which of the following contributes to an increase in labor productivity?
A) An increase in human capital.
B) Technological advances.
C) An increase in physical capital.
D) All of the above contribute to an increase in labor productivity.
Answer: D

Topic: Labor Productivity
Skill: Conceptual
43) Which of the following contributes to an increase in labor productivity?
   A) Increased consumption expenditure.
   B) Decreased investment.
   C) Increased capital stock.
   D) All of the above contribute to an increase in labor productivity.
Answer: C

Topic: Technological Change
Skill: Conceptual
44) Using growth accounting, a factor leading to "technological change" includes
   A) increases in capital per hour of labor.
   B) advances in human capital.
   C) diminishing returns.
   D) None of the above answers are correct.
Answer: B

Topic: Technological Change
Skill: Conceptual
45) Technological change is often calculated as the
   A) difference between potential and actual economic growth.
   B) change in output per unit of labor.
   C) growth in labor productivity not explained by the growth capital per hour of labor.
   D) growth of capital utilization.
Answer: C

Topic: The Productivity Function
Skill: Conceptual
46) If capital per hour of work increases from $10 to $20,
   A) the prices of goods produced using that capital will increase.
   B) GDP per hour of work will decrease.
   C) real GDP will increase.
   D) real GDP will decrease because costs have risen.
Answer: C

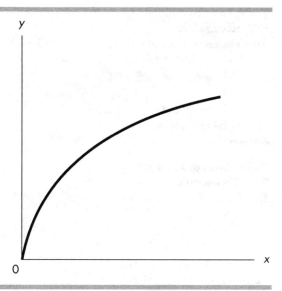

Topic: The Productivity Function
Skill: Analytical
47) The above figure shows a productivity function. _____ is measured along the horizontal axis.
   A) Real GDP per hour of work
   B) Productivity per hour of work
   C) Capital per hour of work
   D) Quantity of labor employed
Answer: C

Topic: The Productivity Function
Skill: Analytical
48) The above figure shows a productivity function. _____ is measured along the vertical axis.
   A) Real GDP per hour of work
   B) Productivity per hour of work
   C) Capital per hour of work
   D) Total output
Answer: A

Topic: The Productivity Function
Skill: Conceptual
49) The productivity function
   A) may shift upward or downward.
   B) shows how real GDP is related to the amount of capital per hour of work.
   C) shows the effects of the law of diminishing returns.
   D) All of the above answers are correct.
Answer: D

Topic: The Productivity Function
Skill: Recognition

50) A technological change _____ and a change in the capital stock _____.

A) shifts the productivity function; shifts the productivity function

B) shifts the productivity function; creates a movement along the productivity function

C) creates a movement along the productivity function; shifts the productivity function

D) does not change the productivity function; creates a movement along the productivity function

Answer: B

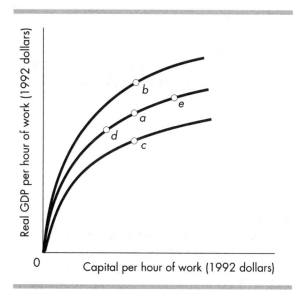

Topic: The Productivity Function
Skill: Analytical

51) In the above figure showing a productivity function, an increase in the number of factories in a country would cause a movement from point *a* to a point such as

A) point *b*.

B) point *c*.

C) point *d*.

D) point *e*.

Answer: D

Topic: The Productivity Function
Skill: Analytical

52) In the above figure showing a productivity function, suppose there are large technological advances. This change would cause a movement from point *a* to a point such as

A) point *b*.

B) point *c*.

C) point *d*.

D) point *e*.

Answer: B

Topic: The Productivity Function
Skill: Analytical

53) In the above figure showing a productivity function, suppose a country is initially operating at point *a*. If the quantity of capital in the economy increases, the economy would move to a point such as

A) point *b*.

B) point *c*.

C) point *d*.

D) point *e*.

Answer: D

Topic: The Productivity Function
Skill: Analytical

54) In the above figure showing a productivity function, suppose a country is initially operating at point *a*. If the employment increases and the quantity of capital stays the same, the economy would move to a point such as

A) point *b*.

B) point *c*.

C) point *d*.

D) point *e*.

Answer: C

Topic: Law of Diminishing Returns
Skill: Conceptual

55) Suppose that in 1999 capital doubles and no other inputs change. Again, in 2000, capital doubles. Which of the following statements is correct?

A) The amount of output will fall between 1999 and 2000.

B) If output increases by 30 percent in 1999 as a result of the increase in capital, it will increase by less than 30 percent in 2000.

C) If output increases by 30 percent in 1999 as a result of the increase in capital, it will increase by 30 percent in 2000.

D) Less labor will be used in 2000.

Answer: B

Topic: The One Third Rule
Skill: Conceptual

56) Which of the following describes the one third rule?

A) A 1/3 percent increase in capital per hour of labor leads to a 1 percent in real GDP per hour.

B) A 1/3 percent increase in capital per hour of work leads to a 1/3 percent increase in labor per hour of capital.

C) If capital per hour of work increases by 3 percent, real GDP per hour of work will increase by 1 percent.

D) If capital per hour of work increases by 3 percent, labor will increase by 1 percent.

Answer: C

Topic: The One Third Rule
Skill: Conceptual

57) The one third rule

A) explains why the productivity function shifts.

B) explains why the productivity function has a negative slope.

C) can be used to show how capital contributes to an increase in output.

D) can be used to show increases in labor contribute to an increase in real GDP per person.

Answer: C

Topic: The One Third Rule
Skill: Conceptual

58) Suppose capital per hour of work grows at 3.0 percent per year and technological change grows at 1.0 percent per year. Using the one third rule, the growth rate of real GDP per hour of work is ____ percent per year.

A) 2.0

B) 1.0

C) 7.0

D) 5.0

Answer: A

Topic: The One Third Rule
Skill: Conceptual

59) Suppose capital per hour of work grows at 1.0 percent per year and technological change grows at 2.0 percent per year. Using the one third rule, the growth rate of real GDP per hour of work is ____ percent per year.

A) 3.0

B) 9.0

C) 4.33.

D) 2.33.

Answer: D

Topic: The One Third Rule
Skill: Conceptual

60) Suppose capital per hour of work grows at 3.0 percent per year and technological change grows at 1.0 percent per year. The growth rate of real GDP per hour of work is ____ percent per year.

A) 5.0

B) 4.0

C) 3.0

D) 2.0

Answer: D

Topic: The One Third Rule
Skill: Conceptual

61) Suppose capital per hour of work grows 3.0 percent per year and the growth rate of real GDP per hour of work is 2.0 percent per year. Thus technological change grows at ____ percent per year.

A) 5.0

B) 3.0

C) 1.0

D) 4.0

Answer: C

Topic: Accounting For Productivity Growth in the United States
Skill: Conceptual
62) Data for the U.S. show that
  A) capital per hour of work has increased for the past several decades.
  B) a productivity growth slowdown occurred in the 1960s.
  C) real GDP per hour of work has decreased.
  D) Both answers A and C are correct.
Answer: A

Topic: Accounting For Productivity Growth in the United States
Skill: Conceptual
63) Which of the following can explain the behavior of the U.S. productivity function between the 1960s and the present?
  A) Increases in capital per hour of work caused a movement along a stationary curve.
  B) Technological progress has shifted the curve upward but there has been no movement along the curve.
  C) Increases in capital per hour of work have caused both upward shifts in the curve as well as movements along the curves.
  D) Technological progress has shifted the curve upward and increases in capital per hour of work have caused movements along the curves.
Answer: D

Topic: Accounting For Productivity Growth in the United States
Skill: Recognition
64) In the last decade in the United States, technological change has
  A) decreased from the decade of the productivity growth slowdown.
  B) increased from the decade of the productivity growth slowdown.
  C) stayed the same from the decade of the productivity growth slowdown.
  D) fallen in the manufacturing sector but risen in the service sector.
Answer: B

Topic: Achieving Faster Growth
Skill: Conceptual
65) Several factors are thought to be important for achieving faster economic growth. Which of the following is one of those factors?
  A) Expansion of international trade.
  B) Increased government spending.
  C) Increased taxes on saving.
  D) Promotion of consumption expenditure.
Answer: A

Topic: Achieving Faster Growth
Skill: Conceptual
66) Which of the following policies improves prospects for more rapid economic growth?
  A) Policies to increase government consumption.
  B) Limitations on international trade.
  C) Policies to increase the educational attainment of the labor force.
  D) Encouragement of political instability.
Answer: C

Topic: Achieving Faster Growth, Saving
Skill: Conceptual
67) Savings is an important economic growth variable because
  A) it can finance new investment and capital formation.
  B) it helps the economy maintain the current level of total expenditures when a recession begins.
  C) it provides a fund for wages needed from any unexpected population growth.
  D) All of the above answers are correct.
Answer: A

Topic: Achieving Faster Growth, Saving
Skill: Conceptual
68) Which of the following statements is CORRECT?
  I.   Higher savings rates can stimulate economic growth.
  II. Limiting international trade can stimulate economic growth.
  A) I only.
  B) II only.
  C) Both I and II.
  D) Neither I nor II.
Answer: A

Topic: Achieving Faster Growth, International Trade
Skill: Conceptual
69) Economic growth will tend to be higher in a country that
   A)   has a low savings rate.
   B)   has an economy open to international trade.
   C)   has an undeveloped system of property rights.
   D)   does not grant patents to inventors.
Answer: B

Topic: Achieving Faster Growth, Education
Skill: Conceptual
70) The relationship between education and economic growth can best be summarized in saying that
   A)   educated people are less apt to consume goods that deplete economic resources, which encourages economic growth.
   B)   educational expenditures tend to divert funds from productive investments, which discourages economic growth.
   C)   educational expenditures tend to be inflationary, which discourages economic growth.
   D)   education has benefits beyond those who receive the education, which encourages economic growth.
Answer: D

■ Growth Theories

Topic: Growth Theories
Skill: Recognition
71) Theories of economic growth include
   I.   Keynesian theory.
   II.   Classical theory.
   III. New growth theory.
   A)   I and II.
   B)   I and III.
   C)   II and III.
   D)   I, II and III.
Answer: C

Topic: Classical Growth Theory
Skill: Recognition
72) Which of the following ideas are included in classical growth theory?
   I.   Subsistence real wage.
   II.   Growth in real GDP per person is temporary.
   III. Technological change induces investment.
   A)   I only.
   B)   I and II.
   C)   II and III.
   D)   I, II and III.
Answer: B

Topic: Classical Growth Theory
Skill: Conceptual
73) The classical model of Malthus predicted that economies would
   A)   continue to grow indefinitely.
   B)   experience rapid technological progress.
   C)   reach a state where the growth of real GDP per person stopped.
   D)   experience significant productivity growth.
Answer: C

Topic: Classical Growth Theory
Skill: Conceptual
74) In the world of Malthus, real GDP per person eventually stops growing. The primary reason for the decrease in economic growth is that
   A)   rising wage rates would severely reduce the rate of growth of labor productivity.
   B)   savings were not required in order for investment to occur.
   C)   the neoclassical growth model had not yet been invented.
   D)   there would be diminishing returns to labor.
Answer: D

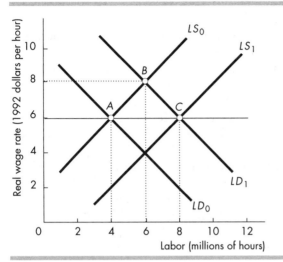

Topic: Classical Growth Theory
Skill: Analytical
75) The above figure illustrates the classical growth model. Suppose the economy is initially at point *A*. Technological advances cause a movement to point *B* and eventually to point *C*. This movement occurs because $6 represents the

A) minimum wage set by the government.
B) subsistence real wage.
C) the equilibrium real wage.
D) the wage that equates the demand for capital to the supply of capital.

Answer: B

Topic: Classical Growth Theory
Skill: Analytical
76) The above figure illustrates the classical growth model. Suppose the economy is initially at point *A*. The movement to point *B* could be caused by _____ while the movement to point *C* is caused by _____.

A) population growth; an increase in technology
B) population growth; a response to the subsistence real wage
C) an increase in technology; the actual wage being greater than the subsistence real wage
D) an increase in technology; a decrease in population

Answer: C

Topic: Neoclassical Growth Theory
Skill: Recognition
77) Which of the following ideas apply to the neoclassical growth theory?

I. The rate of technological change influences the rate of economic growth.
II. Technological change promotes saving and investment.
III. Convergence of economic growth rates across countries.

A) I only.
B) III only.
C) I and II.
D) I, II and III.

Answer: D

Topic: Neoclassical Growth Theory
Skill: Recognition
78) Which of the following ideas apply to the neoclassical growth theory?

I. Technological change results from chance.
II. Growth in real GDP increases saving and investment.

A) I only.
B) II only.
C) Both I and II.
D) Neither I nor II.

Answer: C

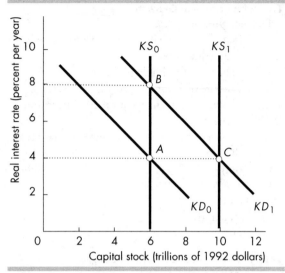

Topic: Neoclassical Growth Theory
Skill: Analytical

79) The above figure illustrates the neoclassical growth model. Suppose the target interest rate is 4 percent and that the economy is at point A. An increase in technology

A) will cause an increase in capital to $10 billion and continual growth in real GDP.

B) will cause an increase in demand for capital, but because of an increase in the interest rate above the target interest rate, there will be no change in the supply of capital.

C) will shift the demand curve for capital rightward and have no effect on the investment demand curve.

D) will cause the interest rate temporarily to rise above 4 percent.

Answer: D

Topic: Neoclassical Growth Theory
Skill: Analytical

80) The above figure illustrates the neoclassical growth model. Suppose the target interest rate is 4 percent and that the economy is at point A. A technological advance causes

A) a movement from point A to point B and then to point C in the long run.

B) a movement directly to point C in the short run.

C) a movement to point B in the long run.

D) a movement from point A to point C and then to point B in the long run.

Answer: A

Topic: New Growth Theory
Skill: Conceptual

81) An important foundation of the new growth theory is that

A) we will get more technological advances the more the government is involved in deciding which technology to pursue.

B) we will get more technological advances the greater the rewards people receive from making technological advances.

C) the growth rate of the capital stock is more important than the growth rate of new knowledge in generating economic growth.

D) improvements in labor productivity are poor measures of technological growth.

Answer: B

Topic: New Growth Theory
Skill: Recognition

82) One of the major tenets of the new growth theory is that

A) technology is not an important determinant of economic growth.

B) economic growth is not as important as leisure time growth.

C) the greater the rewards for technological advances are, the greater the number of technological advances we will have.

D) the rewards associated with technological advances have little to do with the actual rate of invention or innovation.

Answer: C

Topic: New Growth Theory
Skill: Conceptual

83) Firms are more likely to devote resources to research and development when

A) the country is in recession.

B) they expect to earn profits from successful R&D.

C) it is easy to copy new techniques of other firms.

D) the country has limited the amount of international trade it allows.

Answer: B

Topic: New Growth Theory
Skill: Conceptual

84) New growth theory economists believe that

 I. Economic growth can continue as long as we keep finding new ideas.

 II. The marginal product of capital diminishes very rapidly, so we must rely upon technological advances to create economic growth.

 A) I only.
 B) II only.
 C) Both I and II.
 D) Neither I nor II.

Answer: A

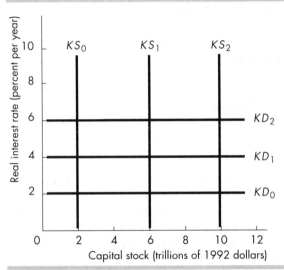

Topic: New Growth Theory
Skill: Analytical

85) The above figure diagram refers to the _____ model of economic growth.

 A) classical
 B) Malthusian
 C) neoclassical growth
 D) new growth

Answer: D

Topic: New Growth Theory
Skill: Analytical

86) In the above figure, suppose that 2 percent is the target interest rate. If technological advances cause the rate of return on capital to rise to 4 percent,

 A) there will be diminishing returns to capital.
 B) the supply of capital curve will shift rightward.
 C) real GDP will grow.
 D) Both answers B and C are correct.

Answer: D

■ True Or False Questions

Topic: Growth in the U.S. Economy
Skill: Recognition

87) Over the last 100 years, real GDP per person in the United States has grown at an average rate of 2 percent per year.

Answer: TRUE

Topic: Real GDP Growth in the World Economy
Skill: Conceptual

88) Because the U.S. is a developed economy, every other country is catching up to the U.S. in terms of real GDP per person.

Answer: FALSE

Topic: Preconditions for Economic Growth
Skill: Conceptual

89) An incentive system is a necessary precondition for economic growth.

Answer: TRUE

Topic: Preconditions for Economic Growth
Skill: Conceptual

90) In order to economic growth to occur, a democratic style of government is necessary.

Answer: FALSE

Topic: Persistent Economic Growth
Skill: Conceptual

91) As long as an economy offers property rights, markets and monetary exchange, economic growth will occur.

Answer: FALSE

Topic: Saving and Investment in New Capital
Skill: Conceptual

92) Saving and investment increase capital per worker and therefore help foster economic growth.

Answer: TRUE

Topic: Growth Accounting
Skill: Conceptual

93) The quantity of real GDP supplied depends only on the amounts of labor and capital in the production process.

Answer: FALSE

Topic: Aggregate Production Function
Skill: Conceptual

94) The equation $Y = F(N, K, T)$ is called the aggregate demand function.

Answer: FALSE

Topic: Labor Productivity
Skill: Conceptual
95) Labor productivity has grown at almost the same rate over the last 35 years in the U.S.
Answer: FALSE

Topic: Achieving Faster Growth, Saving
Skill: Conceptual
96) To achieve faster growth, economies can increase income tax rates in order to increase saving rates.
Answer: FALSE

Topic: Classical Growth Theory
Skill: Conceptual
97) The classical growth theory shows how technology changes continually generate economic growth.
Answer: FALSE

Topic: Neoclassical Growth Theory
Skill: Conceptual
98) The neoclassical growth theory is based on a subsistence real wage rate.
Answer: FALSE

Topic: New Growth Theory
Skill: Conceptual
99) New growth theory claims that economic growth occurs because firms' reap profits from research and add to the stock of capital.
Answer: TRUE

■ Essay Questions

Topic: Real GDP Growth in the World Economy
Skill: Recognition
100) Briefly explain how growth in real GDP differs across economies including the U.S., Japan, Africa and Central America.
Answer:

Topic: Preconditions for Economic Growth
Skill: Conceptual
101) Explain how markets and property rights interact to promote economic growth.
Answer:

Topic: The Productivity Function
Skill: Conceptual
102) Explain the productivity function and how the components interact.
Answer:

Topic: The Productivity Function
Skill: Analytical
103) Draw a productivity function. Show the effects of an increase in capital stock versus a technological advance.
Answer:

Topic: Achieving Faster Growth
Skill: Conceptual
104) Describe three ways that governments can promote faster economic growth.
Answer:

Topic: Classical Growth Theory
Skill: Conceptual
105) What is the main difference between classical economists' ideas about economic growth versus what modern evidence suggests?
Answer:

Topic: Neoclassical and New Growth Theory
Skill: Conceptual
106) What is the role of profits in the neoclassical growth theory versus in the new growth theory?
Answer:

Topic: Neoclassical and New Growth Theory
Skill: Conceptual
107) What is the main shortcoming of the neoclassical growth model and how does the new growth theory address this shortcoming?
Answer:

Chapter 12 EXPENDITURE MULTIPLIERS*

■ Fixed Prices and Expenditure Plans

Topic: Expenditure Plans
Skill: Recognition
1) The components of aggregate expenditure include
   I.   Imports
   II. Consumption
   III. Government transfer payments
   A) I and II.
   B) II only.
   C) II and III.
   D) I, II and III.
Answer: A

Topic: Consumption and Saving
Skill: Recognition
2) Which of the following statements is <u>FALSE</u>?
   A) disposable income – saving = consumption expenditure.
   B) consumption expenditure + saving = disposable income.
   C) saving = disposable income – consumption expenditure.
   D) consumption expenditure = saving – disposable income.
Answer: D

Topic: Saving
Skill: Recognition
3) Saving equals
   A) disposable income minus taxes.
   B) disposable income minus consumption expenditure.
   C) disposable income plus consumption expenditure.
   D) consumption expenditure minus disposable income.
Answer: B

Topic: Consumption Function
Skill: Recognition
4) Which of the following are important influences on consumption?
   I.   nominal interest rate.
   II. disposable income.
   III. expected future income.
   A) II only.
   B) I and II.
   C) II and III.
   D) I, II and III.
Answer: C

Topic: Consumption Function
Skill: Recognition
5) The consumption function
   A) shows how much all households plan to consume at each level of real disposable income.
   B) shows how much all households plan to consume at each possible interest rate.
   C) shows how much real disposable income people will earn at each income tax bracket.
   D) shows how much all households plan to consume at each level of savings.
Answer: A

Topic: Consumption Function
Skill: Recognition
6) The relationship between consumption expenditure and disposable income is called
   A) the consumption function.
   B) the savings function.
   C) the investment function.
   D) the household aggregate demand function.
Answer: A

---

* This is Chapter 29 in *Economics*.

Topic: Consumption Function
Skill: Conceptual

7)   The consumption function shows
A)   a positive relationship between an individual's wealth and his or her consumption expenditure.
B)   a positive relationship between disposable income and consumption expenditure.
C)   a negative relationship between consumption expenditure and aggregate saving.
D)   a negative relationship between disposable income and consumption expenditure.
Answer: B

Topic: Consumption Function
Skill: Conceptual

8)   For a given consumption function, a movement along the function to higher levels of consumption expenditure arises because
A)   the level of disposable income decreases.
B)   household wealth rises.
C)   the level of disposable income increases.
D)   the level of desired saving rises.
Answer: C

Topic: Consumption Function
Skill: Conceptual

9)   The positive slope of the consumption function indicates that
A)   consumers spend less out of each extra dollar of income.
B)   the stock of household wealth is subject to change.
C)   when prices fall consumers spend more.
D)   consumers increase their total consumption expenditure when disposable income increases.
Answer: D

Topic: Consumption Function
Skill: Conceptual

10)   As disposable income increases, consumption expenditures
A)   increase by the same amount.
B)   increase by a smaller amount.
C)   increase by a larger amount.
D)   remain constant.
Answer: B

Topic: Consumption Function
Skill: Conceptual

11)   If real disposable income increases by $1500, consumption expenditures will
A)   stay constant.
B)   decrease by less than $1500.
C)   increase by less than $1500.
D)   increase by more than $1500.
Answer: C

Topic: Consumption Function
Skill: Conceptual

12)   With consumption expenditure on the vertical axis and disposable income on the horizontal axis, the consumption function intersects the 45-degree line at $4 trillion. This result indicates that
A)   autonomous consumption spending is $4 trillion.
B)   consumption spending is $4 trillion when disposable income is $4 trillion.
C)   consumption spending is less than $4 trillion because taxes must be paid.
D)   consumption spending is more than $4 trillion because taxes have been paid.
Answer: B

Topic: Autonomous Consumption
Skill: Recognition

13)   Autonomous consumption is
A)   consumption expenditure that is earned rather than transferred from the government.
B)   consumption expenditure that does not depend on the level of GDP or disposable income.
C)   the amount spent on consumption when saving equals zero.
D)   consumption expenditure when the marginal propensity to consume is 1.
Answer: B

Topic: Autonomous Consumption
Skill: Recognition

14)   _____ consumption is consumption that will occur _____ the level of GDP and disposable income.
A)   Autonomous; independent of
B)   Autonomous; depending on
C)   Induced; independent of
D)   None of the above answers is correct.
Answer: A

Topic: Consumption Function and the 45-Degree Line

Skill: Recognition

15) In a diagram with the consumption function, the 45-degree line

A)   contains only a consumption component.

B)   represents both consumption expenditure and investment.

C)   shows where consumption expenditure equals disposable income.

D)   reflects a decreasing MPC as disposable income rises.

Answer: C

Topic: Consumption Function and the 45-Degree Line

Skill: Recognition

16) In a diagram with the consumption function, the 45-degree line indicates all points where

A)   consumption expenditures and saving are equal.

B)   saving and investment are equal.

C)   consumption expenditures and disposable income are equal.

D)   saving and disposable income are equal.

Answer: C

Topic: Consumption Function and the 45-Degree Line

Skill: Recognition

17) In a diagram with the consumption function, the _____ shows all points where disposable income equals consumption expenditures.

A)   consumption function

B)   aggregate demand curve

C)   45-degree line

D)   saving function

Answer: C

Topic: Consumption Function and the 45-Degree Line

Skill: Recognition

18) Consumption expenditures equal disposable income

A)   at every point on the consumption function.

B)   at every point on the saving function.

C)   at every point on the 45-degree line.

D)   when saving equals disposable income.

Answer: C

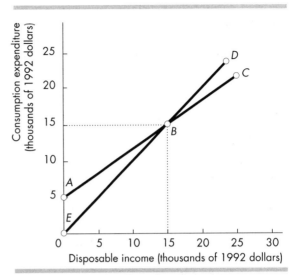

Topic: Consumption Function

Skill: Analytical

19) In the above figure, line *ABC* is called

A)   the 45-degree line.

B)   the consumption function.

C)   the saving function.

D)   aggregate supply.

Answer: B

Topic: Autonomous Consumption

Skill: Analytical

20) In the above figure, autonomous consumption equals

A)   0.

B) $5000.

C) $20,000.

D)   −$5000.

Answer: B

Topic: 45-Degree Line

Skill: Analytical

21) In the above figure, line *EBD* is called

A)   the 45-degree line.

B)   the consumption function.

C)   the saving function.

D)   aggregate demand.

Answer: A

Topic: Consumption Function and Saving Function
Skill: Conceptual

22) As real disposable income increases, consumption expenditure _____ and saving _____.

A) increases; increases
B) increases; decreases
C) decreases; increases
D) decreases; decreases

Answer: A

Topic: Saving Function
Skill: Recognition

23) "Dissaving" occurs when

A) income exceeds consumption expenditure.
B) saving is negative.
C) the consumption function is below the 45-degree line drawn from the origin.
D) saving is positive.

Answer: B

Topic: Saving Function
Skill: Conceptual

24) When disposable income equals consumption expenditure, then

A) saving is zero.
B) the MPC = zero.
C) the MPS = zero.
D) None of the above are correct.

Answer: A

Topic: Saving Function
Skill: Conceptual

25) At the level of disposable income where the consumption function crosses the 45-degree line,

A) saving is negative.
B) consumption equals only autonomous consumption.
C) the marginal propensity to consume is 0.50.
D) saving is zero.

Answer: D

Topic: Saving Function
Skill: Conceptual

26) At a level of disposable income of $0, consumption expenditure is $3500. Then

A) saving equals 0.
B) saving equals –$3500.
C) saving equals $3500.
D) the MPC = zero.

Answer: B

Topic: Saving Function
Skill: Conceptual

27) At a level of disposable income of $0, consumption is $5000. Saving equals

A) 0.
B) $2500.
C) –$5000.
D) an amount that cannot be determined with the information available.

Answer: C

Topic: Saving Function
Skill: Conceptual

28) If the consumption function is below the 45-degree line drawn from the origin, then saving at these levels of disposable income will

A) be positive.
B) be negative.
C) equal zero.
D) be some amount that cannot be determined without additional information.

Answer: A

Topic: Saving Function
Skill: Conceptual

29) The vertical distance between the 45-degree line and the consumption line represents

A) investment.
B) total consumption expenditure.
C) the difference between consumption expenditure and investment.
D) saving or dissaving.

Answer: D

Topic: Saving Function
Skill: Recognition

30) The saving function shows a _____ relationship between _____.

A) positive; disposable income and saving
B) positive; disposable income and dissaving
C) negative; disposable income and consumption
D) negative; real GDP and saving

Answer: A

Topic: Saving Function
Skill: Conceptual
31) Suppose that saving equals $0 when disposable income equals $1 trillion. Along the saving function, _____ occurs to the left of $1 trillion and _____ occurs to the right of $1 trillion.
A) saving; dissaving
B) saving; saving
C) dissaving; saving
D) dissaving; dissaving
Answer: C

Topic: Marginal Propensity to Consume
Skill: Recognition
32) The marginal propensity to consume refers to
A) the additional saving that occurs out of an additional dollar of disposable income.
B) the additional consumption expenditure that occurs out of an additional dollar of disposable income.
C) the additional consumption expenditure that occurs out of an additional dollar of investment.
D) total consumption expenditure divided by total disposable income.
Answer: B

Topic: Marginal Propensity to Consume
Skill: Recognition
33) The marginal propensity to consume equals
A) the change in consumption expenditure divided by the change in disposable income.
B) the change in consumption expenditure divided by disposable income.
C) consumption expenditure divided by the change in disposable income.
D) consumption expenditure divided by disposable income.
Answer: A

Topic: Marginal Propensity to Consume
Skill: Recognition
34) The marginal propensity to consume is found by
A) dividing consumption expenditure by disposable income.
B) dividing disposable income by consumption expenditure.
C) dividing the change in disposable income by the change in consumption expenditure.
D) dividing the change in consumption expenditure by the change in disposable income.
Answer: D

Topic: Marginal Propensity to Consume
Skill: Recognition
35) The *MPC* can be defined as
A) that fraction of total disposable income that is consumed.
B) that fraction of total disposable income that is not consumed.
C) that fraction of a change in disposable income that is consumed.
D) that fraction of a change in disposable income that is saved.
Answer: C

Topic: Marginal Propensity to Consume
Skill: Recognition
36) The change in consumption expenditure divided by the change in disposable income that caused the consumption change is called
A) the consumption factor.
B) the marginal propensity to consume.
C) the average propensity to consume.
D) autonomous consumption.
Answer: B

Topic: Marginal Propensity to Consume
Skill: Recognition
37) The marginal propensity to consume
A) shows how much disposable income changes when consumption expenditure decreases.
B) is greater than 1 only if the marginal propensity to save is greater than 1.
C) shows how much of an extra dollar of disposable income is consumed.
D) shows the percentage of disposable income consumed at each level of income.
Answer: C

Topic: Marginal Propensity to Consume
Skill: Conceptual
38) Suppose disposable income increases from $2 trillion to $3 trillion. At the same time, consumption expenditure increases from $1.8 trillion to _____. Thus the *MPC* must equal _____.
A) $2.8 trillion; 0.80
B) $2.6 trillion; 0.80
C) $2.4 trillion; 0.40
D) $3 trillion; 1.00
Answer: B

Topic: Marginal Propensity to Consume
Skill: Conceptual

39) Suppose disposable income increases from $5 trillion to $6 trillion. As a result, consumption expenditure increases from $4 trillion to _____. This result means the *MPC* equals _____.

A) $4.5 trillion; 4.50
B) $5 trillion; 0.80
C) $4.8 trillion; 0.80
D) $6 trillion; 1.00

Answer: C

Disposable income (dollars)	Consumption expenditure (dollars)
0	100
100	180
300	340
500	500
700	660
900	820

Topic: Saving Function
Skill: Analytical

40) In the above table, savings are positive when income is greater than

A) zero.
B) $100.
C) $300.
D) $500.

Answer: D

Topic: Saving Function
Skill: Analytical

41) In the above table, savings equal zero when real disposable income equals

A) 0.
B) $200.
C) $300.
D) $500.

Answer: D

Topic: Marginal Propensity to Consume
Skill: Analytical

42) In the above table, the marginal propensity to consume equals

A) 0.90.
B) 0.75.
C) 0.80.
D) 0.85.

Answer: C

Disposable income (billions of dollars)	Consumption expenditure (billions of dollars)
400	450
600	600
800	750
1000	900
1200	1050

Topic: Saving Function
Skill: Analytical

43) Based upon the above table, if disposable income is $400 billion, saving equals

A) –$50 billion.
B) $0 billion.
C) $50 billion.
D) $100 billion.

Answer: A

Topic: Saving Function
Skill: Analytical

44) Based upon the above table, saving equals $100 billion when disposable income equals

A) $800 billion.
B) $1000 billion.
C) $1200 billion.
D) some amount but we need more information to calculate the amount.

Answer: B

Topic: Marginal Propensity to Consume
Skill: Analytical

45) Based upon the above table, the *MPC* for the consumption function is

A) increasing as income rises.
B) equal to 1.0 at $600 billion.
C) constant at 0.75.
D) constant at 0.25.

Answer: C

Topic: Marginal Propensity to Save
Skill: Conceptual

46) If the *MPC* equals 0.75, then

A) for every $100 increase in consumption expenditure, disposable income increases by $75.
B) consumption expenditure is always more than disposable income.
C) for every $100 increase in disposable income, saving increases by $75.
D) for every $100 increase in disposable income, saving increases by $25.

Answer: D

Topic: Marginal Propensity to Save
Skill: Recognition
47) The *MPS* equals the ratio of
 A) saving to real GDP.
 B) the change in saving to the change in consumption expenditure.
 C) saving to consumption expenditure.
 D) None of the above answers is correct.
Answer: D

Topic: Marginal Propensity to Save
Skill: Conceptual
48) Suppose real GDP increases from $4 trillion to $5 trillion. As a result, consumption expenditure increases from $4 trillion to $4.75 trillion. This result implies the *MPS* equals
 A) 0.75.
 B) 0.25.
 C) 0.
 D) some amount that cannot be determined without more information.
Answer: D

Topic: Marginal Propensity to Save
Skill: Recognition
49) 1 – *MPC* equals
 A) autonomous consumption.
 B) the marginal propensity to save.
 C) induced consumption.
 D) the net national product.
Answer: B

Topic: Slopes and Marginal Propensities
Skill: Conceptual
50) Which of the following concerning the marginal propensity to consume and the consumption function is true?
 I. The larger the marginal propensity to consume, the greater the amount of autonomous consumption.
 II. The larger the marginal propensity to consume, the steeper the consumption function.
 A) I is true.
 B) II is true.
 C) I and II are true.
 D) Neither I nor II is true.
Answer: B

Topic: Slopes and Marginal Propensities
Skill: Conceptual
51) The slope of the consumption function
 A) is positive and equals 1 — *MPC*.
 B) is negative.
 C) equals the *MPC*.
 D) is undefined below the 45-degree line.
Answer: C

Topic: Shifts in the Consumption Function and Saving Function
Skill: Conceptual
52) When the saving function in an economy shifts downward, which of the following also happens?
 A) The consumption function shifts upward.
 B) The investment function shifts downward.
 C) The consumption function shifts downward.
 D) The consumption function does not shift.
Answer: A

Topic: Shifts in the Consumption Function
Skill: Conceptual
53) All of the following shift the consumption function EXCEPT
 A) a change in wealth.
 B) a change in the rate of interest.
 C) a change in disposable income.
 D) a change in expectations concerning future income.
Answer: C

Topic: Shifts in the Consumption Function
Skill: Conceptual
54) The consumption function shifts upward when
 A) disposable income increases.
 B) saving increases.
 C) the purchasing power of households' net assets increase.
 D) the population decreases.
Answer: C

Topic: Shifts in the Consumption Function
Skill: Conceptual
55) Which of the following shift the consumption function upward?
 A) decreases in wealth.
 B) expectations of harder times ahead.
 C) decreases in the real interest rate.
 D) increases in disposable income.
Answer: C

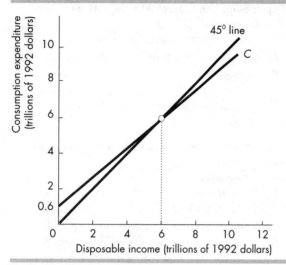

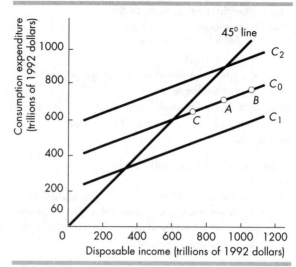

Topic: Saving Function
Skill: Analytical
56) In the above figure, when disposable income is greater than $6 trillion, then

A) savings are negative.
B) the MPC is greater than 1.
C) savings are positive.
D) the MPS is negative.

Answer: C

Topic: Marginal Propensity to Consume
Skill: Analytical
57) In the above figure, the marginal propensity to consume equals

A) 0.80.
B) 0.90.
C) 0.75.
D) 0.85.

Answer: B

Topic: Shifts in the Consumption Function
Skill: Analytical
58) In the above figure, a change in autonomous consumption to $1 trillion with no change to the MPC would cause the consumption function to

A) become steeper.
B) become flatter.
C) shift downward.
D) shift upward.

Answer: D

Topic: Shifts in the Consumption Function, Real Interest Rate
Skill: Analytical
59) In the above figure, initially the economy is at point A on consumption function C_0. What happens when the real interest rate rises?

A) The consumption function shifts upward from C_0 to a consumption function such as C_2.

B) The consumption function shifts downward from C_0 to a consumption function such as C_1.

C) There is a movement from point A to a point such as B along consumption function C_0.

D) There is a movement from point A to a point such as C along consumption function C_0.

Answer: B

Topic: Shifts in the Consumption Function, Real Assets
Skill: Analytical
60) In the above figure, initially the economy is at point A on consumption function C_0. What happens when the price level rises and thus decreases the purchasing power of net assets ?
 A) The consumption function shifts upward from C_0 to a consumption function such as C_2.
 B) The consumption function shifts downward from C_0 to a consumption function such as C_1.
 C) There is a movement from point A to a point such as B along consumption function C_0.
 D) There is a movement from point A to a point such as C along consumption function C_0.
Answer: B

Topic: Shifts in the Consumption Function, Future Incomes
Skill: Analytical
61) In the above figure, initially the economy is at point A on consumption function C_0. What happens when people come to expect their future incomes will be higher?
 A) The consumption function shifts upward from C_0 to a consumption function such as C_2.
 B) The consumption function shifts downward from C_0 to a consumption function such as C_1.
 C) There is a movement from point A to a point such as B along consumption function C_0.
 D) There is a movement from point A to a point such as C along consumption function C_0.
Answer: A

Topic: Shifts in the Consumption Function, Future Incomes
Skill: Analytical
62) In the above figure, initially the economy is at point A on consumption function C_0. Which of the following represents the effect of an expectation that incomes will fall in the future?
 A) The consumption function shifts from C_0 to a consumption function such as C_2.
 B) The consumption function shifts from C_0 to a consumption function such as C_1.
 C) There is a movement from point A to a point such as B along consumption function C_0.
 D) There is a movement from point A to a point such as C along consumption function C_0.
Answer: B

Topic: The U.S. Consumption Function
Skill: Conceptual
63) The U.S. consumption function
 A) has shifted upward over time.
 B) has a positive slope.
 C) has a slope of about 0.75.
 D) All of the above answers are correct.
Answer: D

Topic: Import Function
Skill: Conceptual
64) As a result of NAFTA, the marginal propensity to import has
 A) increased.
 B) decreased.
 C) remained the same.
 D) been about 0.4.
Answer: A

Real GDP with a Fixed Price Level

Topic: Aggregate Expenditure
Skill: Recognition
65) Aggregate expenditure equals
 A) $C + I + G + X - M$.
 B) $G + X - M$.
 C) $C + I + G$.
 D) $C + I + G + X$.
Answer: A

Topic: Aggregate Expenditure Curve
Skill: Recognition
66) The aggregate expenditure curve shows
   A) how consumption changes in response to a change in disposable income.
   B) how planned aggregate expenditure and real GDP are related.
   C) a negative relationship between the price level and real GDP.
   D) Both answers B and C are correct.
Answer: B

Topic: Aggregate Expenditure Curve
Skill: Recognition
67) The relationship between desired aggregate expenditure and real GDP is called the
   A) dissaving function.
   B) consumption function.
   C) equilibrium function.
   D) aggregate expenditure function.
Answer: D

Topic: Induced Expenditures
Skill: Recognition
68) The sum of the components of aggregate expenditure that vary with real GDP is called
   A) induced expenditures.
   B) the *MPC*.
   C) autonomous expenditures.
   D) autonomous consumption.
Answer: A

Topic: Autonomous Expenditures
Skill: Recognition
69) The sum of the components of aggregate expenditure that are not influenced by real GDP is called
   A) induced expenditures.
   B) the *MPC*.
   C) autonomous expenditures.
   D) autonomous consumption.
Answer: C

Topic: Equilibrium Expenditure
Skill: Conceptual
70) At equilibrium expenditure
   A) consumers' purchases of goods and services equal firms' purchases of investment goods.
   B) firms hold no inventories of raw materials or final goods.
   C) aggregate planned expenditure equals total output.
   D) aggregate planned expenditure equals total output minus net exports.
Answer: C

Topic: Equilibrium Expenditure
Skill: Conceptual
71) At the equilibrium expenditure
   A) there can be unplanned inventory accumulation.
   B) purchasers will be prone to bid up prices.
   C) purchasers are willing to buy exactly the amount of output that is produced.
   D) an increase in desired expenditure cannot increase the level of real GDP.
Answer: C

Topic: Equilibrium Expenditure
Skill: Conceptual
72) Equilibrium expenditure occurs where
   A) the aggregate expenditure curve crosses the 45-degree line.
   B) planned expenditures exceed national income.
   C) savings exceed planned investment.
   D) All of the answers are correct.
Answer: A

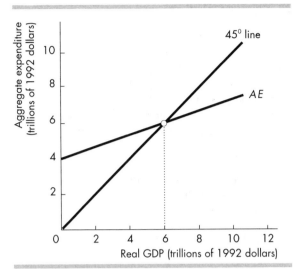

Topic: Equilibrium Expenditure
Skill: Analytical
73) In the above figure, if real GDP equals $6 trillion, there would be
A)   an increase in autonomous consumption expenditure.
B)   an increase in autonomous inventories.
C)   no change in GDP.
D)   an unplanned increase in firms' inventories.
Answer: C

Topic: Actual Expenditure and Planned Expenditure
Skill: Analytical
74) In the above figure, if real GDP equals $8 trillion,
A)   consumption will increase.
B)   unplanned inventories will increase.
C)   actual investment will decrease but planned investment will increase.
D)   unplanned inventories will decrease.
Answer: B

Topic: Actual Expenditure and Planned Expenditure
Skill: Conceptual
75) If aggregate planned expenditure exceeds GDP,
A)   firms are not maximizing their profits.
B)   planned investment is greater than planned savings.
C)   actual inventories decrease below their target.
D)   planned consumption is less than actual consumption.
Answer: C

Topic: Actual Expenditure and Planned Expenditure
Skill: Conceptual
76) If firms' inventories are increasing above their target level, then
A)   the level of real GDP will increase.
B)   the level of real GDP will not change in the foreseeable future.
C)   actual consumption is greater than planned consumption.
D)   actual investment exceeds planned investment.
Answer: D

Topic: Actual Expenditure and Planned Expenditure
Skill: Conceptual
77) If planned expenditures equal $2000 when GDP is $2200, then
A)   inventories will decrease by $200.
B)   actual investment will exceed planned investment.
C)   there will be excess demand for most goods.
D)   the economy must have a trade surplus to sell the excess goods and services.
Answer: B

Topic: Actual Expenditure and Planned Expenditure
Skill: Conceptual
78) Suppose that in 1999, firms discover that their inventories are falling below their target levels. Which of the following statements is correct?
A)   The level of aggregate savings must equal the level of desired investment.
B)   Even though firms are trying, they are unable to maximize profits.
C)   Aggregate demand is less than aggregate supply.
D)   Real GDP is less than equilibrium expenditure.
Answer: D

Topic: Convergence to Equilibrium
Skill: Conceptual
79) When real GDP exceeds aggregate planned expenditures,
A)   actual inventories decrease below their target.
B)   the circular flow will increase.
C)   eventually GDP will decrease.
D)   a higher level of equilibrium income will prevail.
Answer: C

Topic: Convergence to Equilibrium
Skill: Conceptual
80) If aggregate planned expenditures are less than the level of real GDP,
   A) output and income will increase.
   B) output and income remain unchanged.
   C) output and income will either decrease or remain unchanged, depending on the *MPC*.
   D) inventories will increase above their target level and real GDP will decrease.

Answer: D

Topic: Convergence to Equilibrium
Skill: Conceptual
81) Suppose the equilibrium level of expenditure is $600. If real GDP is $500, then inventories are
   A) increasing above their target levels, and output will expand.
   B) increasing above their target levels, and output will contract.
   C) decreasing below their target levels, and output will expand.
   D) decreasing below their target levels, and output will contract.

Answer: C

Topic: Convergence to Equilibrium
Skill: Conceptual
82) Suppose the equilibrium level of expenditure is $1,200. If real GDP is $1,400, then planned expenditures
   A) exceed real GDP, and output will increase.
   B) are less than real GDP, and output will decrease.
   C) are equal to real GDP, and there will be no change in output.
   D) are less than real GDP, and output will increase.

Answer: B

■ The Multiplier

Topic: The Multiplier
Skill: Recognition
83) The multiplier is
   A) the ratio of the change in real GDP to the change in autonomous expenditures.
   B) the ratio of the equilibrium level of real GDP to the change in induced expenditures.
   C) the ratio of the change in induced expenditures to the change in autonomous expenditures.
   D) the ratio of the change in autonomous expenditures to the change in real GDP.

Answer: A

Topic: The Multiplier Effect
Skill: Conceptual
84) The multiplier effect
   A) generates instability in autonomous expenditure.
   B) promotes stability of the general price level.
   C) magnifies small changes in spending into larger changes in output and income.
   D) increases the *MPC*.

Answer: C

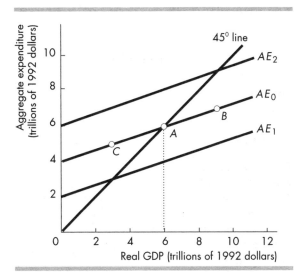

87) If the $MPC = 0.9$, then ignoring any multiplier effect, an increase in household income causes consumption expenditure to

A) rise by more than the full increase in income.

B) rise by the full increase in income.

C) rise by less than the full increase in income.

D) fall, as increases in income will increase saving.

Answer: C

88) The multiplier shows that as _____ changes, real GDP changes by a _____ amount.

A) induced expenditure; larger

B) induced expenditure; smaller

C) autonomous expenditure; larger

D) autonomous expenditure; smaller

Answer: C

89) If the *MPC* increases from 0.75 to 0.80,

A) the multiplier becomes larger.

B) the multiplier becomes smaller.

C) the slope of the consumption function becomes smaller.

D) the slope of the savings function becomes larger.

Answer: A

90) An increase in the size of the multiplier can be caused by

A) an increase in the *MPS*.

B) an increase in the *MPC*.

C) a decrease in induced expenditures.

D) an increase in the marginal propensity to import.

Answer: B

91) In an economy with households and firms but no government or foreign trade, the multiplier equals

A) $1/MPC$.

B) $1/MPS$.

C) $1/(1 - MPS)$.

D) $1/(MPC + MPS)$.

Answer: B

85) In the above figure the economy is initially at point *A* on aggregate expenditure curve AE_0.

Suppose firms expect profits to increase and decide to increase investment. As a result

A) the *AE* curve shifts upward to a curve such as AE_2.

B) the *AE* curve shifts downward to a curve such as AE_1.

C) there is a movement along AE_1 to a point such as *B*.

D) there is a movement along AE_1 to a point such as *C*.

Answer: A

86) In the above figure the economy is initially at point *A* on aggregate expenditure curve AE_0.

Suppose investment decreases. As a result

A) the *AE* curve shifts upward to a curve such as AE_2.

B) the *AE* curve shifts downward to a curve such as AE_1.

C) there is a movement along AE_1 to a point such as *B*.

D) there is a movement along AE_1 to a point such as *C*.

Answer: B

Topic: The Multiplier and the MPS
Skill: Conceptual
92) If the *MPS* increases, the multiplier
A) decreases.
B) increases.
C) stays the same.
D) can either increase or decrease depending on what happens to the *MPC*.
Answer: A

Topic: The Multiplier and the MPS
Skill: Conceptual
93) An increase in the value of the multiplier can be caused by
A) a decrease in the marginal propensity to consume.
B) an increase in the marginal propensity to import.
C) an increase in income-tax rates.
D) a decrease in the marginal propensity to save.
Answer: D

Topic: The Multiplier
Skill: Conceptual
94) If the marginal propensity to consume is 0.8 and there no income taxes or imports, the multiplier equals
A) 0.8.
B) 1.0.
C) 4.0.
D) 5.0.
Answer: D

Topic: The Multiplier
Skill: Conceptual
95) If the *MPC* is .9 and there are no income taxes or imports, the multiplier for a change in autonomous spending equals
A) 0.1.
B) 9.0.
C) 10.0.
D) 100.0.
Answer: C

Topic: The Multiplier
Skill: Conceptual
96) If the multiplier is 10 and there are no income taxes or imports, then the *MPC* is
A) 0.9.
B) 0.1.
C) 1.0.
D) 9.0.
Answer: A

Topic: The Multiplier
Skill: Conceptual
97) If the multiplier is 4 and there are no imports or income taxes, the marginal propensity to consume is
A) 0.25.
B) 0.50.
C) 0.75.
D) 1.00.
Answer: C

Topic: The Multiplier and Imports
Skill: Conceptual
98) The presence of imports ____ the size of the multiplier because with an increase of real GDP, ____.
A) increases; U.S. consumers buy goods from other countries
B) increases; U.S. firms can sell goods to other countries
C) decreases; U.S. consumers buy goods from other countries
D) decreases; U.S. firms can sell goods to other countries
Answer: C

Topic: Slope of the Aggregate Expenditure Curve
Skill: Conceptual
99) A change in which of the following will change the slope of the aggregate expenditure curve?
A) An increase in autonomous government purchases.
B) An increase in the marginal propensity to consume.
C) A decrease in autonomous consumption expenditures.
D) All of the above answers are correct because they all change the slope of the aggregate expenditure curve.
Answer: B

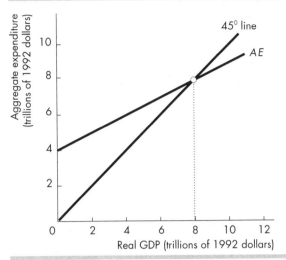

Topic: Slope of the Aggregate Expenditure Curve and The Multiplier
Skill: Analytical
100) In the figure above, the multiplier equals
  A) 0.5.
  B) 2.0.
  C) 10.0.
  D) some amount that cannot be calculated without additional information
Answer: B

Topic: Slope of the Aggregate Expenditure Curve and The Multiplier
Skill: Analytical
101) In the figure above, if income taxes increase,
  A) the *AE* curve becomes steeper.
  B) the *AE* curve becomes flatter.
  C) there is a movement leftward along the *AE* curve.
  D) there is a movement rightward along the *AE* curve.
Answer: B

■ The Multiplier and the Price Level

Topic: *AE, AD*, and the Price Level
Skill: Conceptual
102) An increase in the price level causes
  A) a downward shift in the *AE* curve and a movement up along the *AD* curve.
  B) a downward shift in both the *AE* and *AD* curves.
  C) a downward shift in the *AD* curve and a movement down along the *AE* curve.
  D) a leftward movement along both the *AE* and *AD* curves.
Answer: A

Topic: *AE, AD*, and the Price Level
Skill: Analytical
103) A shift in the aggregate expenditure curve as a result of an increase in the price level results in a
  A) leftward shift in the aggregate demand curve.
  B) movement down along the aggregate demand curve.
  C) rightward shift in the aggregate demand curve.
  D) movement up along the aggregate demand curve.
Answer: D

Topic: *AE, AD*, and Change in Autonomous Expenditure
Skill: Conceptual
104) An increase in investment spending causes
  A) a movement along the aggregate expenditure curve and a shift in the aggregate demand curve.
  B) a shift in the aggregate expenditure curve and a movement along the aggregate demand curve.
  C) a shift in the aggregate expenditure curve but has no effect on the aggregate demand curve.
  D) a shift in the aggregate expenditure and aggregate demand curves.
Answer: D

Topic: *AE*, *AD*, and Change in Autonomous Expenditure
Skill: Analytical
105) Which of the following cause a shift in the aggregate expenditure curve AND a shift in the aggregate demand curve?
I.   A decrease in investment.
II.   A change in the price level.
III.   An increase in exports.
A)   I and II.
B)   I and III.
C)   II and III.
D)   III only.
Answer: B

Topic: The Multiplier and the Change in Aggregate Demand Level
Skill: Conceptual
106) The multiplier measures the
A)   horizontal shift in the aggregate demand curve from an increase in autonomous spending.
B)   vertical shift in the aggregate demand curve from an increase in autonomous spending.
C)   horizontal difference between two points on the same aggregate demand curve.
D)   vertical difference between two points on the same aggregate demand curve.
Answer: A

Topic: *AE*, *AD*, and Change in Autonomous Expenditure
Skill: Analytical
107) The larger the multiplier, the ____ the *AE* curve and the ____ the *AD* curve from an increase in investment.
A)   steeper; smaller the shift in
B)   steeper; larger the shift in
C)   flatter; larger the movement along
D)   flatter; smaller the movement along
Answer: B

Topic: The Multiplier in the Short Run
Skill: Conceptual
108) An economy saves 20 percent of any increase in income and there are no income taxes or imports. Then, an increase in investment of $2 billion can produce a short run increase in real GDP of as much as
A) $2 billion.
B) $10 billion.
C) $0.4 billion.
D) $1.6 billion.
Answer: B

Topic: The Multiplier in the Short Run
Skill: Conceptual
109) Equilibrium real GDP is $400 billion, the *MPC* = 0.9, and there are no income taxes or imports. Investment increases $40 billion. If the price level is constant, after the increase in investment, equilibrium real GDP will be
A) $440 billion.
B) $360 billion.
C) $600 billion.
D) $800 billion.
Answer: D

Topic: The Multiplier in the Short Run
Skill: Conceptual
110) The *MPS* is 0.1 and there are no imports or income taxes. Investment decreases by $100 million and the price level is constant. Real GDP
A)   decreases by $10 million.
B)   increases by $90 million.
C)   decreases by $1 billion.
D)   increases by $1 billion.
Answer: C

Topic: The Multiplier in the Short Run
Skill: Conceptual
111) If the price level is constant and there are no income taxes or imports, a decrease in investment of $100 that occurs when the *MPS* = 0.25 leads to a decrease in real GDP of
A) $25.
B) $100.
C) $400.
D) $800.
Answer: C

Topic: The Multiplier in the Short Run
Skill: Conceptual
112) Suppose the price level is constant and there are no imports or taxes. If the marginal propensity to consume is 0.8 and the real GDP needs to be increased by $500 billion, then

A) consumption spending needs to increase by $500 billion.
B) saving needs to be reduced by $500 billion in order to generate the extra $500 billion.
C) an increase in investment spending of $200 billion is needed to generate the desired increase of $500 billion.
D) an increase in autonomous spending of $100 billion will lead to the increase of $500 billion.

Answer: D

■ True Or False Questions

Topic: Expenditure Plans
Skill: Recognition
113) Components of aggregate expenditure include saving, consumption expenditure, investment and government purchases.
Answer: FALSE

Topic: Consumption Function
Skill: Recognition
114) The positive relationship between consumption expenditure and disposable income is shown in the consumption function.
Answer: TRUE

Topic: Saving Function
Skill: Conceptual
115) As disposable income increases, saving increases.
Answer: TRUE

Topic: Marginal Propensity to Consume
Skill: Conceptual
116) The marginal propensity to consume must increase as disposable income increases.
Answer: FALSE

Topic: Induced Expenditure
Skill: Recognition
117) Components of induced expenditure include government purchases, investment and consumption expenditures.
Answer: FALSE

Topic: Actual Expenditure and Planned Expenditure
Skill: Conceptual
118) When planned aggregate expenditure is greater than real GDP, inventories decrease.
Answer: TRUE

Topic: The Multiplier Effect
Skill: Recognition
119) If the price level is constant, a change in investment has a multiplied impact on real GDP.
Answer: TRUE

Topic: The Multiplier
Skill: Recognition
120) In the short run, the multiplier is typically less than 1.
Answer: FALSE

Topic: The Multiplier
Skill: Conceptual
121) If the change in autonomous investment equals $1 trillion and the change in real GDP equals $4 trillion, the multiplier equals 1/4.
Answer: FALSE

Topic: The Multiplier
Skill: Conceptual
122) If the multiplier is 3, a $750,000 increase in autonomous expenditure increases equilibrium expenditure by $2.25 million.
Answer: TRUE

Topic: The Multiplier, Imports and Income Taxes
Skill: Conceptual
123) The effect of imports and income taxes causes the multiplier to be larger than it would otherwise be.
Answer: FALSE

Topic: Shifts in the Aggregate Demand Curve
Skill: Conceptual
124) An upward shift in the aggregate expenditure curve leads to a leftward shift in the short-run aggregate supply curve in the short run.
Answer: FALSE

Topic: Short-Run Multiplier Versus Long-Run Multiplier
Skill: Conceptual
125) The multiplier in the short run is greater than the multiplier in the long run.
Answer: TRUE

■ Essay Questions

Topic: Consumption Function
Skill: Analytical
126) Draw a consumption function and use it to explain the connection between disposable income, saving and dissaving.

Answer:

Topic: Marginal Propensity to Consume
Skill: Conceptual
127) What is the marginal propensity to consume? Why it is an important concept?

Answer:

Topic: Induced Versus Autonomous Expenditure
Skill: Conceptual
128) Explain the different components of autonomous versus induced expenditures.

Answer:

Topic: Actual Expenditures and Planned Expenditures
Skill: Conceptual
129) Suppose that real GDP is $4 trillion. Explain what happens when planned expenditures are greater than real GDP.

Answer:

Topic: The Multiplier
Skill: Conceptual
130) What is the mathematical formula for the multiplier. What is the multiplier effect?

Answer:

Topic: The Multiplier
Skill: Conceptual
131) Explain the effects of the multiplier when the $MPC = 0.90$. Choose your own values for real GDP and the change in autonomous expenditures.

Answer:

Topic: The Multiplier, Imports and Income Taxes
Skill: Conceptual
132) How do imports and income taxes affect the multiplier? Why do they have this effect?

Answer:

Topic: The Slope of the Aggregate Expenditure Curve and the Multiplier
Skill: Conceptual
133) What is the relationship between the MPC and the slope of the AE curve?

Answer:

Topic: AE and AD Curves
Skill: Analytical
134) Draw two graphs—one showing the AE curve and the 45-degree line and the other showing the aggregate demand curve. How are the two curves related?

Answer:

Topic: Short-Run Multiplier Versus Long-Run Multiplier
Skill: Conceptual
135) Why does the multiplier differ between the long run and the short run?

Answer:

Chapter 13 FISCAL POLICY*

■ The Federal Budget

Topic: The Federal Budget
Skill: Recognition

1) Which of the following is considered a purpose of the federal budget?
   I. To help the economy achieve full employment.
   II. To finance the activities of the federal government.
   III. To promote sustained economic growth.
   A) I and II.
   B) I and III.
   C) II and III.
   D) I, II and III.

Answer: D

Topic: The Federal Budget
Skill: Conceptual

2) In terms of the budget process, place the following events in order for fiscal year 2000.
   I. Congress approves the budget.
   II. The president sends a budget to Congress.
   III. Supplementary budget laws are passed.
   A) III, II, I.
   B) II, III, I.
   C) II, I, III.
   D) I, II, III.

Answer: C

Topic: Fiscal Policy
Skill: Recognition

3) Fiscal policy is
   A) a deliberate attempt to move the economy to full employment and to achieve sustained economic growth.
   B) a deliberate attempt to finance the activities of the federal government.
   C) only the use of federal deficit or surplus to keep the economy at full employment.
   D) a deliberate attempt to get the government involved in as much of the economy as possible.

Answer: A

Topic: Fiscal Policy
Skill: Recognition

4) Fiscal policy can be defined as
   A) use of the federal budget to reach macroeconomic objectives.
   B) government policy with respect to transfer payments such as unemployment compensation and welfare.
   C) government policy to retire the federal government debt.
   D) government spending and tax decisions accomplished using automatic stabilizers.

Answer: A

Topic: The Employment Act of 1946
Skill: Recognition

5) The Employment Act of 1946 made it the responsibility of the federal government to
   A) balance its budget because that policy would create the maximum level of employment.
   B) promote maximum employment.
   C) provide full employment and a stable balance of payments.
   D) improve the distribution of income.

Answer: B

---

* This is Chapter 30 in *Economics*.

Topic: The Employment Act of 1946
Skill: Recognition

6) The Employment Act of 1946 was <u>NOT</u> concerned with

A) price stability.
B) full employment.
C) farming price supports.
D) economic growth.

Answer: C

Topic: Council of Economic Advisers
Skill: Recognition

7) The Council of Economic Advisers

A) proposes the president's budget each year.
B) approves fiscal policy changes.
C) helps the president and the public stay informed about the state of the economy.
D) helps the president make changes in monetary policy.

Answer: C

Topic: Tax Revenues
Skill: Recognition

8) Which of the following is the largest source of federal government revenue?

A) corporate income taxes.
B) social security taxes.
C) personal income taxes.
D) borrowing.

Answer: C

Topic: Tax Revenues
Skill: Conceptual

9) The government receives tax revenues from several sources. Rank the following sources from largest to the smallest.

I. corporate income taxes.
II. personal income taxes.
III. social insurance taxes.

A) I, II, III.
B) II, III, I.
C) I, III, II.
D) III, II, I.

Answer: B

Topic: Government Expenditures
Skill: Conceptual

10) Rank the following government expenditures from the largest to the smallest.

I. debt interest.
II. transfer payments.
III. purchases of goods and services.

A) I, II, III.
B) III, II, I.
C) III, I, II.
D) II, III, I.

Answer: D

Topic: Government Expenditures
Skill: Recognition

11) Government expenditures as a percentage of GDP is currently equal to approximately

A) 10 percent.
B) 20 percent.
C) 50 percent.
D) 66 percent.

Answer: B

Topic: Budget Surplus and Deficit
Skill: Recognition

12) A budget deficit is the difference between

A) what U.S. consumers buy and U.S. producers produce.
B) foreign holdings of American assets and American holdings of foreign assets.
C) government tax receipts and government expenditures.
D) U.S. imports and U.S. exports.

Answer: C

Topic: Budget Surplus and Deficit
Skill: Recognition

13) A government surplus is defined as

A) the government printing money to pay its bills.
B) an excess of government revenues relative to government expenditures.
C) on-budget expenditures.
D) interest payments on the federal government debt.

Answer: B

Topic: Budget Surplus and Deficit
Skill: Recognition
14) If taxes exactly equaled government expenditures in a year

A) the federal government debt would be zero.
B) the federal government debt would decrease.
C) the budget deficit would not change.
D) the budget deficit would be zero.

Answer: D

Topic: The Budget Deficit
Skill: Recognition
15) Which years showed the greatest ratio of government deficit to GDP?

A) the 1960s.
B) the 1970s.
C) the 1980s.
D) the 1990s.

Answer: C

Topic: Deficits and Debt
Skill: Recognition
16) The sum of accumulated annual federal budget deficits minus surpluses equals

A) the federal government debt.
B) the structural deficit.
C) the trade deficit.
D) the federal budget.

Answer: A

Topic: Deficits and Debt
Skill: Recognition
17) The federal government debt is defined as

A) the obligations of benefits from federal taxes and expenditures.
B) the sum of all annual federal expenditures.
C) the cumulative sum of annual federal deficits minus surpluses.
D) the annual difference between federal revenues and expenditures.

Answer: C

Topic: State and Local Budgets
Skill: Conceptual
18) Spending by state and local governments is similar to spending by the federal government in that both

A) help stabilize the aggregate economy.
B) spend most of their budgets on education.
C) have deficits that rise during recessions.
D) None of the above.

Answer: D

Topic: State and Local Budgets
Skill: Conceptual
19) Which of the following are true regarding state and local government spending?

I. State and local government spending is used to stabilize the economy.
II. Some state and local government spending is used on education.
III. State and local government spending tends to increase during recessions.

A) I only.
B) I and II.
C) II only.
D) I and III.

Answer: C

■ Fiscal Policy Multipliers

Topic: Discretionary Fiscal Policy
Skill: Recognition
20) Deliberate changes in government expenditures and taxes to influence GDP

A) are automatic stabilizers.
B) are discretionary fiscal policy.
C) are enacted by the Council of Economic Advisers.
D) operate without time lags.

Answer: B

Topic: Discretionary Fiscal Policy
Skill: Recognition
21) Discretionary fiscal policy is

A) the control of the money supply as a tool of macroeconomic policy.
B) the use of taxation but not government spending to pursue macroeconomic goals.
C) the control of government spending but not taxes.
D) the use of government spending and taxation to pursue macroeconomic goals.

Answer: D

Topic: Discretionary Fiscal Policy
Skill: Conceptual

22) When the economy is hit by spending fluctuations, the government can try to minimize the effects by
   A) changing government spending on goods.
   B) changing taxes.
   C) changing government spending on services.
   D) all of the above.
Answer: D

Topic: Lump-Sum Taxes
Skill: Recognition

23) When incomes and GDP change, the amount of revenue collected by _____ does not change.
   A) discretionary taxes
   B) lump-sum taxes
   C) income taxes
   D) automatic taxes
Answer: B

Topic: Government Purchases Multiplier
Skill: Recognition

24) The government purchases multiplier is defined as
   A) the change in real GDP as a result of a change in government purchases of goods and services.
   B) the change in government purchases of goods and services as a result of a change in real GDP.
   C) the change in government purchases due to a change in taxes.
   D) the change in taxes as a result of a change in government spending.
Answer: A

Topic: Government Purchases Multiplier
Skill: Conceptual

25) The government purchases multiplier will be larger
   A) the larger the *MPC*.
   B) the smaller the *MPC*.
   C) the larger the tax increase used to finance the increase in purchases.
   D) the smaller the slope of the *AE* curve.
Answer: A

Topic: Government Purchases Multiplier
Skill: Recognition

26) In an economy with no international sector and no taxes, the government purchases multiplier equals
   A) $1/(1 - MPC)$.
   B) $1/MPC$.
   C) $MPC/(1 - MPC)$.
   D) $(1 - MPC)/MPC$.
Answer: A

Topic: Government Purchases Multiplier
Skill: Conceptual

27) In an economy with no international sector and no taxes, if the *MPC* equals 0.76, the government purchases multiplier equals
   A) 1.32.
   B) 4.16.
   C) 3.16.
   D) 1.24.
Answer: B

Topic: Government Purchases Multiplier
Skill: Conceptual

28) In an economy with no international sector and no taxes, if the *MPC* equals 0.81, the government purchases multiplier equals
   A) 1.23.
   B) 4.26.
   C) 5.26.
   D) 1.19.
Answer: C

Topic: Government Purchases Multiplier
Skill: Conceptual

29) Suppose real GDP is $4 trillion, and the government wants to increase real GDP to $5 trillion. The marginal propensity to consume is 0.8 and there are no imports or taxes. Assuming that prices do not change, which change in government spending below will generate the extra $1 trillion in real GDP?
   A) $100 billion.
   B) $125 billion.
   C) $200 billion.
   D) $400 billion.
Answer: C

Topic: Lump-Sum Tax Multiplier
Skill: Conceptual

30) A change in lump-sum taxes _____ because it _____ which, in turn, _____ change consumption expenditure.

A) creates a multiplier effect; changes disposable income; can

B) cannot create a multiplier effect; does not affect disposable income; cannot

C) creates a multiplier effect; changes investment; can

D) cannot create a multiplier effect; cannot change investment; cannot

Answer: A

Topic: Lump-Sum Tax Multiplier
Skill: Conceptual

31) Suppose the government increases lump-sum taxes. This change causes

A) disposable income to decrease, which causes consumption expenditure to decrease and aggregate expenditure to decrease.

B) government spending to decrease, which causes aggregate expenditure to decrease.

C) consumption expenditure to decrease and spending on imports to decrease. The effect on aggregate expenditure depends on whether domestic spending or spending on imports decreases the most.

D) disposable income to decrease, which causes aggregate supply to decrease.

Answer: A

Topic: Lump-Sum Tax Multiplier
Skill: Recognition

32) The _____ multiplier equals _____.

A) lump-sum tax; $-MPC/(MPC - 1)$

B) lump-sum tax; $-MPC/(1 - MPC)$

C) government purchases; $-MPC/(1 - MPC)$

D) government purchases; $1/MPC$

Answer: B

Topic: Lump-Sum Tax Multiplier
Skill: Conceptual

33) Suppose real GDP equals $3 trillion and potential GDP equals $3.6 trillion. Prices are constant and there are no imports. If the *MPC* equals 0.75, by how much should the government decrease lump-sum taxes to move GDP to potential GDP?

A) $600 billion.

B) $200 billion.

C) $300 billion.

D) $900 billion.

Answer: B

Topic: Induced Taxes
Skill: Conceptual

34) When the economy grows, _____ increase because real GDP _____.

A) induced taxes; decreases

B) induced taxes; increases

C) lump-sum taxes; decreases

D) lump-sum taxes; increases

Answer: B

Topic: Induced Taxes
Skill: Conceptual

35) Which of the following is true regarding induced taxes?

I.   Induced taxes vary with disposable income.

II. Induced taxes cause the multiplier effect to be greater than it would be otherwise.

III. Induced taxes weaken the link between real GDP and disposable income.

A) I and II.

B) I and III.

C) II and III.

D) I, II and III.

Answer: B

Topic: Induced Taxes and Entitlement Spending
Skill: Conceptual

36) Induced taxes _____ and entitlement spending _____ the size of the government purchases multiplier.

A) increases; decreases

B) increases; increases

C) decreases; decreases

D) decreases; increases

Answer: C

Topic: Induced Taxes and Entitlement Spending
Skill: Conceptual

37) Induced taxes

A) decrease the government purchases multiplier.

B) do not change the government purchases multiplier.

C) increase the government purchases multiplier.

D) may change the government purchases multiplier depending on the magnitude of the marginal propensity of consume.

Answer: A

Topic: Automatic Stabilizers
Skill: Recognition

38) Taxes and government expenditures that, without need for additional government action, change in response to changes in the level of economic activity are called

A) discretionary fiscal variables.

B) automatic stabilizers.

C) built-in monetary stabilizers.

D) cyclically balanced budgets.

Answer: B

Topic: Automatic Stabilizers
Skill: Recognition

39) Automatic stabilizers refer in part to

A) discretionary fiscal policies.

B) deficit-reduction policies.

C) government spending actions that automatically dampen the business cycle.

D) the unemployment effects of recession.

Answer: C

Topic: Automatic Stabilizers
Skill: Recognition

40) One characteristic of automatic stabilizers is that

A) they require no legislative action by Congress to be made effective.

B) they automatically produce surpluses during recessions and deficits during inflation.

C) they have no effect on unemployment.

D) they reduce the size of the federal government debt during times of recession.

Answer: A

Topic: Automatic Stabilizers
Skill: Conceptual

41) Automatic stabilizers

A) do not require any legislative decisions by the Congress.

B) cushion the decrease in after-tax income and consumption when a recession occurs.

C) are, for example, unemployment compensation payments.

D) All of the above answers are correct.

Answer: D

Topic: Automatic Stabilizers
Skill: Conceptual

42) Automatic stabilizers

A) cushion the decrease in after-tax income when a recession occurs.

B) magnify the increase in after-tax income when a boom occurs.

C) require the government to balance the budget.

D) require the government use countercyclical policy, such as increasing or decreasing government purchases.

Answer: A

Topic: Automatic Stabilizers
Skill: Conceptual

43) Income taxes in the United States are automatic stabilizers because

A) tax revenues increase when income increases, thus offsetting some of the increase in aggregate demand.

B) tax revenues decrease when income increases, intensifying the increase in aggregate demand.

C) the President can increase tax rates whenever the President deems such a policy appropriate.

D) tax rates can be adjusted by the Congress to counteract economic fluctuations.

Answer: A

Topic: Budget Deficit Over the Business Cycle
Skill: Conceptual

44) In general, the relationship between the business cycle and the government budget deficit is
A) for the deficit to fall when the economy is growing.
B) only now being studied by macroeconomics.
C) not stable because the relationship depends on consumer confidence.
D) non-existent because the deficit depends on the policy of the current administration toward taxation.

Answer: A

Topic: Cyclical and Structural Balances
Skill: Recognition

45) The structural deficit is that deficit that would exist
A) with the taxes and expenditures that would occur if the economy was at the equilibrium level of real GDP.
B) with the taxes and expenditures that would occur if the economy was at the full employment level of real GDP.
C) if tax rates were set to maximize tax revenues.
D) if there were no discretionary fiscal interventions into the economy.

Answer: B

Topic: Cyclical and Structural Balances
Skill: Recognition

46) The structural surplus is what
A) would be produced if there were no deflationary gap.
B) the government surplus would be if the economy were at potential GDP.
C) people would save at full employment.
D) would happen to employment if the full-employment level of GDP prevailed.

Answer: B

Topic: Cyclical and Structural Balances
Skill: Recognition

47) The cyclical deficit is the portion of the deficit
A) caused by fluctuations in real GDP.
B) that is the result of nondiscretionary federal spending.
C) that would exist if the economy were at potential real GDP.
D) the result of discretionary federal spending.

Answer: A

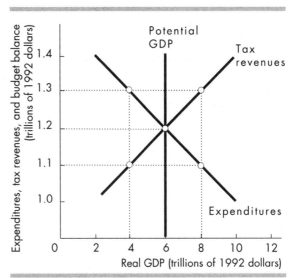

Topic: Cyclical and Structural Balances
Skill: Analytical

48) In the above figure, if actual GDP = $8 trillion, there is a budget _____ equal to _____.
A) surplus; $0.2 trillion
B) surplus; $1.3 trillion
C) deficit; $0.2 trillion
D) deficit; $1.1 trillion

Answer: A

Topic: Cyclical and Structural Balances
Skill: Analytical

49) In the above figure,
A) the structural deficit equals zero.
B) any surpluses are cyclical surpluses.
C) any deficits are cyclical deficits.
D) All of the above answers are correct.

Answer: D

■ Fiscal Policy Multipliers and the Price Level

Topic: Fiscal Policy and Aggregate Demand
Skill: Conceptual

50) Suppose that real GDP equals $2 trillion while potential GDP is $3 trillion. There no imports or taxes and prices are constant. If the government wants to increase aggregate demand to fill the gap, it should increase government spending by _____ if the *MPC* equals _____.

A) $200 billion; 0.80
B) $1 trillion; 0.80
C) $250 billion; 0.75
D) Both answers A and C are correct.

Answer: D

Topic: Expansionary Fiscal Policy
Skill: Recognition

51) The most expansionary fiscal policy would be one that

A) decreases government purchases and lowers taxes.
B) increases the nation's money supply.
C) increases government purchases and lowers taxes.
D) raises tax rates.

Answer: C

Topic: Expansionary Fiscal Policy
Skill: Conceptual

52) Suppose the government lowered marginal tax rates from 40 percent to 30 percent. This change is an example of

A) crowding out.
B) an automatic stabilization.
C) an expansionary fiscal policy.
D) a contractionary fiscal policy.

Answer: C

Topic: Expansionary Fiscal Policy
Skill: Conceptual

53) Suppose the government decreases induced taxes. This change causes

A) government purchases to increase.
B) government purchases to decrease.
C) an increase in aggregate demand.
D) a decrease in aggregate demand.

Answer: C

Topic: Expansionary Fiscal Policy
Skill: Conceptual

54) If the federal government pursues an expansionary fiscal policy, then

A) eventually aggregate demand decreases because private investment decreases.
B) government has reduced taxes less than it has decreased its purchases.
C) government has increased taxes more than it has decreased spending.
D) either government spending has increased or taxes have decreased or both.

Answer: D

Topic: Expansionary Fiscal Policy
Skill: Recognition

55) The aggregate demand curve is shifted rightward by

A) an increase in tax rates.
B) a decrease in government purchases.
C) an increase in the federal budget surplus.
D) an increase in government purchases.

Answer: D

Topic: Contractionary Fiscal Policy
Skill: Conceptual

56) A contractionary fiscal policy

A) shifts the *AE* curve upward.
B) shifts the *AD* curve leftward.
C) includes an increase in government purchases.
D) includes a decrease in induced taxes.

Answer: B

Topic: Contractionary Fiscal Policy
Skill: Conceptual

57) If the government enacts a contractionary fiscal policy, it might

A) increase induced taxes.
B) increase lump-sum taxes.
C) decrease government purchases.
D) All of the above answers are correct.

Answer: D

Topic: Equilibrium GDP and the Price Level in the Short Run
Skill: Analytical

58) Ignoring the supply-side view, an increase in government spending _____ the *AE* curve and _____ the *SAS* curve.

A) shifts upward; does not shift
B) shifts downward; shifts leftward
C) does not shift; does not shift
D) shifts upward; shifts rightward

Answer: A

Topic: Equilibrium GDP and the Price Level in the Short Run
Skill: Analytical

59) Ignoring the supply-side view, an increase in government purchases _____ the *AD* curve and _____ the *SAS* curve.

A) shifts rightward; does not shift
B) shifts leftward; shifts leftward
C) does not shift; does not shift
D) shifts rightward; shifts rightward

Answer: A

Topic: Equilibrium GDP and the Price Level in the Short Run
Skill: Conceptual

60) Contractionary fiscal policy will

A) involve cutting taxes.
B) generate an increase in real GDP.
C) lower the price level.
D) involve increasing government spending.

Answer: C

Topic: Equilibrium GDP and the Price Level in the Short Run
Skill: Conceptual

61) If the economy is at a level of GDP less than potential GDP, which of the following fiscal policies would lead to a higher equilibrium level of real GDP in the short run?

A) only decrease government spending.
B) only increase taxes.
C) increase government spending and/or decrease taxes.
D) decrease government spending and/or increase taxes.

Answer: C

Topic: Equilibrium GDP and the Price Level in the Short Run
Skill: Conceptual

62) Suppose the economy is at a short-run equilibrium beyond the economy's long run potential level of real GDP. Which of the following fiscal policies would decrease output and prices in the short run?

A) an increase in government spending.
B) a decrease in taxes.
C) an increase in taxes.
D) None of the above answers are correct.

Answer: C

Topic: Equilibrium GDP and the Price Level in the Short Run
Skill: Conceptual

63) Suppose the economy is in equilibrium on the *SAS* curve at an output level beyond the economy's potential real GDP. In the short run, if the government decreases its spending, then

A) output will decrease and the price level will rise.
B) output will increase and the price level will fall.
C) output and the price level will both decrease.
D) output and the price level will both increase.

Answer: C

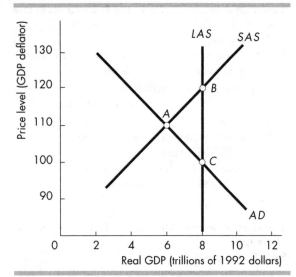

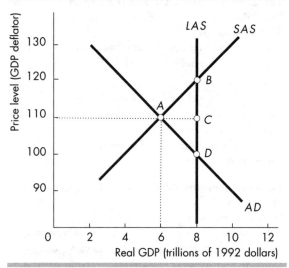

Topic: Equilibrium GDP and the Price Level in the Short Run

Skill: Analytical

64) In the above figure, suppose the economy is a point *A*. The government could ____ to move the economy to point ____.

A) increase government spending; *C*

B) increase government spending; *B*

C) decrease induced taxes; *C*

D) decrease lump-sum taxes; *C*

Answer: B

Topic: Equilibrium GDP and the Price Level in the Short Run

Skill: Analytical

65) In the above figure, suppose the economy is at point *A*. To move the economy so that it is producing at its potential GDP, the government might increase its purchases

A) by $2 trillion.

B) so that the aggregate supply curve shifts so that it goes through point *D*.

C) so that the aggregate demand curve shifts so that it goes through point *B*.

D) so that the aggregate demand curve and the aggregate supply curve both shift so that they both go through point *C*.

Answer: C

Topic: Equilibrium GDP and the Price Level in the Short Run

Skill: Analytical

66) In the above figure, suppose the economy is at point *A*. By the proper use of fiscal policy, the government can

A) shift the *LAS* curve through point *A*.

B) get the economy to point *B*.

C) get the economy to point *C*.

D) get the economy to point *D*.

Answer: B

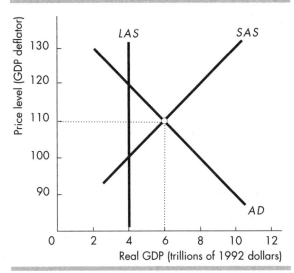

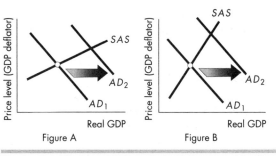

Figure A   Figure B

Topic: Equilibrium GDP and the Price Level in the Short Run

Skill: Analytical

67) In the above figure, which fiscal policy could help move the economy to its long-run equilibrium?

A) Decreasing government purchases.

B) Decreasing taxes.

C) Increasing transfers.

D) Both answers A and B are correct.

Answer: A

Topic: Equilibrium GDP and the Price Level in the Short Run

Skill: Analytical

68) In the above figure, an increase in government purchases increases aggregate demand. In both figures, the rightward shift in the aggregate demand curve is exactly the same. In which of the two figures is the multiplier the largest?

A) Figure A.

B) There is no multiplier effect shown.

C) Figure B.

D) The multiplier is the same in both figures.

Answer: A

Topic: Equilibrium GDP and the Price Level in the Short Run

Skill: Conceptual

69) Once you account for ____, the multiplier effect of an increase in government purchases is ____.

A) price level effects; weakened

B) price level effects; strengthened

C) the MPC; weakened

D) the MPC; strengthened

Answer: A

Topic: Equilibrium GDP and the Price Level in the Short Run

Skill: Conceptual

70) In the ____, the government purchases multiplier is ____.

A) long run; greater than 0

B) long-run; less than 0

C) short-run; less than 0

D) short-run; greater than 0

Answer: D

Topic: Fiscal Expansion at Potential GDP
Skill: Conceptual

71) Ignoring any supply-side effects, when the economy is on its long-run aggregate supply curve and the government initiates an expansionary fiscal policy, the result is

A) a permanent increase in real GDP and a permanent increase in the price level.

B) a temporary increase in real GDP and a temporary increase in the price level.

C) a temporary increase in real GDP and an increase in the price level, followed by a reduction of real GDP to its original level and a further increase in the price level.

D) a temporary increase in real GDP and an increase in the price level, followed by a further increase in the price level and no subsequent change in real GDP.

Answer: C

Topic: Fiscal Expansion at Potential GDP
Skill: Conceptual

72) Suppose the economy is at an equilibrium on the *LAS* curve and the government increases its purchases. In the short run one would expect real GDP to ____ and the price level to ____.

A) increase; increase

B) constant; increase

C) increase; remain constant.

D) remain constant; remain constant

Answer: A

Topic: Fiscal Expansion at Potential GDP
Skill: Conceptual

73) Suppose the economy is in equilibrium on the *LAS* curve and government spending increases. Ignoring any supply-side effects, in the long run

A) the price level and real GDP will return to the original levels.

B) the price level will increase and real GDP will return to the original level.

C) the price level and real GDP will increase.

D) real GDP will increase and the price level will decrease.

Answer: B

Topic: Limitations of Fiscal Policy
Skill: Conceptual

74) The use of fiscal policy is limited because

A) there is never a long enough time lag.

B) the economy is almost always at full employment.

C) the President may have different goals than Congress.

D) time lags associated with fiscal policy may cause the policy to take effect too late to solve the problem it was supposed to address.

Answer: D

Topic: Limitations of Fiscal Policy
Skill: Conceptual

75) Which of the following are a limitation of fiscal policy?

I.   There is a lag between recognizing that fiscal policy might be needed and when it actually takes effect.

II. It is difficult to know where the economy is in relation to potential GDP.

III. Monetary policy might counter fiscal policy.

A) I only.

B) I and II.

C) I and III.

D) I, II and III.

Answer: B

Topic: Limitations of Fiscal Policy
Skill: Conceptual

76) An advantage of automatic stabilizers over discretionary fiscal policy is that

A) automatic stabilizers are not subject to all the same time lags that discretionary fiscal policy is.

B) automatic stabilizers can be easily fine-tuned to move the economy to full employment.

C) only the President is involved in implementing automatic stabilizers instead of both the President and Congress.

D) automatic stabilizers require only a simple majority of Congress to pass whereas discretionary fiscal policy requires a two-thirds majority to pass.

Answer: A

■ Fiscal Policy and Aggregate Supply

Topic: Fiscal Policy and Potential GDP
Skill: Conceptual
77) Which of the following are arguments made by supply-side economists?
   I.   A tax cut will have a relatively large effect on aggregate supply.
   II. A tax cut will increase aggregate demand substantially more than it increases aggregate supply.
   III. Tax cuts will have very little effect on potential GDP.
   A) I only.
   B) I and II.
   C) III only.
   D) I, II and III.
Answer: A

Topic: Fiscal Policy and Potential GDP
Skill: Conceptual
78) Supply-siders assert that tax cuts
   A) cannot affect aggregate demand.
   B) have a relatively small effect on aggregate supply.
   C) increase potential GDP.
   D) cannot influence labor supply.
Answer: C

Topic: Fiscal Policy and Potential GDP
Skill: Conceptual
79) The supply-side theory of economics claims that
   A) tax cuts increase potential GDP.
   B) tax cuts decrease aggregate demand.
   C) tax cuts cannot affect aggregate demand.
   D) Both answers A and B are correct.
Answer: A

Topic: Fiscal Policy and Potential GDP
Skill: Conceptual
80) According to supply-siders, tax cuts can change
   I.   the quantity of labor supplied.
   II. the quantity of capital used.
   III. real GDP.
   A) I only.
   B) I and II.
   C) II only.
   D) I, II and III.
Answer: D

Topic: Fiscal Policy and Potential GDP
Skill: Conceptual
81) According to supply-siders, a tax increase
   A) weakens the incentive to work.
   B) decreases real GDP.
   C) will increase the amount of capital used because people work less.
   D) Both answers A and B are correct.
Answer: D

Topic: Fiscal Policy and Potential GDP
Skill: Conceptual
82) According to supply siders, a(n) _____ in income tax rates will cause the _____.
   A) increase; labor supply curve to shift rightward.
   B) increase; labor supply curve to shift leftward.
   C) decrease; labor demand curve to shift rightward.
   D) decrease; labor demand curve to shift leftward.
Answer: B

Topic: Fiscal Policy and Potential GDP
Skill: Conceptual
83) Supply-side economists stress that an increase in taxes causes the labor supply curve to shift _____ and the _____.
   A) leftward; after-tax wage rate to fall
   B) rightward; before-tax wage rate to rise
   C) leftward; after-tax wage rate to rise
   D) The question errs because tax rates only affect aggregate demand.
Answer: A

Topic: Fiscal Policy and Potential GDP
Skill: Conceptual
84) Supply siders assert that a tax _____ will cause the _____.
   A) increase; before-tax interest rate to rise
   B) increase; after-tax interest rate to rise
   C) decrease; after-tax interest rate to remain constant
   D) decrease; before-tax interest rate to rise
Answer: A

Topic: Supply Effects and Demand Effects
Skill: Conceptual
85) According to supply-side theory, a tax increase will affect
   A) the aggregate demand curve.
   B) the short-run aggregate supply curve.
   C) the long-run aggregate supply curve.
   D) all of the above.
Answer: D

Topic: Supply Effects and Demand Effects
Skill: Conceptual

86) According to the supply-side theory, a tax decrease will shift the

A) long-run aggregate supply curve rightward.
B) short-run aggregate supply curve rightward.
C) aggregate demand curve rightward.
D) all of the above.

Answer: D

Topic: Supply Effects and Demand Effects
Skill: Conceptual

87) Supply siders argue that a tax cut will have a(n) _____ effect on _____.

A) unpredictable; aggregate demand.
B) large; aggregate supply.
C) small; aggregate supply.
D) Both answers A and B are correct.

Answer: B

Topic: Supply Effects and Demand Effects
Skill: Conceptual

88) Suppose the economy is in a recession and supply-side economists convince the President and Congress to pass a tax cut. According to the supply siders, this tax cut will cause

A) aggregate demand to increase.
B) aggregate supply to increase.
C) the supply of capital to increase.
D) all of the above.

Answer: D

Topic: Supply Effects and Demand Effects
Skill: Analytical

89) Suppose the government enacts an income tax cut. According to which view, traditional or supply-side, will the price level increase the most?

A) The price level will increase the most according to the traditional view.
B) The price level will increase the most according to the supply-side view.
C) Both views hold that the price level will increase by the same amount.
D) Both views hold that the price level will not increase.

Answer: A

Topic: Supply Effects and Demand Effects
Skill: Analytical

90) Suppose the government enacts an income tax cut. According to which view, traditional or supply-side, will real GDP increase the most?

A) Real GDP will increase the most according to the traditional view.
B) Real GDP will increase the most according to the supply-side view.
C) Both views hold that real GDP will increase by the same amount.
D) Both views hold that GDP will not increase.

Answer: B

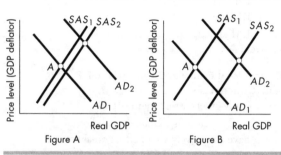

Figure A   Figure B

Topic: Supply Effects and Demand Effects
Skill: Analytical

91) In the above figure, which of the diagrams show the supply-side view rather than the traditional view of an income tax cut?

A) Figure A.
B) Figure B.
C) Both figures show the supply-side view.
D) Neither figure shows the supply-side view.

Answer: B

Topic: Supply Effects and Demand Effects
Skill: Analytical

92) In the above figure, which of the diagrams show the traditional view rather than the supply-side view of an income tax cut?

A) Figure A.
B) Figure B.
C) Both figures show the traditional view.
D) Neither figure shows the traditional view.

Answer: A

■ True Or False Questions

Topic: The Federal Budget
Skill: Recognition
93) Each president can decide when to submit a budget to Congress.
Answer: FALSE

Topic: Fiscal Policy
Skill: Conceptual
94) The main goal of fiscal policy is to produce a balanced budget.
Answer: FALSE

Topic: The Budget Surplus in Global Perspective
Skill: Recognition
95) All developed countries have about the same ratio of the government surplus/GDP.
Answer: FALSE

Topic: Discretionary Fiscal Policy
Skill: Recognition
96) Discretionary policy requires an act of Congress.
Answer: TRUE

Topic: Government Purchases Multiplier
Skill: Recognition
97) $1/(1 - MPC)$ is the government purchases multiplier.
Answer: TRUE

Topic: Lump-Sum Tax Multiplier
Skill: Recognition
98) The lump-sum tax multiplier is $MPC/(1 - MPC)$.
Answer: FALSE

Topic: Induced Taxes and Entitlement Spending
Skill: Conceptual
99) Induced taxes and entitlement payments decrease the multiplier effects.
Answer: TRUE

Topic: Cyclical and Structural Balances
Skill: Conceptual
100) The structural surplus measures whether a budget surplus is cyclical or structural.
Answer: TRUE

Topic: Fiscal Policy and Aggregate Demand
Skill: Conceptual
101) An increase in government spending leads to rightward shift of the AD curve.
Answer: TRUE

Topic: Expansionary Fiscal Policy
Skill: Conceptual
102) Expansionary fiscal policy is used when the economy is expanding too fast.
Answer: FALSE

Topic: Fiscal Policy and Potential GDP
Skill: Conceptual
103) An increase in income taxes can decrease potential GDP and long-run aggregate supply.
Answer: TRUE

Topic: Supply Effects and Demand Effects
Skill: Conceptual
104) The traditional view of fiscal policy claims that there are small effects on aggregate supply.
Answer: TRUE

Topic: Supply Effects and Demand Effects
Skill: Conceptual
105) The supply-side view of fiscal policy claims that an income tax cut has a large effect on aggregate supply.
Answer: TRUE

■ Essay Questions

Topic: Fiscal Policy
Skill: Recognition
106) What is fiscal policy and its purposes?
Answer:

Topic: The Employment Act of 1946
Skill: Recognition
107) What is the Employment Act of 1946?
Answer:

Topic: Budget Surplus and Deficit
Skill: Recognition
108) What is the difference between budget surplus, budget deficit and a balanced budget?
Answer:

Topic: Discretionary Fiscal Policy
Skill: Conceptual
109) What is the difference between discretionary fiscal policy and automatic stabilizers?
Answer:

Topic: Government Purchases Multiplier
Skill: Recognition
110) What is the government purchases multiplier?
Answer:

Topic: Entitlement Spending
Skill: Conceptual
111) How does entitlement spending affect the government purchases multiplier?
Answer:

Topic: Expansionary and Contractionary Fiscal Policy
Skill: Conceptual
112) What are examples of expansionary and contractionary fiscal policies? Name two of each.
Answer:

Topic: Limitations of Fiscal Policy
Skill: Conceptual
113) What are some of the limitations of fiscal policy? Discuss two.
Answer:

Topic: Supply Effects and Demand Effects
Skill: Conceptual
114) Explain the difference between the traditional and the supply-side views of fiscal policy.
Answer:

Chapter 14 MONEY*

■ What Is Money?

Topic: What is Money?
Skill: Recognition
1) Money serves as
A) a medium of exchange.
B) a store of value.
C) a unit of account.
D) all of the above.
Answer: D

Topic: Medium of Exchange
Skill: Recognition
2) A medium of exchange is
A) an object that sellers will accept as payment.
B) a measure by which prices are expressed.
C) an asset that is used to settle future debts.
D) the thing traded when barter takes place.
Answer: A

Topic: Medium of Exchange
Skill: Conceptual
3) Money's function as a medium of exchange means that
A) money is a common denominator for expressing the prices of goods and services.
B) money can be used to store wealth.
C) money serves as an acceptable means of payment.
D) money requires a double coincidence of wants.
Answer: C

Topic: Medium of Exchange
Skill: Conceptual
4) When money is accepted as payment in a market transaction, it is functioning as a
A) store of value.
B) unit of accounting.
C) medium of exchange.
D) unit of investment.
Answer: C

Topic: Medium of Exchange
Skill: Conceptual
5) Matthew purchases a candy bar with his allowance. This purchase represents using money as
A) a medium of exchange.
B) a store of value.
C) an unit of account.
D) none of the above.
Answer: A

Topic: Medium of Exchange
Skill: Conceptual
6) Money as a medium of exchange
  I.   Facilitates the exchange of goods
  II. Reduces or eliminates the need for barter
A) I only.
B) II only.
C) Both I and II.
D) Neither I nor II.
Answer: C

Topic: Medium of Exchange
Skill: Recognition
7) The direct exchange of goods and services for other goods and services is known as
A) primitive trade.
B) nonmarket trade.
C) barter.
D) purchasing power trading.
Answer: C

---

* This is Chapter 31 in *Economics*.

Topic: Medium of Exchange
Skill: Conceptual

8)　Barter is an inefficient means of exchange because
A)　barter transactions require a double coincidence of wants.
B)　barter only occurs in relatively primitive economies.
C)　demand will not necessarily equal supply.
D)　in a barter transaction only one party needs to want what the other party has to sell.

Answer: A

Topic: Unit of Account
Skill: Conceptual

9)　As a unit of account, money is used
A)　to state prices of all goods and services.
B)　to pay off future debts.
C)　to hold purchasing power over time.
D)　to exchange for goods and services.

Answer: A

Topic: Unit of Account
Skill: Conceptual

10)　Cigarettes served as money in some POW camps during World War II. Given this fact, we would expect to observe
A)　no one ever smoking a cigarette.
B)　people usually resorting to barter rather than using cigarettes as money.
C)　prices of other goods expressed in terms of cigarettes.
D)　only government-issued cigarettes being accepted as money.

Answer: C

Topic: Unit of Account
Skill: Conceptual

11)　Pat easily compares the prices of several vacuum cleaners to find the best value. This comparison represents the use of money as
A)　a unit of account.
B)　a medium of exchange.
C)　a store of value.
D)　all of the above.

Answer: A

Topic: Unit of Account
Skill: Conceptual

12)　Catherine compares the prices of candy bars in order to get the "best buy." This comparison represents using money as
A)　a medium of exchange.
B)　a store of value.
C)　a unit of account.
D)　none of the above.

Answer: C

Topic: Store of Value
Skill: Conceptual

13)　Which of the following applies to an object serving as a store of value?
I.　If an object can be held and exchanged later for a good or service, it serves as a store of value.
II.　The less stable an object's value, the better it serves as a store of value.
III.　A work of art can serve as a store of value.
A)　I only.
B)　I and II.
C)　I and III.
D)　I, II and III.

Answer: C

Topic: Store of Value
Skill: Conceptual

14)　Which of the following applies to money when it serves as a store of value?
I.　Money is a store of value because it is an agreed measure for stating goods' prices.
II.　The more stable money's value, the better it serves as a store of value.
III.　When money serves as a store of value, it requires a double coincidence of wants.
A)　I only.
B)　I and II.
C)　II only.
D)　II and III.

Answer: C

Topic: Store of Value
Skill: Conceptual
15) Nicholas is saving money collected from his paper route in order to purchase a new bicycle. His saving represents using money as
A) a medium of exchange.
B) a store of value.
C) an unit of account.
D) none of the above.
Answer: B

Topic: Money in the United States Today
Skill: Recognition
16) Checking deposits are
A) not part of the money supply.
B) part of the money supply.
C) small in volume relative to currency in circulation.
D) quite different from checking accounts.
Answer: B

Topic: Money in the United States Today, M1
Skill: Recognition
17) Which of the following is NOT included in M1?
A) Currency.
B) Checking deposits owned by individuals.
C) Saving deposits.
D) Traveler's checks.
Answer: C

Topic: Money in the United States Today, M1
Skill: Recognition
18) The largest component of M1 is
A) currency.
B) checking deposits.
C) small time deposits.
D) the store of value money.
Answer: B

Topic: Money in the United States Today, M2
Skill: Recognition
19) The definition of M2 includes
   I.   M1.
   II. money market mutual funds.
   III. currency held outside of banks.
A) I and II only.
B) I and III only.
C) II and III only.
D) I, II, and III.
Answer: D

Topic: Money in the United States Today, M1 and M2
Skill: Recognition
20) Checking deposits are included in
A) M1 only.
B) M2 only.
C) M1 and M2.
D) savings balances only.
Answer: C

Topic: Money in the United States Today, M1 and M2
Skill: Recognition
21) The major difference between M1 and M2 is that
A) M1 is a stock variable while M2 is a flow variable.
B) M2 is a stock variable while M1 is a flow variable.
C) time deposits and savings deposits are included in M2.
D) traveler's checks are part of M1.
Answer: C

Component	Amount (billions of dollars)
Currency	235
Checking deposits	570
Savings deposits	416
Traveler's checks	8
Time deposits	1,144
Money market mutual funds	930
Available credit on credit cards	675

Topic: Money in the United States Today, M1 and M2
Skill: Analytical
22) According to the table above, the value of M1 is _____ and the value of M2 is _____.
A) $813 billion; $2490 billion
B) $805 billion; $2490 billion
C) $813 billion; $3303 billion
D) $1,488 billion; $3978 billion
Answer: C

Component	Amount (billions of dollars)
Currency	300
Checking deposits	600
Savings deposits	450
Traveler's checks	10
Time deposits	1,200
Money market mutual funds	1,100
Available credit on credit cards	900

Topic: Money in the United States Today, M1 and M2
Skill: Analytical
23) According to the table above, the value of M1 is _____ and the value of M2 is _____.
A) $860 billion; $2,750 billion
B) $910 billion; $1,960 billion
C) $860 billion; $4,560 billion
D) $910 billion; $3,660 billion
Answer: D

Topic: Liquidity
Skill: Conceptual
24) A highly liquid asset
A) has high transaction costs associated with its sale.
B) is highly leveraged.
C) generally has a very limited market for its resale.
D) can be disposed of easily without loss of value.
Answer: D

Topic: Liquidity
Skill: Conceptual
25) An individual wanting the most liquid asset possible will hold
A) currency.
B) a savings account.
C) gold.
D) U.S. government bonds.
Answer: A

Topic: Liquidity
Skill: Conceptual
26) Which of the following is the most liquid asset?
A) money.
B) land.
C) a government bond.
D) a share of stock.
Answer: A

Topic: Checks Are Not Money
Skill: Conceptual
27) Which of the following is true?
 I.   Checks are considered money because they can be used as a medium of exchange.
 II.   Checks represent a transfer of money.
A) I only.
B) II only.
C) Both I and II.
D) Neither I nor II.
Answer: B

Topic: Credit Cards Are Not Money
Skill: Conceptual
28) Credit cards
A) are not a part of the money supply because they are not a means of payment.
B) are a part of M1 but not of M2.
C) are a part of the money supply because they are used to purchase goods and services.
D) are a part of M2 but not a part of M1.
Answer: A

Topic: Credit Cards Are Not Money
Skill: Conceptual
29) Credit cards are
A) a part of the money supply because they are used in so many transactions.
B) a part of the money supply when the transaction approach is used but not when the liquidity approach is used.
C) not part of the money supply because they represent a loan of money to the user.
D) not part of the money supply because the government has no control over the amount of credit outstanding.
Answer: C

■ Financial Intermediaries

Topic: Financial Intermediaries
Skill: Recognition
30) Which of the following is considered a financial intermediary?
I. The Federal Reserve.
II. A commercial bank like Citibank.
III. A credit union for federal government employees.
A) I only.
B) I and II.
C) II and III.
D) I, II and III.
Answer: C

Topic: Financial Intermediaries
Skill: Recognition
31) Financial intermediation is best defined as the process by which
A) inflation is controlled.
B) corporations issue new stock.
C) liabilities are liquidated.
D) financial institutions accept savings from savers and make loans to borrowers.
Answer: D

Topic: Financial Intermediaries
Skill: Conceptual
32) Which of the following is an example of a financial intermediary?
A) a money market mutual fund.
B) a credit union.
C) a commercial bank.
D) All of the above are examples of a financial intermediary.
Answer: D

Topic: Commercial Banks
Skill: Conceptual
33) Commercial banks
A) are the only financial intermediary providing checking accounts.
B) are licensed by state agencies or the Comptroller of the Currency.
C) deal only with businesses.
D) are the only financial intermediary with a liability that is part of the nation's M2 money supply.
Answer: B

Topic: Commercial Banks
Skill: Conceptual
34) Modern U.S. commercial banks perform all of the following functions EXCEPT
A) accept demand deposits.
B) issue paper currency.
C) make loans to households and business firms.
D) accept time deposits.
Answer: B

Topic: Commercial Banks
Skill: Conceptual
35) Which of the following are correct regarding a bank's balance sheet?
I. Liabilities + Assets = Net worth.
II. People's deposits are part of the bank's assets.
III. Loans made by banks are part of its liabilities.
A) I only.
B) I and II.
C) II and III.
D) neither I, II nor III is correct.
Answer: D

Topic: Commercial Banks
Skill: Conceptual
36) Which of the following are part of a commercial bank's reserves:
I. cash in the bank's vaults.
II. loans.
III. cash in checking accounts.
A) I only.
B) I and II.
C) I and III.
D) I, II and III.
Answer: A

Topic: Commercial Banks
Skill: Conceptual
37) If a bank decided to keep all its deposits as reserves, it would
A) go out of business because it would make no profits.
B) be considered to be operating a very risky business.
C) maximize profits.
D) not have any cash on hand.
Answer: A

Topic: Commercial Banks
Skill: Conceptual

38) Which of the following statements is correct about the commercial banks' reserves kept as deposits at the Federal Reserve?
   A) Commercial banks can make loans to commercial customers out of these reserves.
   B) Commercial banks don't have access to their reserves at the Fed.
   C) The reserves are the banks' only assets.
   D) Commercial banks write checks to other banks on their reserve accounts at the Fed.

Answer: D

Topic: Commercial Banks
Skill: Conceptual

39) Which of the following is true regarding a bank's operations?
   I.   The bank's goal is to collect as many deposits as possible and keep the deposits as reserves.
   II. Loans represent a liability for the bank.
   A) I only.
   B) II only.
   C) Both I and II.
   D) Neither I nor II.

Answer: D

Topic: Commercial Banks
Skill: Conceptual

40) U.S. government Treasury bills are part of a bank's ____ and loans to businesses are part of a bank's ____.
   A) assets; reserves
   B) reserves; assets
   C) assets; assets
   D) reserves; reserves

Answer: C

Topic: Commercial Banks
Skill: Conceptual

41) Which of the following are part of a bank's assets?
   I.   Reserves at the Federal Reserve.
   II. Customers' deposits.
   III. Loans.
   A) III only.
   B) I and II.
   C) II and III.
   D) I and III.

Answer: D

Topic: Reserves
Skill: Recognition

42) The reserves of a commercial bank
   A) consist of vault cash and deposits at the Federal Reserve.
   B) are the funds the bank can use to satisfy the cash demands of its customers.
   C) are a small fraction of the bank's demand and time deposits.
   D) All of the above answers are correct.

Answer: D

Topic: Money Market Mutual Funds
Skill: Conceptual

43) Which of the following is true regarding money market mutual funds?
   I.   Money market mutual funds buy highly liquid assets like Treasury bills.
   II. Shareholders can obtain loans from money market mutual funds.
   A) I only.
   B) II only.
   C) Both I and II.
   D) Neither I nor II.

Answer: A

Topic: Economic Functions of Financial Intermediaries
Skill: Conceptual

44) Which of the following tasks are performed by financial intermediaries?
   I.   They make long-term loans using short-term deposits, thereby creating liquidity.
   II. They efficiently gather funds from a large base of depositors.
   III. They concentrate risk.
   A) I only.
   B) II only.
   C) III only.
   D) I and II.

Answer: D

Topic: Economic Functions of Financial Intermediaries
Skill: Conceptual

45) Financial intermediaries are good at minimizing
   A) the costs of monitoring borrowers.
   B) risky borrowers.
   C) liquidity.
   D) all of the above.

Answer: A

Topic: Economic Functions of Financial Intermediaries
Skill: Conceptual

46) If a savings and loan "pools risk," which of the following must it do?

A) Take funds in from a large number of lenders.

B) Have a large spread between the interest rate it charges borrowers and the interest rate it pays lenders.

C) Lend money to a large number of firms.

D) Both answers A and C are correct.

Answer: D

■ Financial Regulation, Deregulation and Innovation

Topic: Financial Regulation
Skill: Recognition

47) Which of the following are kinds of regulations faced by financial intermediaries?

I. deposit insurance
II. capital requirements
III. lending rules

A) I only.

B) I and II.

C) II and III.

D) I, II and III.

Answer: D

Topic: Financial Regulation
Skill: Recognition

48) A function of the Federal Deposit Insurance Corporation (FDIC) is

A) to insure bank loans.

B) to insure the nation's money supply.

C) to insure bank deposits up to $100,000.

D) to guarantee that no depositor will ever lose any money from a bank failure.

Answer: C

Topic: Financial Regulation
Skill: Conceptual

49) The manner in which FDIC deposit insurance is set up in the United States encourages financial intermediaries to

A) be too conservative in their lending practices.

B) maintain excess reserves that are too great.

C) make riskier loans than they otherwise would.

D) reject some loans that probably would be profitable.

Answer: C

Topic: Financial Regulation, Deregulation and Innovation
Skill: Conceptual

50) Deposit insurance by the FDIC shields depositors from the adverse effects of risky decisions made by the financial intermediary, and thus

A) encourages riskier behavior on the part of managers of financial intermediaries.

B) encourages depositors to monitor the managers of financial intermediaries more closely.

C) encourages moral hazard on the part of depositors.

D) generates a more efficient banking system.

Answer: A

Topic: Financial Regulation
Skill: Conceptual

51) Which of the following is a current balance sheet regulation?

A) Requirements that a certain percentage of deposits be held as cash or safe, liquid deposits.

B) Rules that set the minimum amount of an owner's financial resources that must be invested in a financial intermediary.

C) Regulations that limit the total amount of assets that a financial intermediary may own.

D) Both answers A and B are correct.

Answer: D

Topic: Financial Regulation
Skill: Conceptual

52) In terms of a balance sheet regulation, capital requirements

A) state how much of the bank's assets must be held as stocks or bonds.

B) state the percentage of deposits that financial intermediaries must hold as reserves, cash, liquid assets and loans.

C) mandate the minimum amount of investment an owner of a financial intermediary must have in the institution.

D) were imposed under the 1980s deregulation.

Answer: C

Topic: Deregulation in the 1980s
Skill: Conceptual

53) DIDMCA (the Depository Institutions' Deregulation and Monetary Control Act) was responsible for

A) limiting how banks, savings and loans, savings banks, money market mutual funds and credit unions could compete.

B) allowed more competition between all types of financial intermediaries.

C) restricting the Fed's ability to control bank reserves.

D) Both answers B and C are correct.

Answer: B

Topic: Deregulation in the 1980s
Skill: Conceptual

54) DIDMCA (the Depository Institutions' Deregulation and Monetary Control Act) did which of the following?

I. Promoted competition among financial intermediaries.

II. Gave the Federal Reserve more control over reserve requirements imposed on all depository institutions.

III. Made a greater distinction between banks and nonbank financial institutions.

A) I and III.

B) I and II.

C) II and III.

D) I, II and III.

Answer: B

Topic: Financial Innovation
Skill: Conceptual

55) Financial intermediaries may engage in financial innovation in order to

A) lower the cost of obtaining funds.

B) increase the return from lending.

C) avoid regulation.

D) All of the above answers are correct.

Answer: D

Topic: Deregulation Innovation and Money
Skill: Conceptual

56) As a result of deregulation,

A) the composition of M1 has changed.

B) the composition of M2 has changed.

C) the cost of obtaining deposits has increased.

D) Both answers A and B are correct.

Answer: D

■ How Banks Create Money

Topic: Reserves: Actual and Required
Skill: Recognition

57) The required reserve ratio

A) is the amount of money that banks require borrowers to reserve in their accounts.

B) is the fraction of a bank's total deposits that are required to be held in reserve.

C) increases when withdrawals from a bank are made.

D) is higher for banks that make riskier loans.

Answer: B

Topic: Reserves: Actual and Required
Skill: Conceptual

58) Which of the following is true regarding the required reserve ratio?

A) The ratio determines the legally required amount of reserves a bank must hold.

B) The ratio determines the amount of excess reserves a bank must hold.

C) The ratio is only enforced against banks that are operating in a risky manner.

D) None of the above answers are correct.

Answer: A

Topic: Reserves: Actual and Required
Skill: Recognition

59) Required reserves for a commercial bank

A) are the reserves a bank is legally required to hold to back its deposits.

B) are only the reserves required to be held in the bank's vault.

C) are only the money used by the bank tellers.

D) consist only of deposits at the Fed.

Answer: A

Topic: Reserves: Actual and Required
Skill: Recognition

60) The difference between actual reserves and required reserves is

A) net worth.

B) excess reserves.

C) illegal reserves.

D) borrowings from the Fed.

Answer: B

Topic: Reserves: Actual and Required
Skill: Conceptual

61) A bank with $100 million in deposits has $15 million of cash in the bank, $10 million in deposits with the Fed, and $15 million in government securities in its vault. Its total reserves equal

A) $10 million.
B) $15 million.
C) $25 million.
D) $40 million.

Answer: C

Topic: Reserves: Actual and Required
Skill: Conceptual

62) Suppose a bank has $1,500,000 in deposits and the required reserve ratio is 12 percent. If the bank is currently holding $200,000 in reserves, the excess reserves are equal to

A) zero.
B) $40,000.
C) $120,000.
D) $20,000.

Answer: D

Topic: Reserves: Actual and Required
Skill: Conceptual

63) Suppose a bank is exactly meeting its required reserve ratio of 10 percent and a new deposit of $75,000 is made. Immediately after the deposit is made, the bank's excess reserves equal

A) zero.
B) $7,500.
C) $67,500.
D) It is impossible to determine without additional information.

Answer: C

Topic: Reserves: Actual and Required
Skill: Conceptual

64) Suppose a bank faces a reserve requirement ratio of 12 percent. If someone deposits $1,000 in the bank,

A) immediately after the deposit, excess reserves increase by $880.
B) the bank can make loans of $1,000.
C) the bank's required reserves rise by $1,000.
D) Both answers B and C are correct.

Answer: A

Topic: Reserves: Actual and Required
Skill: Conceptual

65) A bank with $1 billion in deposits holds $70 million in cash, $80 million on deposit with the Fed, and owns $100 million in government securities. If a reduction in the required reserve ratio generates excess reserves of $30 million, and prior to the change the bank had no excess reserves, then the former required reserve ratio was ____ and the new required reserve ratio is ____.

A) 15 percent; 10 percent
B) 15 percent; 12 percent
C) 25 percent; 22 percent
D) 25 percent; 20 percent

Answer: B

Topic: Reserves and Loans
Skill: Conceptual

66) The effect of a new deposit in Bank A-One on the bank's balance sheet is

A) an increase in deposits and an increase in reserves, both of which are assets to the bank.
B) an increase in deposits, which is an asset to the bank, and an increase in reserves, which is a liability to the bank.
C) an increase in deposits and an increase in loans, both of which are liabilities to the bank.
D) an increase in deposits, which is a liability to the bank, and an increase in reserves, which is an asset to the bank.

Answer: D

Topic: Reserves and Loans
Skill: Conceptual

67) When a bank holds excess reserves

A) it can create money.
B) it can make loans.
C) it has too many loans.
D) Both answers A and B are correct.

Answer: D

Topic: Reserves and Loans
Skill: Conceptual

68) Banks create money whenever they

A) accept a deposit.
B) lend excess reserves to a borrower.
C) receive monthly payments on their loans.
D) receive interest on existing loans.

Answer: B

Topic: Reserves and Loans
Skill: Conceptual

69) Commercial banks are able to create money by
A) printing Federal Reserve Notes.
B) making loans.
C) making customers pay back their loans.
D) exchanging their reserves at the Fed for vault cash.

Answer: B

Topic: Reserves and Loans
Skill: Conceptual

70) Given a required reserve ratio of 20 percent, a commercial bank that has received a new deposit of $100 can make additional loans of
A) $0.
B) $20.
C) $80.
D) $400.

Answer: C

Bank of Wealth Balance Sheet			
Assets		Liabilities	
Reserves		Deposits	$250,000
Required	$25,000		
Excess	10,000		
Total reserves	$35,000		
Loans	215,000		_____
Total assets	250,000	Total liabilities	$250,000

Topic: Reserves: Actual and Required
Skill: Analytical

71) In the above balance sheet, the Bank of Wealth is subject to a required reserve ratio of
A) 20 percent.
B) 15 percent.
C) 10 percent.
D) 5 percent.

Answer: C

Topic: Reserves and Loans
Skill: Analytical

72) In the above balance sheet, the Bank of Wealth can make additional loans up to
A) $25,000.
B) $10,000.
C) $5,000.
D) $250,000.

Answer: B

Topic: Reserves: Actual and Required
Skill: Analytical

73) In the above balance sheet, if a customer withdrew $10,000 from her deposits, the bank would
A) have to borrow money to meet the required reserve ratio.
B) have excess reserves of $5,000 after the withdrawal.
C) have zero excess reserves after the withdrawal.
D) have $1,000 in excess reserves after the withdrawal.

Answer: D

ABC Bank Balance Sheet			
Assets		Liabilities	
Reserves		Deposits	$100,000
Required	$20,000		
Excess	5,000		
Total reserves	30,000		
Loans	75,000		_____
Total assets	100,000	Total liabilities	$100,000

Topic: Reserves: Actual and Required
Skill: Analytical

74) According to the above balance sheet, the required reserve ratio for the ABC Bank is
A) 5 percent.
B) 15 percent.
C) 20 percent.
D) 10 percent.

Answer: C

Topic: Reserves and Loans
Skill: Analytical

75) Suppose that $10,000 in new deposits is received by ABC bank, which has the above balance sheet. If there were no other changes in the balance sheet, after the deposit the bank would be in a position to make total new loans in the amount of
A) $13,000.
B) $15,000.
C) $10,000.
D) $30,000.

Answer: A

Topic: The Deposit Multiplier
Skill: Conceptual
76) The deposit multiplier is
   A) the ratio of the change in deposits to the change in reserves.
   B) the ratio of the money supply to excess reserves.
   C) the ratio of reserves to deposits.
   D) the ratio of the money supply to total bank reserves.
   Answer: A

Topic: The Deposit Multiplier
Skill: Conceptual
77) If there are no excess reserves and people want to hold no currency, the deposit multiplier equals
   A) the required reserve ratio.
   B) the inverse of the required reserve ratio.
   C) the total reserve requirement.
   D) the number of dollars on reserve.
   Answer: B

Topic: The Deposit Multiplier
Skill: Conceptual
78) The deposit multiplier gives us
   A) the growth in real GDP when the money supply increases.
   B) the growth in the money supply when real GDP increases.
   C) the maximum potential change in total deposits from a change in reserves.
   D) the maximum potential change in the money supply from a change in deposits.
   Answer: C

Topic: The Deposit Multiplier
Skill: Conceptual
79) If the required reserve ratio is 0.03, there are no excess reserves, and people want to hold no currency, the deposit multiplier equals
   A) 14.29.
   B) 33.33.
   C) 0.03.
   D) 10.0.
   Answer: B

Topic: The Deposit Multiplier
Skill: Conceptual
80) Assuming banks do not wish to hold excess reserves and that there are no cash leakages so that people want to hold no currency, if the required reserve ratio is 10 percent, the deposit multiplier is equal to ____.
   A) 10.
   B) 5.
   C) 20.
   D) 0.
   Answer: A

Topic: The Deposit Multiplier
Skill: Conceptual
81) Suppose that people hold no currency and banks hold no excess reserves. Then, if the Fed decreases the required reserve ratio from 20 percent to 10 percent, the deposit multiplier
   A) increases from 10 to 20.
   B) increases from 5 to 10.
   C) decreases from 20 to 10.
   D) decreases from 10 to 5.
   Answer: B

Topic: Using the Deposit Multiplier
Skill: Conceptual
82) If the required reserve ratio is 10 percent, an extra dollar of reserves will increase banking-system deposits by as much as
   A) $0.10.
   B) $10.
   C) $5.
   D) $1.
   Answer: B

Topic: Using the Deposit Multiplier
Skill: Conceptual
83) Suppose that people want to hold no currency, that banks want to hold no excess reserves, and that the deposit multiplier is 8.33. The required reserve ratio
   A) equals 0.12.
   B) must also be 8.33.
   C) equals 0.88.
   D) cannot be calculated with more information.
   Answer: A

Topic: Using the Deposit Multiplier
Skill: Conceptual

84) If banks have reserve requirements of 20 percent of their deposits, $100 million in excess reserves allows the banking system to create at most

A) $100 million in new money.
B) $20 million in new money.
C) $500 million in new money.
D) $80 million in new money.

Answer: C

Topic: The Deposit Multiplier in the United States
Skill: Conceptual

85) To reach the maximum deposit multiplier of 1/(required reserve ratio), it is assumed that

A) commercial banks keep excess reserves.
B) all loans get redeposited in a checking account.
C) there is insufficient loan demand.
D) loans are diverted into circulating currency.

Answer: B

Topic: The Deposit Multiplier in the United States
Skill: Conceptual

86) The more excess reserves banks decide to keep, then

A) the smaller the deposit multiplier.
B) the larger the deposit supply.
C) the larger the deposit multiplier.
D) the larger the currency drain.

Answer: A

■ Money, Real GDP, and the Price Level

Topic: The Short-Run Effects of a Change in the Quantity of Money
Skill: Conceptual

87) The short-run effect of an increase in the quantity of money

A) increases real GDP only.
B) increases the price level only.
C) increases both real GDP and the price level.
D) increases nominal GDP but decreases real GDP because the price level increases too.

Answer: C

Topic: The Short-Run Effects of a Change in the Quantity of Money
Skill: Conceptual

88) The initial effect of an increase in the quantity of money

A) increases aggregate demand.
B) decreases aggregate supply.
C) increases aggregate supply.
D) decreases the rate of inflation as firms produce more goods and services.

Answer: A

Topic: The Short-Run Effects of a Change in the Quantity of Money
Skill: Conceptual

89) Which of the following is <u>NOT</u> a short-run effect of an increase in the quantity of money?

A) People try to buy more goods and services.
B) Banks have excess reserves.
C) Aggregate supply increases.
D) Price level increases.

Answer: C

Topic: The Short-Run Effects of a Change in the Quantity of Money
Skill: Conceptual

90) If the aggregate demand curve shifts rightward following an increase in the quantity of money, what can be concluded if the short-run aggregate supply curve is rather steep?

A) There will be a significant increase in real GDP with little impact on the price level.
B) There will be a significant increase in both real GDP and the price level.
C) There will be little increase in real GDP but a significant increase in the price level.
D) There is significant unemployment and slack in the economy.

Answer: C

Topic: The Long-Run Effects of a Change in the Quantity of Money
Skill: Conceptual

91) In the long run, a decrease in the quantity of money will

A) increase real GDP.
B) have no lasting impact on real GDP.
C) increase the price level.
D) increase nominal GDP.

Answer: B

Topic: The Long-Run Effects of a Change in the Quantity of Money
Skill: Conceptual

92) The long-run effect of an increase in the quantity of money

   A) increases real GDP with no increase in the price level.
   B) increases the price level with no increase in real GDP.
   C) increases both real GDP and the price level.
   D) increases nominal GDP by decreasing real GDP as the price level increases.

Answer: B

Topic: The Long-Run Effects of a Change in the Quantity of Money
Skill: Conceptual

93) Which of the following is part of the long-run effects of an increase in the quantity of money?

   I.   An increase in money wages.
   II.   A decrease in velocity.
   III. Real GDP increases.

   A) I only.
   B) I and II.
   C) II and III.
   D) I and III.

Answer: A

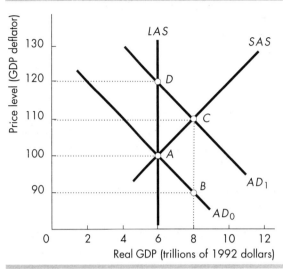

Topic: The Short-Run Effects of a Change in the Quantity of Money
Skill: Analytical

94) In the above figure, suppose point *A* is the original equilibrium. If there is an increase in the quantity of money that shifts the aggregate demand curve to AD_1, the new short-run equilibrium is given by point

   A) *A* (that is, the equilibrium does not change).
   B) *B*.
   C) *C*.
   D) *D*.

Answer: C

Topic: The Long-Run Effects of a Change in the Quantity of Money
Skill: Analytical

95) In the above figure, suppose point *A* is the original equilibrium. If there is an increase in the quantity of money that shifts the aggregate demand curve to AD_1, the long-run price level is

   A) 90.
   B) 100.
   C) 110.
   D) 120.

Answer: D

Topic: Quantity Theory of Money, Velocity of Circulation
Skill: Recognition
96) The velocity of circulation is
A) the relationship between income and spending.
B) the relationship between increases in income and investment.
C) the ratio of currency to demand deposits.
D) the average number of times per year a dollar is spent on goods and services in GDP.
Answer: D

Topic: Quantity Theory of Money, Velocity of Circulation
Skill: Conceptual
97) When macroeconomists say that the velocity of circulation was equal to 4 in 1998, what they mean is that
A) consumers held four dollars in wealth for each dollar they spent in 1998.
B) on average, each dollar of money in the economy purchased four dollars of goods and services in GDP in 1998.
C) for each additional dollar of money injected into the economy, the price level rose 4 percent in 1998.
D) real output of goods and services in GDP rose by four dollars for each additional dollar of money consumers saved.
Answer: B

Topic: Equation of Exchange
Skill: Recognition
98) The equation of exchange
A) is $MV = PY$.
B) becomes the quantity theory if velocity and the price level are constant.
C) cannot be used in an economy with inflation.
D) All of the above answers are correct.
Answer: A

Topic: Equation of Exchange
Skill: Conceptual
99) If $V = 5$, $P = \$3$, and $Y = 50$, then the money supply equals
A) $10.
B) $30.
C) $150.
D) $300.
Answer: B

Topic: Equation of Exchange
Skill: Conceptual
100) According to the equation of exchange, if $M = \$400$, $P = \$8$, and $Y = \$200$, then
A) nominal GDP is $800.
B) V is 4.
C) the price level must fall.
D) V cannot be determined.
Answer: B

Topic: Equation of Exchange
Skill: Conceptual
101) If $M = \$100$, $Y = \$500$ and $P = \$2$, then V is equal to
A) .10.
B) 1.0.
C) 10.
D) 50.
Answer: C

Topic: Equation of Exchange
Skill: Conceptual
102) Suppose that the nominal money supply (M) is $200 billion and the value of aggregate output (PY) is $1 trillion. It must be the case that
A) the economy is suffering from inflation.
B) the average price paid for a "typical" good is $5.
C) there will be a shortage of money balances in the economy.
D) the velocity of circulation is 5.
Answer: D

Topic: Predictions of the Quantity Theory of Money
Skill: Conceptual
103) According to the quantity theory of money, a 10 percent increase in the money supply ultimately leads to
A) a 10 percent increase in real national income.
B) a 10 percent increase in real GDP.
C) a 10 percent increase in the price level.
D) a 10 percent increase in velocity.
Answer: C

Topic: Predictions of the Quantity Theory of Money
Skill: Conceptual

104) According to the quantity theory of money, changes in the price level are usually caused by changes in the
A) prime interest rate.
B) real interest rate.
C) money supply.
D) velocity of circulation.
Answer: C

Topic: Predictions of the Quantity Theory of Money
Skill: Conceptual

105) Other things constant, the quantity theory of money concludes that any increase in the money supply
A) causes a decrease in the demand for money.
B) results in a decrease in the aggregate price level.
C) causes the aggregate level of nominal income to decrease.
D) results in a proportional increase in the price level.
Answer: D

Topic: Predictions of the Quantity Theory of Money
Skill: Conceptual

106) According to the quantity theory of money,
A) an increase in the money supply will increase real output.
B) an increase in the money supply will decrease real output.
C) a decrease in the money supply will decrease the velocity of circulation.
D) a decrease in the money supply will decrease the price level.
Answer: D

Topic: Predictions of the Quantity Theory of Money
Skill: Conceptual

107) Which of the following is true regarding the quantity theory of money?
I. The theory predicts that in the long run the inflation rate equals the money growth rate minus the growth rate of potential GDP.
II. The theory predicts that countries with high growth rates of money will have high inflation rates.
III. In the U.S., the long-run relationship between money growth and inflation supports the theory.
A) I and II.
B) II and III.
C) I and III.
D) I, II and III.
Answer: D

■ True Or False Questions

Topic: Medium of Exchange
Skill: Conceptual

108) Barter eliminates the double coincidence of wants.
Answer: FALSE

Topic: Store of Value
Skill: Conceptual

109) When Patty uses money to buy her lunch, she is showing the use of money as a "store of value."
Answer: FALSE

Topic: Money in the United States Today, M1 and M2
Skill: Conceptual

110) M1 is usually greater than M2.
Answer: FALSE

Topic: Financial Intermediaries
Skill: Recognition

111) A financial intermediary receives deposits from lenders and makes loans to borrowers.
Answer: TRUE

Topic: Commercial Banks
Skill: Conceptual

112) Liquid securities, loans and reserves are assets of a commercial bank.
Answer: TRUE

Topic: Economic Functions of Financial Intermediaries
Skill: Conceptual
113) A financial intermediary creates liquidity and pools risk.
Answer: TRUE

Topic: Deregulation in the 1980s
Skill: Conceptual
114) As a result of banking deregulation in the 1980s, a more competitive environment for banks and savings and loans was created.
Answer: TRUE

Topic: Deregulation, Innovation, and Money
Skill: Conceptual
115) Deregulation in the banking industry led to a change in the composition of the money supply.
Answer: TRUE

Topic: The Deposit Multiplier
Skill: Recognition
116) The reserve requirement ratio helps determine to what degree banks can create money.
Answer: TRUE

Topic: The Deposit Multiplier
Skill: Recognition
117) The deposit multiplier is the amount by which a change in deposits changes the money supply.
Answer: FALSE

Topic: The Deposit Multiplier
Skill: Conceptual
118) When the required reserve ratio equals 10 percent, the deposit multiplier equals 9.
Answer: FALSE

Topic: The Deposit Multiplier in the United States
Skill: Conceptual
119) Because some banks choose to hold excess reserves, the deposit multiplier is increased in size.
Answer: FALSE

Topic: Predictions of the Quantity Theory of Money
Skill: Conceptual
120) The quantity theory of money claims that an increase in the money supply leads to an equal percentage increase in the price level in the long run.
Answer: TRUE

Topic: International Evidence on the Quantity Theory of Money
Skill: Conceptual
121) In comparing growth rates of money growth and inflation across countries, the long-run proposition of the quantity theory of money is supported.
Answer: TRUE

■ Essay Questions

Topic: What is Money?
Skill: Recognition
122) What are the three functions of money?
Answer:

Topic: Unit of Account
Skill: Conceptual
123) Give an example of how money functions as a unit of account.
Answer:

Topic: Financial Intermediaries
Skill: Conceptual
124) What is a financial intermediary? Give two examples.
Answer:

Topic: Economic Functions of Financial Intermediaries
Skill: Recognition
125) What are at least three services of financial intermediaries?
Answer:

Topic: Financial Regulation
Skill: Conceptual
126) What is a positive effect and a negative effect of deposit insurance?
Answer:

Topic: Deregulation in the 1980s
Skill: Conceptual
127) Briefly describe the effects of deregulation on the banking industry since the 1980s.
Answer:

Topic: The Deposit Multiplier
Skill: Conceptual
128) Explain the connection between the required reserve ratio and the deposit multiplier.
Answer:

Topic: The Deposit Multiplier in the United States
Skill: Conceptual
129) What factors affect the actual size of the deposit multiplier in the United States?

Answer:

Topic: The Short-Run Effects of a Change in the Quantity of Money
Skill: Conceptual
130) What short-run effects does a change in the quantity of money have on real GDP? Why do they occur?

Answer:

Topic: International Evidence on the Quantity Theory of Money
Skill: Conceptual
131) What is the relationship between money growth and inflation across countries? Does your answer support the quantity theory of money?

Answer:

Chapter 15 MONETARY POLICY*

■ The Federal Reserve System

Topic: The Federal Reserve System
Skill: Recognition
1) The central bank for the United States is
  A) Bank of America.
  B) the Congressional Bank.
  C) the Federal Reserve System.
  D) First Federal Bank of the United States.
Answer: C

Topic: The Federal Reserve System
Skill: Recognition
2) The Federal Reserve System
  A) is the central bank of the United States.
  B) imposes reserve requirements on all banks.
  C) conducts the nation's monetary policy.
  D) All of the above are correct.
Answer: D

Topic: The Federal Reserve System
Skill: Recognition
3) Which of the following is <u>NOT</u> a function of the Fed?
  A) holding reserves for depository institutions.
  B) supervising member banks.
  C) regulating the money supply.
  D) lending funds to creditworthy private firms.
Answer: D

Topic: The Federal Reserve System
Skill: Recognition
4) Control of the nation's money supply is handled by
  A) Congress.
  B) the Federal Reserve System.
  C) all commercial banks.
  D) Congress, the Federal Reserve System, and all member commercial banks.
Answer: B

Topic: Monetary Policy
Skill: Conceptual
5) When the Fed is ____ it is ____.
  A) adjusting the amount of money in circulation; issuing government bonds
  B) issuing government bonds; conducting monetary policy
  C) adjusting the amount of money in circulation; conducting monetary policy
  D) regulating the nation's financial institutions; conducting monetary policy
Answer: C

Topic: Monetary Policy
Skill: Conceptual
6) Which of the following is a goal of monetary policy?
  A) promote faster long-term economic growth.
  B) maintain full employment.
  C) keep inflation in check.
  D) All of the above answers are correct.
Answer: D

Topic: The Structure of the Federal Reserve System
Skill: Recognition
7) The Federal Reserve system does <u>NOT</u>
  A) consist of 12 regional Federal Reserve banks.
  B) control the U.S. money supply.
  C) approve commercial bank loans.
  D) lend reserves to commercial banks.
Answer: C

---

* This is Chapter 32 in *Economics.*

**Topic: The Structure of the Federal Reserve
System**
Skill: Recognition
8)   Which of the following is <u>NOT</u> a part or compo-
     nent of the Federal Reserve System?
A)   the 12 regional Federal Reserve banks.
B)   the Federal Open Market Committee.
C)   the Federal Deposit Insurance Corporation.
D)   the Board of Governors.
Answer: C

**Topic: The Structure of the Federal Reserve
System**
Skill: Recognition
9)   The Board of Governors of the Federal Reserve
     System consists of
A)   7 members appointed by Congress and 7 ap-
     pointed by the President.
B)   the presidents of each regional Federal Reserve
     bank.
C)   12 members appointed by Congress.
D)   7 members appointed by the President of the
     United States.
Answer: D

**Topic: The Structure of the Federal Reserve
System**
Skill: Recognition
10) The Board of Governors of the Federal Reserve
     System is
A)   appointed by the Congress.
B)   elected by the public.
C)   appointed by the President of the United States
     and confirmed by the U.S. Senate.
D)   elected by members of the American Banking
     Association.
Answer: C

**Topic: The Structure of the Federal Reserve
System**
Skill: Recognition
11) There are _____ regional Federal Reserve banks.
A)   10.
B)   12.
C)   15.
D)   over 10,000.
Answer: B

**Topic: The Structure of the Federal Reserve
System**
Skill: Conceptual
12) Regional Federal Reserve banks
A)   are located in each of the 50 states.
B)   are run by the governors of the states in which
     they are located.
C)   provide general banking services to the public.
D)   None of the above answers are correct.
Answer: D

**Topic: The Structure of the Federal Reserve
System**
Skill: Recognition
13) The Federal Open Market Committee (FOMC)
A)   makes decisions on the Fed's purchase and sale
     of government securities.
B)   has no effect on the money supply.
C)   is headed by the Senate majority leader.
D)   consists of the ranking members of the House of
     Representatives.
Answer: A

**Topic: The Structure of the Federal Reserve
System**
Skill: Recognition
14) The Federal Open Market Committee (FOMC)
A)   determines the government's tax policy.
B)   determines the Fed's monetary policy.
C)   oversees all transactions on the stock market.
D)   lends to the least credit-worthy customers who
     otherwise can't get loans.
Answer: B

**Topic: The Structure of the Federal Reserve
System**
Skill: Conceptual
15) Which of the following is TRUE regarding the
     Federal Open Market Committee (FOMC)?
A)   It is the main policy-making group of the Con-
     gress.
B)   Representatives from each state control its op-
     eration.
C)   It meets about every six weeks to decide on
     monetary policy.
D)   Both answers A and C are correct.
Answer: C

Topic: The Fed's Power Center
Skill: Recognition

16) The Chairman of the Board of Governors of the Fed

A)   has the largest influence on monetary policy actions.

B)   is appointed by the President.

C)   is Alan Greenspan.

D)   All of the above answers are correct.

Answer: D

Topic: The Fed's Policy Tools
Skill: Recognition

17) The tools at the disposal of the Fed for changing the money supply do <u>NOT</u> include

A)   open market operations.

B)   changing the required reserve ratio.

C)   changing discount rates.

D)   increasing the number of commercial banks.

Answer: D

Topic: The Fed's Policy Tools, Required Reserve Ratios
Skill: Recognition

18) The fraction of deposits that banks must keep on hand or at the Federal Reserve is called the

A)   discount rate.

B)   required reserve ratio.

C)   deposit multiplier.

D)   money multiplier.

Answer: B

Topic: The Fed's Policy Tools, Required Reserve Ratios
Skill: Conceptual

19) In 1999, banks

A)   were required to hold 10 percent of checking deposits in excess of about $50 million as reserves.

B)   experienced a change in required reserve ratios.

C)   were not required to hold reserves.

D)   None of the above answers are correct.

Answer: A

Topic: The Fed's Policy Tools, Discount Rate
Skill: Recognition

20) The discount rate is the

A)   interest rate banks charge their best customers.

B)   interest rate on short-term U.S. government securities.

C)   interest rate the Fed charges on loans made to depository institutions.

D)   interest rate the Fed charges to the largest and most secure manufacturing concerns in the country.

Answer: C

Topic: The Fed's Policy Tools, Open Market Operations
Skill: Recognition

21) Open market operations are

A)   the buying and selling of U.S. government securities by the Fed.

B)   the buying and selling of U.S. government securities by citizens, banks and the Fed.

C)   the selling of new government securities by the U.S. Treasury in order to increase the money supply.

D)   the selling of new government securities by the U.S. Treasury in order to finance a budget deficit.

Answer: A

Topic: The Fed's Policy Tools, Open Market Operations
Skill: Recognition

22) When the Fed wants to undertake open market operations, it

A)   can require all commercial banks to buy from or sell to it.

B)   can require all member banks to buy from or sell to it.

C)   buys or sells government securities.

D)   buys from or sells to the U.S. Treasury.

Answer: C

Topic: The Fed's Policy Tools, Open Market Operations
Skill: Conceptual
23) Which of the following statements about the Federal Reserve is most true?
A) It makes loans to large industrial corporations.
B) It is a private, profit-maximizing institution whose ownership is represented in publicly traded shares.
C) It pursues open market operations aimed at influencing the supply of money.
D) It is unable to exert any control, direct or indirect, over commercial banks.
Answer: C

Topic: The Fed's Balance Sheet
Skill: Recognition
24) Which of the following is an asset of the Fed?
A) gold.
B) Federal Reserve notes.
C) banks' deposits.
D) Both answers B and C are correct.
Answer: A

Topic: Monetary Base
Skill: Recognition
25) The monetary base consists of
A) the money supply.
B) Federal Reserve notes, coins, and banks' deposits at the Fed.
C) demand deposits and vault cash.
D) government securities held by the Fed.
Answer: B

■ Controlling the Money Supply

Topic: How Required Reserve Ratios Work
Skill: Recognition
26) To control the money supply, the Fed least frequently uses
A) reserve requirement changes.
B) open market sales of government securities.
C) open market purchases of government securities.
D) discount rate changes.
Answer: A

Topic: How Required Reserve Ratios Work
Skill: Conceptual
27) If the required reserve ratio is increased and the banking system has no excess reserves,
A) the money supply will increase.
B) the money supply will decrease.
C) bank deposits will decrease but there will be no effect on the supply of money.
D) bank loans will increase.
Answer: B

Topic: How Required Reserve Ratios Work
Skill: Conceptual
28) An increase in the required reserve ratio will result in
A) easier credit.
B) lower interest rates.
C) a decrease in the money supply.
D) higher levels of investment.
Answer: C

Topic: How Required Reserve Ratios Work
Skill: Conceptual
29) Which of the following increases the money supply?
A) an individual's cash withdrawal from a bank.
B) an individual's purchase of a bond from the Fed.
C) a decrease in the required reserve ratio.
D) an increase in the required reserve ratio.
Answer: C

Topic: How the Discount Rate Works
Skill: Conceptual
30) To increase the money supply, the Fed can
A) raise the required reserve ratio.
B) forbid loans of reserves from one bank to another.
C) lower the discount rate.
D) sell U.S. government securities on open markets.
Answer: C

Topic: How the Discount Rate Works
Skill: Conceptual
31) To decrease the money supply
A) the Federal Reserve could increase the discount rate.
B) the Federal Reserve could decrease the required reserve ratio.
C) commercial banks could increase their loans.
D) commercial banks could sell government securities.
Answer: A

Topic: How An Open Market Operation Works
Skill: Recognition

32) The most frequently used tool of the Fed's monetary policy is
   A) controlling the discount rate.
   B) controlling the reserve requirements.
   C) controlling bank loans through moral suasion.
   D) buying and selling government securities.

Answer: D

Topic: How An Open Market Operation Works
Skill: Conceptual

33) Open market purchases by the Federal Reserve System (the Fed)
   A) increase the monetary base.
   B) increase bank reserves.
   C) do not change the required reserve ratio.
   D) All of the above answers are correct.

Answer: D

Topic: How An Open Market Operation Works
Skill: Conceptual

34) When the Fed purchases government securities on the open market, bank reserves _____ and the monetary base _____.
   A) increase; increases
   B) increase; decreases
   C) decrease; increases
   D) decrease; decreases

Answer: A

Topic: How An Open Market Operation Works
Skill: Conceptual

35) The Fed buys government securities and gives a bond dealer a check for the amount. After the check has cleared,
   A) reserves remain unchanged because the increase of reserves at the dealer's bank are offset by an increase in reserves at the Fed.
   B) reserves have decreased by the amount of the check because the Fed pays for the check by decreasing the dealer's bank's deposits at the Fed.
   C) reserves have increased by the amount of the check because the Fed pays for the check by increasing the amount of the dealer's bank's deposits with the Fed.
   D) reserves have increased by the amount of the reserves times the required reserve ratio, and the money supply increases by the difference between the amount of the check and the increase in the reserves.

Answer: C

Topic: How An Open Market Operation Works
Skill: Conceptual

36) The Fed's purchase of government securities will
   A) increase loans made by banks.
   B) be an effective anti-inflationary policy.
   C) decrease the price level and have no effect on real GDP.
   D) decrease bank reserves.

Answer: A

Topic: How An Open Market Operation Works
Skill: Conceptual

37) If the Fed wants to increase the quantity of money, it can
   A) raise the required reserve ratio.
   B) sell government securities in the open market.
   C) instruct banks to print more money.
   D) buy government securities on the open market.

Answer: D

38) If the Federal Reserve purchases government securities, all of the following occurs <u>EXCEPT</u>:
A) Commercial bank reserves will increase.
B) The money supply will increase.
C) The discount rate will be forced higher.
D) There will be a multiple expansion of banking deposits.

Answer: C

39) If the Fed sells government securities it previously purchased,
A) commercial bank reserves will decrease.
B) the government debt will be decreased.
C) commercial bank reserves will increase.
D) there will be no effect on the money supply.

Answer: A

40) The initial impact of the Fed's open market sale of government securities to commercial banks is
A) an increase in the money supply by some multiple of the dollar volume of the sale.
B) an increase in commercial bank deposits at the Fed.
C) a decrease in the money supply by some multiple of the dollar volume of the sale.
D) a decrease of the commercial banking system's reserve deposits at the Fed.

Answer: D

41) The Fed buys $1 million in U.S. government securities. A bond dealer sells the securities and deposits its check into Bank ABC. Prior to the transaction, Bank ABC had zero excess reserves. If the required reserve ratio is 20 percent, the bank now has
A) $1 million more in total reserves and $800,000 more in excess reserves.
B) $800,000 more in both total and excess reserves.
C) $1 million more in both total and excess reserves.
D) $800,000 more in total reserves with excess reserves unchanged.

Answer: A

42) Which of the following is true concerning the operation of monetary policy?
A) When the Federal Reserve purchases a government security it withdraws reserves from commercial banks.
B) When the Federal Reserve purchases a government security the debt of the U.S. government is decreased.
C) When the Federal Reserve sells a government security it withdraws reserves from the commercial banking system.
D) The Federal Reserve may only sell government securities to fund government deficits that have been approved by the President of the United States.

Answer: C

43) A decrease in the reserves of commercial banks could be caused by
A) a decision by U.S. households to hold less currency.
B) the sale of government securities by the Federal Reserve.
C) a decrease in the discount rate.
D) an increase in the required reserve ratio.

Answer: B

Banking System Balance Sheet			
Assets		Liabilities	
Reserves		Deposits	$2,00,000
Required	$200,000		
Excess	$0		
Total reserves	$200,000		
Loans	1,800,000		
Total assets	2,000,000	Total liabilities	$2,00,000

44) The required reserve ratio for the entire banking system in the above table is
A) 20 percent.
B) 10 percent.
C) 15 percent.
D) 1 percent.

Answer: B

Topic: How An Open Market Operation Works
Skill: Analytical

45) Using the data in the above table, an open market operation in which the Fed purchased $100,000 of government securities from a bank would

A) create a reserve deficiency for the banking system.

B) lead to a total expansion of the money supply of $100,000.

C) generate $100,000 of excess reserves for the banking system.

D) cause demand deposits to fall by $100,000.

Answer: C

Topic: The Money Multiplier
Skill: Conceptual

46) If the required reserve ratio is doubled, the money multiplier

A) is decreased.

B) is increased but does not double.

C) stays the same.

D) is doubled.

Answer: A

Topic: The Multiplier Effect of an Open Market Operation
Skill: Conceptual

47) The smaller the currency drain, the

A) smaller the increase in the money supply from an increase in reserves.

B) more likely it is that the banking system will hold a larger proportion of excess reserves.

C) the smaller the effect of a change in the discount rate.

D) larger the increase in the money supply from an increase in reserves.

Answer: D

Topic: The Multiplier Effect of an Open Market Operation
Skill: Conceptual

48) After an open market operation, a multiple expansion of deposits can occur because

A) banks typically hold some excess reserves.

B) what one bank can do, the whole system cannot do.

C) one bank's excess reserves are loaned out and end up as excess reserves in other banks.

D) people convert their demand deposits to cash.

Answer: C

Topic: The Multiplier Effect of an Open Market Operation
Skill: Conceptual

49) In the long run, a sale of securities by the Fed causes

A) a contraction of the money supply equal to the amount of the securities sold.

B) an expansion of the money supply equal to the amount of the securities sold.

C) a multiple expansion of the money supply greater than the amount of the securities sold.

D) a multiple contraction of the money supply greater than the amount of the securities sold.

Answer: D

Topic: The Multiplier Effect of an Open Market Operation
Skill: Conceptual

50) In the long run, a purchase of U.S. government securities by the Fed causes

A) an expansion of the money supply equal to the amount of the securities purchased.

B) a contraction of the money supply equal to the amount of the securities purchased.

C) an expansion of the money supply of more than the amount of the securities purchased.

D) a contraction of the money supply of more than the amount of the securities purchased.

Answer: C

Topic: The Multiplier Effect of an Open Market Operation
Skill: Conceptual

51) If the Federal Reserve increases the monetary base by $10 million, eventually the money supply will

A) decrease by $10 million.

B) decrease by more than $10 million.

C) increase by $10 million.

D) increase by more than $10 million.

Answer: D

Topic: The Multiplier Effect of an Open Market Operation
Skill: Conceptual

52) If the Federal Reserve sells $500,000 worth of government securities, in the long run the money supply will
A) decrease by $500,000.
B) decrease by more than $500,000.
C) increase by $500,000.
D) increase by more than $500,000.

Answer: B

■ The Demand for Money

Topic: The Influences on Money Holding
Skill: Recognition

53) Which of the following affect how much money people choose to hold?
A) aggregate expenditure.
B) interest rates.
C) the presence credit cards.
D) All of the above answers are correct.

Answer: D

Topic: The Influences on Money Holding, The Price Level
Skill: Conceptual

54) The demand for nominal money
A) increases as the price level increases.
B) decreases as the price level increases.
C) depends on the supply of money.
D) is the same as the demand for real money.

Answer: A

Topic: The Influences on Money Holding, The Price Level
Skill: Conceptual

55) Which of the following decreases the demand for nominal money?
A) a decrease in the nominal interest rate.
B) an increase in real GDP.
C) an increase in the cost of using automatic teller machines.
D) a decrease in the price level.

Answer: D

Topic: The Influences on Money Holding, The Interest Rate
Skill: Recognition

56) The opportunity cost of holding money balances rather than other assets is
A) the interest rate.
B) the price level.
C) foregone consumption.
D) foregone liquidity.

Answer: A

Topic: The Influences on Money Holding, The Interest Rate
Skill: Conceptual

57) The opportunity cost of holding money refers to
A) the service fees charged to withdraw currency from an ATM.
B) the price level.
C) the interest that could have been earned if the money balances had been changed into an interest-bearing asset.
D) the pleasure that would have been received if the money balances had been used to buy a good or service.

Answer: C

Topic: The Influences on Money Holding, The Interest Rate
Skill: Conceptual

58) The higher the interest rate, the
A) greater the opportunity cost of holding money.
B) lower the quantity of money demanded.
C) more the money demand curve shifts leftward.
D) Both answers A and B are correct.

Answer: D

Topic: The Influences on Money Holding, The Interest Rate
Skill: Conceptual

59) If the interest rate is low, people will want to hold a lot of money balances because
A) the opportunity cost of holding money is high.
B) the opportunity cost of holding money is low.
C) the price of bonds is expected to go up.
D) Both answers B and C are correct.

Answer: B

Topic: The Influences on Money Holding, The Interest Rate
Skill: Conceptual
60) A rise in the interest rate will
A) encourage people to sell bonds and hold money.
B) encourage people buy bonds and decrease the quantity of money they hold.
C) increase the level of money balances desired for medium of exchange purposes.
D) increase the quantity of currency in the economy.
Answer: B

Topic: The Influences on Money Holding, The Interest Rate
Skill: Conceptual
61) The demand for money is
A) positively related to interest rates.
B) negatively related to the price level.
C) negatively related to interest rates.
D) negatively related to transactions in the economy.
Answer: C

Topic: The Influences on Money Holding, Real GDP
Skill: Conceptual
62) Which of the following decreases the demand for money?
A) An increase in the price level.
B) An increase in M1.
C) A decrease in real GDP.
D) A decrease in the cost of printing money.
Answer: C

Topic: The Influences on Money Holding, Financial Innovation
Skill: Conceptual
63) Which of the following directly changes the demand for money?
A) increased use of interest-paying checking accounts.
B) automatic teller machines.
C) a sale of government securities.
D) Both answers A and B are correct.
Answer: D

Topic: The Influences on Money Holding, Financial Innovation
Skill: Conceptual
64) Which of the following causes a leftward shift in the demand for money curve?
A) increased use of credit cards.
B) increased use of automatic teller machines.
C) increase in interest rates.
D) Both answers A and B are correct.
Answer: D

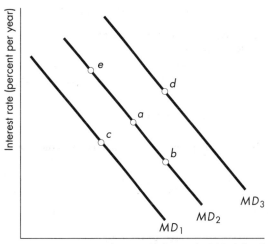

Topic: The Demand for Money Curve
Skill: Analytical
65) In the above figure, suppose the economy is initially at point a. If the interest rates increases, there is a movement to point such as
A) b.
B) c.
C) d.
D) e.
Answer: D

Topic: Shifts in the Demand for Money Curve
Skill: Analytical
66) In the above figure, suppose the economy is at point a. If there is an increase in real GDP, there is a movement to point such as
A) b.
B) c.
C) d.
D) e.
Answer: C

Topic: The Demand for Money in the United States
Skill: Conceptual

67) Since the 1970s, which factors have caused an increase in demand for M1?
A)   increases in real GDP.
B)   increased use of credit cards.
C)   financial innovation.
D)   Both answers A and B are correct.
Answer: A

■ Interest Rate Determination

Topic: Interest Rate Determination
Skill: Recognition

68) Which of the following is a true statement?
A)   The prices of bonds are directly related to the interest rate.
B)   The prices of bonds increase when there is inflation.
C)   The prices of bonds are unrelated to the interest rate.
D)   The prices of bonds are inversely related to the interest rate.
Answer: D

Topic: Interest Rate Determination
Skill: Recognition

69) Bond prices
A)   are unaffected by the Fed's actions.
B)   are unaffected by interest rate changes.
C)   vary directly with interest rates.
D)   vary inversely with interest rates.
Answer: D

Topic: Interest Rate Determination
Skill: Recognition

70) When the interest rate increases,
A)   the market price of bonds will fall.
B)   the demand for money will increase.
C)   real national income will increase.
D)   investment in money increases.
Answer: A

Topic: Interest Rate Determination
Skill: Conceptual

71) If you buy a bond for $750 that pays 10 percent and the interest rate falls to 8 percent, then
A)   the price of the bond is still $750.
B)   the price of the bond has fallen.
C)   the price of the bond has risen.
D)   the price of the bond may rise or fall depending on whether the federal funds rate changed.
Answer: C

Topic: Interest Rate Determination
Skill: Conceptual

72) If you buy a bond for $1,000 that pays 5 percent and the interest rate rises to 8 percent, then
A)   the price of the bond is still $1,000.
B)   the price of the bond has risen.
C)   the price of the bond has fallen.
D)   the price of the bond may rise or fall depending on whether the federal funds rate changed.
Answer: C

Topic: Interest Rate Determination
Skill: Conceptual

73) Suppose that the price of a bond last week was $950 but this week its price is $975. Between last week and this week interest rates
A)   have fallen.
B)   have stayed about the same if inflation is roughly the same.
C)   have risen.
D)   are unaffected by bond prices.
Answer: A

Topic: Interest Rate Determination
Skill: Conceptual

74) Suppose that the price of a bond last week was $750 but this week its price is $700. Between last week and this week interest rates
A)   have fallen.
B)   have stayed the same if inflation is roughly the same.
C)   have risen.
D)   are unaffected by bond prices.
Answer: C

Topic: Money Market Equilibrium
Skill: Conceptual

75) An excess demand for money will lead to a rise in

A)   the interest rate.

B)   investment.

C)   income.

D)   bond prices.

Answer: A

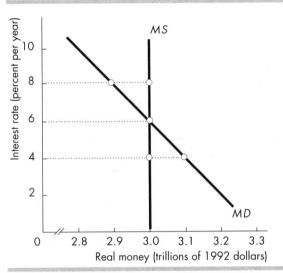

Topic: Money Market Equilibrium
Skill: Analytical

76) In the above figure, if the interest rate is 4 percent, people

A)   sell bonds so as to convert them into cash.

B)   buy bonds so as to have a better store of value.

C)   petition the Fed to tighten the money supply.

D)   buy stocks, because stocks are more liquid than currency.

Answer: A

Topic: Money Market Equilibrium
Skill: Analytical

77) In the above figure, at an interest rate of 8 percent, people

A)   sell bonds so as to convert them into cash.

B)   buy bonds to get rid of excess money.

C)   petition the Fed to tighten the money supply.

D)   buy stocks, because stocks are more liquid than currency.

Answer: B

Topic: Changing the Interest Rate
Skill: Conceptual

78) An increase the quantity of money will lead to

A)   an excess demand for money and a decrease in the interest rate.

B)   an increase in the interest rate.

C)   a movement down along the money demand curve to a lower interest rate.

D)   an leftward shift of the money demand curve and a lower interest rate.

Answer: C

Topic: Changing the Interest Rate
Skill: Conceptual

79) If the central bank increases the supply of money, a new equilibrium is reached by

A)   a rightward shift of the demand for money curve.

B)   a movement down the demand for money curve.

C)   a leftward shift of the demand for money curve.

D)   a movement up the demand for money curve.

Answer: B

Topic: Changing the Interest Rate
Skill: Conceptual

80) An increase in the money supply leads to

A)   a reduction in the interest rate.

B)   a decrease in the price level.

C)   a reduction in the velocity of circulation.

D)   a leftward shift in the money demand curve.

Answer: A

Topic: Changing the Interest Rate, Fed Policy
Skill: Conceptual

81) Open market operations by the Fed cause

A)   changes in the discount rate.

B)   aggregate supply to change.

C)   the prices of bonds to change.

D)   shifts in the demand curve for money.

Answer: C

Topic: Changing the Interest Rate, Fed Policy
Skill: Conceptual

82) The Fed engages in open market operations and sells government securities. The result is

A)   lower interest rates.

B)   higher interest rates.

C)   interest rates remain unchanged because bond prices did not change.

D)   uncertain as far as what happens to the interest rate because more information is needed.

Answer: B

Topic: Changing the Interest Rate, Fed Policy
Skill: Conceptual
83) Bond prices decrease. A possible cause is
  A) the Fed decreasing the reserve requirement ratio.
  B) the Fed decreasing the discount rate, causing other interest rates to decrease and a fall in bond prices.
  C) the Fed selling bonds in the open market.
  D) the Fed buying bonds in the open market.
Answer: C

Topic: Changing the Interest Rate, Fed Policy
Skill: Conceptual
84) To lower interest rates, the Federal Reserve should
  A) buy government securities.
  B) raise the Treasury bill rate.
  C) raise the reserve requirement.
  D) decrease bank reserves.
Answer: A

■ Monetary Policy

Topic: The Fed in Action
Skill: Recognition
85) Which of the following are short-term interest rates that tend to move together?
  I. 3-month Treasury bill rate.
  II. Discount rate.
  III. Required reserve ratio.
  A) I and II.
  B) I and III.
  C) II and III.
  D) I, II and III.
Answer: A

Topic: The Fed in Action
Skill: Recognition
86) Which is true?
  A) The federal funds rate is always equal to the Treasury bill rate.
  B) The discount rate varies inversely with the federal funds rate.
  C) The Fed controls or influences both the federal funds rate and the discount rate.
  D) The federal funds rate and the Treasury bill rate generally move independently.
Answer: C

Topic: Recession of 1990-1991
Skill: Recognition
87) During the recession of 1990-1991, the Federal Reserve
  A) reduced bank reserve requirements.
  B) unsuccessfully tried to persuade banks to reduce excess reserves.
  C) held growth in the money supply constant at 2 percent annually.
  D) lowered interest rates.
Answer: D

Topic: The Ripple Effects of Monetary Policy
Skill: Conceptual
88) Monetary policy can
  A) decrease the money supply, thus raising interest rates, and decreasing investment.
  B) increase the money supply, thus lowering interest rates, and increasing investment.
  C) shift the aggregate demand curve leftward by decreasing the quantity of money.
  D) All of the above answers are correct.
Answer: D

Topic: The Ripple Effects of Monetary Policy
Skill: Conceptual
89) To increase investment, the Federal Reserve should
  A) increase its loans to expanding businesses.
  B) increase the discount rate.
  C) buy government bonds.
  D) sell government bonds.
Answer: C

Topic: The Ripple Effects of Monetary Policy
Skill: Conceptual

90) The Fed increases the money supply. A mechanism through which aggregate demand increases is an increase in the money supply
   A) increases the interest rates, which decrease investment demand, thereby increasing aggregate demand.
   B) decreases interest rates, which decrease investment demand, thereby increasing aggregate demand.
   C) raises the dollar on foreign exchange markets so that net exports decrease, which increases investment demand, thereby increasing aggregate demand.
   D) decreases interest rates, which increase investment demand, thereby increasing aggregate demand.

Answer: D

Topic: The Ripple Effects of Monetary Policy
Skill: Conceptual

91) A decrease in the money supply
   A) increases interest rates, investment, and aggregate demand.
   B) raises interest rates, decreases investment, and decreases aggregate demand.
   C) lowers interest rates, increases investment, and increases aggregate demand.
   D) decreases interest rates, investment, and aggregate demand.

Answer: B

Topic: The Ripple Effects of Monetary Policy
Skill: Conceptual

92) A decrease in the money supply causes the interest rate to _____ and investment to _____.
   A) fall; increase
   B) rise; increase
   C) fall; decrease
   D) rise; decrease

Answer: D

Topic: The Ripple Effects of Monetary Policy
Skill: Conceptual

93) An increase in the money supply increases GDP by
   A) lowering taxes.
   B) directly decreasing government purchases.
   C) increasing the government deficit.
   D) lowering interest rates, and thereby increasing investment and consumption expenditure.

Answer: D

Topic: The Ripple Effects of Monetary Policy
Skill: Conceptual

94) An increase in the money supply will lead to
   A) a decrease in interest rates.
   B) a decrease in the value of the dollar.
   C) an increase in exports.
   D) All of the above answers are correct.

Answer: D

Topic: Effect of Monetary Policy on Aggregate Demand
Skill: Conceptual

95) The direct effect of an increase in the money supply is to
   A) raise interest rates as people increase their saving.
   B) increase potential GDP.
   C) increase aggregate demand.
   D) decrease aggregate demand.

Answer: C

Topic: Effect of Monetary Policy on Aggregate Demand
Skill: Conceptual

96) If the economy is operating below its full employment level, the Fed can
   A) increase aggregate demand by increasing the rate of growth of the money supply.
   B) increase aggregate demand by stimulating the demand for money.
   C) increase aggregate demand by buying bonds and raising interest rates.
   D) increase aggregate supply by raising the price level.

Answer: A

Topic: The Ripple Effects of Monetary Policy
Skill: Conceptual
115) If the Fed sells bonds in the open market, net
exports will increase.
Answer: FALSE

**Topic: Effect of Monetary Policy on Aggregate
Demand**
Skill: Conceptual
116) If the Fed increases the discount rate, aggregate
demand decreases.
Answer: TRUE

■ Essay Questions

Topic: Monetary Policy
Skill: Recognition
117) Describe the goals of the Fed's monetary policy.
Answer:

**Topic: The Structure of the Federal Reserve
System**
Skill: Recognition
118) What is the role of the Federal Open Market
Committee?
Answer:

Topic: How the Discount Rate Works
Skill: Conceptual
119) Describe how changes in the discount rate change
the money supply.
Answer:

Topic: How An Open Market Operation Works
Skill: Conceptual
120) Describe how open market operations change the
money supply.
Answer:

Topic: The Money Multiplier
Skill: Conceptual
121) What is the money multiplier and what affects its
size?
Answer:

Topic: The Influences on Money Holding
Skill: Recognition
122) What factors affect money demand?
Answer:

Topic: Shifts in the Demand Curve for Real Money
Skill: Recognition
123) What causes the demand curve for real money to
shift rightward?
Answer:

Topic: Interest Rate Determination
Skill: Conceptual
124) What relationship exists between interest rates and
bond prices and why?
Answer:

Topic: Alan Greenspan's Fed
Skill: Conceptual
125) Describe the behavior of the Fed as led by Alan
Greenspan.
Answer:

Topic: The Ripple Effects of Monetary Policy
Skill: Conceptual
126) Explain the ripple effects of a sale of government
bonds in an open market operation.
Answer:

Chapter 16 INFLATION*

■ Inflation and the Price Level

Topic: Inflation and the Price Level
Skill: Recognition
1)   Inflation is a process
A)   when the value of real GDP increases.
B)   when the value of real GDP decreases.
C)   when the price level is rising.
D)   when the value of money is rising.
Answer: C

Topic: Inflation and the Price Level
Skill: Conceptual
2)   Which of the following occurs during the process
     of inflation?
A)   People need less money to make transactions.
B)   Firms pay lower money wages.
C)   The price level jumps higher and then stabilizes
     at its new, higher level.
D)   The value of money falls.
Answer: D

Topic: Inflation and the Price Level
Skill: Recognition
3)   Which of the following describes inflation cor-
     rectly?
A)   A one-time jump in the price level.
B)   An increase in real wages.
C)   A persistent increase in the price level.
D)   The fall in the price level from one year to an-
     other year.
Answer: C

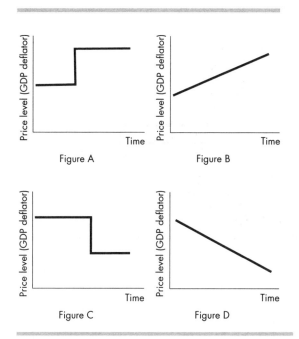

Figure A

Figure B

Figure C

Figure D

Topic: Inflation and the Price Level
Skill: Analytical
4)   In the above, which figure correctly shows an
     economy experiencing inflation?
A)   Figure A.
B)   Figure B.
C)   Figure C.
D)   Figure D.
Answer: B

---

* This is Chapter 33 in *Economics*.

Topic: Inflation Rate
Skill: Recognition

5) Using the notation P_t to designate this period's price level and P_{t-1} to designate last period's price level, the formula for measuring the inflation rate from last period to this period is

A) $[(P_t - P_{t-1}) / P_t] \times 100.$

B) $[(P_{t-1} - P_t) / P_{t-1}] \times 100.$

C) $[(P_t - P_{t-1}) / P_{t-1}] \times 100.$

D) $[(P_{t-1} - P_t) / P_t] \times 100.$

Answer: C

Year	Price level
1996	91
1997	100
1998	110
1999	121

Topic: Inflation Rate
Skill: Analytical

6) In the above table, the inflation rate between 1996 and 1997 is approximately

A) 0.9 percent.
B) 1 percent.
C) 10 percent.
D) 100 percent.

Answer: C

Topic: Inflation Rate
Skill: Analytical

7) In the above table, the inflation rate between 1997 and 1998 is approximately

A) 9 percent.
B) 10 percent.
C) 100 percent.
D) 110 percent.

Answer: B

Topic: Inflation Rate
Skill: Analytical

8) In the above table, the inflation rate between 1998 and 1999 is approximately

A) 10 percent.
B) 11 percent.
C) 121 percent.
D) None of the above answers are correct.

Answer: A

Topic: Inflation
Skill: Conceptual

9) Which of the following can start an inflation?

A) An increase in aggregate demand.
B) An increase in aggregate supply.
C) A decrease in aggregate supply.
D) Both answers A and C are correct.

Answer: D

■ Demand-Pull Inflation

Topic: Initial Effect of an Increase in Aggregate Demand
Skill: Conceptual

10) Which of the following factors could start a demand-pull inflation if the economy is currently operating at potential GDP?

A) An increase in tax rates.
B) A decrease in government purchases.
C) A decrease in wage rates.
D) An increase in exports.

Answer: D

Topic: Initial Effect of an Increase in Aggregate Demand
Skill: Conceptual

11) In demand-pull inflation, at the start

A) the price level and real GDP both increase.
B) the price level rises and real GDP decreases.
C) the price level changes but real GDP remains the same.
D) None of the above answers are correct.

Answer: A

Topic: Initial Effect of an Increase in Aggregate Demand
Skill: Conceptual

12) Demand-pull inflation can start when

A) money wages rise but the price level does not change.
B) money wages rise faster than prices.
C) the short-run aggregate supply curve shifts rightward.
D) the aggregate demand curve shifts rightward.

Answer: D

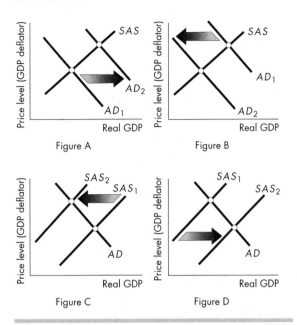

Figure A

Figure B

Figure C

Figure D

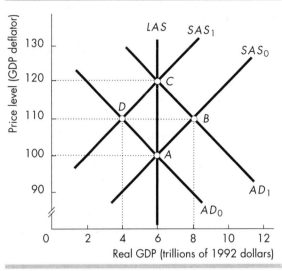

Topic: Initial Effect of an Increase in Aggregate Demand
Skill: Analytical

13) Which of the above figure best shows the start of a demand-pull inflation?

A) Figure A.
B) Figure B.
C) Figure C.
D) Figure D.

Answer: A

Topic: Wage Response
Skill: Conceptual

14) If an economy at potential GDP experiences a demand shock that shifts the aggregate demand curve rightward, there will be

A) an eventual leftward shift in the short-run aggregate supply curve.
B) unemployment below the natural rate.
C) upward pressure on money wage rates.
D) All of the above answers are correct.

Answer: D

Topic: Initial Effect of an Increase in Aggregate Demand
Skill: Analytical

15) In the above figure, suppose that the economy is at point A when the money supply increases. In the short run, the economy will move to point _____.

A) B.
B) C.
C) D.
D) A, that is, the price level and level of real GDP will not change.

Answer: A

Topic: Wage Response
Skill: Analytical

16) In the above figure, suppose that the economy is at point A when foreign countries begin an expansion and buy more U.S.-made goods. In the short run, this change causes a movement to point _____ and an eventual increase in _____.

A) B; money wages
B) D; the natural rate of unemployment
C) B; the natural rate of unemployment
D) D; money wages

Answer: A

Topic: A Demand-Pull Inflation Process
Skill: Conceptual

17) Suppose that a shock causes the aggregate demand curve to shift rightward. If the Fed does nothing,

A) the economy will experience a temporary reduction in employment but will eventually return to full employment.

B) output initially will exceed potential GDP, but the economy will return to potential GDP with a higher price level.

C) the short-run aggregate supply curve will not shift leftward and there will be continued inflation.

D) eventually the short-run aggregate supply curve will shift leftward and there will be continued inflation.

Answer: B

Topic: A Demand-Pull Inflation Process
Skill: Conceptual

18) If the Fed responds to an increase in aggregate demand by increasing the money supply

A) nothing happens because aggregate demand had already increased.

B) output will begin to decrease more rapidly than otherwise.

C) wages will fall to reduce the unemployment.

D) there may be continued inflation.

Answer: D

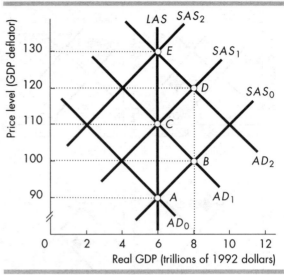

Topic: A Demand-Pull Inflation Process
Skill: Analytical

19) In the above figure, the movement from point A to B to C to D to E represents

A) demand-pull inflation resulting solely from wage responses to excess labor demand.

B) demand-pull inflation resulting from persistent increases in the money supply.

C) cost-push inflation resulting solely from wage responses to excess labor demand.

D) cost-push inflation resulting from persistent increases in the money supply.

Answer: B

Topic: A Demand-Pull Inflation Process
Skill: Analytical

20) In the above figure, suppose the economy is at point A. The movement from point B to C to D to E could result from

A) continual increases in real wages.

B) continual increases in oil prices.

C) continual increases in the money supply.

D) Both answers A and C are correct.

Answer: C

Topic: A Demand-Pull Inflation Process
Skill: Analytical

21) In the above figure, suppose the economy is at point *A* initially. For real GDP to increase to and consistently remain above $6 trillion

 I.   the price level must increase to above 90.

 II. there needs to be continued increases in the money supply.

 A) Only I.

 B) Only II.

 C) Both I and II are correct.

 D) Neither I nor II is correct.

Answer: D

Topic: A Demand-Pull Inflation Process
Skill: Analytical

22) In the above figure, if the economy moves from point *A* to point *E*,

 A) money wages have increased.

 B) there may have been demand-pull inflation.

 C) there has been economic growth.

 D) Both answers A and B are correct.

Answer: D

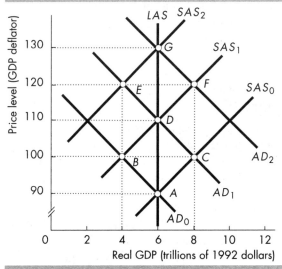

Topic: A Demand-Pull Inflation Process
Skill: Analytical

23) In the above figure, which path represents a demand-pull inflation?

 A) Point *A* to *C* to *D* to *F* to *G*.

 B) Point *A* to *B* to *D* to *E* to *G*.

 C) Point *A* to *C* to *D* to *E* to *G*

 D) Point *A* to *B* to *D* to *F* to *G*.

Answer: A

■ Cost-Push Inflation

Topic: Cost-Push Inflation
Skill: Conceptual

24) Assuming that GDP currently equals potential GDP, a cost-push inflation could result from which of the following?

 A) A decrease in tax rates.

 B) An increase in the labor force.

 C) A large crop failure that boosts the prices of raw food materials.

 D) An increase in the nation's capital stock.

Answer: C

Topic: Initial Effect of a Decrease in Aggregate Supply
Skill: Conceptual

25) Demand-pull and cost-push inflation are different. Specifically cost-push inflation starts with a

 A) falling GDP and unemployment rate.

 B) raising GDP and unemployment rate.

 C) falling GDP and raising unemployment rate.

 D) raising GDP and falling unemployment rate.

Answer: C

Topic: Initial Effect of a Decrease in Aggregate Supply
Skill: Recognition

26) When a cost-push inflation starts

 A) prices fall even though money wages may rise.

 B) real GDP rises faster than the money supply.

 C) the short-run aggregate supply curve shifts rightward.

 D) prices rise and real GDP decreases.

Answer: D

Topic: Initial Effect of a Decrease in Aggregate Supply
Skill: Recognition

27) Initially in a cost-push inflation

 A) only real GDP changes while the price level remains constant.

 B) the price level and real GDP both increase.

 C) the price level rises and real GDP decreases.

 D) All of the above answers are correct.

Answer: C

Topic: Initial Effect of a Decrease in Aggregate Supply
Skill: Conceptual
28) If the prices of crucial raw materials increase,
   A) the short-run aggregate supply curve shifts leftward.
   B) stagflation will probably occur.
   C) a cost-push inflation could occur depending on the behavior of the Federal Reserve.
   D) All of the above answers are correct.
Answer: D

Topic: Initial Effect of a Decrease in Aggregate Supply
Skill: Conceptual
29) An increase in the price of a resource such as oil
   I.   shifts the aggregate demand curve leftward.
   II.   shifts the long-run aggregate supply curve rightward.
   III. shifts the short-run aggregate supply curve leftward.
   IV.   increases the price level and decreases real GDP in the short run.
   A) I only is correct.
   B) both I and II are correct.
   C) III only is correct.
   D) both III and IV are correct.
Answer: D

Topic: Stagflation
Skill: Conceptual
30) Stagflation results from
   A) a leftward shift in the short-run aggregate supply curve.
   B) a rightward shift in the aggregate demand curve.
   C) a rightward shift in the short-run aggregate supply curve.
   D) an increase in government purchases financed by an increase in the money supply.
Answer: A

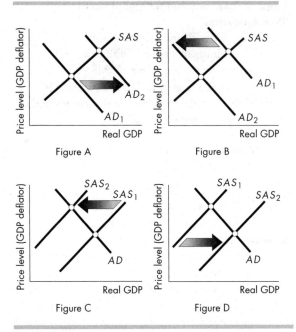

Figure A   Figure B

Figure C   Figure D

Topic: Initial Effect of a Decrease in Aggregate Supply
Skill: Analytical
31) In the above, which figure shows the start of a cost-push inflation?
   A) Figure A.
   B) Figure B.
   C) Figure C.
   D) Figure D.
Answer: C

Topic: Aggregate Demand Response
Skill: Conceptual
32) When the Fed starts a cost-push inflation by responding to a decrease in the short-run aggregate supply by increasing the money supply, the Fed's policy will result in an increase in
   A) employment, but a decrease in costs and prices.
   B) costs and unemployment.
   C) GDP but a decrease in employment.
   D) the price level.
Answer: D

Topic: A Cost-Push Inflation Process
Skill: Conceptual

33) If the Fed responds to repeated decreases in the short-run aggregate supply with repeated increases in the money supply, the economy will be faced with

A) a one-time increase in prices.
B) continuous inflation.
C) alternating periods of inflation and deflation.
D) steady decreases in real GDP.

Answer: B

Topic: A Cost-Push Inflation Process
Skill: Conceptual

34) When there is a cost-push inflation,

A) workers demand higher money wages because of the inflation.
B) the short-run aggregate supply curve shifts left-ward.
C) the aggregate demand curve shifts rightward.
D) All of the above answers are correct.

Answer: D

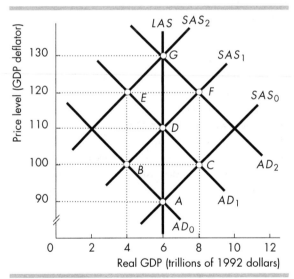

Topic: A Cost-Push Inflation Process
Skill: Analytical

35) In the above figure, which path represents a cost-push inflation?

A) Point A to C to D to F to G.
B) Point A to B to D to E to G.
C) Point A to C to D to E to G.
D) Point A to B to D to F to G.

Answer: B

■ Effects of Inflation

Topic: Unanticipated Inflation in the Labor Market
Skill: Conceptual

36) Which of the following can occur as a result of unanticipated inflation in the labor market?

I.   A redistribution of wealth from firms to workers.
II. Employment and unemployment both fall.
III. Labor turnover because of falling real wages.

A) I and II.
B) I and III.
C) I only.
D) I, II and III.

Answer: B

Topic: Unanticipated Inflation in the Labor Market
Skill: Conceptual

37) Suppose that firms and workers believe the inflation rate will be 3 percent this year. Instead inflation is 6 percent. Which of the following occurs as a result of this unanticipated inflation?

A) The firm will lay off some workers because the real wage rate is too high.
B) Income will be redistributed from firms to workers.
C) Profits will be higher than expected because real wage rates have been set too low.
D) The unemployment rate will not change because people need jobs.

Answer: C

Topic: Unanticipated Inflation in the Capital Market
Skill: Conceptual

38) Lenders gain in the capital market when

A) the inflation rate was more than expected.
B) the inflation rate was less than expected.
C) there is an anticipated decrease in the real interest rate.
D) None of the above answers are correct.

Answer: B

Topic: Unanticipated Inflation in the Capital Market
Skill: Conceptual

39) The anticipated inflation rate is 3 percent, but the actual inflation rate is 5 percent. In this case, lenders _____ and borrowers _____.

A) benefit; benefit
B) benefit; are harmed
C) are harmed; benefit
D) are harmed; are harmed

Answer: C

Topic: Unanticipated Inflation in the Capital Market
Skill: Conceptual

40) Suppose that lenders and borrowers expect the inflation rate to be 4 percent. Instead, the inflation rate turns out to be 6 percent. Which of the following occurs?

A) The real interest rate is higher than expected.
B) Borrowers wish they had borrowed more money.
C) More loans will be made.
D) Borrowers and lenders will set higher interest rates during the next period.

Answer: B

Topic: Unanticipated Inflation in the Capital Market
Skill: Conceptual

41) Suppose that borrowers and lenders believe the inflation rate will be 4 percent this year. Instead the inflation rate during the year turns out to be 2 percent. Which of the following occurs?

A) Too few loans will be made.
B) The real interest rate is higher than expected.
C) Lenders wish they had made fewer loans.
D) Borrowers wish they had borrowed more money.

Answer: B

Topic: Forecasting Inflation
Skill: Recognition

42) Rational expectations are

A) possible to make and are always accurate.
B) impossible to make because they are assumed to be always accurate.
C) based on all relevant information.
D) used in the labor market but not in the financial markets.

Answer: C

Topic: Anticipated Inflation
Skill: Conceptual

43) If people correctly anticipate an increase in aggregate demand, a result is

A) an increase in the real value of outstanding public debt.
B) workers demanding higher money wages to keep the real wage unchanged.
C) a lower rate of inflation in the current time period.
D) there are no predictable results associated with an anticipated increase in aggregate demand.

Answer: B

Topic: Anticipated Inflation
Skill: Conceptual

44) The anticipated inflation rate is 5 percent. In order for purchasing power to remain constant, money wages must rise by

A) 2 percent.
B) 5 percent.
C) 7 percent.
D) 12 percent.

Answer: B

Topic: Anticipated Inflation
Skill: Conceptual

45) When workers and employers correctly anticipate an increase in inflation caused by an increase in aggregate demand,

A) there will be no unemployment.
B) workers will overestimate the real wage.
C) unemployment will be at the natural rate.
D) workers will underestimate the real wage.

Answer: C

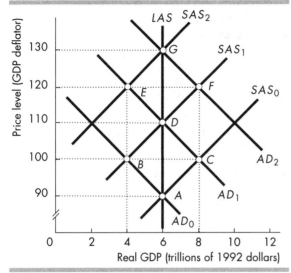

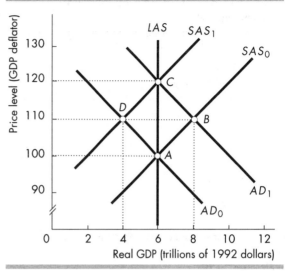

Topic: Anticipated Inflation
Skill: Analytical

46) In the above figure, if people correctly anticipate the increases in aggregate demand and the resulting inflation, the path will be from

A) point A to C to D to F to G.
B) point A to B to D to E to G.
C) point A to D to G.
D) point A to B to D to F to G.

Answer: C

Topic: Anticipated Inflation
Skill: Analytical

47) In the above figure, the economy is initially at point A. If workers and firms correctly anticipate the increase in aggregate demand and the resulting inflation rate, the economy will move to point

A) B.
B) C.
C) D.
D) A, that is, the price level and level of real GDP will not change.

Answer: B

Topic: Unanticipated Inflation
Skill: Conceptual

48) Suppose aggregate demand increases by more than expected. Which of the following describes what will occur?

A) Real GDP will be greater than potential GDP.
B) The price level will increase.
C) Unemployment will fall.
D) All of the above answers are correct.

Answer: D

Topic: Unanticipated Inflation
Skill: Conceptual

49) Suppose aggregate demand increases by less than expected. Which of the following describes what will occur?

A) Real GDP will be less than potential GDP.
B) The price level will fall.
C) Real GDP will be more than potential GDP.
D) Both answers A and B are correct.

Answer: A

Topic: The Costs of Anticipated Inflation
Skill: Conceptual

50) Which of the following are costs of higher antici-
    pated inflation?
    I.   Higher transactions costs as people try to
         avoid holding money.
    II. Larger government budget deficits.
    III. Reduced investment because of increased un-
         certainty.
    A) I only.
    B) I and II.
    C) I and III.
    D) I, II and III.
Answer: C

Topic: The Costs of Anticipated Inflation,
Transactions Costs
Skill: Conceptual

51) Transactions costs of inflation
    A) arise because of anticipated inflation.
    B) arise because people are unwilling to hold as
       much money when anticipated inflation rises.
    C) are higher during periods of rapid inflation.
    D) All of the above answers are correct.
Answer: D

Topic: The Costs of Anticipated Inflation, Tax
Effects
Skill: Conceptual

52) Higher anticipated inflation
    A) has no effect on nominal interest rates.
    B) has no effect on investment.
    C) cannot affect tax rates unless the government en-
       acts fiscal policy.
    D) lowers the after-tax real interest rates.
Answer: D

Topic: The Costs of Anticipated Inflation, Tax
Effects
Skill: Conceptual

53) Suppose the tax rate equals 33 percent and the
    real interest rate equals 3 percent. Additionally,
    suppose the inflation rate is 6 percent. The real
    after-tax interest rate equals _____ and the actual
    tax rate on interest income is _____.
    A) 9 percent; 0 percent
    B) 0 percent; 100 percent
    C) 9 percent; 33 percent
    D) 0 percent; 33 percent
Answer: B

Topic: The Costs of Anticipated Inflation,
Increased Uncertainty
Skill: Conceptual

54) Anticipated inflation
    A) may create uncertainty and decrease investment.
    B) may cause economic growth to increase.
    C) helps make the long-term inflation rate more
       predictable.
    D) raises the after-tax real interest rate.
Answer: A

Topic: The Costs of Anticipated Inflation,
Increased Uncertainty
Skill: Conceptual

55) As a result of anticipated inflation,
    A) people are encouraged to find ways to profit
       from the inflation.
    B) economic growth will be unaffected though it is
       adversely affected from unanticipated inflation.
    C) the long-run aggregate supply curve shifts right-
       ward.
    D) long-term planning is made easier.
Answer: A

■ Inflation and Unemployment: The Phillips Curve

Topic: Inflation and Unemployment: The Phillips Curve
Skill: Recognition

56) Phillips curves describe the relationship between
    A) aggregate expenditures and aggregate demand.
    B) the money supply and interest rates.
    C) unemployment and inflation.
    D) aggregate demand and the price level.
Answer: C

Topic: The Short-Run Phillips Curve
Skill: Recognition

57) The short-run Phillips curve shows the relation-
    ship between unemployment and inflation when
    the natural unemployment rate is constant and
    A) the expected inflation rate is falling.
    B) the expected inflation rate does not change.
    C) the expected inflation rate is rising.
    D) aggregate demand is changing.
Answer: B

Topic: The Short-Run Phillips Curve
Skill: Recognition
58) Along a short-run Phillips curve
  A) a direct relationship exists between the money supply and interest rates.
  B) a direct relationship exists between the price level and desired real output.
  C) an inverse relationship exists between interest rates and the price level.
  D) an inverse relationship exists between the unemployment rate and the inflation rate.
Answer: D

Topic: The Short-Run Phillips Curve
Skill: Conceptual
59) In the short run, unanticipated inflation typically leads to
  A) higher rates of unemployment.
  B) decreases in aggregate demand.
  C) lower rates of unemployment.
  D) workers thinking the real wage has been reduced.
Answer: C

Topic: The Short-Run Phillips Curve
Skill: Conceptual
60) The inflation rate has been 3 percent per year for several years, and the unemployment rate has been stable at 5 percent. Unanticipated changes in monetary policy cause the inflation rate to increase to 6 percent. In the short run, the unemployment rate will
  A) remain constant.
  B) increase to 8 percent.
  C) increase, but the exact amount cannot be known for sure.
  D) decrease.
Answer: D

Topic: The Short-Run Phillips Curve
Skill: Conceptual
61) An increase in the expected inflation rate causes
  A) a movement downward along the short-run Phillips curve.
  B) a movement upward along the short-run Phillips curve.
  C) a downward shift of the short-run Phillips curve.
  D) an upward shift of the short-run Phillips curve.
Answer: D

Topic: The Short-Run Phillips Curve
Skill: Conceptual
62) Which of the following leads to a downward shift in the short-run Phillips curve?
  A) People expect inflation to be 5 percent in 1999 and then expect inflation to be 3 percent in 2000.
  B) People expect the unemployment rate to increase.
  C) The long-run Phillips curve shifts rightward.
  D) Unexpected inflation increases.
Answer: A

Topic: The Short-Run Phillips Curve
Skill: Conceptual
63) Which of the following leads to an rightward shift in the short-run Phillips curve?
  I.   a reduction in inflationary expectations.
  II. an increase in the natural unemployment rate.
  A) I only.
  B) II only.
  C) I and II.
  D) Neither I nor I.
Answer: B

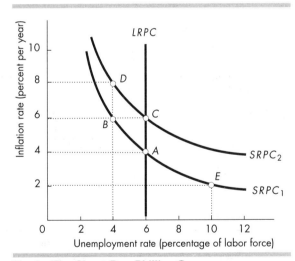

Topic: The Short-Run Phillips Curve
Skill: Analytical
64) In the above figure, suppose the economy is at point *A*. An unexpected increase in the inflation rate to 6 percent will cause a movement to point
  A) *B*.
  B) *C*.
  C) *D*.
  D) *E*.
Answer: A

Topic: The Short-Run Phillips Curve
Skill: Analytical
65) In the above figure, suppose the economy is at point A. An expected increase in the inflation rate to 6 percent will cause a movement to point
A) B.
B) C.
C) D.
D) E.
Answer: B

Topic: The Long-Run Phillips Curve
Skill: Recognition
66) The long-run Phillips curve
A) is vertical at potential GDP.
B) is the horizontal sum of the short-run Phillips curves.
C) is vertical at the natural unemployment rate.
D) is the vertical sum of the short-run Phillips curves.
Answer: C

Topic: The Short-Run and Long-Run Phillips Curve
Skill: Analytical
67) An increase in the natural unemployment rate shifts _____ Phillips curve rightward.
A) only the short-run
B) only the long-run
C) both the short-run and the long-run
D) neither the short-run nor the long-run
Answer: C

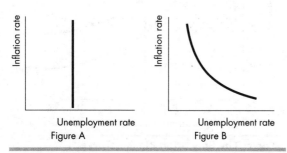

Figure A   Figure B

Topic: The Short-Run Phillips Curve
Skill: Analytical
68) Which of the diagrams in the above figure best illustrates a short-run Phillips curve?
A) Figure A.
B) Figure B.
C) Both Figure A and Figure B.
D) Neither Figure A nor Figure B.
Answer: B

Topic: The Short-Run Phillips Curve
Skill: Analytical
69) In the above figure B, which of the following are being held constant while moving along the curve in the figure?
A) the expected inflation rate.
B) the natural unemployment rate.
C) the AD curve.
D) Both answers A and B are correct.
Answer: D

Topic: The Long-Run Phillips Curve
Skill: Analytical
70) Which of the diagrams in the above figure best illustrates a long-run Phillips curve?
A) Figure A.
B) Figure B.
C) Both Figure A and Figure B.
D) Neither Figure A nor Figure B.
Answer: A

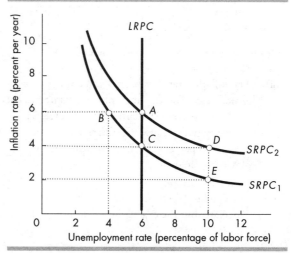

Topic: The Short-Run Phillips Curve
Skill: Analytical
71) In the above figure, the economy is at point A. The inflation rate unexpectedly drops by two percentage points, perhaps because the Fed unexpectedly changed its monetary policy. As a result, the economy moves to point
A) B.
B) C.
C) D.
D) E.
Answer: C

Topic: The Long-Run Phillips Curve
Skill: Analytical

72) In the above figure, the economy is at point *A*. The inflation rate drops by two percentage points and people correctly anticipated the fall, perhaps because they correctly anticipated the Fed's monetary policy. As a result, the economy moves to point

A) *B.*
B) *C.*
C) *D.*
D) *E.*

Answer: B

Topic: The U.S. Phillips Curve
Skill: Conceptual

73) Consider the U.S. data for inflation and the unemployment rate for the last three decades. Which of the following statements describes the relationship between the two variables?

A) The natural unemployment rate did not change but the expected inflation rate did change over these years.
B) Several different short-run Phillips curve representing different natural rates of unemployment and different expected inflation rates existed.
C) There is a positive relationship.
D) None of the above answers are correct.

Answer: B

■ Interest Rates and Inflation

Topic: Interest Rates and Inflation
Skill: Conceptual

74) Which of the following can directly explain why nominal interest rates differ in different countries?

A) Unemployment rates vary across countries.
B) Inflation rates vary across countries.
C) Potential GDP differs.
D) Government fiscal policies differ.

Answer: B

Topic: Interest Rates and Inflation
Skill: Conceptual

75) Which of the following correctly describes the relationship between nominal interest rates and inflation?

A) There is no relationship between the nominal interest rate and the inflation rate.
B) When there are high nominal interest rates, there are low inflation rates.
C) When there are high nominal interest rates, there are high inflation rates.
D) None of the above are correct.

Answer: C

Topic: Interest Rates and Inflation
Skill: Conceptual

76) A basic fact about inflation and nominal interest rates is that

A) high inflation and high nominal interest rates go together.
B) high inflation and low nominal interest rates go together.
C) inflation has little impact on nominal interest rates in the long run.
D) high nominal interest rates and high inflation are always associated with high real interest rates.

Answer: A

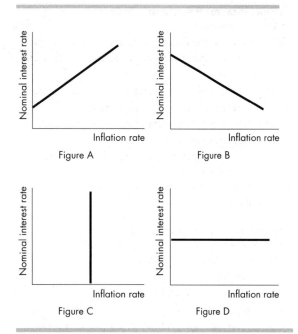

Figure A

Figure B

Figure C

Figure D

Topic: Interest Rates and Inflation
Skill: Analytical
77) In the above, which figure best shows the relationship between nominal interest rates and inflation in the U.S.?
A) Figure A.
B) Figure B.
C) Figure C.
D) Figure D.
Answer: A

Topic: Why Inflation Influences the Nominal Interest Rate
Skill: Conceptual
78) The reason that nominal interest rates rise with anticipated inflation is
A) the wage/price spiral.
B) demand-pull inflation.
C) cost-push inflation.
D) lenders require higher nominal interest rates to offset the fall in the value of money.
Answer: D

Topic: Why Inflation Influences the Nominal Interest Rate
Skill: Conceptual
79) People expect an inflation rate of 5 percent and the real interest rate is positive. Then the nominal interest rate will be
A) more than 5 percent.
B) 5 percent.
C) less than 5 percent.
D) Without more information it is impossible to tell if the nominal interest rate will be more than, less than, or equal to 5 percent.
Answer: A

Topic: Why Inflation Influences the Nominal Interest Rate
Skill: Conceptual
80) If people expect an inflation rate of 3.3 percent, and the real interest rate is 3 percent, the nominal interest rate equals (approximately)
A) 0.3 percent.
B) 8.6 percent.
C) 6.3 percent.
D) 9.9 percent.
Answer: C

■ True Or False Questions

Topic: Inflation and the Price Level
Skill: Recognition
81) Inflation describes the event of increasing output and rising prices.
Answer: FALSE

Topic: A Demand-Pull Inflation Process
Skill: Conceptual
82) Increases in the money supply can create demand-pull inflation.
Answer: TRUE

Topic: A Demand-Pull Inflation Process
Skill: Conceptual
83) For a demand-pull inflation spiral to occur, government spending must persistently increase.
Answer: FALSE

Topic: Demand-Pull Inflation In the United States
Skill: Recognition
84) The early 1990s were the last period of substantial demand-pull inflation in the U.S.
Answer: FALSE

Topic: Cost-Push Inflation
Skill: Conceptual
85) Increases in government purchases can create cost-push inflation.
Answer: FALSE

Topic: Cost-Push Inflation
Skill: Conceptual
86) Increases in the prices of raw materials can create cost-push inflation.
Answer: TRUE

Topic: A Cost-Push Inflation Process
Skill: Conceptual
87) For a cost-push inflation spiral to occur, the Fed must persistently increase the money supply.
Answer: TRUE

Topic: Unanticipated Inflation in the Capital Market
Skill: Conceptual
88) Unanticipated inflation causes income to be redistributed between borrowers and lenders.
Answer: TRUE

Topic: Forecasting Inflation
Skill: Recognition
89) The most accurate forecast that can be made is called a rational expectation.
Answer: TRUE

Topic: Inflation and Unemployment: The Phillips Curve
Skill: Recognition
90) The Phillips curve describes the relationship between real GDP and inflation.
Answer: FALSE

Topic: The Short-Run Phillips Curve
Skill: Conceptual
91) The negative relationship between inflation and unemployment can be explained by the aggregate supply and demand curves.
Answer: TRUE

Topic: The Long-Run Phillips Curve
Skill: Recognition
92) The long-run Phillips curve is vertical at the natural unemployment rate.
Answer: TRUE

Topic: Interest Rates and Inflation
Skill: Conceptual
93) As the inflation rate increases, nominal interest rates increase.
Answer: TRUE

Topic: Interest Rates and Inflation
Skill: Conceptual
94) There is a negative relationship between nominal interest rates and the inflation rate.
Answer: FALSE

■ Essay Questions

Topic: Inflation and the Price Level
Skill: Conceptual
95) Describe what happens to prices and the value of money when there is inflation.
Answer:

Topic: Demand-Pull Inflation
Skill: Recognition
96) What is demand-pull inflation?
Answer:

Topic: Demand-Pull Inflation
Skill: Conceptual
97) Describe how a demand-pull inflation can occur.
Answer:

Topic: Cost-Push Inflation
Skill: Recognition
98) What is cost-push inflation?
Answer:

Topic: A Cost-Push Inflation Process
Skill: Conceptual
99) Describe how a cost-push inflation can occur.
Answer:

Topic: Unanticipated Inflation in the Labor Market
Skill: Conceptual
100) How does unanticipated inflation affect the labor market? Mention two effects.
Answer:

Topic: Effects of Inflation
Skill: Conceptual
101) What are some costs of anticipated inflation? Explain your answer.
Answer:

Topic: Inflation and Unemployment: The Phillips Curve
Skill: Analytical
102) What is the Phillips curve? Draw an example.
Answer:

Topic: The U.S. Phillips Curve
Skill: Conceptual
103) Describe the Phillips curve as it relates to the U.S. economy for the last 30 years.
Answer:

Topic: Interest Rates and Inflation
Skill: Conceptual
104) Describe and explain the relationship between the nominal interest rate, the real interest rate, and the inflation rate.
Answer:

Chapter 17 THE BUSINESS CYCLE*

■ Cycle Patterns, Impulses, and Mechanisms

Topic: Business Cycle Patterns
Skill: Recognition
1) Which of the following is TRUE regarding the business cycle?
   I. It is a regular pattern of increasing and decreasing business activity.
   II. The cycle follows a rising trend.
   III. The NBER dates turning points in recessions and expansions.
   A) I and II.
   B) I and III.
   C) II and III.
   D) I, II and III.
Answer: C

Topic: Business Cycle Patterns
Skill: Recognition
2) The _____ is responsible for identifying _____.
   A) Council of Economic Advisors; phases of the business cycle
   B) Nation Bureau of Economic Research (NBER); phases of the business cycle
   C) Federal Reserve; forecasting changes in the trade balance
   D) Congress; forecasting turning points in the business cycle
Answer: B

Topic: Business Cycle Patterns
Skill: Recognition
3) The NBER has identified _____ recessions and expansions since 1920.
   A) 2.
   B) 5.
   C) 15.
   D) 60.
Answer: C

Topic: Business Cycle Patterns
Skill: Recognition
4) The recession that occurred in _____ was the most severe.
   A) 1990-1991
   B) early 1970s
   C) 1945
   D) 1930s
Answer: D

Topic: Business Cycle Patterns
Skill: Recognition
5) Which of the following is CORRECT regarding business cycles?
   I. Expansions usually last for about 4 years.
   II. Recessions usually last for about 1 year.
   III. The NBER has identified 5 recessions and expansions since 1920.
   A) I and II.
   B) I and III.
   C) II and III.
   D) I, II and III.
Answer: A

---

* This is Chapter 34 in *Economics*.

Topic: Business Cycle Patterns
Skill: Recognition
6) Recessions, on average, last for _____ with the last one occurring in _____.
   A) about 1 year; 1982-1983
   B) about 1 year; 1990-1991
   C) about 5 years; 1982-1983
   D) about 5 years; 1990-1991
Answer: B

Topic: Business Cycle Patterns
Skill: Recognition
7) Expansions, on average, usually last for _____ with the last expansion _____.
   A) about 2 years; ending in 1993.
   B) about 2 years; ongoing in 1995.
   C) about 4 years; ending in 1999.
   D) about 4 years; ongoing in 1999.
Answer: D

Topic: Business Cycle Patterns
Skill: Recognition
8) Analysis shows that
   A) long recessions are followed by long expansions.
   B) long recessions are followed by short expansions.
   C) short recessions are followed by long expansions.
   D) there is no relationship between the length of expansions and the preceding recessions.
Answer: D

Topic: Cycle Impulses and Mechanisms
Skill: Conceptual
9) When economists describe business cycles, they usually
   A) agree that the impulses that start business cycles are similar.
   B) agree that the mechanisms that perpetuate business cycles are similar.
   C) disagree upon which impulses are responsible for starting business cycles.
   D) disagree as to the role investment plays in business cycles.
Answer: C

Topic: Role of Investment and Capital
Skill: Recognition
10) Economists agree that _____ play(s) a crucial role in the development of recessions and expansions.
   A) consumption expenditure
   B) investment
   C) government purchases
   D) net exports
Answer: B

Topic: Role of Investment and Capital
Skill: Conceptual
11) The beginning of a recession coincides with a _____ while an expansion is triggered by a(n) _____.
   A) decrease in investment; decrease in investment
   B) decrease in government purchases; decrease in investment
   C) decrease in investment; increase in investment
   D) decrease in government spending; increase in investment
Answer: C

Topic: Role of Investment and Capital
Skill: Conceptual
12) A recession is caused when _____ and near the end of a recession _____.
   A) investment decreases; investment increases
   B) consumption expenditure decreases; investment increases
   C) government purchases decrease; government purchases increase
   D) net exports decrease; consumption expenditures increase
Answer: A

Topic: Role of Investment and Capital
Skill: Conceptual
13) The country of Belize is experiencing an economic expansion. Place the following events in the proper sequence to describe what will occur.
   I.   The quantity of capital increases.
   II.   Firms increase investment.
   III. Labor productivity increases.
   IV.   Diminishing returns to capital occur.
   A) IV, I, II, III.
   B) II, I, III, IV.
   C) III, I II, IV.
   D) I, II, IV, III.
Answer: B

Topic: Role of Investment and Capital
Skill: Recognition
14) If capital per hour of labor ____, we can expect ____.
   A) increases; the economy to experience an expansion
   B) increases; the economy to enter a recession
   C) decreases; the economy to enter an expansion
   D) decreases; diminishing returns to capital to occur
Answer: A

Topic: Central Roles of Investment and Capital
Skill: Conceptual
15) Suppose a recession is starting in South Korea. Place the following events in the correct sequence to describe what will occur as part of the recession and subsequent recovery.
   I.   The amount of capital per hour of labor decreases.
   II. Investment in new capital decreases.
   III. Profitable opportunities arise.
   IV. Investment increases.
   A) I, II, III, IV.
   B) II, I, III, IV.
   C) II, I, IV, III.
   D) IV, I, II, III.
Answer: B

Topic: The *AS-AD* Model
Skill: Conceptual
16) Business cycle impulses can
   A) affect only aggregate demand.
   B) affect only aggregate supply.
   C) affect both aggregate supply and aggregate demand.
   D) always be classified as part of the real business cycle theory.
Answer: C

■ Aggregate Demand Theories of the Business Cycle

Topic: Aggregate Demand Theories of the Business Cycle
Skill: Recognition
17) Which of the following are aggregate demand theories of the business cycle?
   I.   Keynesian Theory
   II. Real Business Cycle Theory
   III. Rational Expectations Theory
   A) I only.
   B) I and II.
   C) I and III.
   D) I, II and III.
Answer: C

Topic: Keynesian Theory
Skill: Conceptual
18) The impulse in the Keynesian model is ____.
   A) expected future sales and profits.
   B) a speed up in money growth.
   C) unanticipated changes in aggregate demand.
   D) unanticipated changes in aggregate supply.
Answer: A

Topic: Keynesian Theory
Skill: Conceptual
19) The Keynesian explanation of the business cycle is based on
   A) the inability of government policy-makers to predict the future course of the economy.
   B) shifts in monetary policy undertaken by the Federal Reserve.
   C) volatile expectations about future sales and profits.
   D) unstable inflationary expectations.
Answer: C

Topic: Keynesian Theory
Skill: Conceptual
20) Keynesians believe that
   A) wage adjustments will quickly eliminate unemployment.
   B) aggregate demand changes tend to induce aggregate supply changes, offsetting any effect from changes in government purchases.
   C) the economy will normally operate at full employment.
   D) a change in expected future sales can affect the amount of investment in the economy.
Answer: D

Topic: Keynesian Theory
Skill: Conceptual

21) The Keynesian explanation of the business cycle rests on several concepts, including

A) sticky wages.

B) unstable monetary policy by the Fed.

C) shocks to the rate of technological change.

D) the desire of politicians to be re-elected.

Answer: A

Topic: Keynesian Theory
Skill: Recognition

22) Which of the following are elements of the Keynesian theory of the business cycle?

I. multiplier effects.

II. rational expectations

III. a horizontal short-run aggregate supply curve

A) I and III.

B) II and III.

C) I and II.

D) I, II and III.

Answer: A

Topic: Keynesian Theory
Skill: Conceptual

23) Given the Keyneisan view of a flat short-run aggregate supply curve, a $20-billion decrease in aggregate demand causes real GDP to

A) not change.

B) decrease by less than $20 billion.

C) decrease by $20 billion.

D) decrease by more than $20 billion.

Answer: C

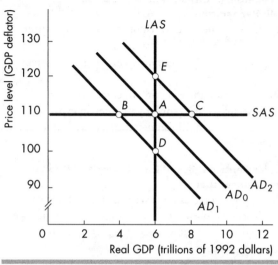

Topic: Keynesian Theory
Skill: Analytical

24) The curves in the above figure show the economy as viewed from a

A) real business cycle viewpoint.

B) Keynesian viewpoint.

C) monetarist viewpoint.

D) new classical rational expectations viewpoint.

Answer: B

Topic: Keynesian Theory
Skill: Analytical

25) In the above figure, suppose the economy is initially at point A. If firms expect profits to decrease, in the Keynesian theory the economy will move to point

A) B.

B) C.

C) D.

D) E.

Answer: A

Topic: Keynesian Theory
Skill: Analytical

26) In the above figure, suppose the economy is initially at point *A* when firms come to expect that future tax rate changes will reduce the profitability of investment. In the Keynesian theory, which of the following occur?

I. Investment will decrease.

II. There will be a movement to point *D*.

III. Money wages will not fall.

A) I only.

B) II and III.

C) I and III.

D) I, II and III.

Answer: C

Topic: Monetarist Theory
Skill: Recognition

27) Which of the following are elements of the monetarist theory of the business cycle?

I. The "impulse" is a change in the growth rate of the money supply.

II. The "mechanism" initially affects only the *SAS* curve.

III. Prices are temporarily sticky.

A) I and III.

B) II and III.

C) I and II.

D) I, II and III.

Answer: A

Topic: Monetarist Theory
Skill: Conceptual

28) Which of the following is TRUE regarding the monetarist theory of the business cycle?

I. Monetarists assume that the money supply increases at a constant rate.

II. Fluctuations in interest rates cause business cycles.

III. Changes in money growth affect aggregate demand.

A) I only.

B) III only.

C) I and II.

D) II and III.

Answer: B

Topic: Monetarist Theory
Skill: Conceptual

29) According to monetarist theory, the force that starts a recession is

A) a decrease in investment in stocks and bonds.

B) a slowdown in the growth rate of the quantity of money.

C) a decrease in spending money on goods.

D) an fall in interest rates that makes people decrease their saving.

Answer: B

Topic: Monetarist Theory
Skill: Conceptual

30) Monetarists contend that

A) wages are "sticky" the entire time that the economy is in a recession.

B) increases in money growth cause investment to increase.

C) exports decrease as a result of an increases in money growth.

D) the Keynesian multiplier is too small.

Answer: B

Topic: Monetarist Theory
Skill: Conceptual

31) Suppose the economy is initially at full employment. In response to an increase in money growth, a monetarist claims that

A) aggregate demand will increase.

B) money wage rates eventually will rise.

C) the economy moves away from and then back towards full employment as the economy reacts to changes in money growth.

D) All of the above are TRUE.

Answer: D

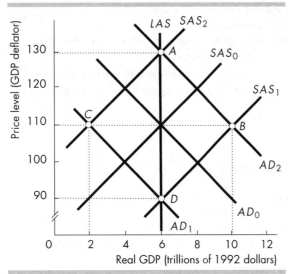

Topic: Monetarist Theory
Skill: Analytical

32) In the above figure, suppose the economy has moved from point *A* to point *C*. According to the monetarist theory of the business cycle, what could have caused this movement?

A)   An increase in money wages.
B)   An increase in money growth.
C)   A decrease in money growth.
D)   An increase in uncertainty.

Answer: C

Topic: Monetarist Theory
Skill: Analytical

33) In the above figure, suppose the economy has moved from point *D* to point *B*. According to the monetarist theory of the business cycle, what could have caused this movement?

A)   A decrease in money wages.
B)   An increase in uncertainty about future sales and profits.
C)   An increase in money growth.
D)   An increase in money wages.

Answer: C

Topic: Monetarist Theory
Skill: Analytical

34) In the above figure, suppose the economy has moved from point *C* to point *D*. According to the monetarist theory of the business cycle, what could have caused this movement?

A)   A decrease in money wages.
B)   An increase in money growth.
C)   A decrease in money growth.
D)   An increase in uncertainty.

Answer: A

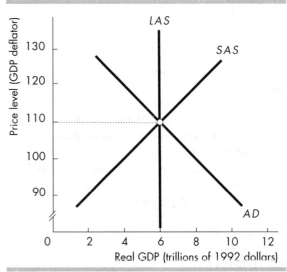

Topic: Monetarist Theory
Skill: Analytical

35) Using the above figure, a recession in the monetarist model would start with

A)   a rightward shift in the *AD* curve.
B)   a leftward shift in the *AD* curve.
C)   a leftward shift in the *SAS* curve.
D)   a leftward shift in the *LAS* curve.

Answer: B

Topic: Monetarist Theory
Skill: Analytical

36) In the above figure, according to the monetarist view of the business cycle, in the long run after all adjustments have been made, an expansion would cause

A)   an increase in real GDP above $7 trillion.
B)   an increase in the price level above 110.
C)   a decrease in real GDP below $7 trillion.
D)   a decrease in the price level below 110.

Answer: B

Topic: New Classical Theory
Skill: Conceptual

37) According to new classical theory of the business cycle, the business cycle is caused by

A) shifts in the aggregate supply curve.
B) anticipated changes in policy.
C) the fixed duration of price and wage contracts.
D) unanticipated changes in aggregate demand.

Answer: D

Topic: New Classical Theory
Skill: Conceptual

38) One assumption of the new classical model is that

A) wages are "sticky" downward.
B) prices are "sticky" upward.
C) people make rational expectations about aggregate demand.
D) markets are not purely competitive.

Answer: C

Topic: New Classical Theory
Skill: Conceptual

39) According to the new classical model, changes in aggregate demand change real GDP

A) all of the time.
B) only when the short-run aggregate supply curve is vertical.
C) only when the changes in aggregate demand are anticipated.
D) only when the changes in aggregate demand are unanticipated.

Answer: D

Topic: New Classical Theory
Skill: Recognition

40) Suppose the data show that an unanticipated change in tax rates caused a recent recession. These data support which model of the business cycle?

A) new classical.
B) new Keynesian.
C) real business cycle.
D) Both answers A and B are correct.

Answer: D

Topic: New Classical Theory
Skill: Conceptual

41) A larger than expected increase in aggregate demand will cause a(n) _____ in the _____ model of the business cycle.

A) recession; new Keynesian
B) recession; Keynesian
C) expansion; new classical
D) expansion; real business cycle

Answer: C

Topic: New Classical Theory
Skill: Recognition

42) Which of the following correctly describes the new classical theory of the business cycle?

A) An unanticipated change in the money supply can trigger a business cycle.
B) An anticipated tax rate change can trigger a business cycle.
C) An anticipated change in the level of exports can trigger a business cycle.
D) Rational expectations keep the money wage from changing quickly.

Answer: A

Topic: New Classical Theory
Skill: Conceptual

43) According to the new classical theory, an unexpected increase in aggregate demand causes the unemployment rate to _____ and the price level to _____.

A) stay the same; stay the same
B) fall; stay the same
C) fall; rise
D) rise; rise

Answer: C

Topic: New Classical Theory
Skill: Conceptual

44) According to the new classical theory, an unanticipated increase in the money supply that unexpectedly increases aggregate demand will _____ the price level and _____ real GDP.

A) raise; increase
B) raise; not affect
C) not affect; increase
D) lower; decrease

Answer: A

Topic: New Classical Theory
Skill: Conceptual
45) In the new classical theory, anticipated shifts in the aggregate demand curve
  A) also change the short-run aggregate supply curve.
  B) change prices but not real GDP.
  C) do not change unemployment.
  D) All of the above answers are correct.
Answer: D

Topic: New Classical Theory
Skill: Conceptual
46) Which of the following is TRUE regarding the new classical view of the business cycle?
  A) If firms and workers anticipate an increase in aggregate demand, money wages can be adjusted.
  B) Long-term contracts cause sticky wages.
  C) If firms and workers expect the money supply to increase, aggregate demand will decrease.
  D) Long-term contracts cause business cycles.
Answer: A

Topic: New Keynesian Theory
Skill: Conceptual
47) The _____ theory of the business cycle asserts that anticipated and unanticipated changes in aggregate demand cause fluctuations in real GDP.
  A) real business cycle.
  B) monetarist.
  C) new Keynesian.
  D) new classical.
Answer: C

Topic: New Keynesian Theory
Skill: Conceptual
48) The new Keynesian theory of the business cycle asserts that _____ generate changes in _____.
  A) both anticipated and unanticipated events; aggregate demand
  B) anticipated events only; aggregate demand
  C) anticipated events only; aggregate supply
  D) both anticipated and unanticipated events; aggregate supply
Answer: A

Topic: New Keynesian Theory
Skill: Conceptual
49) According to the new Keynesian model of the business cycle, which of the following can trigger an expansion?
  I. An unanticipated increase in the money supply.
  II. An anticipated increase in the money supply.
  III. An anticipated increase in government purchases.
  A) I only.
  B) II and III.
  C) I, II and III.
  D) none of the three will trigger an expansion.
Answer: C

Topic: New Keynesian Theory
Skill: Conceptual
50) New Keynesian economists believe that
  A) money wages are sticky at least in the short run.
  B) money wages are flexible in the short run but prices are sticky.
  C) money wages rise when the price level falls.
  D) money wages are fully flexible in the short run.
Answer: A

Topic: New Keynesian Theory
Skill: Conceptual
51) New Keynesian economics differs from the new classical theory with respect to its assumptions concerning
  A) the slope of the aggregate demand curve.
  B) wage flexibility.
  C) the importance of interest rates in determining investment spending.
  D) the slope of the short-run aggregate supply curve.
Answer: B

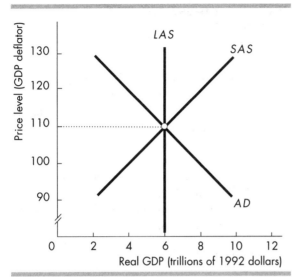

Topic: New Keynesian Theory
Skill: Analytical

52) In the above figure, suppose the economy is in equilibrium at potential GDP in the diagram. According to new Keynesian theorists, an unanticipated increase in the money supply that creates an unanticipated increase in aggregate demand will (initially)

A) increase real GDP and leave the price level at 110.
B) leave real GDP at its potential level but increase the price level.
C) increase real GDP and the price level.
D) have no effect on real GDP or the price level.

Answer: C

Topic: New Classical and New Keynesian Theories
Skill: Recognition

53) An unanticipated decrease in aggregate demand will trigger a recession in the _____ theory of the business cycle.

A) new Keynesian.
B) new classical.
C) Keynesian.
D) Both answers A and B are correct.

Answer: D

Topic: New Classical and New Keynesian Theories
Skill: Conceptual

54) Which of the following are TRUE regarding the rational expectation theory of the business cycle?

I. New Keynesian economists believe that money wages are influenced by rational expectations of the price level.
II. New classical economists believe that money wages are influenced by rational expectations of the price level.
III. New classical economists believe anticipated changes in aggregate demand trigger business cycles.

A) I and II.
B) I and III.
C) II and III.
D) I, II and III.

Answer: A

Topic: New Classical and New Keynesian Theories
Skill: Conceptual

55) The new classical theory predicts that when aggregate demand changes, money wages change _____ and the new Keynesian theory predicts that when aggregate demand changes, money wages change _____.

A) immediately; immediately
B) immediately; slowly
C) slowly; slowly
D) slowly; immediately

Answer: B

Topic: New Classical and New Keynesian Theories
Skill: Conceptual

56) According to the new classical theory, _____ policy changes have no effect on real GDP and according to the new Keynesian theory, _____ policy changes have an effect on real GDP.

A) anticipated; anticipated
B) unanticipated; anticipated
C) expansionary; expansionary
D) expansionary; contractionary

Answer: A

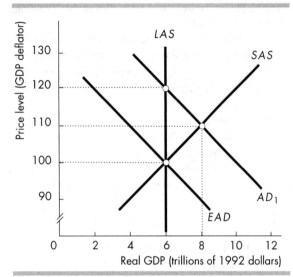

Topic: New Classical Theory
Skill: Analytical

57) In the above figure , according to the _____ model, an increase in GDP can occur because of a(n) _____ change in the money supply.
A) new classical; anticipated
B) new classical; unanticipated
C) real business cycle; anticipated
D) real business cycle; unanticipated

Answer: B

Topic: New Classical Theory
Skill: Analytical

58) In the above figure, the economy has a real GDP of $6 trillion and a price level of 100 when an un-anticipated demand shock shifts the aggregate demand curve to AD_1. The new classical theory of the business cycle concludes that the demand shock will
A) cause policy makers to implement countercyclical policy.
B) raise real GDP to $8 trillion and the price level to 110.
C) have no effect on real GDP level or the price level because the demand shock is unanticipated.
D) have no effect on real GDP because the short-run aggregate supply will also shift but the price level will rise to 120.

Answer: B

Topic: New Classical Theory
Skill: Analytical

59) In the above figure, the economy has a real GDP of $6 trillion and a price level of 100 when an *anticipated* demand shock shifts the aggregate demand curve to AD_1. The new classical theory of the business cycle concludes that the anticipated change in aggregate demand will
A) cause real GDP to equal $6 trillion and the price level to equal 100.
B) cause real GDP to equal $8 trillion and the price level to equal 110.
C) cause real GDP to equal $6 trillion and the price level to equal 120.
D) cause real GDP to fall, but the precise value of real GDP cannot be determined.

Answer: C

Topic: New Classical and New Keynesian Theories
Skill: Analytical

60) In the above figure, the economy has a real GDP of $6 trillion and a price level of 100 when an *anticipated* demand shock shifts the aggregate demand curve to AD_1. According to the new Keynesian theory, the anticipated increase in aggregate demand will cause real GDP to equal _____ and according to the new classical theory, the anticipated increase will cause real GDP to equal _____.
A) $6 trillion; $6 trillion
B) $6 trillion; $8 trillion
C) $8 trillion; $6 trillion
D) $8 trillion; $8 trillion

Answer: C

Topic: New Classical and New Keynesian Theories
Skill: Analytical

61) In the above figure, the economy has a real GDP of $6 trillion and a price level of 100 when an *unanticipated* demand shock shifts the aggregate demand curve to AD_1. According to the new Keynesian theory, the unanticipated increase in aggregate demand will cause real GDP to equal ____ and according to the new classical theory, the unanticipated increase will cause real GDP to equal ____.

A) $6 trillion; $6 trillion
B) $6 trillion; $8 trillion
C) $8 trillion; $6 trillion
D) $8 trillion; $8 trillion

Answer: D

■ Real Business Cycle Theory

Topic: RBC Impulse
Skill: Recognition

62) Real business cycle theory explains changes in employment and output by focusing on

A) changes in productivity.
B) changes in monetary policy.
C) changes in fiscal policy.
D) the interaction of fiscal and monetary policies.

Answer: A

Topic: RBC Impulse
Skill: Recognition

63) Real business cycle theory explains the business cycle as the result of

A) excess growth of the money supply.
B) unstable investment demand.
C) shocks to consumer spending habits.
D) fluctuations in productivity.

Answer: D

Topic: RBC Mechanism
Skill: Conceptual

64) Real business cycle economists claim that the intertemporal substitution effect

A) plays a small role in the labor market.
B) depends on the real interest rate.
C) plays a large role in the economy only during expansions.
D) has unpredictable effects on the economy.

Answer: B

Topic: RBC Mechanism
Skill: Conceptual

65) According to the real business cycle theory, which do people consider when deciding when to work?

A) the real interest rate.
B) the nominal interest rate.
C) the inflation rate.
D) the current money wage rate only.

Answer: A

Topic: RBC Mechanism
Skill: Conceptual

66) Suppose that the U.S. becomes involved in an international disturbance like a Mideast war that causes firms to think that future profits and productivity will fall. Which of the following do real business cycle economists predict will occur?

I. Investment demand decreases.
II. The quantity of money will increase as banks make more loans.

A) Only I.
B) Only II.
C) Both I and II.
D) Neither I nor II.

Answer: A

Topic: RBC Mechanism
Skill: Conceptual

67) Suppose that a severe shock that decreases investment demand hits the U.S. Which of the following can we expect to occur according to the real business cycle model?

A) the real interest rate will fall.
B) people will work fewer hours.
C) the real wage will fall.
D) All of the above are true.

Answer: D

Topic: Real Business Cycle Theory
Skill: Conceptual

68) Unlike the other models of the business cycle, the real business cycle model claims that

A) fluctuations in real GDP can be prevented.
B) fluctuations in real GDP show the economy is working efficiently.
C) real wages are sticky.
D) changes in the money supply can cause changes in real GDP.

Answer: B

Topic: Real Business Cycle Theory
Skill: Conceptual

69) The real business cycle model proposes, unlike other models of the economy, that

A) there is no short-run aggregate supply, only a long-run aggregate supply.

B) changes in real GDP cause changes in technology.

C) changes in the money supply cause changes in real GDP.

D) intertemporal substitution effects are unimportant.

Answer: A

Topic: Real Business Cycle Theory
Skill: Analytical

70) In the real business cycle model, there is no

A) *SAS* curve.

B) *AD* curve.

C) *LAS* curve.

D) price level.

Answer: A

Topic: Real Business Cycle Theory
Skill: Conceptual

71) According to the real business cycle theory, an increase in the price of a resource, such as oil, that decreases investment demand will

A) increase both real GDP and the price level.

B) increase real GDP but not change the price level.

C) decrease real GDP.

D) decrease real GDP and increase the money supply.

Answer: C

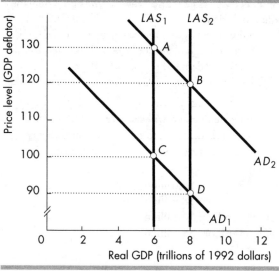

Topic: Real Business Cycle Theory
Skill: Analytical

72) In the above figure, assume that the economy is at point *C*. According to the real business cycle theory, an increase in productivity that increases investment demand will cause the economy to move to point such as _____ as _____.

A) *B*; employment increases

B) *B*; the real interest rate falls

C) *C*; the real interest rate increases

D) *D*; employment decreases

Answer: A

Topic: Real Business Cycle Theory
Skill: Analytical

73) In the above figure, assume that the economy is at point *B*. According to the real business cycle theory, a negative shock to productivity causes a movement to point such as _____ as real _____.

A) *A*; interest rates fall

B) *C*; interest rates rise

C) *D*; interest rates fall

D) *D*; interest rates rise

Answer: B

Topic: Real Business Cycle Theory
Skill: Analytical

74) In the above figure, assume that the economy is at point *C*. According to the real business cycle theory, an increase in the money supply will cause the economy to a move to a point such as

A) point *A*.

B) point *B*.

C) point *C*, that is, there will be no change.

D) point *D*.

Answer: A

Topic: Criticisms of Real Business Cycle Theory
Skill: Conceptual

75) Critics of the real business cycle theory claim that

A) both real and nominal variables change during the business cycle.

B) the intertemporal substitution effect is too weak to account for changes in labor supply.

C) changes in technology cannot cause economic growth.

D) Both answers B and C are correct.

Answer: B

■ Recessions and Expansions During the 1990s

Topic: U.S. Recession of 1990-1991
Skill: Recognition

76) Which of the following played a role in creating the business cycle recession of 1990-1991?

I.   Oil prices rose.

II. The government raised taxes.

III. Firms decreased investment.

A) I and II.

B) I and III.

C) II and III.

D) I, II and III.

Answer: B

Topic: U.S. Recession of 1990-1991
Skill: Recognition

77) Which of the following are elements of the U.S. 1990-91 recession?

I.   a negative shock to aggregate supply.

II. a decrease in investment.

III. increases in the prices of fuel and raw materials.

A) I and III.

B) I and II.

C) II and III.

D) I, II, and III.

Answer: D

Topic: U.S. Recession of 1990-1991
Skill: Recognition

78) The recession in 1990-1991 occurred as a result of

I.   a decrease in short-run aggregate supply.

II. a decrease in aggregate demand.

III. increased investment.

IV. a fall in oil prices.

A) I only.

B) I and IV.

C) I and II.

D) II and III.

Answer: C

Topic: U.S. Recession of 1990-1991
Skill: Recognition

79) In the 1990-1991 recession,

A) the *LAS* curve shifted leftward.

B) the *AD* curve shifted rightward.

C) the *SAS* curve shifted leftward.

D) the *SAS* curve shifted rightward.

Answer: C

Topic: U.S. Recession of 1990-1991
Skill: Recognition

80) Which of the following describes what occurred during the 1990-1991 recession?

A) A decline in labor productivity caused the long-run aggregate supply curve to shift leftward.

B) The government decreased its purchases.

C) Firms' uncertainty regarding profits caused investment to decrease.

D) Both answers B and C are correct.

Answer: C

Topic: U.S. Expansion of 1990-1991
Skill: Recognition
81) _____ has been a feature of the U.S. expansion in the 1990s.
A)   Low inflation
B)   Large increases in government spending
C)   Increases in the budget deficit
D)   Unanticipated changes in the money supply
Answer: A

Topic: U.S. Expansion in the 1990s
Skill: Recognition
82) Which of the following models best describes the U.S. expansion of the 1990s?
A)   the Keynesian model.
B)   the rational expectations model.
C)   the new Keynesian model.
D)   the real business cycle model.
Answer: D

Topic: Japanese Recession of the 1990s
Skill: Recognition
83) Which of the following have contributed to the Japanese recession in the 1990s?
A)   the lack of efficient markets.
B)   large increases in government spending.
C)   unanticipated increases the growth rate of the money supply.
D)   lack of technological advances.
Answer: A

■ The Great Depression

Topic: The Great Depression
Skill: Recognition
84) During the Great Depression, by the year 1933 real GDP had fallen by _____ percent compared to 1929.
A)   1.8
B)   15
C)   29
D)   60
Answer: C

Topic: The Great Depression
Skill: Recognition
85) Which of the following statements regarding the Great Depression is correct?
A)   If a person was able to keep his or her job, the person's real wage generally increased.
B)   Real GDP fell by about 10 percent.
C)   Increased government spending helped to spur consumer spending.
D)   Evidence collected by Milton Friedman and Anna Schwartz show that the stock market crash was the primary cause of the depression.
Answer: A

Topic: Why the Great Depression Happened
Skill: Recognition
86) The Great Depression occurred due to several factors. Which of the following were considered sources of international uncertainty?
A)   The decline of Britain's stock market.
B)   Free trade policies among world powers.
C)   The decline of the U.S.'s traditional economic power.
D)   International currency fluctuations and the introduction of restrictive trade policies.
Answer: D

Topic: Why the Great Depression Happened
Skill: Recognition
87) The stock market crash contributed to the Great Depression by
I.   increasing people's consumption expenditure rather than saving because people feared another stock market crash.
II.   increasing interest rates.
III. helping to create uncertainty, causing firms to cut back on investment.
A)   I and II.
B)   I and III.
C)   III.
D)   II and III.
Answer: C

Topic: Why the Great Depression Happened
Skill: Recognition

88) Which of the following contributed to the collapse of the economy during the Great Depression?
   I.   A severe decrease in government spending.
   II. A decrease in investment.
   III. A large decrease in the monetary base.
   A) I and II.
   B) I and III.
   C) II and III.
   D) II only.
Answer: D

Topic: Why the Great Depression Happened
Skill: Recognition

89) Between 1929 and 1933, aggregate demand _____ and aggregate supply _____.
   A) increased; increased
   B) increased; decreased
   C) decreased; decreased
   D) decreased; increased
Answer: D

Topic: Why the Great Depression Happened
Skill: Recognition

90) Which of the following is correct concerning the behavior of the money supply during the Great Depression?
   A) Peter Temin has cited a severe monetary contraction as a chief cause of the Great Depression.
   B) The monetary base decreased by 50 percent.
   C) A decrease in bank deposits constituted a large portion of the decrease in the money supply.
   D) The Fed directed the decrease in the money supply.
Answer: C

Topic: Can the Great Depression Happen Again?
Skill: Recognition

91) Another severe depression is unlikely to occur because of
   I.   bank deposit insurance.
   II. stable international currency markets.
   III. the Fed's role as a lender of last resort.
   A) I and II.
   B) I and III.
   C) II and III.
   D) III only.
Answer: B

Topic: Can the Great Depression Happen Again?
Skill: Recognition

92) Another severe depression is unlikely to occur because of
   I.   the larger fraction of GDP accounted for by government purchases.
   II. the existence of more dual-income families.
   III. European and American-based trade-agreement alliances.
   A) I only.
   B) I and II.
   C) I and III.
   D) II and III.
Answer: B

■ True Or False Questions

Topic: Business Cycle Patterns
Skill: Recognition

93) Recessions and expansions have turning points dated by the National Bureau for Economic Research (NBER).
Answer: TRUE

Topic: Business Cycle Patterns
Skill: Recognition

94) On average, recessions last for just over 1 year.
Answer: TRUE

Topic: Keynesian Theory
Skill: Conceptual

95) The Keynesian theory of business cycle views volatile expectations of future sales and profits as the main source of economic fluctuations.
Answer: TRUE

Topic: Monetarist Theory
Skill: Conceptual

96) The monetarist theory of the business cycle views fluctuations in the growth rate of the quantity of money as the main source of economic fluctuations.
Answer: TRUE

Topic: New Classical Theory
Skill: Conceptual

97) The new classical theory of the business cycle views anticipated fluctuations in aggregate demand as the main source of economic fluctuations.
Answer: FALSE

Topic: New Keynesian Theory
Skill: Conceptual
98) The new Keynesian theory of the business cycle views only anticipated changes in aggregate demand as the source of economic fluctuations.
Answer: FALSE

Topic: RBC Impulse
Skill: Conceptual
99) The real business cycle theory views fluctuations in productivity as the main source of business cycles.
Answer: TRUE

Topic: RBC Mechanism
Skill: Conceptual
100) The intertemporal substitution effect is the impulse in the Keynesian theory of the business cycle.
Answer: FALSE

Topic: Real Business Cycle Theory
Skill: Conceptual
101) The short-run aggregate supply curve and the aggregate demand curve both are upward sloping in the real business cycle model.
Answer: FALSE

Topic: U.S. Recession of 1990-1991
Skill: Conceptual
102) During the 1990-91 recession, both the short-run aggregate supply and aggregate demand curves shifted leftward.
Answer: TRUE

Topic: Why the Great Depression Happened
Skill: Conceptual
103) During the Great Depression, the monetary base increased, causing a surge in inflation.
Answer: FALSE

Topic: Can the Great Depression Happen Again?
Skill: Conceptual
104) The existence of bank deposit insurance is one factor that will probably prevent another depression.
Answer: TRUE

■ Essay Questions

Topic: Keynesian Theory
Skill: Conceptual
105) Explain the impulse in the Keynesian theory of the business cycle.
Answer:

Topic: Monetarist Theory
Skill: Conceptual
106) Explain the impulse in the monetarist theory of the business cycle.
Answer:

Topic: New Classical Theory
Skill: Conceptual
107) Explain the impulse in the new classical theory of the business cycle.
Answer:

Topic: New Keynesian Theory
Skill: Conceptual
108) Explain the impulse in the new Keynesian theory of the business cycle.
Answer:

Topic: RBC Impulse
Skill: Conceptual
109) Explain the impulse in the real business cycle theory of the business cycle.
Answer:

Topic: RBC Mechanism
Skill: Conceptual
110) What is the intertemporal substitution effect and what role does it play in the real business cycle model?
Answer:

Topic: Criticisms of Real Business Cycle Theory
Skill: Conceptual
111) What are criticisms of the real business cycle theory?
Answer:

Topic: Why the Great Depression Happened
Skill: Conceptual
112) Peter Temin, Anna Schwartz and Milton Friedman have conflicting theories as to the causes of the Great Depression. Briefly discuss their disagreement.
Answer:

Chapter 18 MACROECONOMIC POLICY CHALLENGES*

■ Policy Goals

Topic: Policy Goals
Skill: Recognition
1) Which of the following are domestic macroeconomic policy goals?
   I. Achieve a growth rate of potential GDP equal to 2.0 percent.
   II. Smooth avoidable fluctuations in real GDP.
   III. Maintain an inflation rate equal to zero percent.
   A) I only.
   B) II only.
   C) I and II.
   D) I, II and III.
Answer: B

Topic: Policy Goals
Skill: Recognition
2) Monetary and fiscal policies aim to keep
   A) real GDP above potential GDP.
   B) the inflation rate low.
   C) unemployment at its natural rate.
   D) Both answers B and C are correct.
Answer: D

Topic: Potential GDP Growth
Skill: Recognition
3) Which of the following plays a role in determining economic growth?
   II. Saving.
   III. Investment by firms.
   A) Only I.
   B) Only II.
   C) Both I and II.
   D) Neither I nor II.
Answer: C

Topic: Potential GDP Growth
Skill: Recognition
4) Between 1988 and 1998, the rate of growth of potential GDP in the U.S. economy has been, on average, equal to approximately
   A) 2.0 percent.
   B) 5.0 percent.
   C) 8.0 percent.
   D) 12.0 percent.
Answer: A

Topic: The Business Cycle
Skill: Conceptual
5) Which of the following is TRUE regarding the business cycle?
   I. Potential GDP grows at a constant rate.
   II. Economists believe that most fluctuations can be removed from real GDP.
   III. Fluctuations in technological advances contribute to fluctuations in real GDP.
   A) I only.
   B) I and II.
   C) II and III.
   D) III only.
Answer: D

Topic: The Business Cycle
Skill: Conceptual
6) _____ will cause fluctuations in the growth rate of potential GDP.
   A) Variations in the pace of technological advances.
   B) Variations in the real wage
   C) Changes in the pace of new capital investment
   D) Both answers A and C are correct
Answer: D

---

* This is Chapter 35 in *Economics*.

Topic: The Business Cycle
Skill: Conceptual

7)   Which of the following is TRUE regarding the variations in real GDP growth?

   A)   Real business cycle theorists claim fluctuations are due to changes in potential GDP.

   B)   Aggregate demand theories claim that changes in government spending are the cause of the fluctuations.

   C)   Variations in real GDP growth create reductions in the natural rate of unemployment.

   D)   Potential GDP and trends in real GDP growth are negatively related.

Answer: A

Topic: The Business Cycle
Skill: Conceptual

8)   By keeping real GDP growth steady, the economy can avoid

   A)   bottlenecks as real GDP exceeds potential GDP.

   B)   losses in output when real GDP growth slows to less than that of potential GDP.

   C)   inflation.

   D)   Both answers A and B are correct.

Answer: D

Topic: The Business Cycle
Skill: Conceptual

9)   Suppose the growth rate of real GDP increases. Which of the following can we expect to occur?

   A)   The unemployment rate will fall.

   B)   Bottlenecks will disappear.

   C)   The money supply will increase.

   D)   The growth rate of potential GDP will increase by more than the growth rate of real GDP.

Answer: A

Topic: The Business Cycle
Skill: Conceptual

10)   Suppose real GDP growth slows. Which of the following can we expect to occur?

   A)   The unemployment rate will be greater than the natural rate of unemployment.

   B)   The duration of unemployment will decrease.

   C)   Bottlenecks in production.

   D)   The natural rate of unemployment will be greater than the actual unemployment rate.

Answer: A

Topic: Unemployment
Skill: Recognition

11)   Most economists estimate the natural rate of unemployment in the U.S. is about

   A)   1 percent.

   B)   5 percent.

   C)   10 percent.

   D)   15 percent.

Answer: B

Topic: Inflation
Skill: Conceptual

12)   Suppose the inflation rate becomes extremely unpredictable. Which of the following may occur?

   A)   People will tend to use money for exchange.

   B)   The unemployment rate will fall.

   C)   Nominal GDP will become MORE predictable.

   D)   Some borrowers and lenders may not use money for transactions.

Answer: D

Topic: Inflation
Skill: Conceptual

13)   Which of the following is TRUE regarding the choice of an inflation rate?

   A)   Most economists would choose an inflation rate equal to zero.

   B)   Most economists would choose an inflation rate less than zero.

   C)   Most economists would choose an inflation rate between zero and three percent.

   D)   Choosing an inflation rate means that an unemployment rate also must be chosen.

Answer: C

Topic: Two Core Policy Indicators
Skill: Recognition

14)   The macroeconomic policy goal of _____ is linked to _____ in the short run.

   A)   lowering the inflation rate; smoothing the business cycle

   B)   smoothing the business cycle; increasing exports

   C)   maintaining low unemployment; smoothing the business cycle

   D)   increasing the growth rate of real GDP; lowering the inflation rate

Answer: C

Topic: Two Core Policy Indicators
Skill: Conceptual
15) The growth in real GDP and the inflation rate are
 A) closely related in less developed nations but not developed ones.
 B) closely related in the long run.
 C) closely related in the short run and long run.
 D) largely unrelated in the long run.
Answer: D

Topic: Two Core Policy Indicators
Skill: Recognition
16) _____ and _____ are considered core targets of macroeconomic policy.
 A) Inflation; smoothing the business cycle
 B) Real GDP growth; inflation
 C) Real GDP growth; smoothing of the business cycle
 D) Smoothing the business cycle; maintaining low unemployment
Answer: B

■ Policy Tools and Performance

Topic: Policy Tools
Skill: Recognition
17) Which of the following are tools available to policy makers as they try to achieve macroeconomic goals?
 I. Government purchases and taxes.
 II. International trade.
 III. Changes in the money supply.
 A) I and II.
 B) I only.
 C) I and III.
 D) I, II and III.
Answer: C

Topic: Policy Tools
Skill: Recognition
18) Fiscal policy consists of
 A) changes in the money supply.
 B) balancing the budget.
 C) government purchases and tax policies.
 D) the federal government.
Answer: C

Topic: Policy Tools
Skill: Recognition
19) The use of government purchases and taxes to manipulate the economy is known as
 A) anti-stabilization policy.
 B) fiscal policy.
 C) federal expenditure.
 D) balancing the budget.
Answer: B

Topic: Policy Tools
Skill: Recognition
20) Adjusting the quantity of money and the interest rate characterize
 A) monetary policy.
 B) fiscal policy.
 C) both monetary and fiscal policy.
 D) budget deficit and budget surplus activities.
Answer: A

Topic: Policy Tools
Skill: Conceptual
21) Monetary policy includes adjustments in _____ so as to change _____.
 A) interest rates; short-run aggregate supply
 B) interest rates; long-run aggregate supply
 C) the money in circulation; short-run aggregate supply
 D) the money in circulation; aggregate demand
Answer: D

Topic: Monetary Policy Since 1960
Skill: Conceptual
22) Measures of monetary policy include:
 I. the growth rate of M2.
 II. the growth rate of the budget deficit or surplus.
 III. the real federal funds rate.
 A) I only.
 B) II only.
 C) I and III.
 D) I and II.
Answer: C

Topic: Monetary Policy Since 1960
Skill: Conceptual

23) A change in the M2 growth rate indicates how the Fed intends to influence
   A) short-run aggregate supply.
   B) aggregate demand.
   C) fiscal policy.
   D) long-run aggregate supply.

Answer: B

■ Long-Term Growth Policy

Topic: Long-Term Growth Policy
Skill: Recognition

24) _____ and _____ are sources of long-term growth of potential GDP.
   A) Fixed-rule policy; feedback-rule policy
   B) Saving; technology
   C) Technology; international markets
   D) Both answers A and B are correct

Answer: B

Topic: Long-Term Growth Policy
Skill: Conceptual

25) Suppose the government wants to promote long-term growth in potential GDP. Policy actions can do this by
   A) increasing government saving.
   B) increasing international trade.
   C) cutting taxes on private saving.
   D) Both answers A and C are correct.

Answer: D

Topic: Long-Term Growth Policy
Skill: Conceptual

26) Monetary policy can contribute to long-term economic growth by
   A) directly promoting increased consumption expenditure.
   B) increasing saving.
   C) keeping the inflation rate low.
   D) raising interest rates.

Answer: C

Topic: Long-Term Growth Policy
Skill: Conceptual

27) Suppose the government decides to enhance long-term economic growth of potential GDP by using fiscal policy. Fiscal policy accomplishes this by
   A) raising inflation rates.
   B) lowering interest rates.
   C) promoting increased saving.
   D) generating government deficits.

Answer: C

Topic: National Saving
Skill: Conceptual

28) Savings is an important economic growth variable because
   A) it is the principal source of new investment and capital formation.
   B) it helps the economy maintain the current level of total expenditures when a recession begins.
   C) it provides a fund for wages given any unexpected population growth.
   D) All of the above answers are correct.

Answer: A

Topic: National Saving
Skill: Recognition

29) Private saving plus government saving equals
   A) national saving, if government saving is greater than zero.
   B) investment.
   C) national saving, regardless of whether government saving is positive or negative.
   D) net national saving.

Answer: C

Topic: National Saving
Skill: Recognition

30) Over the past 35 years, which of the following is TRUE regarding saving behavior in the U.S.?
   A) In recent years, national saving has increased as a percentage of GDP.
   B) National saving, on average, has been about 40 percent of GDP.
   C) Private saving has been less than government saving.
   D) Private saving has always been less than national saving.

Answer: A

Topic: National Saving
Skill: Recognition
31) Since 1993, national saving as a percent of GDP has
A) fallen.
B) risen.
C) been negative.
D) been rather steady.
Answer: B

Topic: National Saving
Skill: Conceptual
32) In order to increase its growth, the U.S. economy
A) must use its own saving.
B) can use both foreign and domestic saving.
C) should refrain from using fiscal policy.
D) should refrain from using monetary policy.
Answer: B

Topic: National Saving
Skill: Conceptual
33) It is important for the U.S. to foster saving because
A) saving is used for investment, which contributes to economic growth.
B) an increase in the U.S. saving rate would cause world saving to increase.
C) an increase in the U.S. saving rate could decrease world real interest rates.
D) All of the above answers are correct.
Answer: D

Topic: National Saving
Skill: Conceptual
34) An advantage of increased saving in the U.S. is that
A) economic growth in the U.S. will probably increase.
B) aggregate demand would stop changing, thereby helping smooth the business cycle.
C) other countries will save more as well.
D) long-run aggregate supply will increase, which will help smooth the business cycle.
Answer: A

Topic: National Saving
Skill: Conceptual
35) Suppose the government wants to increase *national* saving. This goal can be accomplished by
A) increasing the government's surplus.
B) increasing the return on saving.
C) cutting the capital gains tax.
D) All of the above answers are correct.
Answer: D

Topic: National Saving
Skill: Conceptual
36) If government policies reduce the after-tax return to saving, the result will be
A) a decrease in government saving.
B) a decrease in national saving.
C) a decrease in the inflation rate.
D) an increase in Individual Retirement Accounts (IRAs).
Answer: B

Topic: National Saving
Skill: Conceptual
37) If the government wants to increase national saving, the government could
A) cut taxes on interest income.
B) cut taxes on capital gains.
C) use a consumption tax instead of an income tax.
D) All of the above answers are correct.
Answer: D

Topic: Investment in Human Capital
Skill: Conceptual
38) Suppose the government decides to promote long-term economic growth. What are some actions the government can undertake to accomplish this goal?
A) Subsidizing college education.
B) Increasing the growth rate of the money supply.
C) Increasing government purchases.
D) Both answers A and B are correct.
Answer: A

Topic: Investment in Human Capital
Skill: Conceptual

39) The U.S. government has a policy to encourage investment in human capital because

A) left to their own, people would acquire too little human capital.

B) there are no private returns to human capital.

C) interest rates are too high.

D) people are unwilling to invest on their own.

Answer: A

Topic: Investment in Human Capital
Skill: Conceptual

40) Which of the following does the U.S. government do to increase human capital?

I. Subsidizes education.

II. Sets standards of achievement for the school system.

III. Increases the private returns to human capital.

A) I only.

B) I and II.

C) I and III.

D) I, II and III.

Answer: B

Topic: Investment in New Technologies
Skill: Conceptual

41) One reason the government supports investment in new technology is that this investment

A) lowers interest rates.

B) does not suffer diminishing returns.

C) lowers the inflation rate.

D) decreases aggregate demand.

Answer: B

Topic: Investment in New Technologies
Skill: Conceptual

42) One reason the government promotes investment in new technology is that this investment

A) tends to have positive effects on ALL sectors of the economy.

B) decreases the amount of foreign investment in the U.S. economy.

C) lowers interest rates.

D) decreases the need for labor.

Answer: A

Topic: Investment in New Technologies
Skill: Conceptual

43) In order to promote long-term economic growth via investment in new technologies, the government can

A) increase the money supply.

B) raise interest rates.

C) provide tax incentives for research and development activities.

D) use discretionary fiscal policy.

Answer: C

■ Business Cycle and Unemployment Policy

Topic: Business Cycle and Unemployment Policy
Skill: Recognition

44) Monetary policies can be _____ and fiscal policies can be _____.

A) only a fixed-rule policy; only a fixed-rule policy

B) either a fixed-rule or a feedback-rule policy; only a fixed-rule policy

C) only a fixed-rule policy; either a fixed-rule or a feedback-rule policy

D) either a fixed-rule or a feedback-rule policy; either a fixed-rule or a feedback-rule policy

Answer: D

Topic: Fixed-Rule Policies
Skill: Conceptual

45) Which of the following are TRUE regarding fixed-rule policies?

I. Fixed-rule policies are frequently used by policy makers.

II. A fixed-rule policy operates independently of the economy's behavior.

III. Keynesian-based policies are a good example of fixed-rule policies.

A) I only.

B) II only.

C) I and III.

D) II and III.

Answer: B

Topic: Fixed-Rule Policies
Skill: Conceptual
46) Which type of theory suggests introducing a fixed rate of monetary growth to replace discretionary monetary policy in the economy?
A) Keynesian theory.
B) monetarist theory.
C) rational expectations theory.
D) both monetarist and Keynesian theories.
Answer: B

Topic: Fixed-Rule Policies
Skill: Conceptual
47) Suppose a constitutional amendment is passed that mandates a balanced federal budget every year, and the President and Congress consistently carry this mandate out. This would be an example of
A) active policymaking.
B) flexible-rule policymaking.
C) fixed-rule policymaking.
D) feedback-rule policymaking.
Answer: C

Topic: Feedback-Rule Policies
Skill: Recognition
48) Which of the following statements are TRUE regarding feedback-rule policies?
I. The actions from a feedback-rule policy depend on the behavior of the economy.
II. Monetarists generally support the use of feedback-rule policies.
A) Only I.
B) Only II.
C) Neither I nor II.
D) Both I and II.
Answer: A

Topic: Feedback-Rule Policies
Skill: Conceptual
49) An example of a feedback-rule policy includes
A) increasing the money supply during an economic recession.
B) adjusting the federal budget so that it balances every year.
C) increasing taxes during an economic expansion.
D) Both answers A and C are correct.
Answer: D

Topic: Feedback-Rule Policies
Skill: Conceptual
50) Suppose the United States is in a recession. If the Fed decreases interest rates because of this fact, the Fed is conducting a
A) flexible-rule policy.
B) feedback-rule policy.
C) nondiscretionary policy.
D) fixed-rule policy.
Answer: B

Topic: Feedback-Rule Policies
Skill: Conceptual
51) A(n) ____ policy to stabilize the economy specifies how policy actions respond to changes in the state of the economy.
A) economic
B) supply-shock
C) feedback-rule
D) fixed-rule
Answer: C

Topic: Fixed-Rule and Feedback-Rule Policies
Skill: Conceptual
52) Which answer accurately describes the two policies described below?
I. A constant growth rate of the money supply.
II. The Fed decreasing the money supply during an economic expansion and increasing the money supply during an economic recession.
A) I and II are both fixed-rule policies.
B) I is a fixed-rule policy and II is a feedback-rule policy.
C) I is a feedback-rule policy and II is a fixed-rule policy.
D) I and II are both feedback-rule policies.
Answer: B

Topic: Fixed-Rule and Feedback-Rule Policies
Skill: Conceptual

53) Which answer accurately describes the two policies described below?

I.   A constant growth rate of the money supply.
II.   Decreasing government purchases during an
      economic expansion and increasing govern-
      ment purchases during an economic recession.

A)   I and II are both fixed-rule policies.
B)   I is a fixed-rule policy and II is a feedback-rule
     policy.
C)   I is a feedback-rule policy and II is a fixed-rule
     policy.
D)   I and II are both feedback-rule policies.

Answer: B

Topic: Stabilizing Aggregate Demand Shocks
Skill: Conceptual

54) As firms expect future profits to increase, they
increase their investment. As a result, real GDP
rises above potential GDP. A monetarist following
a fixed-rule policy would recommend

A)   increasing the money supply.
B)   decreasing government purchases.
C)   doing nothing.
D)   Both answers A and B are correct.

Answer: C

Topic: Stabilizing Aggregate Demand Shocks
Skill: Conceptual

55) Consumer confidence in the economy falls, and as
a result, aggregate demand decreases. As real GDP
falls below potential GDP, a monetarist using a
fixed rule would recommend

A)   increasing the money supply.
B)   increasing government purchases.
C)   doing nothing.
D)   Both answers A and B are correct.

Answer: C

Topic: Stabilizing Aggregate Demand Shocks
Skill: Conceptual

56) Suppose that several European countries enter a
recession decreasing U.S. exports. As real GDP in
the U.S. decreases below potential GDP, a
monetarist following a fixed rule would recommend

A)   increasing the money supply.
B)   increasing government purchases.
C)   doing nothing.
D)   reducing tariffs.

Answer: C

Topic: Stabilizing Aggregate Demand Shocks
Skill: Conceptual

57) Suppose that several European countries enter a
recession decreasing U.S. exports. As real GDP in
the U.S. decreases below potential GDP, a
Keynesian following a feedback rule would recommend

A)   increasing the money supply.
B)   decreasing government purchases.
C)   doing nothing.
D)   decreasing the money supply.

Answer: A

Topic: Stabilizing Aggregate Demand Shocks
Skill: Conceptual

58) According to a Keynesian economist using a feedback rule, an increase in aggregate demand that
increases real GDP so that it exceeds potential
GDP should be met with a(n) _____ in tax rates or
a(n) _____ in government spending.

A)   increase; increase
B)   increase; decrease
C)   decrease; increase
D)   decrease; decrease

Answer: B

Topic: Stabilizing Aggregate Demand Shocks
Skill: Conceptual

59) According to a Keynesian economist using a feedback rule, a decrease in aggregate demand should
be met with a(n) _____ in tax rates or a(n) _____ in
government purchases.

A)   increase; increase
B)   increase; decrease
C)   decrease; increase
D)   decrease; decrease

Answer: C

Topic: Stabilizing Aggregate Demand Shocks
Skill: Conceptual

60) Consumer confidence in the economy rises, and as a result, real GDP increases above potential GDP. A Keynesian economist using a feedback rule would recommend

A)   increasing government spending.
B)   decreasing government spending.
C)   increasing the money supply.
D)   decreasing taxes.

Answer: B

Topic: Stabilizing Aggregate Demand Shocks
Skill: Conceptual

61) A worldwide recession reduces the amount of U.S. exports, and as a result, aggregate demand decreases. A Keynesian economist using a feedback rule would recommend that the appropriate monetary policy is

A)   increasing government spending.
B)   increasing the money supply.
C)   decreasing the money supply.
D)   doing nothing.

Answer: B

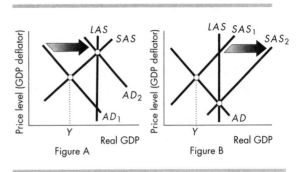

Figure A   Figure B

Topic: Stabilizing Aggregate Demand Shocks
Skill: Analytical

62) In both parts of the above figure, the economy is in a recession—the equilibrium real GDP is only *Y*. The two diagrams illustrate different approaches toward macroeconomic policy. Which of the following statements is correct?

A)   Figure A represents a nonactivist, fixed-rule approach; Figure B represents an activist, feedback-rule approach.
B)   Figure A represents a feedback-rule approach; Figure B represents the discretionary approach.
C)   Figure A represents an activist, feedback-rule approach; Figure B represents a nonactivist, fixed-rule approach.
D)   Figure A represents the fiscal policy approach; Figure B represents the monetary policy approach.

Answer: C

Topic: Stabilizing Aggregate Demand Shocks
Skill: Analytical

63) In both parts of the above figure, the economy is in a recession—the equilibrium real GDP is only *Y*. If the Fed responds by increasing the money supply, it would be using a _____ approach and the outcome of this policy is shown in _____.

A)   monetarist; Figure A
B)   Keynesian activist, Figure A
C)   rational expectations; Figure B
D)   real business cycle; Figure B

Answer: B

Topic: Feedback Rules are Better?
Skill: Conceptual

64) Monetarists believe that activist policy might prove destabilizing because
A) the private economy is basically unstable so that anything the government does must be destabilizing.
B) the effects of monetary and fiscal policy are known with certainty.
C) fiscal and monetary policy have no effect on real GDP.
D) long lags characterize the effect of monetary policy on the economy.
Answer: D

Topic: Feedback Rules are Better?
Skill: Conceptual

65) Which of the following is a problem in pursuing an activist monetary policy?
A) The lag between a change in the money supply and its effect on economic activity may be long.
B) We often don't know we're in a recession until it has occurred.
C) It's not certain we are aiming at the correct potential GDP target.
D) All of the above answers are correct.
Answer: D

Topic: Stabilizing Aggregate Supply Shocks
Skill: Conceptual

66) A real business cycle theorist contends that the best response to a productivity growth slowdown would be
A) an increase in the money supply.
B) targeting nominal GDP growth.
C) increasing government purchase.
D) allowing the decrease in potential GDP to correct itself.
Answer: D

Topic: Stabilizing Aggregate Supply Shocks
Skill: Conceptual

67) Suppose England experiences a negative shock to aggregate supply and its government subscribes to the real business cycle theory. To keep changes in the real GDP to a minimum, policy makers would
A) use expansionary monetary policy.
B) use contractionary monetary policy.
C) use expansionary fiscal policy.
D) do nothing.
Answer: D

Topic: Stabilizing Aggregate Supply Shocks
Skill: Conceptual

68) Suppose the United States experiences a decrease in long-run aggregate supply. If the real business cycle theory is correct, the use of a fixed-rule policy that keeps monetary and fiscal policy unchanged will result in
A) a less severe recession.
B) unnecessary inflation.
C) an increase in aggregate demand.
D) no change in aggregate demand.
Answer: D

Topic: Nominal GDP Targeting
Skill: Conceptual

69) Which of the following is TRUE regarding nominal GDP targeting?
I. Supporters of the policy use a monetarist fixed rule.
II. Supporters choose a fixed growth rate of nominal GDP.
III. During a recession, a proper response is a reduction in taxes.
A) I and II.
B) I and III.
C) II and III.
D) I, II and III.
Answer: C

Topic: Nominal GDP Targeting
Skill: Conceptual

70) Suppose the government decides to pursue a policy of nominal GDP targeting. If the policy is successful, we would expect
A) an absence of excessive inflation.
B) an absence of severe recession.
C) use of a target inflation rate.
D) Both answers A and B are correct.
Answer: D

Topic: Nominal GDP Targeting
Skill: Conceptual

71) Suppose the government decides to pursue a policy of nominal GDP targeting. This decision implies that it will use
A) fixed-rule policies.
B) feedback-rule policies.
C) nondiscretionary policies.
D) flexible-rule policies.
Answer: B

Topic: Natural Rate Policies
Skill: Conceptual

72) A natural rate policy aims to
   A) decrease the natural real interest rate.
   B) increase the natural real interest rate.
   C) decrease the natural rate of unemployment.
   D) Both answers A and C are correct.

Answer: C

Topic: Natural Rate Policies
Skill: Conceptual

73) Suppose the government decided to pursue a policy of reducing the natural rate of unemployment. Which of the policies might it use?
   I.   Reducing unemployment benefits.
   II. Lowering the minimum real wage.
   III. Increasing the inflation rate.
   A) I only.
   B) I and II.
   C) II and III.
   D) I, II and III.

Answer: B

■ Inflation Policy

Topic: Avoiding Cost-Push Inflation
Skill: Conceptual

74) Suppose a Mideast war pushed up the price of oil. This event
   A) alone can generate inflation.
   B) can generate inflation if the Fed also increases the quantity of money.
   C) results in demand-push inflation.
   D) has no effect on the inflation rate.

Answer: B

Topic: Avoiding Cost-Push Inflation
Skill: Conceptual

75) Monetarists would try to control inflation by
   A) a constant rate of growth of the money supply.
   B) decreasing government purchases.
   C) letting the money supply vary with needs.
   D) increasing tax rates.

Answer: A

Topic: Avoiding Cost-Push Inflation
Skill: Conceptual

76) Suppose unions in the country of Rateland are able to win money wage increases of 10 percent for *all* workers. How can cost-push inflation be avoided in Rateland?
   A) If the central bank follows a fixed-rule policy.
   B) If the central bank follows a flexible-rule policy.
   C) If the government reduces tax rates.
   D) If the central bank lowers interest rates.

Answer: A

Topic: Avoiding Cost-Push Inflation
Skill: Conceptual

77) Suppose that oil prices increase by 25 percent. If the Fed follows a fixed-rule policy, _____ will result.
   A) stagflation.
   B) a lower price level.
   C) a budget deficit.
   D) an unemployment rate below the natural rate.

Answer: A

Topic: Avoiding Cost-Push Inflation
Skill: Conceptual

78) Suppose unions in the country Flioca win 10 percent money wage increases for *all* workers. The central bank in Flioca follows a monetarist fixed-rule policy. As a result,
   A) real GDP will decrease in the short run.
   B) the price level will rise.
   C) a cost-push inflation will occur.
   D) Both answers A and B are correct.

Answer: D

Topic: Avoiding Cost-Push Inflation
Skill: Conceptual

79) Suppose OPEC increases the price of oil and the Fed follows a fixed-rule policy. As a result,
   A) stagflation will occur.
   B) money wages will eventually fall.
   C) the natural rate of unemployment will rise.
   D) Both answers A and B are correct.

Answer: D

Topic: Avoiding Cost-Push Inflation
Skill: Conceptual

80) An oil price hike generates a recession. In response, the Fed follows a feedback rule. As a result
of this policy,

A) the United States may experience cost-push in-
flation.
B) long-run aggregate supply will increase.
C) fiscal policy will be ineffective.
D) the natural rate of unemployment will fall.

Answer: A

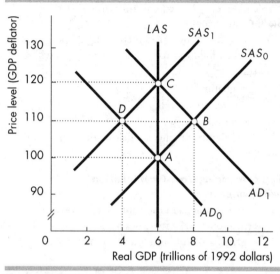

Topic: Avoiding Cost-Push Inflation
Skill: Analytical

81) In the above figure, suppose the economy is at
point A when the country experiences an increase
in energy costs. If the central bank follows a
monetarist fixed rule and does not change the
quantity of money, the economy will

A) remain at point A.
B) move to point B.
C) move to point C.
D) move to point D.

Answer: D

Topic: Avoiding Cost-Push Inflation
Skill: Analytical

82) In the above figure, suppose the economy is at
point A when the country experiences an increase
in energy costs. If the central bank has a feedback-
rule policy that takes effect when energy costs rise,
the effect of the energy price hike *and* feedback
rule

A) keeps the economy at point A.
B) moves the economy to point B.
C) moves the economy to point C.
D) moves the economy to point D.

Answer: C

Topic: Avoiding Cost-Push Inflation
Skill: Analytical

83) In the above figure, suppose the economy is at
point A when the Fed incorrectly thinks that the
economy is heading into a recession. If the Fed
follows a fixed-rule policy, the economy will

A) remain at point A.
B) move to point B.
C) move to point C.
D) move to point D.

Answer: A

Topic: Avoiding Cost-Push Inflation
Skill: Analytical

84) In the above figure, suppose the economy is at
point A when the Fed incorrectly thinks that the
economy is heading into a recession. If the Fed
follows a feedback-rule policy, the economy will

A) remain at point A.
B) move to point B.
C) move to point C.
D) move to point D.

Answer: B

Topic: Avoiding Cost-Push Inflation
Skill: Analytical

85) In the above figure, suppose the economy is at
point A when the Fed incorrectly thinks that potential GDP is $8 trillion. If the Fed follows a
feedback-rule policy, the economy will

A) remain at point A.
B) move to point B.
C) move to point C.
D) move to point D.

Answer: B

Topic: Slowing Inflation
Skill: Conceptual
86) A credible plan to gradually decrease the rate of growth of the money supply
A) would not lower the anticipated rate of inflation.
B) would lower inflation but raise unemployment.
C) would not lower inflation unless unemployment would fall.
D) would lower the anticipated rate of inflation.
Answer: D

Topic: Slowing Inflation
Skill: Conceptual
87) The Fed's *credible* announced intention of lowering inflation results in
A) a decrease in real GDP.
B) a higher unemployment rate.
C) lower inflation.
D) possible higher inflation.
Answer: C

Topic: Inflation Reduction in Practice
Skill: Conceptual
88) The Greenspan Fed has a reputation for
A) unpredictable behavior.
B) maintaining stable prices.
C) generating shifts in the Phillips curve.
D) reversing the actions of the Volcker Fed.
Answer: B

Topic: An Independent Fed
Skill: Conceptual
89) Central banks in Switzerland, Germany and New Zealand all have something in common. What is it?
A) They all follow monetarist policies.
B) They all have only one responsibility—maintaining stable prices.
C) They have very little independence from the government.
D) They are very successful at helping real GDP grow steadily.
Answer: B

Topic: An Independent Fed
Skill: Conceptual
90) Research shows that independent central banks are successful at
A) maintaining a constant money supply growth rate.
B) generating growth in real GDP.
C) maintaining a lower average inflation rate.
D) decreasing unemployment.
Answer: C

■ True Or False Questions

Topic: Policy Goals
Skill: Recognition
91) Smoothing out avoidable business cycle fluctuations is a macroeconomic policy goal.
Answer: TRUE

Topic: Potential GDP Growth
Skill: Conceptual
92) Potential GDP grows at a constant, smooth rate.
Answer: FALSE

Topic: Unemployment
Skill: Recognition
93) Most economists believe the natural unemployment rate is about 5 percent.
Answer: TRUE

Topic: Unemployment
Skill: Recognition
94) Real business cycle economists believe the natural unemployment rate is equal to the actual unemployment rate.
Answer: TRUE

Topic: Policy Tools
Skill: Conceptual
95) Fiscal policy and monetary policy tools work by changing aggregate supply.
Answer: FALSE

Topic: Monetary Policy Tools
Skill: Recognition
96) Measures of monetary policy include M2 and investment.
Answer: FALSE

Topic: National Saving
Skill: Conceptual

97) Long-term economic growth could be promoted by cutting taxes on interest income and capital gains.

Answer: TRUE

Topic: Investment in Human Capital
Skill: Conceptual

98) By subsidizing education, the government aims to increase human capital.

Answer: TRUE

Topic: Investment in New Technologies
Skill: Conceptual

99) Investment in new technology is a way to encourage long-term growth, but the federal government has no ability to influence it.

Answer: FALSE

Topic: Business Cycle and Unemployment Policy
Skill: Recognition

100) Monetary policy and fiscal policy can both be conducted using fixed rules or feedback rules.

Answer: TRUE

Topic: Fixed-Rule Policy
Skill: Recognition

101) An example of a fixed-rule policy is to balance the federal budget each year.

Answer: TRUE

Topic: Feedback-Rule Policy
Skill: Recognition

102) A feedback-rule policy is favored by monetarists.

Answer: FALSE

Topic: Feedback Rules are Better?
Skill: Conceptual

103) Economists usually agree that fixed-rule policies are better for the economy than feedback-rule policies.

Answer: FALSE

Topic: Slowing Inflation
Skill: Conceptual

104) For a decrease in inflation not to affect real GDP, the Fed needs to make sure the inflation-reduction policy is anticipated.

Answer: TRUE

■ Essay Questions

Topic: Policy Goals
Skill: Conceptual

105) There are four macroeconomic policy goals. Discuss at least two of them.

Answer:

Topic: Long-Term Growth Policy
Skill: Conceptual

106) What are ways that fiscal policy can be used to promote long-term economic growth?

Answer:

Topic: Investment in Human Capital
Skill: Conceptual

107) How can the government encourage investment in human capital?

Answer:

Topic: Fixed-Rule Policies
Skill: Conceptual

108) What is an example of a fixed-rule policy?

Answer:

Topic: Feedback-Rule Policies
Skill: Conceptual

109) What is an example of a feedback-rule policy?

Answer:

Topic: Stabilizing Aggregate Demand Shocks
Skill: Conceptual

110) Compare how a Keynesian and a monetarist would handle a decrease in aggregate demand.

Answer:

Topic: Feedback Rules are Better?
Skill: Conceptual

111) Explain why economists find it difficult to say whether fixed-rule or feedback-rule policies are better for the economy.

Answer:

Topic: Nominal GDP Targeting
Skill: Conceptual

112) Describe nominal GDP targeting.

Answer:

Topic: An Independent Fed
Skill: Conceptual

113) What would be the benefits of a more independent Fed?

Answer:

19 TRADING WITH THE WORLD*

■ Patterns and Trends in International Trade

Topic: Patterns and Trends in International Trade
Skill: Recognition
1) Manufactured goods compose _____ of our exports and compose _____ of our imports.
   A) most; most
   B) most; very little
   C) very little; very little
   D) very little; most
Answer: A

Topic: Patterns and Trends in International Trade
Skill: Conceptual
2) Which of the following is CORRECT regarding the United States' international trade?
   I.   The U.S. exports mainly raw materials.
   II. If a German citizen gets her hair cut in New York City, the haircut is counted as a U.S. export of a service.
   III. Canada is the United States' biggest trading partner.
   A) I and II.
   B) I and III.
   C) II and III.
   D) I, II and III.
Answer: C

Topic: Trade in Services
Skill: Conceptual
3) Suppose you buy a plane ticket on Swiss Air, travel to Zurich, buy chocolate, and bring it back to the U.S. The plane ticket is an _____ for the U.S. and the chocolate is an _____ for the U.S.
   A) export of a service; export of a good
   B) import of a service; import of a good
   C) import of a good; import of a service
   D) export of a good; export of a service
Answer: B

Topic: Trade in Services
Skill: Conceptual
4) Suppose a Mexican citizen takes a Greyhound bus trip from Mexico City to Kansas City. While on her trip, she gets sick and receives treatment at a hospital. Which of the following represents the trade that took place?
   A) The bus trip and the medical care are counted as a Mexican imported service.
   B) The trip is a U.S. export and the medical service is not counted.
   C) The trip is not counted in the balance of trade and the medical service is a U.S. export.
   D) Neither the trip nor medical service appears in the balance of trade accounts.
Answer: A

Topic: Balance of Trade
Skill: Recognition
5) The value of exports minus the value of imports is called the _____. Most recently, this value has been _____ for the United States.
   A) balance of payments; positive
   B) balance of trade; negative
   C) balance of trade; positive
   D) balance of payments; negative
Answer: B

---

* This is Chapter 36 in *Economics*.

Topic: Balance of Trade
Skill: Recognition
6)   In 1998, the balance of trade was _____ which means that the U.S. _____.
A)   negative; loaned money to foreigners
B)   positive; loaned money to foreigners
C)   positive; borrowed money from foreigners
D)   negative; borrowed money from foreigners
Answer: D

■ Opportunity Cost and Comparative Advantage

Topic: Comparative Advantage
Skill: Conceptual
7)   Comparative advantage implies that a country will
A)   import those goods in which the country has a comparative advantage.
B)   export those goods in which the country has a comparative advantage.
C)   find it difficult to conclude free trade agreements with other nations.
D)   export goods produced by domestic industries with low wages relative to its trading partners.
Answer: B

Topic: Comparative Advantage
Skill: Conceptual
8)   When the principle of comparative advantage is used to guide trade, then a country will
A)   specialize only in goods with the highest opportunity cost.
B)   specialize only in goods with the lowest opportunity costs.
C)   specialize only in that good for which production is less per worker-hour than another country.
D)   specialize only in that good for which production costs are more than average total costs.
Answer: B

Topic: Comparative Advantage
Skill: Conceptual
9)   If two countries produce wool and cotton, we know that the country with the lower opportunity cost for cotton (in terms of wool) will also have
A)   an absolute advantage in the production of wool.
B)   a comparative advantage in the production of cotton.
C)   a comparative advantage in the production of wool.
D)   an absolute advantage in the production of cotton.
Answer: B

Topic: Comparative Advantage
Skill: Conceptual
10) If country A has a lower opportunity cost for product X than does country B, then we know definitely that
A)   country B has an absolute advantage in the production of product X.
B)   country B has a comparative advantage in the production of product X.
C)   country A has an absolute advantage in the production of product X.
D)   country A has a comparative advantage in the production of product X.
Answer: D

Topic: Comparative Advantage
Skill: Conceptual
11) If country A has a comparative advantage in the production of good X over country B, then
A)   country A also has an absolute advantage in the production of this good.
B)   the opportunity cost of producing X in country A is higher than in country B.
C)   the opportunity cost of producing X in country A is lower than in country B.
D)   we do not have enough information to say anything about relative opportunity costs.
Answer: C

■ Gains From Trade

Uppa		Downa	
Peaches (bushels per year)	Cream (gallons per year)	Peaches (bushels per year)	Cream (gallons per year)
80	0	40	0
60	20	30	15
40	40	20	30
20	60	10	45
0	80	0	60

Topic: Comparative Advantage
Skill: Analytical
12) The table above gives production possibilities in the two nations of Uppa and Downa. Based on the information in the table, we can conclude that
A) Uppa has a comparative advantage in both goods.
B) Downa has a comparative advantage in cream.
C) Uppa has a comparative advantage in neither good.
D) Downa has a comparative advantage in peaches.
Answer: B

Topic: Comparative Advantage and Trade
Skill: Analytical
13) The table above gives production possibilities in the two nations of Uppa and Downa. Based on the information in the table, according to the principle of comparative advantage
A) Uppa should produce both peaches and cream.
B) there is no basis for trade between these two nations.
C) Uppa should produce cream and Downa should produce peaches.
D) Uppa should produce peaches and Downa should produce cream.
Answer: D

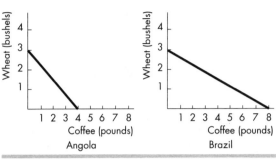

Topic: Opportunity Cost
Skill: Analytical
14) The figure above shows the *PPF*s for Angola and Brazil. The opportunity cost of a pound of coffee is
A) 3/4 of a bushel of wheat in Angola and 3/8 of a bushel of wheat in Brazil.
B) 4/3 of a bushel of wheat in Angola and 8/3 of a bushel of wheat in Brazil.
C) 3 bushels of wheat in Angola and 3 bushels of wheat in Brazil.
D) 4 bushels of wheat in Angola and 8 bushels of wheat in Brazil.
Answer: A

Topic: Comparative Advantage
Skill: Analytical
15) The figure above shows the *PPF*s for Angola and Brazil. The comparative advantage is held by
A) neither country in either good.
B) Brazil in both goods.
C) Angola in wheat, Brazil in coffee.
D) Angola in coffee, Brazil in wheat.
Answer: C

Topic: Comparative Advantage and Trade
Skill: Analytical
16) The figure above shows the *PPF*s for Angola and Brazil. Using the figure, when trade begins, it is profitable to
A) export wheat from Angola to Brazil and coffee from Brazil to Angola.
B) export wheat from Brazil to Angola and coffee from Angola to Brazil.
C) export both wheat and coffee from Angola to Brazil.
D) export both wheat and coffee from Brazil to Angola.
Answer: A

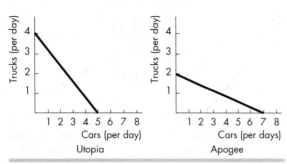

Utopia   Apogee

Topic: Opportunity Cost
Skill: Analytical
17) The figure above shows the *PPF*s for Utopia and
     Apogee. The opportunity cost of a truck is
  A)   5/4 of a car in Utopia.
  B)   2/7 of a car in Apogee.
  C)   5 cars in Utopia.
  D)   4/5 of a car in Apogee.
Answer: A

Topic: Comparative Advantage and Trade
Skill: Analytical
18) Based on the above figure that shows the pre-trade
     *PPF*s for the nations of Utopia and Apogee, when
     trade begins between Utopia and Apogee, it will
     be profitable
  I.   for Utopia to export cars.
  II.   for Utopia to export trucks.
  III.   for Apogee to export cars.
  A)   I only.
  B)   II and III.
  C)   I and III.
  D)   II only.
Answer: B

Topic: Comparative Advantage and Trade
Skill: Conceptual
19) Suppose Country A has land that is a relatively
     poor producer of agricultural products, but has
     large amounts of labor and capital. Other factors
     equal, Country A
  A)   is likely to find it has a comparative advantage in
       the production of food.
  B)   will implement trade protection policies for
       capital-intensive manufactured goods.
  C)   is likely to import food and other agricultural
       products.
  D)   will consume less food.
Answer: C

Topic: Comparative Advantage and Trade
Skill: Conceptual
20) Suppose Mexico has a comparative advantage
     relative to the U.S. in clothing manufacturing and
     the U.S. has a comparative advantage in produc-
     ing agricultural products. Which of the following
     options is most likely to occur?
  A)   Mexico and the U.S. will not trade agricultural
       products or clothing.
  B)   Mexico will sell clothing to the U.S. and the
       U.S. will sell agricultural products to Mexico.
  C)   Mexico will sell agricultural products to the U.S.
       and Mexico will buy clothing from the U.S.
  D)   Mexico will sell clothing to the U.S. but not buy
       any agricultural products from the U.S.
Answer: B

Topic: Gains From Trade
Skill: Conceptual
21) According to the principle of comparative advan-
     tage, the gains from trade
  A)   can be obtained only by a country with an ab-
       solute advantage in the production of some
       good.
  B)   can be obtained by only one of two trading
       countries.
  C)   can be obtained by both trading countries only if
       they both export all the goods being traded.
  D)   can be obtained by both trading countries.
Answer: D

Topic: Gains From Trade
Skill: Conceptual
22) Comparative advantage implies that
  A)   the most inefficient countries cannot export
       profitably.
  B)   every country can gain from exporting and im-
       porting.
  C)   the most efficient countries cannot import prof-
       itably.
  D)   All of the above.
Answer: B

Topic: Gains From Trade
Skill: Conceptual

23) If shoes can be produced relatively more cheaply in Brazil, Italy, or other nations, the United States will experience a gain if it

A) buys its shoes from other nations, using U.S. resources to produce other items.

B) places a quota on imported shoes sufficient to maintain desired domestic levels of production.

C) subsidizes its shoe industry, allowing them to effectively compete with foreign shoemakers.

D) places a tariff on the import of shoes produced by cheap foreign labor.

Answer: A

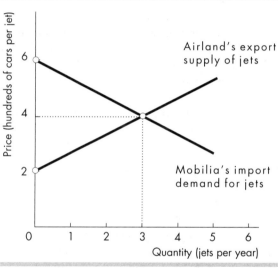

Topic: International Trade
Skill: Analytical

24) In the above figure, if no international trade takes place, the price of a jet in Mobilia is

A) 2 hundred cars per jet.

B) 4 hundred cars per jet.

C) 6 hundred cars per jet.

D) 20 cars per jet.

Answer: C

Topic: International Trade
Skill: Analytical

25) In the above figure, if the countries agree to free trade, the price that people in Mobilia pay for a jet will

A) be 6 hundred cars per jet.

B) be 2 hundred cars per jet.

C) be 4 hundred cars per jet.

D) some amount that cannot be determined from the figure.

Answer: C

Topic: International Trade
Skill: Analytical

26) In the above figure, with free trade how many cars per year does Mobilia export?

A) 1,200 cars.

B) 1,800 cars.

C) 600 cars.

D) 400 cars.

Answer: A

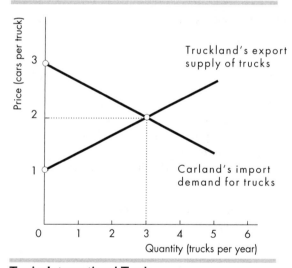

Topic: International Trade
Skill: Analytical

27) In the above figure, if no international trade occurs, the price of trucks in Truckland is

A) 1 car per truck.

B) 2 cars per truck.

C) 3 cars per truck.

D) none of the above.

Answer: A

Topic: International Trade
Skill: Analytical
28) In the above figure, if the countries agree to trade,
   A) the price paid for a truck in Carland will rise.
   B) the price of a truck is 2 cars per truck, if trade is free.
   C) 3 trucks per year are exported from Truckland, if trade is free.
   D) Both answers B and C are true.
Answer: D

Topic: International Trade
Skill: Analytical
29) In the above figure, how many cars per year does Carland export if trade is free?
   A) 1.
   B) 2.
   C) 3.
   D) 6.
Answer: D

Topic: Gains from Trade, Changes in Production
Skill: Conceptual
30) The gains from trade that are possible when two countries have different opportunity costs for wheat and coffee are realized when
   A) trade occurs and resources are reallocated within the two countries.
   B) the two countries continue to produce the same quantities of wheat and coffee.
   C) each country has an absolute advantage in one of the two commodities.
   D) the production possibility curves shift inward.
Answer: A

Topic: Consumption Possibilities
Skill: Conceptual
31) Which of the following correctly completes this statement? Gains from trade are
   A) obtained when a country can consume beyond its production possibility frontier.
   B) unrelated to the terms of trade.
   C) the same as decreasing costs of production.
   D) All of the above answers are correct.
Answer: A

Topic: Consumption Possibilities
Skill: Conceptual
32) International trade permits a country
   A) to produce and consume beyond its production possibility frontier.
   B) to lower the per-unit production cost of the good in which it is specializing.
   C) shift its production possibility frontier outward.
   D) to consume beyond its production possibility frontier.
Answer: D

Topic: Consumption Possibilities
Skill: Recognition
33) The theory of comparative advantage states that a country
   A) with relatively low wages will only export goods.
   B) with relatively high wages can expect no gains from international trade.
   C) can increase its consumption of all goods through trade.
   D) can only trade freely and fairly with another country if the wage levels of the two countries are comparable.
Answer: C

Topic: Consumption Possibilities
Skill: Conceptual
34) The gains of trade can be demonstrated by a consumption point that is
   A) on the production possibility frontier.
   B) inside the production possibility frontier.
   C) beyond the production possibility frontier.
   D) none of the above.
Answer: C

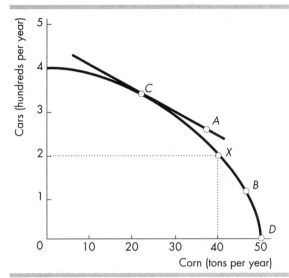

Topic: Changes in Production
Skill: Analytical

35) In the above figure, suppose point *X* represents the "no-trade production and consumption" point for Carland, and Carland enjoys lower opportunity costs in the production of cars. Point _____ represents a typical production point where the economy would move if it decides to trade.

A) *A.*
B) *B.*
C) *C.*
D) *D.*

Answer: C

Topic: Consumption Possibilities
Skill: Analytical

36) In the above figure, suppose point *X* represents the "no-trade production and consumption" point for Carland. Point _____ represents a typical consumption point for Carland if it decides to trade.

A) *A.*
B) *B.*
C) *C.*
D) *D.*

Answer: A

■ Gains from Trade in Reality

Topic: Trade in Similar Goods
Skill: Recognition

37) Which of the following explain why a country can both import and export the same good?
  I.   economies of scale.
  II. different tastes.
  III. different opportunity costs of producing versus consuming the good.

A) I only.
B) I and II.
C) I and III.
D) I, II and III.

Answer: B

Topic: Trade in Similar Goods
Skill: Conceptual

38) Which of the following explain why the U.S. exports cars and imports cars at the same time?

A) By specializing in the production of sport utility vehicles, the U.S. can lower costs and achieve a comparative advantage.
B) Car consumers get to satisfy their tastes for diversity.
C) Other countries specialize in the production of high-end luxury cars, achieving a comparative advantage and selling these cars to U.S. buyers.
D) All of the above answers are correct.

Answer: D

Topic: Trade in Similar Goods; Economies of Scale
Skill: Conceptual

39) Economies of scale help explain
A) tariffs.
B) quotas.
C) trade in similar goods.
D) All of the above.

Answer: C

Topic: Trade in Similar Goods; Economies of Scale
Skill: Conceptual

40) The fact that Canada both imports and exports wine can be explained by
A) tariffs.
B) quotas.
C) the consumption possibility frontier.
D) economies of scale.

Answer: D

■ Trade Restrictions

Topic: Trade Restrictions
Skill: Recognition
41) A tariff
   A)   is a tax imposed on imported goods.
   B)   is a tax imposed on exported goods.
   C)   encourages worldwide specialization according to the principle of comparative advantage.
   D)   has no effect on prices paid by domestic consumers even though it raises the revenue collected by domestic producers.
Answer: A

Topic: Trade Restrictions
Skill: Recognition
42) Countries can resort to _____ to protect domestic industries from foreign competition.
   A)   the use of tariffs
   B)   comparative advantage
   C)   voluntary export restraints
   D)   Both answers A and C are correct.
Answer: D

Topic: Trade Restrictions
Skill: Recognition
43) Which of the following is TRUE regarding non-tariff barriers?
   I.   Voluntary export restraints are examples of a non-tariff barrier.
   II.   A quota is an example of a non-tariff barrier.
   III. Non-tariff barriers can be used to protect domestic industries.
   A)   I and II.
   B)   I and III.
   C)   II and III.
   D)   I, II and III.
Answer: D

Topic: History of Tariffs
Skill: Recognition
44) The Smoot-Hawley Act of 1930 introduced
   A)   opportunities for expanding U.S. foreign trade.
   B)   the highest tariffs set by the United States in the last 70 years.
   C)   a framework promoting international free trade.
   D)   revenue tariffs as a major source of U.S. government revenues.
Answer: B

Topic: History of Tariffs
Skill: Recognition
45) Since 1930, tariff levels in the U.S. have
   A)   generally declined.
   B)   steadily risen.
   C)   increased during expansions.
   D)   decreased during recessions.
Answer: A

Topic: History of Tariffs
Skill: Recognition
46) The General Agreement on Tariffs and Trade (GATT) is an international agreement
   A)   to establish North American as a free trade area.
   B)   to encourage peaceful settlements of trade disputes, but has no particular point of view about the desirability of higher or lower tariffs.
   C)   to encourage world trade by lowering tariffs and other trade barriers.
   D)   to make all tariffs illegal.
Answer: C

Topic: History of Tariffs
Skill: Recognition
47) The Tokyo Round, the Kennedy Round and the Uruguay Round refer to
   A)   periods of dramatic increases in tariff rates.
   B)   tariff reductions under the auspices of GATT.
   C)   tariff wars between countries.
   D)   the initiators of tariff increases.
Answer: B

Topic: History of Tariffs
Skill: Recognition
48) The Uruguay Round of GATT which ended in _____ led to _____.
   A)   1986; the creation of the WTO
   B)   1988; an increase in agreed upon quota levels
   C)   1994; the creation of the WTO
   D)   1996; fewer countries agreeing to free trade
Answer: C

Topic: Effects of a Tariff
Skill: Conceptual
49) Lowering the tariff on good X will
   A)   increase domestic employment in industry X.
   B)   increase the domestic imports of good X.
   C)   increase the domestic price of good X.
   D)   have no effect unless the nation's trading partner lowers its tariff on good X.
Answer: B

Topic: Effects of a Tariff
Skill: Conceptual
50) Reducing a tariff will ____ the domestic production of the good and ____ the total domestic consumption of the good.
  A) increase; increase
  B) increase; decrease
  C) decrease; increase
  D) decrease; decrease
Answer: C

Topic: Effects of a Tariff
Skill: Conceptual
51) Increasing a tariff will ____ the domestic quantity consumed of the good, while ____ the domestic production of the good.
  A) increase; increasing
  B) increase; decreasing
  C) decrease; increasing
  D) decrease; decreasing
Answer: C

Topic: Effects of a Tariff
Skill: Conceptual
52) If a tariff is imposed, the price paid by domestic consumers will ____ and the price received by foreign producers will ____.
  A) increase; decrease
  B) increase; not change
  C) not change; increase
  D) increase; increase
Answer: A

Topic: Effects of a Tariff
Skill: Conceptual
53) If the U.S. imposes a tariff on $1 per imported shirt, the higher tariff will
  A) raise the price of a shirt to U.S. consumers.
  B) benefit U.S. shirt producers.
  C) decrease exports of some products from the United States.
  D) All of the above.
Answer: D

Topic: Effects of a Tariff
Skill: Conceptual
54) Imposition of a U.S. tariff on imported shoes
  A) benefits consumers in the United States by guaranteeing a high-quality product.
  B) benefits shoe producers in the United States by reducing competition.
  C) benefits foreign production of shoes by increasing the amount available for their production.
  D) harms shoe workers in the United States who now face a more hectic production schedule.
Answer: B

Topic: Effects of a Tariff
Skill: Conceptual
55) The free-trade agreement between Canada, Mexico and the U.S. reduced tariffs on goods traded between all three countries. Hence, the agreement will
  A) economically benefit all three countries.
  B) only be beneficial if all three countries experience economies of scale in producing some goods.
  C) create substantial economic gains for the U.S. but not Canada and Mexico.
  D) have little effect on trade patterns between the three countries.
Answer: A

Topic: Effects of a Tariff
Skill: Conceptual
56) A U.S. tariff imposed on items that can be produced more cheaply abroad
  A) benefits Americans by making these goods cheaper.
  B) makes the goods more expensive in foreign markets.
  C) decreases the benefits of international trade.
  D) equalizes the cost of production between the United States and foreign producers.
Answer: C

Topic: Effects of a Tariff; Trade Remains Balanced
Skill: Conceptual
57) Restricting imports leads to
A) a country producing beyond its production possibility frontier.
B) a country consuming even further beyond its production possibility frontier.
C) a decrease in exports and employment.
D) a higher per capita level of real consumption.
Answer: C

Topic: Effects of a Tariff
Skill: Conceptual
58) An increase in the imports of good X could result from
A) an increase in the tariff imposed on good X.
B) an increase in the domestic supply of good X.
C) an increase in the domestic demand for good X.
D) a decrease in the domestic cost of producing good X.
Answer: C

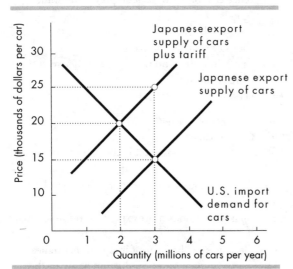

Topic: Effects of a Tariff
Skill: Analytical
59) In the above figure, as a result of the U.S. imposition of a tariff on Japanese cars, the quantity of Japanese cars imported into the U.S. will
A) be 0 cars per year.
B) be 2 million cars per year.
C) be 3 million cars per year.
D) no longer be represented by the demand curve illustrated in the figure.
Answer: B

Topic: Effects of a Tariff
Skill: Analytical
60) The above figure shows the effect of a $10,000 per car tariff imposed by the United States. How much tax revenue does the tariff generate?
A) 0.
B) $20 billion.
C) $30 billion.
D) $40 billion.
Answer: B

Topic: Quota
Skill: Analytical
61) The above figure shows the results of a tariff. What quota would generate the same quantity of imports?
A) A quota of 0 cars.
B) A quota of 1 million cars.
C) A quota of 2 million cars.
D) A quota of 3 million cars.
Answer: C

Topic: Quota
Skill: Recognition
62) A quota is
A) a tariff imposed on goods that are dumped in the country.
B) a law that prevents ecologically damaging goods from being imported into a country.
C) a market-imposed balancing factor that keeps prices of imports and exports in equilibrium.
D) a government-imposed restriction on the quantity of a specific good that can be imported.
Answer: D

Topic: Quota
Skill: Recognition
63) A quota specifies
A) the amount of money that can be charged for any imported good.
B) the amount of taxes that must be paid on any imported good.
C) the maximum amount of a good that may be imported during a specified period.
D) the minimum amount of a good that may be imported during a specified period.
Answer: C

Topic: Quota
Skill: Recognition
64) An import quota protects domestic producers by
A)   setting a limit on the amount of imports.
B)   placing a prohibitive tax on imports.
C)   encouraging competition among domestic pro-
     ducers.
D)   increasing the total supply of the product.
Answer: A

Topic: Quota
Skill: Conceptual
65) The effect of a quota is to
A)   increase the supply of the good and lower its
     price.
B)   increase the supply of the good and increase its
     price.
C)   increase the demand for the good and increase
     its price.
D)   decrease the supply of the good and raise its
     price.
Answer: D

Topic: Quota
Skill: Conceptual
66) Quotas and tariffs both serve the purpose of
A)   increasing foreign trade.
B)   restricting foreign trade.
C)   causing domestic producers to lose revenues.
D)   lowering prices on imported goods.
Answer: B

Topic: Quota
Skill: Conceptual
67) The key difference between a quota and a tariff is
    that
A)   a tariff generates a higher price than does a
     quota.
B)   a tariff generates a greater reduction in exports.
C)   a quota increases profits of domestic producers
     more.
D)   the government collects revenues from a tariff,
     which does not happen with a quota.
Answer: D

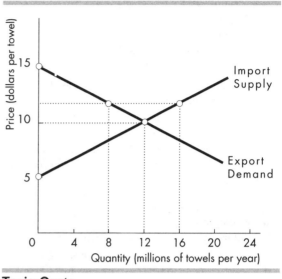

Topic: Quota
Skill: Analytical
68) In the above figure, suppose towel manufacturers
    convince the U.S. government to protect its in-
    dustries' firms by imposing a quota on towel im-
    ports. As a result of the quota of 8 million towels,
A)   the price paid by U.S. consumers is $10 per
     towel.
B)   the price paid by U.S. consumers is more than
     $10 per towel.
C)   the price paid by U.S. consumers is $15 per
     towel.
D)   the price paid by U.S. consumers is more than
     $15 per towel.
Answer: B

Topic: Quota
Skill: Analytical
69) Using the above figure, suppose towel manufac-
    turers convince the U.S. government to protect its
    industries' firms by imposing a quota on towel
    imports. Which of the following statements is
    CORRECT?
A)   The supply curve shifts rightward.
B)   The demand curve shifts leftward.
C)   If the quota is set at 8 million towels, the price
     of towels will be at least $15 per towel.
D)   Importers of towels will earn larger profits.
Answer: D

Topic: Voluntary Export Restraints
Skill: Recognition
70) Voluntary export restraint agreements are
   A) a type of tariff in which the tax is a fixed amount per unit of the good imported.
   B) a type of tariff in which the tax is based on the value of the good.
   C) a type of quota that actually benefits the firms facing the restrictions.
   D) a type of quota in which the government of the exporting nation agrees to limit its exports.
Answer: D

Topic: Voluntary Export Restraints
Skill: Recognition
71) Voluntary export restraints (VERs)
   A) do not protect domestic producers.
   B) raise revenue for the governments involved.
   C) raise the prices paid by domestic consumers.
   D) Both answers B and C are correct.
Answer: C

■ The Case Against Protection

Topic: The Case Against Protection
Skill: Conceptual
72) Which of the following is TRUE regarding protection of domestic firms from foreign competition?
   A) Protecting new industries by imposing tariffs is supported by economists.
   B) Subsidies are a more efficient use of resources to protect strategic industries than are quotas.
   C) Global monopolies can occur naturally and therefore tariffs are a valid response to "dumping".
   D) Both answers A and B are correct.
Answer: B

Topic: The Case Against Protection
Skill: Recognition
73) Valid reasons for protecting trade include which of the following?
   I. The economies of scale argument.
   II. The saving jobs argument.
   III. The protection of high wages argument.
   A) I only.
   B) I and II.
   C) I and III.
   D) None of the reasons are valid.
Answer: D

Topic: The Case Against Protection
Skill: Recognition
74) Which of the following are valid reasons advanced by economists in favor of trade protection? Protection
   A) saves jobs.
   B) prevents rich countries from exploiting poorer countries.
   C) is a good way for governments in developed nations to raise revenue.
   D) Economists would not support any of the above reasons.
Answer: D

Topic: The Case Against Protection
Skill: Recognition
75) Which of the following are reasons economists consider valid for trade protection?
   I. Protection penalizes countries that have weak environmental standards.
   II. Protection protects our national culture.
   III. Protection prevents low-wage jobs in foreign countries from lowering wages in the U.S.
   A) I and II.
   B) II and III.
   C) I, II, and III.
   D) none of the above.
Answer: D

Topic: The Case Against Protection
Skill: Conceptual
76) Economists agree that it would be wise to protect certain industries in the U.S.
   A) so that the U.S. economy becomes more diverse.
   B) to make the U.S. economy more stable.
   C) to create a comparative advantage.
   D) The statement errs because economists make no arguments for protection.
Answer: D

Topic: The Case Against Protection
Skill: Conceptual
77) Without trade protection
   A) rich countries will take advantage of poor countries.
   B) trade wars can be triggered.
   C) wages of U.S. workers will fall.
   D) U.S. consumers will benefit from lower prices for imported goods.
Answer: D

Topic: The Case Against Protection; National Security
Skill: Conceptual
78) Economists argue that to protect industries vital to national defense,
A) tariffs should be imposed.
B) those industries should receive subsidies.
C) quotas should be imposed.
D) Both answers A and C are correct.
Answer: B

Topic: The Case Against Protection; National Security
Skill: Conceptual
79) Some industries argue that they should receive protection because they are vital to national security. Economists respond that
A) this is a valid argument for using tariffs.
B) consumers would be better off if the government subsidized the industry.
C) this is a valid argument for using quotas but not tariffs.
D) Both answers B and C are correct.
Answer: B

Topic: The Case Against Protection; Infant-Industry
Skill: Recognition
80) A new industry develops and we want to protect it from foreign competition until it is able to compete in world markets. Which one of the following arguments *best* describe this type of protection?
A) National security.
B) Cartel formation.
C) Infant industry.
D) Protecting American jobs.
Answer: C

Topic: The Case Against Protection; Infant-Industry
Skill: Conceptual
81) An assumption behind the infant-industry argument for tariff protection is that
A) foreign competitors are selling output below average cost.
B) the domestic industry will be facing an upward adjustment in its average cost.
C) the domestic industry will eventually gain a comparative advantage in producing the good.
D) the market needs additional competition to satisfy consumer demand.
Answer: C

Topic: The Case Against Protection; Infant-Industry
Skill: Recognition
82) A business that contends that it needs temporary protection so that it can grow large enough to compete with foreign producers is using an argument known as the
A) national defense case for tariffs.
B) social advantages case for tariffs.
C) infant-industry case for tariffs.
D) price fluctuations case for tariffs.
Answer: C

Topic: The Case Against Protection; Dumping
Skill: Recognition
83) When a product is sold in a foreign country at a price that is lower than the domestic price, it is called
A) dumping.
B) an escape clause.
C) voluntary export restriction.
D) a countervailing duty.
Answer: A

Topic: The Case Against Protection; Dumping
Skill: Conceptual

84) When a firms "dumps" some of its products in another country, it

A) creates an environmental hazard in the receiving country.
B) sells its products abroad at a price lower than it costs to produce the goods.
C) increases the total level of employment in the receiving country.
D) is specializing according to comparative advantage.

Answer: B

Topic: The Case Against Protection; Saves Jobs
Skill: Conceptual

85) Tariffs that decrease imports to "protect American jobs" will also

A) stimulate exports.
B) decrease exports.
C) decrease import prices.
D) decrease domestic production of import-competing goods.

Answer: B

Topic: The Case Against Protection; Saves Jobs
Skill: Conceptual

86) Increasing tariffs

A) ensure resources are used by the most efficient workers.
B) decreases jobs in industries that export goods and services.
C) save jobs in the United States at no cost.
D) Both answers A and C are correct.

Answer: B

Topic: The Case Against Protection; Saves Jobs
Skill: Conceptual

87) When free trade occurs between the U.S., Mexico and Canada,

A) export-based jobs will be created in all three countries.
B) high-wage workers in the U.S. will see their wages fall.
C) low-wage workers in Canada will see their wages fall.
D) Both answers A and B are correct.

Answer: A

Topic: The Case Against Protection; Cheap Foreign Labor
Skill: Conceptual

88) The reason that average labor costs are higher in the U.S. than in Haiti is that

A) workers are more productive in the U.S.
B) U.S. workers have a comparative advantage.
C) Haitian workers have a comparative advantage.
D) Haitian workers do not have union representation.

Answer: A

Topic: The Case Against Protection; Cheap Foreign Labor
Skill: Conceptual

89) Which of the following are TRUE regarding the argument that trade barriers protect U.S. workers from cheap foreign labor?

I. Low-wage foreigners are just as productive as U.S. workers.
II. U.S. workers have a comparative advantage in low-wage jobs.

A) I only.
B) II only.
C) I and II.
D) Neither I nor II is correct.

Answer: D

Topic: The Case Against Protection; Cheap Foreign Labor
Skill: Conceptual

90) The activities in which U.S. workers are relatively more productive

A) pay higher wages.
B) are those in which the U.S. has a comparative advantage.
C) are at risk of disappearing from the U.S. when NAFTA is completed.
D) Both answers A and B are correct.

Answer: D

**Topic: The Case Against Protection;
Environmental Standards**
Skill: Conceptual

91) Most economists agree that trade protection is
_____.

A) wise in order to protect the environment.

B) harmful because free trade promotes prosperity
while protection is inefficient.

C) necessary in order to protect our national culture.

D) required to make sure all countries meet some
environmental standards.

Answer: B

**Topic: The Case Against Protection;
Environmental Standards**
Skill: Conceptual

92) A reason for trade protection that most economists support include

A) other countries have lax environmental standards.

B) a poor country cannot spend resources on
"green" production techniques.

C) poor countries have low wages and advanced
nations cannot compete because their wages are
higher.

D) None of the above.

Answer: D

■ Why Is International Trade Restricted?

Topic: Tariff Revenue
Skill: Conceptual

93) Because governments in _____ these governments
are _____ to support free trade.

A) developing countries have an easier time collecting tax revenue rather than tariff revenue;
more likely

B) developing countries have an easier time collecting tariff revenue rather than tax revenue; less
likely

C) industrialized countries have an easier time collecting tax revenue rather than tariff revenue; less
likely

D) industrialized countries have an easier time collecting tariff revenue rather than tax revenue; less
likely

Answer: B

Topic: Rent Seeking
Skill: Conceptual

94) The reason tariffs and quotas are imposed is that

A) their costs are spread among many people and
their benefits are concentrated.

B) their costs are concentrated and their benefits are
spread among many people.

C) they create net benefits in the long run.

D) they reduce import dependence.

Answer: A

Topic: Rent Seeking
Skill: Conceptual

95) Which of the following is a TRUE statement?

A) Everyone benefits from free trade.

B) Only exporters benefit from trade.

C) All producers benefit from trade and but not all
consumers benefit.

D) Free trade harms domestic producers of goods
that face import competition.

Answer: D

Topic: Rent Seeking
Skill: Conceptual

96) Trade barriers are politically popular because

A) they are a way to avoid trade wars and still protect domestic producers.

B) people recognize their use as a negotiating tool
in international relations.

C) their benefits are widespread, while their costs
are highly concentrated.

D) their benefits are concentrated, while their costs
are widespread.

Answer: D

Topic: Compensating Losers
Skill: Conceptual

97) When NAFTA was approved, Congress at-
tempted to soften the losses suffered by some industries by

A) creating new jobs to hire workers who lost their
jobs because of NAFTA.

B) setting aside funds to support and retrain workers who lost their jobs because of NAFTA.

C) reducing tariffs.

D) imposing quotas.

Answer: B

Topic: Compensating Losers
Skill: Conceptual
98) Trade is restricted because
  A) we cannot compensate all those people who claim to be harmed by free trade.
  B) anti-free trade groups spent a lot of money to lobby for protection.
  C) it is the most effective way to deal with countries that "dump" their goods in the U.S.
  D) Both answers A and B are correct.
Answer: D

■ True Or False Questions

Topic: Patterns and Trends in International Trade
Skill: Recognition
99) Most of U.S. exports are services.
Answer: FALSE

Topic: Patterns and Trends in International Trade; Balance of Trade
Skill: Recognition
100) The value of exports minus the value of imports is the balance of trade.
Answer: TRUE

Topic: Comparative Advantage
Skill: Recognition
101) A country has a comparative advantage in producing a good if it can produce that good at a lower opportunity cost than any other country.
Answer: TRUE

Topic: Gains from Trade; Consumption Possibilities
Skill: Conceptual
102) By trading, countries are able to consume at a point beyond their production possibility frontier.
Answer: TRUE

Topic: Gains from Trade; Consumption Possibilities
Skill: Conceptual
103) Typically, when two countries trade, the country with the lower opportunity cost is the only country to obtain any of the gains from trade.
Answer: FALSE

Topic: Gains from Trade in Reality; Economies of Scale
Skill: Conceptual
104) One reason countries may both export and import some of the same goods is because of economies of scale.
Answer: TRUE

Topic: Trade Restrictions; Effects of a Tariff
Skill: Conceptual
105) As a result of an increase in tariffs, imports decrease and government revenue increases.
Answer: TRUE

Topic: Trade Restrictions; Quota
Skill: Conceptual
106) Quotas are less damaging to an economy than are tariffs.
Answer: FALSE

Topic: The Case Against Protection; Dumping
Skill: Recognition
107) Dumping occurs when a foreign firm sells its exports at a lower price than it costs to produce them.
Answer: TRUE

Topic: The Case Against Protection; Saving Jobs
Skill: Conceptual
108) Most economists would agree that "saving jobs" is a valid reason for restricting trade.
Answer: FALSE

Topic: Why Is International Trade Restricted?; Tariff Revenue
Skill: Conceptual
109) Less developed countries, compared to industrialized ones, are more likely to have higher tariff rates.
Answer: TRUE

■ Essay Questions

Topic: Trends in International Trade
Skill: Conceptual
110) Explain recent trends in the U.S. balance of trade. In your answer, include the role played by manufactured goods and services.
Answer:

Topic: History of Tariffs
Skill: Recognition
111) Give a brief description of the history of tariffs in the U.S.
Answer:

Topic: Comparative Advantage
Skill: Conceptual
112) Consider two countries, A and B, that produce apples and bananas, respectively. Using your own numbers for production, give an example of country A having a comparative advantage in apples.
Answer:

Topic: Comparative Advantage
Skill: Conceptual
113) Define comparative advantage and discuss its role in international trade.
Answer:

Topic: Gains from Trade
Skill: Analytical
114) Draw production possibility frontiers for two countries, Plano and Tanko. In your diagram, make clear that Plano has a comparative advantage in airplanes and Tanko has a comparative advantage in the production of tanks.
Answer:

Topic: Gains from Trade
Skill: Analytical
115) Draw a production possibility frontier for a country, Xeno, that can produce bombs or butter. Draw another *PPF* for another country, Udder that can produce bombs or butter. Assuming that Udder has a comparative advantage in butter production, show three points in each diagram:
  1. a no-trade production and consumption point.
  2. a production with trade point.
  3. a consumption with trade point.
Answer:

Topic: Gains from Trade; Consumption Possibilities
Skill: Conceptual
116) Explain how countries can gain from international trade.
Answer:

Topic: Gains from Trade in Reality
Skill: Conceptual
117) Explain why countries export and import the same good.
Answer:

Topic: Quotas
Skill: Analytical
118) Using a diagram, explain the effects of a quota.
Answer:

Topic: Why Is International Trade Restricted?
Skill: Conceptual
119) Discuss three reasons why we see trade restrictions. Do YOU agree or disagree with these ideas?
Answer:

Chapter 20 INTERNATIONAL FINANCE*

■ Financing International Trade

Topic: Balance of Payments Accounts
Skill: Recognition
1) A country's statement of all international transactions—trading, borrowing, lending—is called its
A) current account balance.
B) balance of payments accounts.
C) balance of trade.
D) net export statement.
Answer: B

Topic: Balance of Payments Accounts
Skill: Conceptual
2) Which of the following is recorded in the U.S. balance of payments account?
I. Foreign investment in the U.S.
II. U.S. investment abroad.
III. The U.S. government deficit or surplus.
A) III only.
B) I and II.
C) I and III.
D) I, II and III.
Answer: B

Topic: Balance of Payments Accounts
Skill: Recognition
3) Which of the following is included in a nation's current account?
I. The import of services.
II. A change of foreign currency holdings.
III. Net transfers, such as foreign aid payments.
A) I and III.
B) I and II.
C) II and III.
D) III only.
Answer: A

Topic: Balance of Payments Accounts
Skill: Recognition
4) The largest single U.S. balance of payments account is the
A) import of goods and services account.
B) U.S. investment abroad.
C) net interest income.
D) change in official U.S. reserves.
Answer: A

Topic: Balance of Payments Accounts
Skill: Conceptual
5) Which of the following contributes to a positive current account balance for a country?
A) Having tourists visit the country.
B) Importing textiles.
C) Having foreigners buy government securities from the country's government.
D) Importing financial services.
Answer: A

Topic: Balance of Payments Accounts
Skill: Conceptual
6) Which of the following is included in a nation's capital account?
I. The purchase of foreign stocks and bonds.
II. The sale of foreign stocks and bonds.
III. Importing a piece of capital equipment.
A) I only.
B) I and II.
C) III only.
D) I, II and III.
Answer: B

---

* This is Chapter 37 in *Economics*.

Topic: Balance of Payments Accounts
Skill: Conceptual

7) Which of the following transactions leads to a surplus on the U.S. capital account?
A) An American purchases a share of stock on the Tokyo exchange.
B) An American sells wheat to an African nation.
C) A Japanese resident purchases a U.S. government bond.
D) A resident of France visits the United States.
Answer: C

Topic: Balance of Payments Accounts
Skill: Conceptual

8) If the U.S. government increased its holdings of British pounds, definitely
A) the capital account would increase.
B) the capital account would decrease.
C) there would be an increase in U.S. official reserves.
D) there would be a decrease in U.S. official reserves.
Answer: C

Topic: Balance of Payments Accounts
Skill: Conceptual

9) If the U.S. government decreased its holdings of Mexican pesos, definitely
A) the capital account would increase.
B) the capital account would decrease.
C) there would be an increase in U.S. official reserves.
D) there would be a decrease in U.S. official reserves.
Answer: D

Topic: Balance of Payments Accounts
Skill: Recognition

10) When there is a current account deficit, and the official settlements account equals 0, then
A) exports exceed imports for the country.
B) the country is an exporter of capital.
C) the capital account has a surplus.
D) the country has a budget surplus.
Answer: C

Topic: Balance of Payments Accounts
Skill: Conceptual

11) If the official settlements account equals zero, the fact that the United States has a current account deficit means that
A) the U.S. has a deficit in its capital account.
B) the U.S. has a surplus in its capital account.
C) the economy in our country is weak, and we cannot compete with the Japanese.
D) the U.S. is a bad place to invest capital.
Answer: B

Topic: Balance of Payments Accounts
Skill: Conceptual

12) If the United States' imports increase, the sum of the balance of payments accounts (the sum of the current account plus capital account plus official settlements account)
A) becomes negative.
B) becomes positive.
C) becomes negative or positive depending on the government budget deficit or surplus.
D) does not change.
Answer: D

Topic: Balance of Payments Accounts
Skill: Conceptual

13) Suppose the current account of a country is in balance and the official settlements account equals 0. A new transaction occurs so that the current account is now in surplus, but the official settlements account does not change. From this we know that
A) the balance of trade is now in surplus.
B) the government is running a budget deficit.
C) the capital account is now in deficit.
D) the government must make official reserve transactions.
Answer: C

Item	Billions of dollars
Exports of goods	1000
Imports of goods	−665
Exports of services	410
Imports of services	−590
Net interest income	0
Net transfers	−15
U.S. investment abroad	−600
Foreign investment in the U.S.	400
Official settlements account	60

Topic: Balance of Payments Accounts
Skill: Analytical
14) The data in the table above are the U.S. balance of payments. The current account balance is
A) $140 billion.
B) $155 billion.
C) $170 billion.
D) −$45 billion.
Answer: A

Topic: Balance of Payments Accounts
Skill: Analytical
15) The data in the table above are the U.S. balance of payments. The data show that
A) the U.S. has a current account surplus.
B) the U.S. has a capital account surplus.
C) The U.S. loaned $400 billion to the rest of the world.
D) Both answers A and B are correct.
Answer: A

Topic: Balance of Payments Accounts
Skill: Analytical
16) The data in the table above are the U.S. balance of payments. The capital account balance is
A) $0.
B) −$80 billion.
C) −$200 billion.
D) +$200 billion.
Answer: C

Topic: Balance of Payments Accounts
Skill: Analytical
17) The data in the table above are the U.S. balance of payments. The sum of the current account plus capital account plus official settlements account is equal to
A) $0.
B) −$335 billion.
C) $140 billion.
D) −$60 billion.
Answer: A

Item	Billions of dollars
Imports of goods and services	750
Exports of goods and services	1,000
Net interest income	−50
Net transfers	−50
U.S. investment abroad	−350
Foreign investment in the U.S.	200

Topic: Balance of Payments Accounts
Skill: Analytical
18) The data in the table above are the U.S. balance of payments. What is the current account balance?
A) $0.
B) $150 billion.
C) −$100 billion.
D) −$150 billion.
Answer: B

Topic: Balance of Payments Accounts
Skill: Analytical
19) The data in the table above are the U.S. balance of payments. What is the capital account balance?
A) $0.
B) $150 billion.
C) −$350 billion.
D) −$150 billion.
Answer: D

Topic: Balance of Payments Accounts
Skill: Analytical
20) The data in the table above are the U.S. balance of payments. If there is no statistical discrepancy, what is the balance in the official settlements account?
A) $150 billion.
B) −$150 billion.
C) $50 billion.
D) $0.
Answer: D

Topic: Borrowers and Lenders, Debtors and Creditors
Skill: Conceptual

21) Suppose Angola borrows $100 million in 1998 from foreign countries while it lends $15 million. Angola definitely would be considered a

A) net borrower.
B) net lender.
C) creditor nation.
D) debtor nation.

Answer: A

Topic: Borrowers and Lenders, Debtors and Creditors
Skill: Conceptual

22) Suppose Italy lends 1.5 billion lira in 1998 while it borrowed 1 billion lira. Italy definitely would be considered a

A) net borrower.
B) net lender.
C) creditor nation.
D) debtor nation.

Answer: B

Topic: Borrowers and Lenders, Debtors and Creditors
Skill: Conceptual

23) If a country lends more to foreign countries than it borrows from foreign countries in a year, then definitely that year

A) it has a current account deficit.
B) it is a creditor nation.
C) it is a debtor nation.
D) it is a net lender.

Answer: D

Topic: Borrowers and Lenders, Debtors and Creditors
Skill: Recognition

24) Which of the following countries are net lenders?

I.   Japan.
II. United States.

A) I only.
B) II only.
C) Both I and II.
D) Neither I nor II.

Answer: A

Topic: Borrowers and Lenders, Debtors and Creditors
Skill: Conceptual

25) Over its history, Spain has loaned more money than it has received. Spain is considered

A) a net lender.
B) a net borrower.
C) a creditor nation.
D) a debtor nation.

Answer: C

Topic: Borrowers and Lenders, Debtors and Creditors
Skill: Conceptual

26) Over its history, Brazil has borrowed more than it has loaned. Brazil

A) eventually will have a balance of payments account that does not balance.
B) is a debtor nation.
C) is a creditor nation.
D) has no current account balance.

Answer: B

Topic: Borrowers and Lenders, Debtors and Creditors
Skill: Recognition

27) The United States is a

I.   net lender.
II.   net borrower.
III. debtor nation.
IV.   creditor nation.

A) II only.
B) II and III.
C) I and IV.
D) III only.

Answer: B

Topic: Borrowers and Lenders, Debtors and Creditors
Skill: Recognition

28) A developing county is usually a

I.   net lender.
II.   net borrower.
III. debtor nation.
IV.   creditor nation.

A) II only.
B) II and III.
C) I and IV.
D) III only.

Answer: B

Topic: Current Account Balance
Skill: Recognition
29) The current account balance is defined as
A) the value of exports – the value of imports.
B) the amount of exported capital assets + net interest income.
C) the value of exports – the value of imports + net interest income + net transfers.
D) the difference between the import and export of official reserves.
Answer: C

Topic: Current Account Balance
Skill: Conceptual
30) Which of the following are included in the U.S. current account balance?
 I. Exports to Japan.
 II. Interest payments made to Canada.
 III. Transfer payments made to Israel.
A) I only.
B) I and II.
C) I and III.
D) I, II and III.
Answer: D

Topic: Current Account Balance
Skill: Recognition
31) All of the following are a current account transaction EXCEPT
A) importing services.
B) exporting goods.
C) investing abroad.
D) importing goods.
Answer: C

Topic: Current Account Balance
Skill: Recognition
32) Income that a nation earns from previous investments in foreign nations is included in its
A) capital account.
B) unilateral transfers account.
C) current account.
D) statistical errors account.
Answer: C

Topic: Current Account Balance
Skill: Conceptual
33) If net interest and net transfers are $0, and a nation's purchases of foreign goods and services are $3.5 billion while its sales of goods and services to foreigners are $4.5 billion,
A) it has a $1 billion surplus in its balance of payments.
B) it has a $1 billion deficit in its current account.
C) it has a $1 billion surplus in its current account.
D) its capital account shows a surplus.
Answer: C

Topic: Current Account Balance
Skill: Recognition
34) If net interest and net transfers are zero, and a country's exports exceed its imports, the country definitely has a (an) ____.
A) current account surplus
B) current account deficit
C) capital account surplus
D) official settlements account surplus
Answer: A

Topic: Net Exports, the Government Budget, Saving, and Investment
Skill: Conceptual
35) Which of the following help(s) determine net exports?
 I. private saving.
 II. the government budget surplus or deficit.
 III. private investment.
A) I and II.
B) II and III.
C) all of the above.
D) none of the above.
Answer: C

Topic: Net Exports, the Government Budget, Saving, and Investment
Skill: Recognition
36) Suppose $X - M$ = net exports; $T - G$ = government sector surplus or deficit; and $S - I$ = private sector surplus or deficit. What relationship exists among these variables?
A) $(X - M) + (T - G) + (S - I) = 0$.
B) $(X - M) = (T - G) + (S - I)$.
C) $(T - G) + (X - M) = (S - I)$.
D) $(T - G) = (X - M) + (S - I)$.
Answer: B

Topic: Net Exports, the Government Budget, Saving, and Investment
Skill: Conceptual

37) If net exports is a negative number, the government sector must _____ if the private sector is in a _____.

A) run a surplus; surplus
B) equal zero; deficit
C) run a deficit; surplus
D) The statement errs because the accounts are not related.

Answer: C

Topic: Net Exports, the Government Budget, Saving, and Investment
Skill: Analytical

38) If $X - M = \$0$ and the government sector has a deficit of $250 billion, the private sector

A) has a deficit that equals $0.
B) has a deficit that equals $250 billion.
C) has a surplus that equals $250 billion.
D) has a surplus that equals $500 billion.

Answer: C

Item	Billions of dollars
Exports of goods and services, X	500
Imports of goods and services, M	
Net taxes, T	750
Government purchases, G	
Saving, S	1,000
Investment, I	

Topic: Net Exports, the Government Budget, Saving, and Investment
Skill: Analytical

39) In the above table, suppose imports = $750 billion and government purchases = $1,000 billion. Hence investment equals

A) −$500 billion.
B) $1,000 billion.
C) $500 billion.
D) $0.

Answer: B

Topic: Net Exports, the Government Budget, Saving, and Investment
Skill: Analytical

40) Using the data in the above table, suppose imports equals $250 billion and investment equals $1,000 billion. Hence government purchases equal

A) $1,000 billion.
B) $750 billion.
C) $500 billion.
D) $250 billion.

Answer: C

Topic: Net Exports, the Government Budget, Saving, and Investment
Skill: Analytical

41) Using the data in the above table, if the private sector runs a surplus of $250 billion, imports will equal $1,000 billion if

A) government purchases equal −$750 billion.
B) investment equals −$1000 billion.
C) government purchases equal −$1000 billion.
D) the government sector runs a deficit of $750 billion.

Answer: D

Item	Billions of dollars
Exports of goods and services, X	
Imports of goods and services, M	1,000
Net taxes, T	
Government purchases, G	1,300
Saving, S	
Investment, I	650

Topic: Net Exports, the Government Budget, Saving, and Investment
Skill: Analytical

42) Using the data in the above table, if exports = $1,150 billion and the private sector runs a surplus of $300 billion, the government sector will run

A) a surplus of $150 billion.
B) a surplus of $450 billion.
C) a deficit of $150 billion.
D) a deficit of $450 billion.

Answer: C

Topic: Net Exports, the Government Budget, Saving, and Investment
Skill: Analytical
43) Using the data in the above table, if the government sector runs a deficit of $250 billion and net exports equal –$500 billion, then saving must equal

A) $450 billion.
B) $250 billion.
C) $1,350 billion.
D) $400 billion.

Answer: D

Topic: Net Exports, the Government Budget, Saving, and Investment
Skill: Analytical
44) Using the data in the above table, if net exports = –$500 billion and the government balances its budget,

A) the private sector must balance its budget.
B) savings must equal $150 billion.
C) the private sector runs a surplus of $850 billion.
D) saving must equal $650 billion.

Answer: B

Topic: Net Exports, the Government Budget, Saving, and Investment
Skill: Analytical
45) Using the data in the above table, if saving equals $650 billion and exports are greater than imports,

A) the government sector must run a deficit.
B) net taxes will be greater than $1300 billion.
C) net taxes will be less than $650 billion.
D) government purchases must increase.

Answer: B

Topic: The Twin Deficits
Skill: Recognition
46) The twin deficits are the

A) current and capital account deficits.
B) government budget and net exports deficits.
C) fiscal and monetary deficits.
D) federal and local government deficits.

Answer: B

Topic: The Twin Deficits
Skill: Conceptual
47) The tendency of the government sector deficit and _____ to be positively related creates a phenomenon known as the _____.

A) the private sector deficit; twin deficits
B) capital account; capital account deficit
C) net exports deficit; twin deficits
D) current account; current account deficit

Answer: C

Topic: The Twin Deficits
Skill: Conceptual
48) Over time, we see evidence that the government sector deficit and the net exports deficit

A) are negatively related during recessions.
B) are positively related.
C) are negatively related during recessions.
D) are not related.

Answer: B

Topic: The Twin Deficits
Skill: Conceptual
49) One reason that the government sector deficit and the net export deficit are positively related is because

A) capital is very mobile across countries.
B) saving in the U.S. is too low.
C) the U.S. imports too many goods.
D) The statement errs because the deficits are negatively related.

Answer: A

Topic: Is U.S. Borrowing for Consumption or Investment?
Skill: Conceptual
50) According to the textbook, the net export deficit is acceptable because it arises from _____ and therefore, this spending increases the nation's

_____.

A) investment; imports
B) investment; productivity
C) consumption; exports
D) consumption; productivity

Answer: B

■ The Exchange Rate

Topic: The Exchange Rate
Skill: Recognition
51) The exchange rate is the
  A) opportunity cost of pursuing a nation's comparative advantage.
  B) price of one country's currency expressed in terms of another country's currency.
  C) ratio between imports and exports.
  D) interest rate that is charged on risk-free international capital flow.
Answer: B

Topic: The Exchange Rate
Skill: Conceptual
52) Americans demand Japanese yen in order to
  A) buy Japanese products.
  B) supply American goods in Japanese markets.
  C) allow the Japanese to buy U.S. products.
  D) balance the current account.
Answer: A

Topic: The Exchange Rate, Currency Depreciation
Skill: Recognition
53) A decrease in the value of a currency in terms of other currencies is known as a(n)
  A) appreciation.
  B) depreciation.
  C) par value.
  D) gold point.
Answer: B

Topic: The Exchange Rate, Currency Appreciation
Skill: Recognition
54) An increase in the value of a domestic currency in terms of other currencies is known as
  A) an appreciation.
  B) a depreciation.
  C) a flexible exchange rate.
  D) a term not given in the above answers.
Answer: A

Topic: The Exchange Rate, Currency Appreciation
Skill: Conceptual
55) Suppose the exchange rate of the U.S. dollar was 1.00 German mark = $0.50 on Thursday, and on Friday the exchange rate was $1.00 = 2.10 German marks. Which of the following best explains what has happened between Thursday and Friday?
  A) The U.S. dollar appreciated against the German mark.
  B) The German mark appreciated against the U.S. dollar.
  C) The U.S. dollar depreciated against the German mark.
  D) Both answers B and C are correct.
Answer: A

Topic: The Exchange Rate, Currency Appreciation and Depreciation
Skill: Conceptual
56) Suppose the exchange rate of the U.S. dollar was 1.50 British pounds = $1.00 on Wednesday, and on Monday the exchange rate was $0.75 = 1.00 British pound. Which of the following best explains what has happened between Wednesday and Monday?
  A) The U.S. dollar appreciated against the British pound.
  B) The British pound appreciated against the U.S. dollar.
  C) The U.S. dollar depreciated against the British pound.
  D) Both answers B and C are correct.
Answer: D

Topic: Demand in the Foreign Exchange Market
Skill: Recognition
57) The quantity of U.S. dollars _____ in the foreign exchange market is the amount that _____.
  A) demanded; traders plan to buy
  B) demanded; traders plan to sell
  C) supplied; traders plan to buy
  D) supplied; brings equilibrium in the foreign exchange market
Answer: A

Topic: Law of Demand for Foreign Exchange
Skill: Conceptual
58) Which of the following increases the quantity of dollars demanded?
    I.   Firms expect a larger profit from holding dollars.
    II.   NAFTA encourages Mexicans to buy more U.S. made goods.
  A) I only.
  B) II only.
  C) Both I and II.
  D) Neither I or II.
Answer: C

Topic: Law of Demand for Foreign Exchange, Exports
Skill: Conceptual
59) As the value of U.S. exports ____, the quantity of ____ demanded increases.
  A) increases; foreign currencies
  B) increases; dollars
  C) decreases; dollars
  D) None of the above is correct because the value of U.S. exports has nothing to do with the quantity of dollars or foreign currency demanded.
Answer: B

Topic: Law of Demand for Foreign Exchange, Exports
Skill: Conceptual
60) The quantity of dollars demanded by foreign nations increases as
  A) U.S. residents purchase more foreign goods.
  B) foreigners purchase more U.S. goods.
  C) U.S. residents travel abroad more.
  D) U.S. exports fall.
Answer: B

Topic: Law of Demand for Foreign Exchange, Exports
Skill: Conceptual
61) Exports of U.S. goods creates a
  A) demand for dollars with no effect on markets for foreign currencies.
  B) supply of foreign currency with no effect on the market for dollars.
  C) supply of foreign currency and demand for dollars.
  D) demand for foreign currency and supply of dollars.
Answer: C

Topic: Law of Demand for Foreign Exchange, Expected Profit
Skill: Conceptual
62) As the expected profit from holding dollars ____, the quantity of ____.
  A) increases; dollars demanded increases
  B) increases; dollars demanded decreases
  C) decrease; foreign currency demanded decreases
  D) None of the above answers are correct.
Answer: A

Topic: Changes in the Demand for Dollars, Interest Rates
Skill: Conceptual
63) The interest rate in Canada rises while the interest rate in the United States does not change. The demand curve(s) for
  A) Canadian dollars will shift leftward.
  B) Canadian dollars will shift rightward.
  C) U.S. dollars will shift rightward.
  D) Canadian and U.S. dollars will remain unchanged.
Answer: B

Topic: Changes in the Demand for Dollars, Interest Rates
Skill: Conceptual
64) If the U.S. interest rate rises while interest rates in the rest of the world do not change, the higher U.S. interest rate
  A) decreases the demand for dollars.
  B) increases the demand for dollars.
  C) has no effect on the demand for dollars.
  D) will stop all trading between the currencies of the U.S. and other countries.
Answer: B

Topic: Changes in the Demand for Dollars, Interest Rates
Skill: Conceptual
65) An increase in the interest rate in the U.S. compared to the interest rate in Great Britain will
  A) increase the U.S. interest rate differential.
  B) increase the demand for pounds.
  C) shift the demand curve for dollars rightward.
  D) Both answers A and C are correct.
Answer: D

Topic: Changes in the Demand for Dollars, Expected Future Exchange Rates
Skill: Conceptual

66) Today, the dollar is worth 5 francs. In one month you expect the dollar to be worth 6 francs. This belief causes
   A)   an increase in the demand for dollars.
   B)   a decrease in the demand for dollars.
   C)   an increase in the demand for francs.
   D)   an increase in the value of exports to France.
Answer: A

Topic: Changes in the Demand for Dollars, Expected Future Exchange Rates
Skill: Conceptual

67) Today the U.S. dollar is worth 1.5 Canadian dollars. By the end of the month, it's expected that the U.S. dollar will be worth 1.2 Canadian dollars. This belief causes
   A)   an increase in the demand for U.S. dollars.
   B)   a decrease in the demand for U.S. dollars.
   C)   a decrease in the demand for Canadian dollars.
   D)   a decrease in the value of exports to Canada.
Answer: B

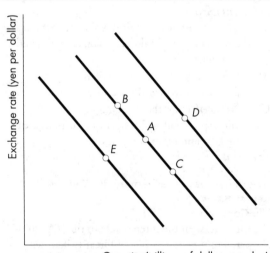

Topic: Law of Demand for Foreign Exchange
Skill: Analytical

68) In the above figure, as the economy moves from point *A* to point *B*,
   A)   the quantity supplied of dollars has increased.
   B)   the quantity demanded of dollars has increased.
   C)   the quantity demanded of dollars has decreased.
   D)   the quantity demanded of pounds has decreased.
Answer: C

Topic: Law of Demand for Foreign Exchange, Exports
Skill: Analytical

69) In the above figure, suppose the economy initially is at point *A*. If the quantity of U.S. exports has increased because of a change in the exchange rate, we expect a movement from point *A* to a point such as _____.
   A)   point *B*
   B)   point *C*
   C)   point *D*
   D)   point *E*
Answer: B

Topic: Changes in the Demand for Dollars, Interest Rates
Skill: Analytical

70) In the above figure, suppose the economy is initially at point *A*. The interest rate in Japan rises relative to the interest rate in the U.S. We can expect a change from point *A* to a point such as

   ____.
   A)   point *B*
   B)   point *C*
   C)   point *D*
   D)   point *E*
Answer: D

Topic: Changes in the Demand for Dollars, Expected Future Exchange Rate
Skill: Analytical

71) In the above figure, suppose the economy is initially at point *A*. People come to expect the future U.S. exchange rate to be lower. As a result, there is a change from point *A* to a point such as ____.
   A)   point *B*
   B)   point *C*
   C)   point *D*
   D)   point *E*
Answer: D

Topic: Changes in the Demand for Dollars, Expected Future Exchange Rate
Skill: Analytical

72) In the above figure, suppose the economy is initially at point *A*. People come to expect the future U.S. exchange rate to be higher. As a result there is a change from point *A* to a point such as _____.

A) point *B*
B) point *C*
C) point *D*
D) point *E*

Answer: C

Topic: Supply in the Foreign Exchange Market
Skill: Conceptual

73) When you arrive at the airport in Paris and go to the bank window to exchange dollars into francs, you are

A) selling francs to the French.
B) avoiding the use of foreign exchange markets.
C) contributing to U.S. exports.
D) None of the above answers is correct.

Answer: D

Topic: Law of Supply for Foreign Exchange
Skill: Conceptual

74) The demand for Dutch tulip bulbs by an American florist creates a

A) demand for the U.S. dollar.
B) demand for an interest rate differential.
C) supply of Dutch guilders.
D) supply of U.S. dollars.

Answer: D

Topic: Law of Supply for Foreign Exchange
Skill: Conceptual

75) Consider the market for dollars. If the price of the dollar rises from 2 marks per dollar to 4 marks per dollar,

A) the supply curve of dollars shifts leftward.
B) the supply curve of dollars shifts rightward.
C) there is an upward movement along the supply curve for dollars.
D) there is a downward movement along the supply curve for dollars.

Answer: C

Topic: Law of Supply for Foreign Exchange, Imports
Skill: Conceptual

76) When a good is imported into the United States, there is created a

A) supply of foreign currency with no effect on the market for the dollar.
B) demand for dollars with no effect on markets for foreign currencies.
C) supply of foreign currencies and a demand for dollars.
D) demand for foreign currencies and a supply of dollars.

Answer: D

Topic: Law of Supply for Foreign Exchange, Expected Profit
Skill: Conceptual

77) Consider the market for dollars. The higher the current exchange rate, the _____ is the expected profit from holding foreign currency and the greater is the _____.

A) larger; quantity of dollars supplied
B) larger; leftward shift in the demand curve for dollars
C) smaller; quantity of dollars supplied
D) smaller; leftward shift in the demand curve for dollars

Answer: A

Topic: Changes in the Supply of Dollars, Interest Rates
Skill: Conceptual

78) Interest rates in the U.S. rise relative to interest rates in other countries. As a result,

A) the supply curve of dollars shifts leftward.
B) the supply curve of dollars shifts rightward.
C) the demand curve for dollars shifts leftward.
D) there is an upward movement along the supply curve of dollars.

Answer: A

Topic: Changes in the Supply of Dollars, Interest Rates
Skill: Conceptual
79) If interest rates in Japan rise and those in the U.S. do not change, there is
A) a decrease in the supply of dollars.
B) an increase in the supply of dollars.
C) a downward movement along the supply curve for dollars.
D) None of the above answers are correct.
Answer: B

Topic: Changes in the Supply of Dollars, Expected Future Exchange Rate
Skill: Conceptual
80) People come to expect the exchange rate for the dollar to rise from 90 yen per dollar to 111 yen per dollar in a month. As a result,
A) the supply curve of dollars shifts leftward.
B) the supply curve of dollars shifts rightward.
C) the demand curve for dollars shifts leftward.
D) there is a downward movement along the supply curve of dollars.
Answer: A

Topic: Changes in the Supply of Dollars, Expected Future Exchange Rate
Skill: Conceptual
81) People come to expect the exchange rate for dollars will soon rise from 75 yen per dollar to 82 yen per dollar. As a result, there is
A) a decrease in the quantity of dollars supplied.
B) an increase in the quantity of dollars supplied.
C) a upward movement along the supply curve of dollars.
D) None of the above answers are correct.
Answer: A

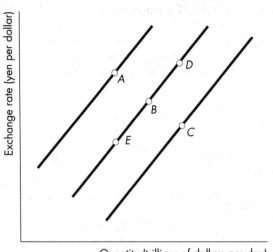

Topic: Changes in the Supply of Dollars, Interest Rates
Skill: Analytical
82) In the figure above, suppose the economy is initially at point B. Then the interest rate in Japan rises relative to the interest rate in the U.S. This change causes the supply of dollars to____ and the market would move to a point such as ____.
A) decrease; A
B) decrease; E
C) increase; D
D) increase; C
Answer: D

Topic: Changes in the Supply of Dollars, Expected Future Exchange Rate
Skill: Analytical
83) In the figure above, suppose the economy is initially at point B. If people come to believe that the exchange rate will fall in the future, the supply of dollars will ____ and the market will move to point such as ____.
A) decrease; A
B) decrease; E
C) increase; D
D) increase; C
Answer: D

Topic: Equilibrium Exchange Rate
Skill: Conceptual

84) Consider the market for lira. Suppose the exchange rate is _____ its equilibrium. This means that the quantity of lira _____ is greater than the quantity of lira _____ and the exchange rate will _____.

A) above; supplied; demanded; fall
B) below; supplied; demanded; rise
C) above; demanded; supplied; fall
D) below; demanded; supplied; fall

Answer: A

Topic: Equilibrium Exchange Rate
Skill: Conceptual

85) In the foreign exchange market for dollars, suppose the equilibrium exchange rate is 120 yen per dollar and $1.2 trillion are traded. Currently, though, the quantity supplied of dollars is $1.5 trillion while the quantity demanded is $1.1 trillion. Hence

A) the current exchange rate is above 120, and the exchange rate will rise.
B) the current exchange rate is above 120, and the exchange rate will fall.
C) the current exchange rate is below 120, and the exchange rate will rise.
D) the current exchange rate is below 120, and the exchange rate will fall.

Answer: B

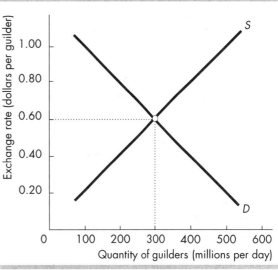

Topic: Equilibrium Exchange Rate
Skill: Analytical

86) Using the above figure, which of the following is correct?

A) 1 guilder will sell for $2.
B) 1 dollar will sell for 1/2 guilder.
C) a shortage of guilders will exist at an exchange rate above $0.60.
D) a surplus of guilders will exist at an exchange rate above $0.60.

Answer: D

Topic: Changes in the Exchange Rate
Skill: Analytical

87) Using the above figure, an increase in the demand for Dutch goods by U.S. consumers will lead to

A) a depreciation in the Dutch currency.
B) an appreciation in the Dutch currency.
C) an increase in the supply of Dutch currency as foreign exchange.
D) a decrease in the supply of Dutch currency as foreign exchange.

Answer: B

Topic: Changes in the Exchange Rate
Skill: Conceptual

88) The U.S. dollar will depreciate in value if

A) the demand for the dollar increases.
B) the demand for the dollar decreases.
C) the supply of foreign exchange decreases.
D) U.S. citizens choose to buy fewer foreign goods.

Answer: B

Topic: Law of Demand for Foreign Exchange
Skill: Conceptual
109) *Ceteris paribus*, a rise in the exchange rate leads to a decrease in the quantity of dollars demanded.
Answer: TRUE

Topic: Changes in the Demand for Dollars, Interest Rates
Skill: Conceptual
110) *Ceteris paribus*, an increase in the U.S. interest rate differential leads to an increase in the demand for dollars.
Answer: TRUE

Topic: Law of Supply for Foreign Exchange
Skill: Conceptual
111) A decrease in the exchange rate leads to an increase in the quantity of dollars supplied.
Answer: FALSE

Topic: The Fed in the Foreign Exchange Market
Skill: Conceptual
112) The exchange rate is not influenced by monetary policy.
Answer: FALSE

■ Essay Questions

Topic: Balance of Payments Accounts
Skill: Conceptual
113) Briefly describe the three balance of payments accounts.
Answer:

Topic: Balance of Payments Accounts
Skill: Conceptual
114) How do the capital account and the current account differ?
Answer:

Topic: Borrowers and Lenders, Debtors and Creditors
Skill: Conceptual
115) What is the difference between a net borrower nation, a net lender nation, a debtor nation and a creditor nation?
Answer:

Topic: Net Exports, the Government Budget, Saving, and Investment
Skill: Conceptual
116) What is the relationship between net exports, the government sector surplus or deficit, and the private sector surplus or deficit?
Answer:

Topic: The Twin Deficits
Skill: Conceptual
117) What are the twin deficits? How are they related?
Answer:

Topic: The Exchange Rate, Currency Depreciation and Appreciation
Skill: Conceptual
118) Give an example of currency depreciation and appreciation.
Answer:

Topic: Law of Demand for Foreign Exchange
Skill: Conceptual
119) What will cause a movement along the demand curve for dollars?
Answer:

Topic: Change in the Demand and Supply of Dollars
Skill: Conceptual
120) How will an increase in the expected future exchange rate affect the current supply and demand curves for dollars?
Answer:

Topic: The Exchange Rate
Skill: Recognition
121) What is purchasing power parity?
Answer:

Topic: The Fed in the Foreign Exchange Market
Skill: Conceptual
122) What role can the Fed play in the foreign exchange market?
Answer: